A GUIDE TO
OPERA RECORDINGS

A GUIDE TO
OPERA
RECORDINGS

ETHAN MORDDEN

New York   Oxford
OXFORD UNIVERSITY PRESS
1987

Oxford University Press

Oxford   New York   Toronto
Delhi   Bombay   Calcutta   Madras   Karachi
Petaling Jaya   Singapore   Hong Kong   Tokyo
Nairobi   Dar es Salaam   Cape Town
Melbourne   Auckland

and associated companies in
Beirut   Berlin   Ibadan   Nicosia

Library of Congress Cataloging-in-Publication Data
Mordden, Ethan
A guide to opera recordings.
Includes index.
1. Operas—Discography.   2. Sound recordings—Reviews.   I. Title.
ML156.4.046M7   1987   789.9′13621   86-32429
ISBN 0-19-504425-8

1 3 5 7 9 8 6 4 2

Printed in the United States of America
on acid-free paper

To
Christopher,
David,
and Matthew,
in collegiate nostalgia

PREFACE

⚄

This is a critical review of a near-century's worth of opera recordings, comprehensive but not all-inclusive, designed to monitor the development of performing stylistics even as it measures the quality of the performances themselves. I assume that readers want to know which is the most fulfilled *Trovatore*, the most theatrical *Carmen*, the most complete *Huguenots*, the most authentic *Boris Godunof*, the most enlightening *Figaro*, even the least expensive *Ring* or the sonically most elaborate *Turandot*; and perhaps pick up a note or two on the less familiar fields of the repertory. There is much to be learned, too, about how over the decades musicians have altered their views on vocal entitlement in various roles, on the use of embellishments in Baroque and bel canto opera, on the purification of corrupt traditions and texts, on the editing of ancient music. To hear, say, the Lucia of Nellie Melba or Amelita Galli-Curci side by side with that of Montserrat Caballé, or the 1928 Bayreuth *Tristan* and then Herbert von Karajan's 1972 *Tristan*, is to realize how differently two eras may take works we thought we could take for granted.

The book moves chronologically, from opera's beginnings to the present era. I have imposed no set structure on the chapters as a whole, partly for readability and, mainly, to let each composer, genre, or era dictate its unique themes of inquiry. Obviously, there is no room in a single volume to treat every recording—not when the most popular titles count upward of twenty-five complete sets each. Nor have I attempted to cover every title. I have not even listed full casts for those recordings that I have discussed: logistical practicalities demand a certain shorthand. As for catalogue numbers, these impede reading and are unnecessary in any case. One locates recordings by title of work, then by conductor and lead singers of a given performance—not by factory ordering codes. Moreover, in this age of digital remastering and CD reissues, catalogue numbers quickly become obsolete. The Furtwängler-Flagstad *Tristan und Isolde* first came out on Victor, saw reissue on Angel, then EMI, then Seraphim, and has just reappeared again in a digital enhancement. Each issue carries a different catalogue number—but the performance will remain the Furtwängler-Flagstad *Tristan* for life. This book is not meant as an index of what is temporarily available, but as a permanent retrospective of opera's discography.

I have decided to include "underground" recordings, most immediately because their recently increased visibility has made them generally available. Also, they are crucial in the phonograph's history, influential as an insistent reminder to record company producers that live performances make home listening more vital. Perhaps most important, they reach back to the 1930s to document opera history as 78 excerpts and studio-made complete sets cannot. (More on this in the following introductory essay.)

Now, some small points. Cited labels refer to the firm of American issue, except when a recording was not released here but simply imported in its European format. Records made in the 78 era are marked by two great periods, the acoustic and the electric, respectively 1900 to 1925 and 1925 to 1950. All LPs cited are in stereo unless otherwise designated as monophonic or digital. (The sole exception are the undergrounds, almost invariably released in single-channel delivery.) Major reissues are cited, chronologically, in parentheses after the label of original issue. For example, "Victor (Angel, Seraphim)" means that the original Victor pressing was reissued, first on Angel and later on Seraphim. Russian composers, operas, and aria titles appear in my own phonography of the language as spoken, not in the inconsistent and incorrect transliteration of Cyrillic spelling favored in the West. I except the names of Russian singers and conductors, as these have already established themselves in print. In the matter of libretto texts and English translations, bear in mind that major American labels have included these as a rule since the dawn of LP. Underground labels at first furnished only notes, at most, but BJR and MRF now include text booklets for the unusual items. Foreign labels are variable, often including texts only in the language of the nation of release. I have noted significant instances of variation.

As I write, in August of 1985, the record industry is undergoing another of its periodic transitions. The vessels of sonic information and the reproductive equipment have been under modification from the beginning, and the rise of the compact disc (CD) may be viewed as merely the latest innovation. At the same time, we have been seeing an astonishing growth of interest in old recordings, in the anthologizing of 78s and the technical improvement of predigital master tapes—not to mention the upsurge in underground issues, often, apparently, of any tape available, but also of such important performances as Dimitri Mitropoulos's *La Forza del Destino* at the Florence May Festival, Otto Klemperer's Covent Garden *Fidelio*, and the world premiere of *The Rake's Progress*. Never has the operatic repertory been so widely covered, or our vocal heritage so densely present.

It seems the right time, then, for a comprehensive look at the history of opera on disc. This book was two years in the writing but twenty years in the making, from the day I bought my first opera set (the Albanese-Björling *Manon Lescaut*, by hap) and began to think about the experiential difference between going to opera and listening to it. I shall refer to the phonograph's peculiar "take" (and influence thereby) on the opera world in the text as we proceed.

All the opinions in this book, unless clearly noted otherwise, are my own.

I wish to acknowledge the support and guidance of my editor Sheldon Meyer, with whom I have published six books, to my vast profit as a writer. And I note with pleasure the continuing cooperation of the house team, editor Leona Capeless and superintendent Joellyn Ausanka. Thanks, finally, to copyeditor Gilda Abramovitz and designer Leslie Phillips; and to my parents, for fostering the interest in theatre and music that made this book not only possible but irresistible.

New York   E.C.M.
March 1987

CONTENTS

A GUIDE TO
OPERA RECORDINGS

OPERA ON DISC:
A BRIEF HISTORY

※

Taking in the remote, crackly sounds fighting up from the hissing surfaces of the discs, no one in the early 1900s could have foreseen a day when opera recordings would complement—even authentically document—the living art, opera in the theatre. Invented in 1877, sound recording was still a primitive technology twenty-five years later. Audio material had to be fed into a recording horn that did not "read" sounds universally. Some sounds it rejected; some that it accepted it fed back disguised. Instruments came through variably; full-sized orchestras were beyond reach. Voices changed color and tone, the highest ones overtopping valid reproduction and the lowest ones slipping into the abyss.

Add to this the limited possibilities in side duration that the ten- or twelve-inch disc allowed and one had little more than a "souvenir of the opera": accompanied on piano (usually, for some reason, very badly played), without textual or annotative matter, and recorded at a speed of anywhere from 60 to 85 revolutions per minute. (We speak of the "78," but speed was not internationally standardized till well into the 1930s.) Of course, playing machines of the day came with adjustable turntables—but the records themselves were not generally marked as to speed. One listened, one guessed, one hastened or slowed the turntable. And one hoped.

Only the favorite scenes were recorded, at that cut down for the fit. Yet opera buffs would stubbornly try to assemble their own "complete" operas by gathering singles by various artists into one album. Obviously, "number" operas adapted best—*Norma, Il Trovatore, Faust, Carmen.* Mozart was largely unavailable; Wagner, in bits, unlistenable. But complete studio sets, despite the strangled orchestral sound and the bulky albums, quickly became a routine event—the earliest set discussed in this book hails from 1907. These albums of course made no attempt to reproduce the atmosphere of the theatre. On the contrary, early opera recordings perforce observed technological etiquette that never troubled theatre performances, such as persuading singers to back up or even turn away from the horn when they hit a big note, or computing the geometry of a quartet so that each of the voices could slide into the horn without bumping the others.

There were occasional attempts to record theatre performances—literally record: set down as testimony. For instance, two companies took down extensive highlights of La Scala's 1904 *Don Pasquale* production, not because the opera's time had come or because a singer or two urged the project, but in response to general agreement that the revival was too good to miss. Why not catch legend fresh, in the making? Granted, the usual studio precautions robbed the show of much color, size, spontaneity. But one hears a fetching vitality on these discs, a smattering, so to say, of theatre.

American labels, unfortunately, left the recording of complete operas to their European affiliates, content simply to import French and Italian sets. There is no Rosa Ponselle–Enrico Caruso *La Forza del Destino* to recall the diva's frantic, historic Met debut; no Geraldine Farrar *Königskinder* or *Madame Sans-Gêne* to explain why she made these titles sellouts; no Mary Garden *Pelléas et Mélisande,* no Nellie Melba *La Bohème.* None of these artists appeared in any complete sets; stars didn't in those days. With a few notable exceptions—Antonio Paoli's Canio, Emmy Destinn's Carmen and Marguerite, Agustarello Affre's Roméo—singers of supplementary celebrity tended to make the complete sets during the first two decades of the century. Economics favored the single cut, especially of a well-known aria or duet. A great deal of money could be made on an album of twenty or twenty-five discs, of course, but these sold to a much smaller market, and seldom sustained a long life in the catalogue, while excerpt sides by the stars might sell well for decades. Victor could easily have secured a complete *Madama Butterfly* with the Met's sensational lineup of Farrar and Caruso backed up by Louise Homer and Antonio Scotti. All were Victor artists. But why tie up a bundle in fees and royalties on a package that few wanted in the first place? Why not simply drive the four singers to Victor's recording studio in Camden, New Jersey, where a makeshift band of local musicians would help them take down the big solos and duets? Thus we do have a sort of Farrar-Homer-Caruso-Scotti *Butterfly*, about thirty minutes' worth; and somewhat more of a Farrar-Caruso *Faust* with Marcel Journet's Mephistofélès; and samples as well of how Met Verdi sounded then.

Someone even attempted to capture the Met company live in performance—Lionel Mapleson, nephew of the famous impresario "Colonel" J. H. Mapleson, and the Met's librarian at the turn of the century. Perched on a catwalk above the stage or huddled with the prompter in his box in front of it, Mapleson recorded snippets of Met performances on cylinders, and through the roar of these badly overplayed artifacts we hear an *involved* virtuosity from singers who were sedate in the studio. The singing is even more exciting, the sense of character sometimes astonishing. Mapleson makes it clear that early studio opera never was intended to mirror live opera; it never was anticipated that, eighty years later, we would stalk those tidy Victor or Fonotipia or La Cigale extracts, searching for representations of style and interpretation, of the thrust of those great voices as they rang through the house. Sadly, it appears that Mapleson was only having fun with his cylinders, not saving a piece of history for us, for he treated them recklessly, wearing them out with use, rerecording some with idiotic household chatter, and apparently giving away or losing others.

Note one advantage that the cylinder had over the flat disc: one could make one's own records. Cylinder players—specifically termed "phonographs"—were also cylinder recorders. But the flat disc was played on equipment—"gramophones"—that only reproduced what had been cut into the discs at the factory. At first this gave the cylinder a leg up in its race with the disc, especially in the earliest years of recording, when the whole business was regarded as something of a toy. However, the influence of opera as the essential material of the recording industry reordered the patterns of commerce. Cylinders were, at first, limited to little more than two minutes' duration and wore out relatively quickly, losing the music in a whooshing turbulence. But one side of a twelve-inch disc took in nearly five minutes of sound, and gave many playings before giving out (that is, as long as the prudent listener didn't "steel" the grooves with worn-out needles, best changed after two or three tours). Opera, even in excerpt, needed more than the cylinder's two minutes, and sat well on the disc's five. Most telling of all, cylinders were cheap, while discs were costly. So, from the start, cylinders concentrated on the inconsequential pop market, while the disc appealed to serious collectors of serious music. Cylinders did make an occasional sortie into the classical world, and of course discs did a strong business in popular music, especially of headline performers and lighter theatre music. But most of the market divided into cheap cylinders for the unpretentious customer and high-priced discs for the discerning. It is typical of the cylinder-disc battle that when Columbia made its great stab at the elite market with its Grand Opera Series in 1903, it issued the takes on discs rather than cylinders—even though Columbia was one of the firms attempting to establish the cylinder's preeminence.

That is what killed off the cylinder, even after improvements in sonics and length of delivery: the disc had opera, the Carusos and Melbas, the archons of an imposing middle-class parlor . . . the status. In main-street America, a gramophone stocked with Met names was as potent a mark of good taste and high culture as a Book-of-the-Month-Club shelf and a few playbills on the coffee table are today. There are many reasons why Americans bought opera records in the early 1900s: to keep favorite works or voices close at hand, to bring the art to places where it wasn't otherwise available, to become intimate with an overwhelming system of titles, scenes, acts, languages, events. But what domesticated opera discs was the measure of upscale respectability it lent the average household. By about 1910, the album of single opera discs had become a staple of the American home, the most popular player being Victor's Victrola, and the most representative records Victor's "red seal" discs, the color denoting work by top-of-the-line artists, recorded only on one side, the verso blank or printed with annotations.

By 1915, the cylinder was on its way out, red seals were two-sided, and "phonograph" and "gramophone" (along with "Victrola" a trade name but, like "Frigidaire," used as common noun) were interchangeable, Americans preferring the former and Britons the latter. Complete sets were increasingly popular, more so in Europe than in America, where they remained a special import item. For Pathé, artists of the Paris Opéra had embarked on a series of complete sets of French classics, plus some Italian works in translation; La Scala served HMV (His Master's Voice, Victor's British affiliate) and Columbia in the Italian repertory. The record had become acculturated. Singers no longer looked upon recording as a purely monetary perquisite of little artistic value, for the discs proved useful in establishing a reputation. In fact, they could be a formidable agent of renown. Caruso's world eminence rested on the popularity of his records among people who seldom if ever heard him live.

Strangely, given the record's broad advance as a cultural symbol, the technology itself had not developed comparably. Much of Caruso's charisma lay in the mysterious affinity that the horn had for his voice. Other singers were not so lucky. Olive Fremstad, one of the greatest Wagnerians of the day, left records dull enough to question her legend. Why Caruso and not Fremstad? Or, to put it another way: what did work on early 78s and what didn't?

To understand the acoustic age, roughly 1900 to 1925, one must come to terms with the paradoxical vitality of acoustic sound. (The term "acoustic" refers to the process by which sound waves were "mapped" in wax through amplification in a horn, as opposed to the "electric" method of recording into a microphone, introduced in 1925). Acoustic transcription was unreliably selective, yes. Fremstad's voice may simply have been too grand for the horn, too brilliant for the wax. She may further have marred her art by toning down her interpretive force in order, so to speak, to soothe herself into the rustic technology. However, what the horn did pick up came out with a remarkable resonance, a virtually physical presence that we have never had since. Acoustic records—indeed, all 78s, electrics as well—were made through a direct-to-disc method that avoided the distancing, the shrouding or artificial souping-up, that our modern through-tape-to-disc method makes necessary. To hear these old 78s—but *only* on their own, contemporary equipment, not on LP rerecording—is to understand why, despite the drawbacks, opera recording became so insistent a theme in phonograph history. These discs are so vital a reproduction that, standing directly in front of the horn (or the reverberator that replaced the unsightly metal speaker), one actually feels the sound leaping out of the machine. Even the most careful of LP reissues cannot duplicate the sensation.

Record collectors became so attuned to the lean penetration of acoustic sound that some predicted disaster when electric recording came in, in the late spring of 1925. But this was a lunatic fringe. Electric recording revolutionized the recording of opera, and all for the better. Surface noise was considerably lessened, and the "body" of the recorded material, the density of the pickup, was vastly increased. Full-sized orchestras could now be accommodated. Certain voices still failed to take (indeed, a very few still do), but the acoustic horn's problems with volume and sounds at the upper and lower extremes of the human voice were forever put by.

Immediately, HMV and European Columbia expanded their catalogue of complete sets. As before, the two Paris houses and La Scala supplied the pit and choral forces, but now the casts were more distinguished. Where HMV's 1920 *Tosca* offered a truly terrible performance by singers of obscure reputation, the 1930 remake gathered three front-rank stars in Carmen Melis, Piero Pauli, and Apollo Granforte, and Columbia's *Tosca* of the year before boasted names of comparable weight. More titles were recorded, too. There had been an acoustic *Manon,* but no other Massenet; now, along with a new electric *Manon,* came a *Werther* with the outstanding Charlotte and Werther of the day, Ninon Vallin and Georges Thill. Best of all, the electric sets sold much better than the acoustics had, partly in response to the impressive casting but also because the public, raised on 78 excerpts, was in the mood for fuller readings.

The emphasis lay on the French and Italian repertory, however. There was no complete *Boris Godunof* or *Yevgyeni Onyegin* till the very end of the 78 era, in the late 1940s, no *Fidelio* or *Der Freischütz* till the LP years, and of Strauss there was only a *Rosenkavalier* highlights album. Moreover, the single-disc repertory became more conservative, focused on the classic titles, where the acoustic delighted in the *objet trouvé*—a duet from an unpopular verismo work, a solo from some long-defunct grand opera, a touch of Gluck, Reyer, Goldmark. But there was, at last, Wagner.

The electric microphone made Wagner not only possible but necessary, for its invention occurred in the midst of a Wagnerian golden age, the era of Frida Leider, Florence Austral, Lauritz Melchior, Friedrich Schorr, Ivar Andrésen. Of extended Wagner, the whole twenty-five years of acoustic recording produced only *Tannhäuser's* Act Two and highlights albums of *Die Meistersinger* and *Parsifal.* In just the first five years of electric recording, the three big *Ring* operas came out in substantial highlights, the third act of *Parsifal* was taken down complete, and, at Bayreuth, most of *Tristan* and very nearly all of *Tannhäuser* entered the catalogue, with the casts (not, alas, the conductor, Arturo Toscanini) that had just sung their way into Bayreuth lore.

The cutting of discs right at the site of the art is an important development, as an attempt to regear the phonograph's aesthetic from studio "echoes" of opera to nearly the real thing. Obviously, this was not possible till the electric process could reproduce a facsimile of the full sound of opera in the theatre. Yet companies were slow to seize the advantage. After all, it was much easier to bring the artists into the studio than to set up shop at, say, Bayreuth, to create a studio from scratch—encountering, it turned out, various logistical problems. For another thing, the next possible step, that of recording opera live in the house during a performance, entailed even greater difficulties. HMV tried it at Covent Garden in the late 1920s, with some success, releasing discs of, among others, Fyodor Shalyapin in *Boris Godunof*, *Mefistofele*, and *Faust*, of Giovanni Zenatello in *Otello*, and, uniquely, Nellie Melba's farewell gala, including her touching curtain speech. EMI has assembled these discs (and a few others that had not been released) on its three-LP set *Royal Opera House Covent Garden: Historic Recordings of Actual Performances*. Grateful as we must be that these readings were preserved, a comparison of these live cuts and any studio take of the same era shows us why so little of the live art was recorded. Sonically, they are perceptibly inferior to studio discs, a bit distant, boxed in; the body of sound is shallow. Artistically, they lack the polish that listeners were used to from the studio presentations, wherein voices were free of opera-house pressures and imperfect takes might be corrected. There was a catch-22 in all this: studio opera, a mere imitation of live opera, had become over the decades a thing-in-itself, not only different from but in certain ways preferable to full-out performances.

Still, a continuing relationship between phonograph and opera house suggested that the recording industry had developed a sense of purpose: the ideal of preserving important history. There were misfires. Victor's studio highlights of Giovanni Martinelli's Met *Otello* failed to capture the concentration he applied onstage. HMV's take of Kirsten Flagstad and Lauritz Melchior live in a near-complete *Tristan* infuriated the two stars, as each felt the other had received favorable microphone placement. (Flagstad was so peeved that she reportedly threw her test pressings into a fjord.) But there were achievements as well, as in HMV's series of Mozart operas taken down at England's Glyndebourne Festival—not live, but with a theatrical verisimilitude remarkable for the time. Thus began one of the phonograph's most enduring and profitable associations with an opera company, a relationship that eventually gave us not only the house specialties, Mozart and Rossini, but works by Monteverdi and Cavalli, Busoni and Britten. Only Bayreuth has been as influential as a corroborator of history. Granted, HMV and Columbia had been recording at La Scala since acoustic days, but these were simply studio sets made with Scala forces, not attempts to preserve specific Scala productions. (This held true in LP days, on Angel's Scala series, which even included operas not in the theatre's active repertory. Not till Deutsche Grammophon joined forces with Claudio Abbado's Scala regime was a serious attempt made to document in toto a Scala event, most notably Abbado's *Simon Boccanegra*.)

There were no major technological developments during the electric era, but in 1949, when the long-playing record was introduced, the doomsayers spoke up again. Their objections, mainly concerned with sound quality, seemed absurd in the face of the advantages. If a symphony that previously required four or five rather breakable discs in a bulky album now sat on one svelte and virtually unbreakable LP, with a single interruption at the turnover instead of constant attendance, think of the benefits in opera. Victor's by-then classic *Aida* with Dusolina Giannini and Aureliano Pertile filled nineteen discs and weighed about fifteen pounds; now it might fit on three discs and weigh little more than a mushroom with a pixie on it, box and all.

The potential was quickly exploited, and within a few years we had our first complete recordings of such works as *Die Entführung aus dem Serail, La Cenerentola, La Sonnambula, Nabucco, Der Fliegende Holländer, Lohengrin, Lakmé, Dalibor, Salome, Gianni Schicchi, Wozzeck, Oedipus Rex,* and *The Turn of the Screw.* Put simply, the LP and its conveniences had widened the record market in a time of prosperity, and most consumers blithely junked their 78s and equipment for the new technology. Labels that hedged on the LP revolution, such as Britain's EMI, found themselves cut out of business. EMI's co-national rival, Decca (London Records in America), was smarter, not only moving immediately into LP but locking up arrangements with various opera theatres in order to expedite the rapprochement of work and performance. Thus, London held handy franchises in Russian opera in its series of Belgrade National Opera albums, in French opera in its Opéra-Comique albums, and in Wagner in its Bayreuth albums.

In America, Columbia made a second attempt to challenge Victor's virtual monopoly on the classical vocal market by hooking up with the Metropolitan Opera. Moreover, it was Columbia that pioneered the LP. Victor countered with the 45, lighter and smaller than the LP and relating the consumer back to the 78 in its four- to five-minute side duration. The 45 eventually became the medium for pop singles, but it proved a bit dainty for the classical market. Viewing, say, the Roger Desormière *Pelléas et Mélisande* in its very thick, very tiny box of seventeen 45s—not only red-sealed but red all over, from the pickup to the lurid spindle hole—the consumer made pause. This didn't look substantial enough for an opera. The singers might sound like mice; perhaps they *were* mice. This is what is called an image problem. Yet Victor held its historic advantage over Columbia in terms of getting top singers into the studio. As Victor had signed Caruso, Farrar, Amelita Galli-Curci in acoustic years, so did it now grab Zinka Milanov, Jussi Björling, Robert Merrill, Leonard Warren, and Toscanini's NBC broadcasts. Columbia brought out America's first homemade complete opera, an English-language Met *Hänsel und Gretel,* in 1947, first released on 78s but planned to ease the firm into LP competition. Other Columbia operas followed. But Victor's weight of talent crushed Columbia as it had back in 1903, underlining what would become the identifying feature of LP opera: formidable casting. Less and less would operas be recorded with merely available voices. HMV had paved the way for this in the electric era, remaking the Scala titles conducted by Carlo Sabajno with more notable casts built around Beniamino Gigli. Accordingly, Victor's LP sets made a point of trying to equal the Met's most impressive casts—a *Carmen* with Risë Stevens, Licia Albanese, Jan Peerce, and Robert Merrill under Fritz Reiner, or Milanov, Fedora Barbieri, Björling, and Warren in *Il Trovatore.*

Perhaps this was good salesmanship rather than the practice of an aesthetic: one spends more money to sell more units. But when EMI organized its classical label, Angel (Columbia in the United Kingdom and France), producer Walter Legge—the man who had put Glyndebourne Mozart in the catalogue—hit upon what now seems simple common sense, but then was revolutionary: as recordings are more or less permanent, why not record operas with . . . well, perfect casts, so the albums would deserve to last forever? Thus, while (American) Columbia's *Hänsel und Gretel* preserves what amounts to a humdrum evening at the Met, at that with mostly second-line singers, Legge's *Hänsel* had Elisabeth Schwarzkopf and Elisabeth Grümmer under Herbert von Karajan—the utmost in imaginative musicianship.

Legge's choice of repertory was daring at a time when the catalogue ran to the cautious. Angel proudly flourished *Il Matrimonio Segreto, Der Barbier von Bagdad, I Puritani, Ariadne auf Naxos, Les Mamelles de Tirésias;* as for classic repertory, Legge's idea of *Tosca* was Maria Callas, Giuseppe di Stefano, and Tito Gobbi under Victor de Sabata, perhaps the greatest performance of an Italian opera made in the first fifty years of opera recording. Legge's packaging was similarly innovative in its sophistication, emphasizing well-informed annotators and literate translations—this in an age when, in three successive recordings of *Rigoletto,* Victor failed to correct its translator's mistaking Sparafucile's "un uom di spada" (a swordsman) for "a man with a spade." Sparafucile is an assassin, not a gardener.

The record business, then, was strengthening its imperatives, widening its goals. The arrival of stereo—practicable by 1955 but not marketed until 1957—further opened up the repertory, as the electric microphone had. Best of all, to persuade consumers to adopt the new equipment only ten years after they had disposed of their 78 kits, the companies glamorized stereo opera by opening up the traditional cuts that had been as usual on disc as in the theatre. Note-complete recordings had become the rule by the early 1960s, and they proved so successful that not only did they remain a feature of opera-on-disc: they began to tell in theatre practice as well. Weaned on complete texts at home, critics and the informed public began to demand them onstage. Thus, opera recording had ceased to reflect the opera scene and was now influencing it. Hearing out-of-the-way titles at one's ease sharpened the appetite for revivals of special material; and surely Legge's championing of Callas as a bel canto stylist helped bring the bel canto revival to America. One odd facet of phonograph opera was to have widespread and hazardous influence later on, in the 1970s: singers began to learn roles for records that they might otherwise never have touched. In the case of Callas trying out Carmen or Manon Lescaut, or of Schwarzkopf sampling operetta, this seemed reasonable, the equivalent, if not the copy, of theatre casting. In the case of a major singer's gallant filling in on a secondary part, this seemed refreshing, a chance to better opera-house business-as-usual, as when Legge had Nicolai Gedda turn a cameo as the Italian Tenor in *Der Rosenkavalier.* In fact, this sort of star-as-comprimario has remained one of the phonograph's unique pleasures, yielding festival casts beyond the resources of any festival, as for instance in the Ping-Pang-Pong trio scene of von Karajan's *Turandot,* rendered by voices of greater polish than any theatre company would think necessary or practical.

But what of smallish voices tackling big parts in the safety of the studio? We have heard, on disc, Turandots, Otellos, Isoldes, Siegfrieds, and Carmens whom we wouldn't likely encounter in the theatre, at least not willingly. Yet, the logic runs, if a singer records a role, the singer has sung the role: why *not* sing it, then? This practice has developed during a shortage of big voices—or has it helped create that shortage by encouraging tender instruments to take dangerous risks?

Records once were a dim echo of live opera, later an alternate kind of opera, separate but equal. Have we reached a point at which records direct live opera, teach it how to sound? At times, certain critics blame a theatre performance for being too theatrical, as if they were disappointed that von Karajan didn't mix the tapes. Yet, in its first days of power, when stereo was new, LP opera appeared to be attempting to separate itself from the theatre as much as possible, especially in John Culshaw's sonic spectaculars on London. Other firms had tried to stall the new system. As it had dragged its feet on LP, so did EMI again on stereo, leaving it a bit dazedly releasing mono opera sets as late as in 1959, after all the other major labels had hurriedly regeared for two-channel sound. London had sagely crossed over in 1955, which allowed it to fill store shelves with genuine stereo versions of older sets—and gave it several years' experience over its rivals in sheer technique.

London seized the day, most notably with the first integral recording of Wagner's *Ring*. In most ways, the four albums followed the procedures of the era, casting prominent specialists with arresting novelties in Joan Sutherland's Woodbird and Kirsten Flagstad in the only Fricka of her life and the preservation, bowing to history, of Hans Hotter's Wotan. However, Culshaw went further in his *Elektra*, fiddling a bit with the sonics to create a kind of nonvisual live opera. Till then, the guiding theory was, the less you notice the sound, the better it is. Now sound became an element in the presentation, distancing the taped performance from the live one. Stereo was not to be merely an expansion of the reproductive mechanics, but an alternative mode of production, its own theatre. Culshaw not only exploited studio tape technology: he reveled in it. No theatre Siegfried could pose as Gunther as persuasively as Culshaw's Siegfried did, for Culshaw's engineers manipulated the dials and "made" the tenor a baritone: as if the Tarnhelm itself had not only turned Wolfgang Windgassen into Dietrich Fischer-Dieskau, but had given Windgassen Dieskau's voice. Here was a true home stereo theatre.

Culshaw's approach was challenged, oddly, by amateurs who saw the phonograph as nothing more than an organ for the preservation of theatre performances. Dismayed by the stolidity of studio tapings, bored with the "same old" singers who turned up on title after title, and eager to explore neglected repertory, a small group of buffs centered in New York formed an informal underground for the under-the-counter marketing of issues made from performance tapes. The practice was illegal, sheer piracy. But as the years went on and issues made available such essential documents as the aborted HMV Flagstad-Melchior *Tristan* or Callas developing her Norma from date to date, or Wilhelm Furtwängler's Scala and RAI *Rings*, or even turbulent repertory nights of unfamiliar Verdi, grand opera, or Singspiel in native expertise, one saw the wisdom in the zeal of these *espontaneos*. Call them "undergrounds," "private discs," or "pirates," as they are interchangeably called: these records held the mandate to perpetuate the art of opera in its greatness, its color, its variety. The pirates were living up to history.

Some of the undergrounds looked and sounded homemade; others rivaled the pros in sonics and packaging. Most of them bore their makers' initials as a label name (one wag dubbed his line of pirates Penzance Records), and thus one identifies them. EJS, the pioneer of the underground, was Edward J. Smith; his discs came in paper sleeves and frequently ran off pitch. But he was omnivorous, issuing everything from Monteverdi to Tippett. MRF, in handsome boxes with, after ten years or so, text-and-notes booklets for the unusual titles, favored the nineteenth century and the verismo era. While EMI officials were tearing Europe apart hunting down everyone who took part in Furtwängler's RAI *Ring* (or the heirs) to get clearance to release the performance legally, MRF quietly put it out, cheating the law but not the music. Voce lacked texts but put forth many an original version of a later revised opera, including an uncut *Don Carlos* in French. BJR was the most advanced in sonics, with an emphasis on bel canto and Verdi. It is worth noting that, while the commercial labels strongly resented the piracy of their artists, many of their producers collected the undergrounds themselves. There was simply no denying the vitality of the live performance. If one loved opera, one delighted in undergrounds.

The legal situation took an unexpected turn when Italian law limited performance copyright to twenty years. After that, any operatic tape could be marketed. Insistently, new labels sprang up to exploit the advantage, not only of Italian tapes, but generally: the underground went public. Salzburg, Bayreuth, La Scala, the Met, Covent Garden, the Florence May Festival—virtually every site of modern opera history was exploited, pillaged . . . documented. A century from now, if someone should wonder what a Toscanini or Walter *Magic Flute* sounded like, or Knappertsbusch's *Ring* or Muti's *Vespri Siciliani,* he'll know.

If only to protect themselves in this mushrooming of legal pirates, the commercial labels began to release live tapes—to record in the opera house rather than in the studio. Even the marmoreal Met disgorged its archival splendor, twenty years after Eddie Smith first sold the tapes. Increasingly, live opera has become the mode of recording, especially as our modern no-frills style—inspired by von Karajan's high-polish Salzburg productions and Muti's austere, joyless bel canto and supported by spineless critics, terrified of individuality—duplicates the rigid purity of a studio reading.

The arrival of direct-to-disc recording and the CD have not affected opera. Direct-to-disc did not prove popular, and was technically suited only to smallish operations, such as jazz or a Lieder recital. The CD is essentially an alternate vessel of reproduction, not a breakthrough as the electric microphone or stereo recording were. As with the acoustic and the 78, the LP has its defenders, resolutely denouncing and boycotting the new technology. But the CD also has undiscerning boosters who think it a cure-all. No. The CD can improve on the LP's delivery of sound, but does not invariably do so; it depends on the quality of engineering. The CD also can reveal a faulty performance to a . . . well, fault. A wobbly voice or sloppy ensemble comes through with irritating clarity on the CD where the LP inadvertently obscures it.

Perhaps the major lesson that the phonograph can teach us is that some important measure of individuality has been poured out of opera since the early years of the century. Singers were less disciplined then, but more expressive. This may explain the current interest in our 78 heritage: are we applying to the imaginative singers of the past as an antidote to the often sterile purity of the modern style? Once the province of the helter-skelter buff and Victor's least enterprising staffers, carelessly transcribing 78s onto LP without testing speed against pitch and blotting out the discs' original brilliance with tape hiss, our 78 heritage is now being carefully treated. We recognize it as a kind of practice history, uncouth but revelatory. On Austria's Preiser and England's Rubini (after Giovanni Battista Rubini, Bellini's favorite tenor), 78s sing at the appropriate speed in approximations of the original resonance. Victor, finally wising up, made a decisive stab at filtering the noise out of Caruso's cuts and invigorating the vocal body with its Soundstream process. Complete 78 sets are increasingly made available on LP, especially long-lost acoustics.

This is an age of retrospection. We have begun to step as far back as forward: to view the past as we lay down new records of the present. In the end, the undergrounds beat Culshaw down, drove out the notion of a separate-but-better phonograph. Records are opera's servants, retaining, illustrating, keeping available. Discs of the early 1900s tell us how they *didn't* sing opera; discs today preserve style. They have become strategic in the opera business, introducing singers to a broad audience (or, by neglect, limiting their renown), affirming the rediscovery of a particular repertory, publicizing a stylistic tilt (Leppard's Monteverdi, say, or von Karajan's Wagner), even playing politics (in DG's recognition of Finnish opera or Hungaroton's attempt to make international stars of Hungarian singers). Records have power. Still, at base opera's discography is at once a souvenir shop and a museum, history with a human face.

And a voice.

1

THE FIRST OPERAS

⊰⊱

"Begin," Lewis Carroll's King of Hearts directs, "at the beginning." This is difficult in the present context, for much of opera's beginnings have been lost. Its key voice, the castrato, is defunct; its scoring was not written down note for note, and now is a matter of conjecture; some of the instruments of its day have, with improvement, become virtually different instruments; and even major music itself has vanished.

Thus, the discography of Claudio Monteverdi or Henry Purcell is quite unlike that of Wagner or Puccini, whose operas are fixed text (albeit with certain variations of revision, as in *Tannhäuser*'s "Paris version" or Alfano's two published completions of *Turandot*). With *L'Incoronazione di Poppea* or *The Fairy Queen*, different recordings yield different compositions, the reconstructions varying greatly not only in performing style but in the very sound of the orchestra and voices.

We see this most vividly in recordings of Monteverdi's operas, which in essence favor one of two possible approaches: that exemplified by Nikolaus Harnoncourt, strictly attentive to the stylistic procedures of the Baroque era; or that exemplified by Raymond Leppard, who splits the difference between what was probable in the 1600s and what is palatable today. *Poppea*, Monteverdi's last opera, offers an ideal basis for comparison. Angel (Seraphim) caught Leppard's *Poppea* at Glyndebourne in 1964, with Magda Laszlo, Frances Bible, Richard Lewis, and Carlo Cava under John Pritchard, while Telefunken made a studio set of Harnoncourt's *Poppea* ten years later, with Helen Donath, Cathy Berberian, Elisabeth Söderström, and Paul Esswood, Harnoncourt himself leading the Concentus Musicus of Vienna. The variations are remarkable: in Leppard's flowing strings and suave harpsichord textured by lute, guitar, harp, and organs as opposed to Harnoncourt's austerely quaint use of the same instruments, further stylized, distanced from modern ears, by the use of tooting recorders and antique oboe.

Or consider the vocal casting. Leppard prefers voices one might hear in Rossini or Britten, while Harnoncourt recruits specialty singers with an interest in this repertory, even a specialty voice, the countertenor, who lacks the castrato's trumpeting brilliance but at least approximates his otherworldly timbre. Leppard's cast is resourceful, struggling to accommodate the Baroque's fascination for recitative to our present-day preference for the aria and duet, but Harnoncourt's experts outdo them, reveling in the Baroque belief that intensity of expression rather than all-out melody yields highest eloquence. Glyndebourne's Nero, tenor Richard Lewis, cuts a fine figure, but he is sturdy rather than, as needed, lascivious. Harnoncourt's Nero is Söderström, stunning in the recklessness of her sensuality. Glyndebourne fields a bass Seneca, the moral force who opposes Nero till ordered to commit suicide; Harnoncourt casts a counter-tenor, and plays his death scene as a ritual rather than as, at Glyndebourne, the climax of the plot. Then, too, in the disposition of Arnalta, Poppea's nurse, Harnoncourt honors the ancient Venetian tradition of the comically obnoxious duenna played by a man, whereas Leppard assigns the role to a mezzo, Oralia Dominguez. She sounds somewhat like a silly Amneris. Harnoncourt's Arnalta, Carlo Gaifa, brings a piquant quality (as well as historical authenticity) to the part. Lastly, Harnoncourt gives us the work complete, on five discs, where Leppard cut the text considerably. Angel cut it further, for two LPs, but we can hear Leppard's score in full on LR's underground of a 1978 performance at the Paris Opéra on three stuffed discs—stuffed with an astonishing aggregate of international stars: Gwyneth Jones, Christa Ludwig, Valerie Masterson, Jon Vickers (a querulously impetuous Nero), Richard Stilwell, and Nicolai Ghiaurov, with, again, a mezzo Arnalta, Jocelyne Taillon, all under Julius Rudel. Note that once more we find general-repertory singers rather than Harnoncourt's elite reciters. In short, Leppard works with what is current on the operatic scene. Harnoncourt raids the museums and the offbeat Lieder parlors.

The Harnoncourt-Leppard opposition is less distinct in Monteverdi's *Il Ritorno d'Ulisse in Patria* (Ulysses' Return to His Homeland), for Leppard's cast, under his own leadership and again fresh from

Glyndebourne performances (Columbia), is much more stylish than Glyndebourne's *Poppea* crew. Indeed, Frederica von Stade and Richard Stilwell hold an informal world copyright on Penelope and Ulysses for the opulent sensitivity with which they invest their parts. Harnoncourt, in another studio project on Telefunken, again takes in more of the score than Leppard, and in a more judicious reconstruction, but the admirable Norma Lerer and Sven Olof Elisasson lack the von Stade–Stilwell glamour.

At that, *Ulisse,* like *Poppea* a product of Monteverdi's last years, has not proved popular with most opera buffs. It is an exemplary piece, taking the axioms of early opera to their extremes, a passionately inward work. But it has little of *Poppea*'s colorful vitality. For a spryer Monteverdi—and a look into opera's earliest days—try his first opera, *Orfeo,* dating from 1607. This gentle retelling of the Orpheus myth points up early opera's search for a Classical simplicity within a framework of festive ceremony, as court entertainment that, paradoxically, was originally devised as an art for art's sake. From *Orfeo*'s first measures, the officious toccata summoning us to attend, we sense a unique blend of pageantry and song.

Four sets serve *Orfeo* best, all in antique style. Harnoncourt's, with Lajos Kozma and Rotraud Hansmann (Telefunken), is the most antique, playing the toccata without drums for a rather dainty effect, and holding the soloists to a spare declamation. Kozma's Orfeo suits the approach, with an almost *dolce far niente* flavor in his portrayal, but the important scene in which a messenger, in the old Greek style, reports on Euridice's death, is somewhat underpowered by modern theatrical standards. On Victor (Erato), Michael Corboz leads a more forceful reading with Eric Tappy and Magali Schwartz, the toccata sternly celebratory and the messenger scene most persuasive. It works by understatement: Orfeo sighs at the bad news rather than keens. Harnoncourt takes it too far, smoothing it down; Corboz respects its shyness, but points it up. Corboz has the delicacy, too, for the scene in which Orfeo softens Charon's heart with song, so austerely performed in Harnoncourt's version that it loses its magic. Jürgen Jürgens's Archiv recording with Nigel Rogers and Emilia Petrescu falls somewhat between Harnoncourt and Corboz, combining the former's stylistic clarity with the latter's storytelling baton. Jürgens's toccata is a no-nonsense fanfare, and his rustic dances have a lovely swing. Better, his messenger scene is touching, and he encourages Rogers to pile on the embellishments when confronting Charon, giving this prototypal musician a properly mythic sense of extremism. Last and lightest of these four *Orfeo*s is Angel's digital set of 1984, closely miked to emphasize intimacy and spontaneity. A strong cast and two chamber groups, the London Baroque (under Charles Medlam) and the London Cornett and Sackbutt Ensemble (under cornettist Theresa Caudle), combine under Nigel Rogers to present what sounds like an expert improvisation, as opposed to the sometimes studied historicism of the other three sets. Rogers knows his *Orfeo:* he not only sang the hero for Jürgens, but played small parts for Harnoncourt's reading, and his almost absurdly small company truly suggests a performance of the early 1600s.

Monteverdi wrote *Orfeo* for Mantua, but he finished his years in Venice. It was there that opera was first given in theatres to a paying public. The subjects were still myth (as in *Orfeo* and *Ulisse*) or history (as in *Poppea*), but *Poppea*'s steamy hedonism quickly replaced *Orfeo*'s innocence. In the operas of Monteverdi's successor, Francesco Cavalli, all life is courtship, disguise, infidelity, and reunion. The curious might sample Erato's *Ercole Amante* (Hercules in Love) for the album's wonderfully detailed notes and Corboz's decisive conducting, with the arranger of the edition, Luciano Sgrizzi, prudently keeping an eye on things at the harpsichord. The singers are a varied lot, Yvonne Minton and Ricardo Cassinelli most spirited. But Ulrik Cold's rough Hercules is somewhat less than *amante*. Another worthy Cavalli set is Vox's *Erismena*, notable for its refreshing use of an ancient English translation, well projected through close miking of the singers, Carole Bogard, Delreen Hafenrichter, Paul Esswood, and Melvin Brown under Alan Curtis.

Most listeners, however, will favor Argo's two Glyndebourne Cavallis in Leppard editions, *Ormindo* and *Calisto*,* especially *Calisto* for its notable diva trio of Ileana Cotrubas, Teresa Kubiak, and Janet Baker, along with counter-tenor James Bowman, baritone Peter Gottlieb, bass Ugo Trama, and tenorino Hughes Cuénod (also in *Ormindo*) as the typical grouchy duenna. *Calisto* gives us the Venetian style at its most luxurious, and Leppard responds with an at times breathtaking beauty of arrangement. Baker's "Ardo, sospiro, e piango" (I burn, I sigh, I weep) claims a pulsing of strings almost certainly unthinkable

---

* These and other titles of seventeenth-century opera usually appear with the definite article: *L'Ormindo, La Calisto, L'Orfeo,* and so on. This is like speaking of Verdi's operas as *L'Aida* or *Il Rigoletto*. Italian, like other romance languages, does not comfortably render nouns without some establishing particle, so librettos of the first operas, published in conjunction with the performances, routinely applied the article on the title page. However, *L'Ormindo* is not the work's title; it means, roughly, "the work entitled *Ormindo*." In fact, Italians do speak of "*L'Aida*" and "*Il Rigoletto*." But this is grammar, not nomenclature.

in Cavalli's day. But, as the sexy elegy of Leppard's setting goads Baker on to a spectacular rendering of the text, only a pedant would complain. Cotrubas, as the local nymph of choice—Jove's anyway—is in the bloom of eager youth, sensitive and vivacious. Gottlieb's Mercury is imaginative. Trama's woolly Jove is the set's defect, but luckily he courts Cotrubas, in typical Baroque plotting, disguised as Diana. Thus, Baker ends up singing much of Trama's role in a dual part: as Diana and, in Italian, "Giove in Diana." Perhaps more than *Poppea*, *Calisto* is the newcomer's best entree to Venetian opera, a most delightful performance of a highly picturesque work. Those who would browse more generally in this arena might try Leppard's disc of Monteverdi and Cavalli highlights (Angel, Vanguard) with Heather Harper, Gerald English, and Hughes Cuénod. (Note the Baroque's emphasis on high voices: one soprano and two tenors.) Leppard includes nonoperatic vocal pieces as well as opera matter, reminding us how close secular music and theatre music were at this time.

Early English opera flirted with and eventually succumbed to the Italian influence. But it had its own form, developed from the court masque, in semi-opera, essentially song-and-dance suites designed to fill out a play. Thus, Henry Purcell's *The Fairy Queen* is not *A Midsummer Night's Dream* set to music, but *A Midsummer Night's Dream* with added musical scenes of no direct bearing on the plot. The emphasis is on full-out musical structures with as little recit as possible, an important difference between the English and Italian styles. Archiv's digital *Fairy Queen* under John Eliot Gardner is tidy and authentic (and somewhat distantly recorded). But Benjamin Britten's completely artificial revision (London) is delightful. Britten plays havoc with order and completeness, but the result stands on its own—just as well, for semi-opera adaptations of Shakespeare are rather out of date today. Britten also has bright sound and an outstanding cast—Jennifer Vyvyan, Alfreda Hodgson, James Bowman, Peter Pears, and John Shirley-Quirk. For something between semi-opera and opera, Purcell's *King Arthur* makes a nice impression, though not in Gardner's overly dutiful archeology (Erato digital), much less in Alfred Deller's (Harmonia Mundi, Music Heritage Society), rhythmically slack and dramatically unrealized. Anthony Lewis, back in the dawn of stereo on Oiseau-Lyre, leads a fiery performance with the valiant Elsie Morison, Heather Harper, and Hervey Alan. As with Angel's Monteverdi-Cavalli survey, the same label offers Yehudi Menuhin's four concert renderings of Purcell in *Music for the Theatre*: suites of *The Fairy Queen*, *King Arthur*, and *The Indian Queen*, plus a mixed bag of bits. Here's a tidy panorama of dances, incidental accompaniments, and songs (sweetly delivered by Joan Carlyle). Given the dim dramatic content of the originals, the nontheatrical presentation is reasonable.

Purcell composed one out-and-out opera, *Dido and Aeneas*. A short piece designed for the students of Josiah Priest's School for Young Gentlewomen in Chelsea, *Dido and Aeneas* claims an instructive discography, from the 78 era of catch-as-catch-can anachronisms through stereo romanticizations up to very recent attempts to reconstruct the temper of the original. Not that HMV's 1945 album under Constant Lambert is wholly out of style—note the free articulation of the harpsichord, faithful to the work but a bit daring for 1945. The singing, however, is very post–Vaughan Williams, denuded of the embellishments that Baroque art luxuriated in. At least we do hear the great Joan Hammond in her only complete opera recording—a noble heroine in the grand diva manner—and the no less great Edith Coates, direly capering as the Sorceress. Geraint Jones's mono disc (HMV, EMI) of a (London) Mermaid Theatre production has Kirsten Flagstad and Elisabeth Schwarzkopf, a somewhat stately reading except in the witches' scenes. By stereo years, editions tend to hedge between authenticity and the spare modern approach, as in Angel's (de los Angeles, Harper, Johnson, Glossop; Barbirolli), decorated here and there with a smidgeon of the Baroque but marred by a lovely yet distinctly unacculturated Dido; or in Oiseau-Lyre's (Baker, Sinclair, Clark, Herincx; Lewis), a brilliant reading that respectfully leaves the middle act unfinished, as its last pages have vanished. (Most other performances borrow a stray bit of Purcell to bring the curtain down.)

Dame Janet rerecorded *Dido* under Steuart Bedford in 1978 (London), a darker, stronger portrayal, vocally less stirring than before. What ring, under Lewis in 1962, she brought to "What storms, what battles did he sing?" In 1978, Baker has impressive support from Alfreda Hodgson, Felicitys Palmer and Lott, and Robert Tear in very small parts; but Peter Pears's Aeneas is embarrassing, more like Turandot's father than Virgil's hero. Leppard's edition (Victor), also from 1978, plays a keener Baroque, as one might expect, in sonics as rich as brocade. Tatiana Troyanos and Richard Stilwell, similarly backed up by comprimarios of quality, are ideal lovers, and Felicity Palmer, promoted to second soprano, makes the most avid of Belindas. This is a very spirited Dido, sweetly embellished and always atmospheric, from sweethearts' court to helldames' cave to ship outward bound and back to court for Dido's great solo, "When I am laid in earth," one of the few Baroque opera solos to claim a substantial 78 history. It is not a great history, reflecting the opportunistic field expedients various singers employ to get through it. Contraltos lower it, thespians oversing it, Baroque adventurers diddle it. Remember, this opera was written for schoolgirls. Troyanos emphasizes its plangent nobility, especially telling after the vitality Leppard gives to the preceding scenes.

What, now, of *Dido and Aeneas*, the schoolgirls' opera? Two fine recordings of 1979 and 1980 attempt to present the piece in its history, so to say, with adults of both sexes but in a manner suggestive of "young gentlewomen" doing the school play. On Harmonia Mundi, Joel Cohen leads D'Anna Fortunato and Mark Baker in a sprightly reading with more orchestral color than we hear on other discs, the Boston Camerata taking in woodwind and percussion (with a woodblock for the hornpipe). How light Cohen's chorus sounds next to Lambert's or Jones's crew! Note the rakish tilt of the orchestral ritornello in "Fear no danger to ensue," a veritable pipes-and-tabor. Referring to Venetian opera's travesty duenna, Cohen casts Bruce Fithian as the Sorceress. Andrew Parrott's digital reading on Chandos with Emma Kirkby and David Thomas is similarly conceived, delighting in reedy, adolescent timbres. Parrott's young witches, amusingly cackly, really sound like kids Halloweening, though his Sorceress, Jantina Noorman, is quite chilling. Thomas's Aeneas is something of a lout, but Kirkby is excellent, the vulnerability of her youth especially moving in "When I am laid in earth" after decades of contraltos.

After Purcell, England's native opera tradition collapsed in deference to the artistic colonialism of the Italian style. But French opera began and remained French, though organized and somewhat developed by Italian composers. Jean-Baptiste Lully, a Florentine contemporary with Cavalli, laid down an informing oeuvre like, yet not like Italian opera, with a unique emphasis on ballet and spectacle, a strategic use of the chorus, and librettos reflecting the influence of the spoken theatre. Lully's *Alceste*, with Felicity Palmer, Anne-Marie Rodde, Renée Auphan, Bruce Brewer, Max von Egmond, and Marc Vento under Jean-Claude Malgoire (Columbia), is illustrative. This is a livelier piece than, say, *Calisto*, more energetically plotted on a more serious theme, with the principals intently interrelated. Italian characters tend to address the audience; French characters address each other. Yet, if Malgoire's performance is poised, still his singers lack the expressive vitality of Leppard's *Calisto* cast. A certain monotony creeps in, till Francois Loup's eccentric Charon wakes things up in Act Four. Erato's digital set of Lully's *Armide et Renaud* under Philippe Herreweghe is cut but much livelier than Malgoire's *Alceste*, Rachel Yakar glamorous as the pagan witch (especially in her sexy lower-middle register), Zeger Vandersteene delicately fervent as the Crusader who falls under her spell. Unlike Malgoire's people, Herreweghe's are irregular in embellishing; but then Malgoire's cast may overdo it, for the French liked relatively clean lines.

On the other hand, the Italians found the French approach dry and unmusical, especially once *opera seria* instituted the aria, with its embellished *da capo*, as opera's essential structural element. Halfway through an opera by Lully's great successor, Jean-Philippe Rameau, *seria* star Faustina Bordoni cried out, "When are we to hear a tune?" Yet Rameau's critics found "too much music" in his operas, too much accompanimental material for the orchestra. In Rameau's *Les Indes Galantes* (Love in the Indies) we hear bagpipes, trumpets and drums, the Provençal *tambourin* percussion, and swirling woodwind triplets for a storm scene. Lully seldom dared such suggestive scoring, and listeners who fear the turgid gaiety of Lully's *tragédie* may prefer to cop their history with *Les Indes*, handsomely served on Columbia (though in a cut text) under Malgoire. The conductor attacks this task with greater gusto than usual for him, eagerly double-dotting the melodies in late-Baroque style to retrieve the music's characteristic bounce, nimble even when majestic. Again we get a cast out of the run of the Caballé-Pavarotti-Bruson axis favored today in repertory titles: Sonia Nigoghossian, Anne-Marie Rodde, Rachel Yakar, Bruce Brewer, and two notable veterans, Janine Micheau and Jean-Christophe Benoit.

Those in search of more conventional glamour might consider two of Rameau's *tragédies,* strictly narrative as compared with the episodic opera-ballet *Les Indes: Hippolyte et Aricie* and *Dardanus.* Malgoire has a very idiomatic *Hippolyte* (Columbia), but Anthony Lewis (Oiseau-Lyre) has Janet Baker, heading, along with Robert Tear and John Shirley-Quirk, a boldly theatrical performance. "Lully needs singers," Rameau once explained. "I need actors." As for *Dardanus,* Leppard turns up on the French scene, too, here in an Opéra production with Frederica von Stade, José van Dam, and Roger Soyer, better played than Lewis's *Hippolyte,* if not as beautifully sung. The search for authenticity is inspiring, especially in Rameau, for he made textual absolutism difficult for archeologists by revising his works on each revival. The Malgoire and Lewis *Hippolytes,* for instance, vary strongly not only in idiom of performance but in the inclusion or omission of whole scenes. In the end, though, it is the great performance that keeps the ancient alive—not the ancient performance.

For this reason, I believe the great Rameau recording to be Pathé's mono set of *Platée* (EMI), neither *tragédie* nor opera-ballet but a comedy, rather a low one at that. Virtually a spoof of the courtly love plots that animated so many early operas, *Platée* finds Jupiter feigning advances to the ugliest (yet vainest) woman on earth, sung—like the Venetian duenna—by a tenor. As with Leppard's *Poppea,* the recording preserves an important festival revival, from Aix-en-Provence in 1956, in a, shall we say, inauthentically stylish production with Michel Sénéchal, Janine Micheau, Nadine Sautereau, Nicolai Gedda, Huc Santana, and Jean-Christophe Benoit. Hans Rosbaud superintends from the clavecin. There are cuts, especially in the ballet music, but the show is wonderfully spirited, Sénéchal's nimble but almost toneless voice perfect for Platée and Gedda's Mercury amusingly *boulevardier* in his readings. Rashly impressionistic, as always, Rameau scores frogs, cuckoos, and ducks into the piece, as if spoofing *tragédie* and its encoded procedures. Other operas of the day take place in groves and temples; *Platée* takes place in a swamp. It may seem an odd work to end the chapter with, after the valiant sense of mission with which opera began. But it does prepare us for the imaginative novelties that will, as we proceed, firm up the outline of opera's history.

2

OPERA SERIA
AND OPERA BUFFA

❧

Many opera buffs, on their first exposure to the oldest operas, find the long stretches of recitative wearisome. As we move into the next century, we find much less recit, much more outright singing. But now the singing can seem wearisome, for composers of the 1700s built opera almost entirely of the so-called *da capo* aria, in ABA form: the first section, a contrasting interlude, then the opening again (*da capo:* "from the top"), this time to be embellished as the singer chose. It was the heyday of the star virtuoso, of castrati and divas, of entrance arias and metaphor arias and exit arias, of opera-as-song. Story, poetry, characterization, scoring, production all were secondary. Singing came first; the aria was everything, allowing for the odd duet or chorus here and there. With opera's maximum creator—the composer—thus limited, opera became static.

This form of aria-opera was called *opera seria*, meaning "serious" (in effect, heroic) opera, as opposed to the comic Italian form, *opera buffa.* It may be that *opera seria* is even harder to revive than Monteverdi and Cavalli. They need only a reconstruction of the scores and replacements for the castrati. *Opera seria* needs, as well, dynamic virtuosos to sing it and ingenious directors to stage it.

On records, of course, staging problems are irrelevant, and the phonograph has been strategic in the last few decades in reclaiming opera's heritage, virtually forcing *opera seria* upon the stage by building up the repertory of the form's outstanding master, George Frideric Handel. On disc, Handel *is opera seria,* for his genius infused the strait format with a penetrating sense of character and sheer exuberance of music. Handel overflows—which is perhaps why the stately *Ariodantes* of conductors Stephen Simon (Victor) and Raymond Leppard (Philips), however well sung, so disappoint. Interestingly, where Philips gives us the top-of-the-line cast of Janet Baker, Edith Mathis, Norma Burrowes, David Rendall, and Samuel Ramey, with counter-tenor James Bowman in the castrato role of the villainous Polinesso, Victor holds its own with the less starry voices of Sofia Steffan, Graziella Sciutti, Carole Bogard, Ian Partridge, and Marius Rintzler, with Bernadette Greevey tackling Polinesso, no little challenge for a mezzo. Philips's *Ariodante* is one disc longer and more complete, with more stylish embellishments of the *da capo*s. It has presence, entitlement. It is a fair reading. So is Victor's. But both sets lack a sense of purpose.

One might say as much for Westminster's *Rodelinda,* made in Vienna in 1964. Brian Priestman conducts Teresa Stitch-Randall, Hilde Rössl-Majdan, Maureen Forrester, Helen Watts, and Alexander Young— all typical vocal escorts of the early-middle Handel Revival. Yet here is another musical and admirable and strangely undashing performance. Not till we turn to an underground, HRE's *Rodelinda* at the English National Opera in 1959, do we begin to comprehend the vitality of Handel's music theatre. Charles Farncombe conducts Joan Sutherland, Janet Baker, Margreta Elkins, Patricia Kern, and Alfred Hallett, all so lively that the recits, where *opera seria* so often sags, are almost as much fun as the arias. *Almost*—for some of the full-out singing is spectacular, in clean sound that lets the English translation come through. (Just as well, as HRE provides no booklet.) Even the often mush-mouthed Sutherland spits her lines out neat, so inspired is the reading.

Note the preponderance of women in the cast, a concomitant of *opera seria*'s emphasis on castrato principals (for which, today, read "mezzos") and trouser roles. London's *Alcina* is almost a nunnery— Sutherland, Mirella Freni, Graziella Sciutti, Teresa Berganza, Monica Sinclair, and, happy wanderer, Luigi Alva, under Bonynge. This is stylish and vivid, and something of a likeness of the famous Zeffirelli production that set the amorous intrigues at the sorceress Alcina's court amid an onstage audience of baroque nobles, an attractive conceit that forgave *opera seria*'s lugubrious construction by reveling in it. At that, some of the arias are cut down, losing their middle sections as well as the repetitive *da capo*s, which gives *Alcina*'s three discs a fleet narration we don't get in more faithful resuscitations such as Raymond Leppard's *Samson* (Victor, Erato), ploddingly complete with the Brittenesque cast of Baker, Helen Watts, Robert Tear, John Shirley-Quirk, and Benjamin Luxon. Then, too, Bonynge's *Alcina* crew apply their embellishments with characterological panache, aiding Handel rather than interfering with him, especially in their use of the climactic cadenzas to cap the emotional "hook" of each solo. Perhaps it is worth noting that, in a repertory that emphasizes English- or German-speaking singers, Bonynge uses a goodly number of Italians, as if placing *Alcina* back in *opera seria*'s ethnic and cultural roots. True, Handel wrote the bulk of his operas for London, but these were Italian operas, in form, in language, and, largely, in casting.

We can sit in on the very start of this transcultural phenomenon in *Rinaldo*, Handel's salutatory work on his arrival in London in 1711. The story, from Tasso, is one of opera's favorites, on the witch Armida's attempt to stalemate a Crusade by vamping a knight. Lully had set it; Gluck, Haydn, Rossini, and Dvořák, among others, would do so. Handel's version is formally rather imaginative for *opera seria*, with choruses and ensembles to vary the aria structures, and Jean-Claude Malgoire brings it to life most authentically (Columbia) with an international cast—Armida is American, her lover Argante is Swedish, and Rinaldo's Christian fiancée is Romanian. Everyone sings in Italian. Malgoire took such trouble to re-create the sound of Handel's day that Columbia listed the orchestra players on the album, down to the recorders and harpsichord that were to vanish from opera's pit. Purists have tried to debunk the set, but its sense of era is so acute that, in Armida's "Molto voglio, molto spero," the instrumentalists adorn the *da capo* right along with the singer, a wonderful effect. Jeanette Scovotti (Armida), Ileana Cotrubas (Almirena), Carolyn Watkinson (Rinaldo), Paul Esswood (Goffredo), and Ulrik Cold (Argante) head the accomplished cast.

The most telling review of Handel's opera recordings may be heard in *Giulio Cesare* (Julius Caesar), a work destined to change the old cliché that Gluck's *Orfeo* is the oldest opera in the standard repertory. Even more than Monteverdi's *L'Incoronazione di Poppea*, the highly stageable *Julius Caesar* inveigles newcomers and veterans alike, albeit in productions and editions that might have given Handel pause. One wonders what he would have thought of Karl Richter's reading (DG), absolutely complete but *without a single embellished da capo!* This is like giving *Swan Lake* without dancers. Virtuoso embellishments are not an excrescence of bel canto. They are a function of its art, and a major source, in its day, of its prestige. To perform bel canto opera without decorations is performing the music "as written"—but not as intended. A shameful business: for Tatiana Troyanos's timbre projects a husky sexiness apt for Cleopatra, and Dietrich Fischer-Dieskau is welcome as Caesar even if castrato roles sound best today in the mezzo's range, not the baritone's. Perhaps Richter ought to study Bonynge's highlights disc (London), *molto virtuoso,* and not just on the part of Sutherland and Marilyn Horne. In "Sì spietata, il tuo rigore," Monica Sinclair (Tolomeo) caps the *da capo* with a run of three octaves. Unfortunately, Bonynge regards this as a star show rather than as selections from a theatre piece; the arias are out of story order, and Caesar (Margreta Elkins) gets only one solo, shorn of its middle section and *da capo.*

It might be better to cut an aria altogether than to shred it, though even in Handel's time such assaults were not uncommon. So, also, were wholesale cuts, borrowings, interpolations, and what have you—in which spirit the New York City Opera mounted its *Giulio Cesare* for Beverly Sills and Norman Treigle under Julius Rudel, the production that most thoroughly publicized the Handel Revival. Purists, again, felt as if they had been racked, but the show carried an immensely persuasive vitality, fairly caught on Victor. But perhaps the English National Opera's aesthetic was more reliable: cut down the windy recits and omit some arias, but otherwise play it as it should be played. Better yet, the ENO gave the piece in English, yielding an advantage that Handel's London public, smugly gaping at the alien art, did not have. Even in digital sound (Angel), Brian Trowell's fine translation comes through variably, but the text booklet is a pleasure to follow, filled with instructive photographs of the production, another landmark in the reinstitution of *opera seria.* Charles Mackerras's singers are a bit less showy than Rudel's, perhaps, but Valerie Masterson's Cleopatra sounds (and looks) truly beautiful, James Bowman's counter-tenor Ptolemy adds a bite of the Baroque, Sarah Walker's Cornelia nearly pounds with widowed despair, and, in the trouser role of Cornelia's son Sextus, Della Jones astonishes with the fire of her coloratura in her first aria. "Come *rouse* yourselves!" she cries, to the gods of vengeance; and the italics, I assure you, are hers. Janet Baker ought to have recorded her Caesar some years earlier. But if "Qual torrente!," another metaphor aria, edges her up a bit with its torrents of divisions, Baker is magnificent in the wheedling "Aure, deh, per pietà." Moreover, Mackerras, imaginatively expert, agrees with Malgoire that the orchestra may decorate right along with the singers, as when the "hunting"-metaphor aria, "Va tacito e nascosto" (Seek silent and hidden), finds the horn and Baker working out the cadenza in tandem, or when, in "Se in fiorito ameno prato" (In the pleasant, flowery meadow), the solo violin rises out of the pit to imitate Baker's embellishments. It is Victor, then, for flash, Angel for a purer Handel.

This much is *opera seria*, the heroic art. *Opera buffa*, bourgeois farces of courtship, calls for less strenuous musicality, tidier talents. Where *Giulio Cesare* tells of ruthless boudoir politics among the royals of Rome and Egypt, Domenico Cimarosa's *Il Matrimonio Segreto* gives us sisters, an aunt, a father, and nothing more ruthless than a betrothal on the sly. This is a typical, not a great *opera buffa*, though it so impressed Leopold II of Austria that he had the entire piece encored for his courtiers, a captive audience. Angel's mono set under Nino Sanzogno, from an all-Italian Piccola Scala production, defers to DG's better-sung stereo box of internationals under Daniel Barenboim.

Cimarosa allows us to comprehend *buffa*. To appreciate it, we turn to Philips's marvelous series of Haydn's comedies, issued from 1975 to 1980, all under Antal Dorati and employing outstanding young singers of what might be called the "style and art" discipline: Jessye Norman, Frederica von Stade, Lucia Valentini Terrani, Claes Haken Ahnsjö, and Benjamin Luxon are typical. This is opera between Handel and Mozart, observing the former's recit-aria structure but also the latter's distaste for the sedentary *da capo* aria. (From its inception, *opera buffa* limited the use of the full-strength solo as unfit for the modest character of its themes.)

English *"buffa"* is different from Italian: not *buffa* at all, scarcely comic, and less operatically fashioned, virtually a play picking up songs here and there. William Shields's *Rosina*, first given at Covent Garden in 1782, is useful here, short enough to hold a single LP, once the amusing country-dialect script is cut down to song cues. Bonynge's gang (Elkins, Harwood, Sinclair, and Tear, for once without Sutherland) give it a lively reading on London, embellishing the lines more than must have been the case in Shields's day. These rustic comedies, so popular in the late 1700s (much later, Vaughan Williams's *Hugh the Drover* revived the form), grew out of ballad opera, basically a play studded with songs, the lyrics new and the tunes borrowed from anywhere. Ballad opera was never opera, and the most famous of them was in fact written as a spoof of the Italian style: John Gay's *The Beggar's Opera*, first given in 1728, prime Handel time. As an early form of musical comedy, *The Beggar's Opera* does not suit the scope of this book, but perhaps Handelians owe it to history to hear this anti-*seria seria* about the royals of the London underworld, set to the simplest melodies available (including one from Handel's own *Rinaldo*, a crusaders' march here given to thieves as "Let us take the road"), and

containing a duet of brawling divas designed to recall the battle between Handel's star sopranos Faustina Bordoni and Francesca Cuz-
zoni—onstage, during Bononcini's *Astianatte*—the year before.

As with so many early operas, the original score has vanished, leaving a vocal line and figured bass to the hands of an arranger. The
most popular such is Frederic Austin, who prepared Nigel Playfair's
celebrated production of 1920 at the Lyric, Hammersmith, an old jewel
of a theatre on the outskirts of London. Austin's chamber orchestra
(including harpsichord) and "light opera" voices hit the mark somewhere between austere scholarship and creative antiquing, and the
revival's run of 1,463 performances—phenomenal for a suburban theatre—instituted "the Austin version" as a valid *Beggar's Opera* for the
twentieth century. Records helped instill the sound of Austin, for, as
Playfair's original Peachum, Austin joined the cast members on HMV's
several albums of the production (songs only) and added good measure
in conducting the overoptimistically named "Eighteenth Century Orchestra" in a two-sided medley. EMI's subsidiary label, World, stuffed
the whole kaboodle onto one LP, complete with texts and handsome
reproductions of Claude Lovat Fraser's original costume designs. The
performances have the air of a slightly faded Gilbert and Sullivan troupe,
an approach replicated, in better sound, on Victor's 78 album of John
Gielgud's 1940 Glyndebourne staging of the Austin version, with Audrey Mildmay's lovely Polly and—for acting smarts—Michael Red-
grave as Macheath.

In recent years, Austin has been swept aside by newer versions,
recorded with some of the dialogue. The 1968 West End revival with
Jan Waters, Frances Cuka, and Peter Gilmore (Columbia) is sassy and
contemporary, as in the waggish use of the ritornello of "A Police-
man's Lot Is Not a Happy One" (from *The Pirates of Penzance*) in
"When you censure the age," and is the most theatrical disc of all.
Richard Bonynge and Douglas Gamley's arrangement calls, like Gielgud's staging, for a mixed opera-and-theatre cast: Kiri Te Kanawa,
James Morris, Angela Lansbury, Michael Hordern, and, graciously, as
Lucy, Dame Joan (London digital). Lush and sugary, even soupy, this
orchestration offends the spirit of ballad opera, handing it over to the
sort of people Gay was burlesquing. In effect, Bonynge has romanticized satire. For wholesale recomposition of *The Beggar's Opera*, most
prefer Benjamin Britten's version, as yet unrecorded, though tapes of
the superb 1963 Edinburgh Festival mounting, with Janet Baker, Heather
Harper, and Peter Pears (plus Edith Coates, as usual going over the
top, as Mrs. Trapes), deserve underground issue. For now, the best
Beggar's Opera—the best performance in the correct spirit—returns us

to Austin for Malcolm Sargent's two-disc mono set (Victor mono; Seraphim stereo), the sort of phonograph classic that is bound to sit on CD in due course.

True, Sargent fields one cast to sing and one to act. Worse yet, the singers—Elsie Morison, Monica Sinclair, John Cameron, Ian Wallace, and Owen Brannigan—work in that good-natured prettiness that marked their work for Sargent on Angel's Gilbert and Sullivan series, while the actors—including Rachel Roberts, John Neville, and Paul Rogers—deliver the text with the dirty zest of a back-street Restoration comedy. The actors bear the playwright's cynicism, the singers the musician's heart. But then this problem is built into the Austin version, with its sweet songs for vicious characters. At least Sargent delivers it with taste and vitality. In a moment such as "In the days of my youth," Mrs. Trapes's alarmingly vigorous salute to her amorous past, the show pulls script and music together in rich symbiosis.

3

GLUCK

❧

Christoph Willibald von Gluck is a magic name in opera history: the Great Reformer, who realigned the corrupt circus of star singers with the high principles of opera's founders, the strangely nationless composer who centered world interest on the French form of opera for a century, the controversial tamer of spectacle and reinventor of the aria, from chance vocal showpiece to precise characterological study. However, Gluck was not only an avant-garde composer, but an avant-garde stager as well. A producer. "The best things," he explained, "become insupportable in a bad performance." Thus we may connect with Gluck: in his desire to make singing actors of opera singers.

Gluck gravitated to Paris for his reform years, so we deal with French opera in this chapter, with, we presume, French singers. Yet Gluck launched his reform in Vienna—musically speaking, an Italian colony at the time. So there will be alternate versions in different languages, and an international character to the singing. This is confusing enough, though comparison of the Italian and French versions of Gluck's *Orfeo* sheds light on the two different opera styles of Gluck's age. The real trouble lies in finding performances that give what Gluck himself asked for in rehearsals: a characterological urgency that would, when necessary, smash standards of good taste in singing. Remember, these reform operas are almost all drawn from Greek myth and deal with profound questions of the human condition. Orpheus dares enter hell to retrieve his beloved; Alceste volunteers to die in place of her husband; Agamemnon prepares to kill his daughter to promote security in time

of national emergency; Orestes suffers guilt for matricide. We expect
to hear howls and groans as well as *canto*—Gluck did, anyway, though
his singers often disappointed him.

Orfeo ed Euridice, long celebrated as the "oldest opera in the repertory" (before Monteverdi's *Poppea* came into fashion), is in fact most
frequently given in renovations dating from Verdi's day and even later.
It's younger than it used to be. Conductors choose from the revisions
or make their own hybrid, so each recording offers a slightly different
text. A good place to start is Riccardo Muti's committed reading of
the original 1762 Vienna *Orfeo* (Angel digital), shorter and more austere than the 1774 Paris *Orphée.* We must do without Euridice's Elysian Fields aria, the d minor Elysian Dance, and Orfeo's interpolated
bravura aria at the end of Act One. (Marilyn Horne had to drop out
of a Muti *Orfeo* at the Florence May Festival because she insisted on
singing the aria.) At least Muti's ruthless ban on emendations gives
us a chance to sit in on history just as Gluck begins his reform—with
one compromise, for the original Orfeo, Gaetano Guadagni, was a
castrato. Muti, *force majeure,* substitutes Agnes Baltsa, with Margaret
Marshall as Euridice and Edita Gruberova as Amor. No howling or
groaning; but the recits are quite fervently delivered.

In the more familiar big diva approach, Georg Solti (London stereo)
leads Horne, Pilar Lorengar, and Helen Donath; and this time Horne
sings the contested aria, "Addio, o miei sospiri," whether Muti likes
it or not. One must admit, it enlivens a work otherwise heavily given
over to *lento* and *andantino,* and while bravura is surely wrong for Gluck,
Horne is terrific in the showpiece, as she is throughout the role. Janet
Baker (Erato digital) under Raymond Leppard is as natural as Horne
yet very unlike her, though she too includes the "Addio" and is not
shy about embellishing. Perhaps the aptest comparison is that Horne
is grander in "Che farò?", Baker more moving in the scene with the
Furies. Both make the most of the part, in the most persuasive sur-
roundings.

With *Orphée,* the Paris version of 1774, Gluck began the castrato's
retirement from opera by recasting the part for a tenor. Angel's Nicolai Gedda rides the surprisingly high line with ease, unfortunately
in a flawed mono performance. Janine Micheau's Euridice sounds senior and lacks passion; and why, after a vital reading of the Furies'
dance, does Louis de Froment allow them to sing with all the tension
of a college glee club? An alternative, in the revision Berlioz made in
1859 for Pauline Viardot (retaining the more fully developed additions
and rescoring of the Paris version but substituting a mezzo for the
tenor), is Columbia's classic 78 set of 1936 (Vox) with Alice Raveau,

Germaine Feraldy, and Jany Delille under Henri Tomasi. The sixteen twelve-inch sides yield something between highlights and a shredded complete performance by deleting much of the recit. Feraldy sounds as if she can't wait to get back to her Manons and Juliettes, and Tomasi has little to work with, given the cuts and sonics. But Raveau's majestic vitality is enthralling.

Gluck's reform really took wing with *Alceste,* another piece available in versions relating to 1767 Vienna (Italian) and 1776 Paris (French) premieres. In the first days of stereo, London released the Italian version on four discs, with Kirsten Flagstad, suffering a cold at taping time and off form, though hers was the ideal Alceste instrument. Her Admeto, Raoul Jobin, is also out of sorts, if spirited, and the whole is inconclusive. Vastly better is Orfeo's digital set of the French version, with Jessye Norman, Nicolai Gedda, Bernd Weikl, Tom Krause, and Siegmund Nimsgern under Serge Baudo, a vigorous performance—and note how Baudo improves upon Gluck's reform by omitting the closing ballet, a convention Gluck was eager but unable to dispose of. One hears something of Gluck's intended naturalism here: in Norman's beautifully undervoiced poignancy at "O dieux! soutenez mon courage"; in Gedda's exploitation of the shocking falling sevenths in the melody of "Barbare! Non, sans toi je ne puis vivre!" as if they were groans. Gedda misses the desperation hidden in the tenderness that makes "Alceste, au nom des dieux" one of Gluck's great extravagances. But he has the ringing high Bs for the Infernal Scene, in which his wife is carried to hell, and the delicacy for the last trio, after she has been returned to earth. Listeners, be warned: the two *Alcestes* are virtually two different operas.

Iphigénie en Aulide, the first opera Gluck wrote specifically for Paris, has been ill-served on a Victor set (in German!) with Anna Moffo, Ludovic Spiess, Dietrich Fischer-Dieskau, and Thomas Stewart. Penzance preserves the famous Salzburg cast of 1962, also in German but at least very listenable: Christa Ludwig, Inge Borkh, James King, Walter Berry, and Otto Edelmann under Karl Böhm. There is no complete recording in French. Worse yet, till recently Gluck's most distinctly reformist work lay unrecorded in any language: *Armide.* The tale is Tasso's (a pagan witch enchants, then loses a Crusader), the libretto Quinault's, from the days (and oeuvure) of Lully, and the vocal characterization Gluck's greatest achievement till then, at least according to Gluck. *Alceste* may be Gluck's epic of reform, and the two *Iphigénie* operas deal with truly weighty affairs. But *Armide* most successfully reveals opera's potential for stimulating the expression of human character.

Armide's history on disc is worth noting, as a study in how unready the century has been to deal with Gluck. A very few great singers recorded 78 excerpts: Agustarello Affre and Joseph Rogatchewsky each trying Renaud's discovery of Armide's magic garden, "Plus j'observe ces lieux," about two decades apart in the acoustic era, Affre preferable for the stylish way he reins in his heroic voice. In electric years, Frida Leider and Suzanne Brohly shared Armide's "Ah! si la liberté," Gluck's simplification of the *da capo* aria, Leider more forceful, Brohly more thoughtful. Janet Baker, in stereo on an all-Gluck recital under Raymond Leppard (Philips), left a smashing performance of the finale, a forerunner of the "mad scenes" of late bel canto. But this—other than an undistinguished highlights LP in Italian with Gloria Davy and Giuseppe Zampieri—was all of *Armide*. The participation of top-line singers indicates Gluck's fascination for the most exacting talents— the power of Affre and Leider, the textual brilliance of Baker. But the highlights disc—in the wrong language, sluggishly delivered, and so halfheartedly published that many lifetime record buffs never knew of it—reveals Gluck's lack of fascination for the record companies. By 1980, two complete undergrounds had appeared, one another forgettable Italian performance and the other drawn from a 1974 RAI concert with Viorica Cortez and Jean Dupouy under Wilfred Boettcher (Voce). The voices are apt and pleasant, but the singers lack imagination, and there is no libretto booklet. It's just the opposite on the sole commercial *Armide*, EMI's digital preservation of the 1982 staging—an odd one, with everyone in what appeared to be *Star Wars* karate suits—at London's Christ Church, Spitalfields. Here the voices are less good; the delivery is rapt and pointed. But Gluck warned us that, in this work, he was less "the musician" than "the poet and painter." Under Richard Hickox's sensitive conducting, Felicity Palmer draws an arresting Armide, disappointing only at the end of Act Three, the one moment for which Gluck felt the need to emend Quinault's ninety-one-year-old text with new lines, outlining her mingled despair and excitement at the pull of love that Hatred, with all her sorcerer's suite, has been unable to still. Anthony Rolfe Johnson's Renaud is more conventionally successful—a smoother sound of less vivacity—and there is but one outright failure, the Hidraout, Armide's consort, here taken by a horribly out-of-voice baritone.

EMI's *Armide* makes an interesting comparison with Erato's recording of Lully's setting of the same text (see Chapter 1). After all, Gluck reset Quinault at least partly to demonstrate how much more a reform opera could do with the same material. There are obvious differences: Lully's Hatred is a baritone, not a soprano; Lully's Hidraout is suave where Gluck's is bellicose; Lully sets as little songs lines that Gluck sees as recit, and vice versa. The larger differences, gradually revealed as one listens, identify Gluck's reform precisely: Lully employs one vocal style for all characters, while Gluck defines their individuality melodically, besides following their shifts in mood; and Gluck's orchestra works harder than Lully's as psychological commentator. In short, Lully's *Armide et Renaud* is a sort of musicale on the theme of love. Gluck's *Armide* is theatre about the different ways love affects people.

Gluck's last great opera, *Iphigénie en Tauride,* largely retires the chorus and ballet of the earlier operas for a taut quartet of principals. The orchestra is most outspoken here, sometimes howling and moaning for the singers: in the opening storm, a pre-Romantic Romantic's view of nature as psychopathic phenomenon, as reflector of the human condition; or in Oreste's scene with the Furies, in which his pathetic attempt to rationalize his matricidal depression, "Le calme rentre dans mon coeur," is contradicted by the violas' nagging on an obsessive monotone, an effect so shocking in its day that at the first rehearsal the orchestra gave up in confusion. "He's lying!" Gluck explained. "He killed his mother!" Such a moment, in which narrative honesty overwhelms convention, freezes Gluck's reform at its center.

Iphigénie en Tauride needs a strong conductor more than Gluck's other operas do. Carlo Maria Giulini (EMI), for all his tense control, lacks singers of temperament, and various undergrounds of Callas's 1957 Scala *Iphigénie* suffer poor sound, three dull males, an Italian translation, and Nino Sanzogno's flabby conducting. Georges Sebastian, leading Régine Crespin, Guy Chauvet, and Robert Massard at the Colon in Buenos Aires in 1964 (Chant du Monde), is unstylish, his singers transposing many of their solos downward; and Massard conveys Oreste's passion by scanting the music. Nor is Orfeo's 1985 digital album an improvement, except in sound and as a complete reading in French. Conductor Lamberto Gardelli offers a kind of needlework Gluck, metrically plying his baton, busy music. Pilar Lorengar's heroine lacks the solid middle voice of Arnould, Falcon, Viardot, Gerville-Réache, Delna, the very history of the French dramatic soprano, and while Franco Bonisolli's Pylade is vital in unexpectedly good French, Dietrich Fischer-Dieskau's Oreste is tamely tasteful for a man who killed his mother.

Angel's early stereo highlights disc remains the choice in this work, for, though it gives but half the opera, it delivers fully in Gluckian style. Georges Prêtre has an erratic track record on disc, but here he superbly leads a cast that might have been chosen to illustrate the state of vocal characterization in Gluck's time. Rita Gorr rather drives the pile here and there, but her sopranoish mezzo is precisely what Iphigénie was composed for, and her sincerity is beyond question. Louis Quilico's Oreste is Classical, balanced, Nicolai Gedda's Pylade a brilliant foil—and note that the hero is a baritone and the tenor his sidekick, typical of the ancient French preference for the lower male voices, but so contrary to later operatic procedure that Angel's libretto sheet accidentally switched the two men's roles in the cast listing. Ernest Blanc's dire Thoas upholds the company average, in a "bass" role (actually the formidable *basse chantante*) that lies higher than some Verdi baritone parts.

Unfortunately, no historian chose Angel's program. How could Prêtre have agreed to delete Oreste's scene with the Furies, or let side two die out in minor choruses, never reaching the C Major finale, a forerunner of that to *Fidelio?* Moreover, it must be said that Prêtre's conducting has a modern edge, however Gluckian his singers may be. Yet hear how grandly he unfurls the strangely fanlike grace notes in the accompaniment to Pylade's "Unis dès la plus tendre enfance." We cannot recapture Gluck's performing practices with certainty, but a stately tour through myth's most grisly tales is surely not what he had in mind. The best things become insupportable in a bad performance.

4

MOZART

⊁⥅⥆

The perfection of Mozart's greatest operas carries a built-in guarantee of failure: what cast, what production team could realize the ideal? This had made them popular festival pieces, on the theory that the extraordinary talent and time that festival conditions afford take us closer to the profound, eliciting Mozart we dream of than business-as-usual repertory conditions can. Many of the best-known festivals have bound at least part of their reputations around this dream of an ideal Mozartean reading—Salzburg, Glyndebourne, Aix-en-Provence. For its part, the phonograph, from its first attempts at complete Mozart operas, has tied in with festivals, at the same time attempting to outdo them, drawing elite singers of Mozartean style into a kind of festival studio for a revelatory *Figaro*, a best-yet *Don Giovanni*, a once-in-a-century *Così fan Tutte*, the unique *Zauberflöte*.

There is more to Mozart, of course, than this Big Four. Some Mozarteans insist that *Idomeneo* makes it five, and *Die Entführung aus dem Serail* has important advocates. Moreover, as with Monteverdi, Handel, and Haydn, the stereo years have seen Mozart's heretofore obscure works securely invested in the phonograph's repertory, as in a delightfully sweet-toned *Il Re Pastore* (The Shepherd King) on Victor (Arabesque), with Lucia Popp, Reri Grist, Arlene Saunders, Nicola Monti, and Luigi Alva under Denis Vaughan. The *opera seria La Clemenza di Tito* (The Mercy of Titus) counts three worthy sets—and note that each takes a different tone, suggesting the rich ambiguity we shall reencounter when we reach the Big Four. Under Istvan Kertesz (London), *Titus* is austerely dramatic; Colin Davis (Philips) tempers the drama with an inward beauty, typified in Janet Baker's formidable Vitellia, one of the most movingly sung villainesses on disc; but Karl Böhm (Philips) hears a lighter *Titus,* albeit with a largely German cast.

Nevertheless, interest centers on the six major works, insistently recorded with perhaps the most consistently distinguished casts in phonograph history. We have had more than a little of rough-and-ready Verdi, or unqualified Carmens, and one complete *Ring* cycle—nineteen records' worth of music—was cast with the most mediocre Wagnerians in Europe. Mozart, too, has suffered indignities, even at Glyndebourne, whose *Idomeneo* was recorded in 1956 in a watered-down version (Angel mono, Seraphim stereo) of what was originally an impressive production, with only Sena Jurinac's meltingly lovely Ilia and Richard Lewis's masterly Idomeneo worth hearing.

However. Later *Idomeneo* sets stress the storytelling potential that Mozart found in *opera seria.* Cuts, though few, remain a nuisance, and no label has yet dared to re-create the *Idomeneo* that Mozart's coevals heard, with the appropriate embellishments and, *force majeure,* for the castrato role of Idamante, a mezzo instead of the tenor invariably heard in this part. Nevertheless, the dynamic Davis (Philips), the stirring, classically Germanic Hans Schmidt-Isserstedt (Eurodisc, Arabesque), and the princely, nostalgic Böhm (DG) give us performances modeled less on the youthful than on the mature Mozart, whose song has purpose. Eurodisc's company (Rothenberger, Moser, Gedda, Dallapozza) might have slipped out of a stirring *Don Giovanni,* especially Moser's star-flaming Electra. She sounds about to step directly into Strauss, at least in temperament. Davis fields the most impressively musical thespians, however, Margherita Rinaldi putting bite into Ilia's ingenue honey and George Shirley majestically tortured as the king who has sworn to sacrifice the first being he meets when he returns home . . . his son.

Die Entführung aus dem Serail (The Abduction from the Seraglio) poses virtually no problems, stylistically or dramatically, though its two soprano-tenor couples, the noble pair and the servants, call for a vocal contrast that we seldom hear. Consider "Martern aller Arten." When Lilli Lehmann (in 1905), Elisabeth Schwarzkopf (on a Urania tape long ascribed to Maria Cebotari), Eleanor Steber (with piano at Carnegie Hall, on ST/and), or Maria Callas (in concert on undergrounds) sings the aria, it has fire, as befits a heroine defying an Eastern potentate. But Beecham's lyrical cast (Angel mono) suave their way through the piece as if it were a *Liederabend.* Too bad: for, from the second measure of the overture, when the strings put a delightfully grouchy burr into their appoggiaturas on the downbeats, we sense a special reading.

At least Beecham's superb Osmin, Gottlob Frick, carries over to Josef Krips's Vienna set (Seraphim), with Anneliese Rothenberger, Lucia Popp, Nicolai Gedda, and Gerhard Unger. Rothenberger's prudent "Martern" lacks Arten, but it's a spirited show in general, the singers gamboling happily in the dialogue. (Beecham's album slots actors in for some of the singers, a sometimes necessary ploy that, somehow, the phonograph has never been able to pull off convincingly.) Colin Davis's Osmin, Robert Lloyd, is as flavorful as Frick—but the rest of the performance (Philips) is rather on the sweet side. Yehudi Menuhin makes a rare appearance on the opera podium leading Angel's English-language *Abduction*—an amusing switchoff, as this work marks one of German opera's first assertions of native energy in both music and language. It's a handsome performance, even if the Blonde (Jennifer Eddy) sounds more like a Konstanze than the Konstanze (Mattiwilda Dobbs) does. Moreover, only Gedda, the sole "foreigner" in the English-speaking cast, expends the diction to put the translation over; and Angel, like Seraphim, supplies no booklet.

We now come, chronologically, to the Big Four, and to the epochal Mozart Society Recordings that introduced the idea of preserving festival performances. The "society" approach, organized by HMV's Walter Legge on a basis of public subscriptions to capitalize the recording of unusual repertory, was launched with a volume of songs by Hugo Wolf. The second project, a complete cycle of Beethoven sonatas by Artur Schnabel, turned out to be one of the phonograph's most enduring achievements. But the four Mozart opera sets, in the middle 1930s, made the most significant history, as three of them, built around Glyndebourne productions under Fritz Busch, marked the first attempts not only to document a specific production but to capture its spirit, even measure its theatricality, as, here, in the wind machine that heralds the entrance of Don Giovanni's stone guest, or the rhythmic clinking of glasses on "Bevi, tocca!" in *Così fan Tutte*'s finale. The use of piano for recit, typical of the day (as in the Busch *Brandenburg Concertos*), startles modern listeners, and few of these early Glyndebourne singers command important reputations. But, over the years, they have stood up to competition from highly resourceful casts in increasingly superior sound, in reissue on Victor (decent), Turnabout (poor), and, most recently, Seraphim—and they are very much alive and well in their best transfer yet.

The Glyndebourne *Figaro*, first of the series, in 1934, omits the recits, and is generally the least imposing of the three sets, an agreeable but lightweight performance. *Le Nozze di Figaro* is, in a way, the most important of Mozart's operas, based on a play of vast social reach, a frankly revolutionary play in an increasingly revolutionary era, adapted by one of the three or four greatest composer-librettist teams in the annals, Mozart and Lorenzo da Ponte. Like Beaumarchais's play, the opera *Figaro* may be light in part, but never lightweight. Its at times dark strains of social commentary and humanistic inquiry ask for more of its performance than merry, poised *canto*. Too much can go wrong in even the best-intentioned *Figaros*—as in Columbia's mono set from Vienna, a classic cast (Schwarzkopf, Seefried, Jurinac, London, Kunz) undone by von Karajan's unyielding tempos, *Figaro* as a *concerto grosso* for voices; or in Victor's 1955 Glyndebourne remake, beautifully paced by Vittorio Gui, with Jurinac's intelligent Countess, but otherwise dulled by uncompelling voices.

Five sets seem to me to bring out all that is in this amazing work— the five all together, for each emphasizes a different aspect. London's Vienna entry under Erich Kleiber is the best-humored, *Figaro* as *opera buffa*. Cesare Siepi accords with the baritones we hear on 78s in taking "Aprite un po' quegli occhi" wryly. But this is, after all, an outburst, a rash attack on women by a man who thinks one has wronged him. Tito Gobbi's 78 acts the solo as well as sings it, and after him Siepi's approach, a mocking address of the men in the house, sounds wrongheaded. It does fall in with the vaudeville-turn air of the scene, for Kleiber includes Marcellina's and Basilio's solos, often cut as "sherbet arias" of no relevance to the action. Nevertheless, the set generally plays as sentimental comedy, egged on by Hilde Gueden's delightful Susanna (she also steps in for Marcellina's aria) and Suzanne Danco's ravishing Cherubino, very confidential in "Non so più," aided by Kleiber's delicate accompaniment.

On the other hand, the agents of narrative dynamics in London's digital set under Solti are Susanna (Lucia Popp) and the *Count* (Thomas Allen), replacing Kleiber's *Gemütlichkeit* with sexual-political confrontation. Kiri Te Kanawa's Countess and Samuel Ramey's Figaro are more passive, Ramey ordinary in "Aprite," though the piece especially flatters his bright-hued timbre. However, Frederica von Stade, repeating the Cherubino that she sang for von Karajan (London), is as vital as Popp and Allen, and again we note changing performing traditions in a single number, "Non so più." Amelita Galli-Curci's acoustic 78 is hasty, characterless, and rises to an unnecessary top B flat. Conchita Supervia's electric performance is more stylish, but makes no attempt to disguise the singer's very womanly charm—exploits it, indeed, in the imploring caress on "di colore." Schwarzkopf's version, on her Mozart recital (Angel mono), reflects postwar stylistic rectitude in a no-nonsense reading, firmly acted and cleanly sung. But Danco's persuasive alternative backs up von Stade in a reading of great warmth and thoughtfulness—witness the moment of musing wonder at the penultimate phrases, bouncing back triumphantly at the last.

Colin Davis's set (Philips) is darkly contentious, the closest to Beaumarchais. With Jessye Norman, Mirella Freni, Yvonne Minton, Ingvar Wixell, and Vladimiro Ganzarolli, it has more voice than Kleiber, more character than Solti. It is, perhaps, an acquired pleasure, because so different from other *Figaros*; yet subtly so. Certainly, Otto Klemperer's *Figaro* (EMI) is very obviously different, though a pleasure for the few. This is the Germanic approach, *Figaro* as symphony, with tempos on the lofty side, shaped act by act rather than from number to number. Few critics enjoyed it—it is more to be admired than enjoyed—but it does count important portrayals in Elisabeth Söderström's Countess and Geraint Evans's celebrated Figaro, a fixture of postwar British music history. Evans's "Aprite," strictly in character, is as well sung as many others, but Evans was another of those "live" performers, hobbled by the microphone, and the scene, here on disc, fails to give a sense of the artist as he was.

The best of the five *Figaros* is, not coincidentally, the most Italian, Giulini's (Angel) with Schwarzkopf, Anna Moffo, Fiorenza Cossotto, Eberhard Wächter, and Giuseppe Taddei. Solti's set boasts one Italian, Klemperer's none. But Giulini's has two Germans, one American (of Italian descent), and *seven* Italians (including the young Piero Cappuccilli as Antonio). In short: *Figaro* as Mozart–da Ponte rather than Beaumarchais. Sunny, boisterous, and charming in imaginative stereo separations, the performance delights from the very rise of the curtain, Taddei and Moffo creating an atmosphere different from all others. This Figaro has an ease of flow—a fluency in the musical language—that even the fast-recit sets lack. Interestingly, as we lose Marcellina's and Basilio's arias, "Aprite" is set in a more thespian context; and Taddei, who till then has been reading too much of the *buffa* handbook shtick into his near-ideal Figaro, opens up with a splendidly biting harangue. Schwarzkopf's Countess was a great portrayal of the day, aristocratic of phrasing to contrast with the servant characters but also with Eberhard Wächter's oafishly *Junker* Count, a very German view of the role. (German Don Giovannis similarly underline the rogue's loutishness.) Only Klemperer's Söderström rivals Schwarzkopf, mainly for her Ingmar Bergmanesque perspective. In the second-act finale, when the Count is temporarily apologetic, Schwarzkopf delivers her aside to Susanna, "Son dolce di cuore" (roughly: I'm too good-natured), blithely, glad the trouble is over. Söderström reads it in despair, to voice the tragedy of the "second" sex. "Di donne al furore chi più crederà?" she goes on: Who will ever credit a woman's anger again?

Schwarzkopf's Donna Elvira, however, reverses the terms. Now she is a fury, confronting—not importuning—Don Giovanni with her love. Sena Jurinac, on the other hand, is all wistful vulnerability. Both are equally valid—as are dashing or philosophical Giovannis, knowing or untried Zerlinas, affable or contentious Leporellos, and so on. Thus the richness of *Don Giovanni*, its eternal regeneration. Half its characters hail from *opera seria*, half from *buffa*, as the music reflects— Elvira's grandly double-dotted "Ah, fuggi il traditor!" as opposed to Masetto's lumpy "Ho capito." But at times the tone crosses itself—in the suave middle section of the Catalogue Aria, rather deft for the egregious Leporello, or in "Là ci darem la mano," elegant but with a swing. From Molière's day to Mozart's, the Don Juan legend was regarded as comic material; Mozart termed his version a *dramma giocoso*, a comedy. In the nineteenth century, however, *Don Giovanni* was treated as a Byronesque tragedy, the closing sextet cut away and forgotten lest it dilute the flow of alienated doom so fiercely decanted in the Banquet Scene.

Today we try to compehend both sides of the opera—though, as with *Figaro*, recordings show quite some variation of emphasis. There is again a preponderance of festival work, both live on stage and duplicated in the studio—Aix-en-Provence; Edinburgh; Bruno Walter, Wilhelm Furtwängler and Karl Böhm at Salzburg; and, of course, the 1936 Glyndebourne set. This holds up better than the *Figaro*, despite John Brownlee's uncharismatic Giovanni, through its pervasive theatricality. The beating of Masetto, for instance, often perfunctory even in the theatre, is vivid here, giving propulsion for the ensuing recit for Masetto and Zerlina and thus setting up for the most truly consoling "Vedrai, carino" on disc, though Audrey Mildmay is anything but a classic Zerlina. These old Glyndebourne sets are weak in sheer vocal distinction. Nowhere do they rival even an ordinary cast of the LP years, much less such classic 78s as John McCormack's seamless "Il mio tesoro" or Lilli Lehmann's ferociously poised "Or sai chi l'onore" (way back in 1905, with piano, complete with recit and appoggiaturas). In fact, Koloman von Pataky makes an unusually forceful Ottavio and Ina Souez (Donna Anna) dares a slow, lyrical, yet authoritative "Or sai." Still, it is not sheer singing that endears this set to us, but presence—something we miss in such smoothly vocalized sets as Josef Krips's

(London, Jubilee) or Leinsdorf's (Victor), both with Cesare Siepi's celebrated Giovanni. Even Aix (Pathé, Vox), for all the sparkle of its youthful cast, lacks grip. However, Teresa Stitch-Randall's Anna is worth hearing for the passion that she puts into the recit before "Or sai," and for the light but very focused tone she uses in the aria, probably more like the Annas of Mozart's time than the dramatic so-pranos who took it over in the wake of Wagnerism—Lilli Lehmann, for instance, and, more to the point, Leinsdorf's Birgit Nilsson.

Glyndebourne's casts form a kind of Mozart repertory company, re-cruited and initiated. After a single performance, we know what to expect from them in anything. Other festivals may surprise us, col-lecting experts from all over and letting the chemistry pour itself. Karl Böhm's 1977 Salzburg team (DG), live onstage, looks good on pa-per—Sherrill Milnes, Anna Tomowa-Sintow, Teresa Zylis-Gara, Ed-ith Mathis, Peter Schreier, and Walter Berry—and comes off rather well, Berry's coarse Leporello enlivening Milnes's Giovanni and Schreier's unexpectedly vivacious Ottavio dovetailing with Sintow's vulnerable Anna. Going back to 1937, Bruno Walter's Salzburg *Gio-vanni* (Melodram), despite direly "historic" sound, promises a stately gala, with Ezio Pinza's rake, Elisabeth Rethberg's Anna, Luise Hellets-gruber's Elvira (as at Glyndebourne), and Dino Borgioli's Ottavio. Surprisingly, this show really *moves*, the most mercurial *Don* on disc. On the other hand, Furtwängler's 1954 Salzburg reading, handsomely transferred onto Seraphim in 1986, fails its own legend despite a not-able cast (Siepi, Grümmer, Schwarzkopf, Berger, Dermota, Edel-mann). Staged not on the main stage but at the Felsenreitschule, where Paul Czinner filmed it, the production was to have marked a summit of modern Middle European Romanticism, pulling heavy-hitting no-bles, quaint commoners (Walter Berry, twenty-five that year, plays Masetto), and Siepi's alluring Giovanni into Furtwängler's majestic conception. This is certainly a fine performance. But the majesty is more a tone than a spirit, the Romanticism more a hook than a con-ception. There are a few unique moments. The Commendatore's death, scarcely a page of score, conjures up the horror of a great man's death at the hands of a waster. And Grümmer's Anna matches even Schwarzkopf and Siepi in perhaps their greatest roles. Still, this is a commendable reading at best—though for a truly disappointing festi-val *Giovanni* one turns to Daniel Barenboim's 1973 Edinburgh outing (Angel). The casting is not hackneyed—Roger Soyer, Antigone Sgourda, Heather Harper, Helen Donath, Luigi Alva, Geraint Ev-ans—and the text gives us not the usual composite of the Prague pre-miere with the Vienna additions but Prague itself, with the Vienna pieces ("Dalla sua pace," "Mi tradì," and the seldom heard Leporello-Zerlina duet, "Restati qua") tacked on by way of appendix. For once, we hear the original Mozart–da Ponte *Don Giovanni*, liberated from concessions made to singers' abilities or public taste. But the performance is a misfire of sluggish voices and aimless tempos.

Richard Bonynge's studio *Giovanni* (London) is even more authentic in approach, conflating Prague and Vienna in a performance designed to re-create the performing style of Mozart's time. A genuine chamber orchestra (complete with harpsichord continuo and an occasional *concertante* elaboration) accompanies singers of the Old School, playing not only appoggiaturas and cadenzas but all-out bel canto decorations, which make a few of the solos into veritable *da capo* arias. But the orchestra, alas, no more than accompanies, supporting a performance in which singing is everything; and we have grown dependent on a narrative orchestra, a Böhm, a Walter, a Furtwängler. Next to other *Giovannis*, Bonynge's is tendentiously limpid, despite a resourceful cast: Gabriel Bacquier, Joan Sutherland, Pilar Lorengar, Marilyn Horne, Werner Krenn, and Donald Gramm. Critics held Horne's mezzo Zerlina to be a flaw in Bonynge's authenticity, especially as Horne's deep-dish soubrette necessitated some downward transposition. In fact, Horne is not only a fine Zerlina but a correct one, as Mozart's age did not draw hard distinctions among the soprano *Fächer*. Sopranos of mezzo range and timbre routinely sang roles now assigned to the higher voice; Maria Malibran, a mezzo, sang Norma, Amina, and Beethoven's Leonore as well as Rossini's Colbran parts, and if she needed a transposition, she took one.

One wonders what sort of *Don Giovanni* Bonynge's cast might have given us in a reading geared to modern taste. Certainly, Colin Davis's gutlessly beautiful crew (Wixell, Arroyo, Te Kanawa, Freni, Burrows, Ganzarolli) brings us no closer to Mozart than Bonynge's. Von Karajan's 1986 Berlin reading (DG digital)—surprisingly his first *Don Giovanni* on disc—is heavy and dull, an overmiked orchestra bringing us closer and closer to von Karajan. Lorin Maazel's sound track to Joseph Losey's film (Columbia) is muscular, an attempt to extrapolate Mozartean intensity with international stars. The performance sounds better on disc than on screen, away from Losey's often irrelevant visuals. If Edda Moser's Anna is less lovely than forceful, and if Te Kanawa's Elvira lacks point (as she also did for Davis), the men are quite good: Ruggero Raimondi another very Italian bass Giovanni, cooler than Pinza and lighter than Siepi, Kenneth Riegel a lively Ottavio, and José van Dam a trim, wry Leporello, rich with niceties in his Catalogue Aria. For Maazel, it seems, the opera's combination of *seria* and *buffa* is more a face-off than a blend, which hobbles the score's mercurial pacing. What other four-disc opera passes by so quickly?

Two notable performances go further than Maazel in separating *Giovanni*'s comic and heroic elements—in fact, shaping the action entirely around one or the other. Carlo Maria Giulini (Angel) gives us a *Giovanni* rather like his *Figaro*, fleet, nimble, touching. All the better: for when the Judgment finally arrives, it truly appalls. The cast yields an arresting blend of German and Italian styles, especially in the two central figures, Eberhard Wächter less feisty than most northern Giovannis (though he bangs out, rather than tosses off, the Champagne Aria) and Giuseppe Taddei a savagely sarcastic Leporello. Above all, the set is extremely musical, Schwarzkopf in more commanding form than for Furtwängler, Sutherland in such gala voice as Anna that she tosses off rather than bangs out the treacherous "Or sai," and Graziella Sciutti, as Zerlina, holding a master class in the projection of character through phrasing. "Là ci darem la mano" typifies Giulini's deftness, the 6/8 coda more delightful than any other, especially as Sciutti's hesitation resolves in a tensely cheerful "Andiam!"

Otto Klemperer (Angel), on the other hand, feels the tension more than the cheer. He doesn't actually scant the comedy, but contains it; here is the grandly Romanticized Giovanni we expected from Furtwängler. As Giulini's cast is largely Italian, Klemperer's is more northern in temper: Nicolai Ghiaurov, Claire Watson, Ludwig, Freni, Gedda, and Berry. While he woos suavely, Ghiaurov generally delivers a hoodlum Giovanni, not just a hedonist but a scourge. Such an approach would throw Giulini's pure *dramma giocoso* off its pins, but it suits Klemperer's morality parable, and he and Ghiaurov goad each other into a titanic Judgment Scene. The rest of the cast may disappoint those who appreciate Giulini's dashing team. Yet Klemperer's cast carries the freight musically: Watson a sweet-toned Anna, Gedda vastly improved from his Aix days, and Ludwig's mezzo Elvira matching Horne's London Zerlina for unusual role coloration (and field-expedient transposing).

Giulini's set is a classic, the favorite *Giovanni* of many a Mozartean. Klemperer's set is rather disliked. However, I would recommend Klemperer as Giulini's complement, the *seria* to his *buffa*. And for a most dynamic *Don Giovanni*, I recommend yet a third Angel set, under Bernard Haitink, this one also from Glyndebourne, digitally recorded in 1984 and generously held to three LPs. Taped in the studio, the reading nevertheless tells of the theatre, saluting a tradition that Glyndebourne itself inaugurated back on the old Mozart Society sets fifty years before. But note an aspect of shifting values in phonograph history: where the 1936 *Don Giovanni* counted a highly international cast, the new one is almost all British and American. What a contrast with Giulini's and Klemperer's Continental headliners: Thomas Allen, Carol Vaness, Maria Ewing, Elizabeth Gale, Keith Lewis, and Richard Van Allan. It's arguable whether any of these delivers the greatest recorded portrayal of his part; what counts, more than individual contributions, is the ingenious fluency of the whole. Even Giulini's set is not livelier, even Klemperer's not darker. As in the Peter Hall production that this set records, *buffa* and *seria* merge, and there are moments when one feels one has for the first time truly heard, *understood* a passage: as in the way the velvet sensuality of "Andiam, andiam, mio bene" cedes to a disturbingly decisive finish, or the way that Ewing carries the questioning nature of the recit before "Mi tradì" into the aria itself, so that we listen, for once, to da Ponte as well as to Mozart (even if the aria's hazardous final lines find Ewing, as so many, in difficulties), or the way that Van Allan shows us how terrifying the stone statue is, the comic shuddering out of his shtick. The stereo separation is creative, affecting a stage perspective at Leporello's call to the maskers. There is one drawback. Lewis's Ottavio was staged as a bearded oldster rather than an ardent fiancé, arrestingly tinting Anna's relationship with Giovanni but rendering Ottavio as ineffectual on disc. Moreover, Haitink's businesslike conducting is a letdown. (The CDs let more orchestra detail shine through, at least.) Still, the set is absorbing, authentic *dramma giocoso*—and, like its predecessor of 1936, a document of what it is like to be alive, operatic, and in the vicinity of Glyndebourne when the history was made.

Recordings of *Così fan Tutte* (All Women Do So) similarly hold close to theatre productions. Busch's old Glyndebourne set (Souez, Helletsgruber, Eisinger, Nash, Domgraf–Fassbaender, Brownlee) might be the best in the series, and even the Met enters the lists, in 1953, in Alfred Lunt's production (Columbia mono), with good work from Eleanor Steber, Roberta Peters, and Richard Tucker. It's embarrassing to compare this blatant sitcom version with the sophisticated European crews; worse yet, the close-miked singers have good diction, revealing an English translation of lurid drivel. Angel's live digital tape of Riccardo Muti's 1983 Salzburg reading (Marshall, Baltsa, Battle, Araiza, Morris, van Dam) greatly advances on Glyndebourne's in vocalism and Columbia's in elegance. From the querulous tone of the opening, suggesting a hot quarrel in session; or the sound of real desperation when the women learn that their lovers are going to war; or the worrisome pause after "Un aura amorosa," to show us, as the characters are learning, how fiercely fragile love is, we get a strong sense of the opera's contradictory nature, of its humanism framed in farce.

Angel's 1954 mono set under von Karajan, another of Walter Legge's attempts to concoct perfect chemistry in the studio, did not derive from the theatre. Rather, it entered the theatre, when half the cast met Guido Cantelli at the Piccola Scala two years later. Cetra preserves the theatre reading, astonishingly effervescent (alas, in boorish sound). Von Karajan, by comparison, is constrained—or, let us say, confidential. He enjoys the farce, but caresses the humanism, so we sense a tug of attention after the spirited first scene gives way to the sisters' first duet. And von Karajan's cast—Elisabeth Schwarzkopf, Nan Merriman, Lisa Otto, Léopold Simoneau, Rolando Panerai, and Sesto Bruscantini—is excellent. That of Angel's stereo remake is even more notable, Christa Ludwig, Hanny Steffek, Alfredo Kraus, Giuseppe Taddei, and Walter Berry joining the returning Schwarzkopf under Karl Böhm. This is a beautiful Così, but a serious one; perhaps too serious: inconclusive. For von Karajan, Schwarzkopf delivered "Come scoglio" organically, as part of the complex system of tones the conductor was constructing. Now, for Böhm, she turns the aria into a diva caricature. Moreover, though one disc longer, the stereo makes the same cuts as the mono, deleting "Al fato da legge" and "Ah, lo veggio."

Victor's set under Erich Leinsdorf placed the fashion for complete Cosìs. But this one is unsubtle despite good work from Leontyne Price, Tatiana Troyanos, and George Shirley. Solti's set (London: Lorengar, Berganza, Berbié, Davies, Krause, Bacquier), a bit surprisingly, is quite tender, if grand-scaled, but short on humor, even if one of the women sings a pair of squeals into the last section of the first-act finale. (Some business from a stage production?) Of complete stereo Cosìs, only one rivals von Karajan, may even surpass him, albeit with the same approach: a fine cast treading the delicate line between self-revelation and self-ridicule. This is Philips's set under Colin Davis, with Montserrat Caballé, Janet Baker, Ileana Cotrubas, Nicolai Gedda, Vladimiro Ganzarolli, and Richard Van Allan. Here is, above all, a natural performance—no forcing of the comedy, no "playing" the parts. Listen to Caballé's "Come scoglio," amusing us not because she doesn't believe in its titanic defiance, but because she does. Or to Cotrubas's "Una donna a quindici anni," not the usual soubrette turn but veteran advice on how a woman can take power in a man's world. The blend of the six voices is uniquely satisfying, not least because Caballé is so seldom heard in Mozart. Indeed, perfect chemistry.

Legge was setting his standards of perfection long before he came to

Angel: his 1937 Mozart Society *Zauberflöte*, from Berlin rather than Glyndebourne, remains for many the all-time great one. Legge is the second reason why, for this is surely the most aptly cast *Magic Flute* on disc, everyone not only expert in his role but bearing the spirit of his character in the timbre of his voice. Thomas Beecham's conducting, however, is the *first* reason why this is the great *Flute*, in a congenially vigorous reading, almost an earthy one, taking Gerhard Hüsch's Papageno as the *genus loci*. Tiana Lemnitz and Helge Roswaenge are an inspiring pair of lovers, Wilhelm Strienz a forgiving Sarastro. To some listeners, Erna Berger's Queen of the Night is insufficient, dependable on the top notes (though Beecham endearingly slows down for her as she approaches the first high F) but without character. How much more persuasive, in this era, is Gwen Catley, so angry in her single of "I'll have vengeance" ("Der Hölle Rache") that she yelps some of the notes. Nonetheless, given Beecham's approach, Berger's sweet Queen is correct, a kind of doll-like fairy-tale villainess. Certainly, Toscanini's Queen, Julie Ostvath, live at Salzburg the same year, could use some of Berger's virtuosity. The rest of Toscanini's cast outstars Beecham's: Jarmila Novotna, Willi Domgraf-Fassbaender, Alexander Kipnis, and Alfred Jerger along with Roswaenge again. But Toscanini's hammering tempos—"Bei Männern" comes off as a gavotte—strip away the work's gentility. Disappointed listeners come away from the set recalling only Ostvath's spectacular mishap in her first aria, perhaps the three wrongest consecutive notes in opera history.

More than any other Mozart opera—more than any other opera, possibly—*Die Zauberflöte* is subject to interpretive bias. There is the Viennese performance, in which this sublimely interconnected work is factored into its constituents. Thus, Hilde Gueden's Pamina is sensitive (but flips up to high notes by using lower notes as launching pads, in the Viennese manner), Wilma Lipp's Queen is mildly bossy, Walter Berry's Papageno is an oafish card, and Paul Schoeffler's speaker is an art-devoted star cameo, all for Karl Böhm (London mono, Richmond stereo). A *gemütlich* presentation. Comparable, but not as well conducted, is von Karajan's mono set (Columbia, EMI mono) with an if possible even more Viennese ensemble: Irmgard Seefried, Lipp again, Anton Dermota, Erich Kunz (a classic Papageno), and Ludwig Weber.

There are the dramatic performances, with a grouchy Queen and stern Masons, perhaps a threatening or grotesque Monostatos. Solti's *Flute* (London) is a good example, with Cristina Deutekom's scornful Queen, Martti Talvela's lovingly unyielding Sarastro, and Gerhard Stolze's ghoulish Monostatos. The *Flutes* cited above stand without dialogue, but Solti's is theatre, and needs script as well as songs. This is a general stereo-era trend, resisted only by Otto Klemperer (Angel), an archon of the profound performance. Tempos are stately, the comedy is less funny than quaint, and Sarastro becomes the central figure, his weight and color affecting all the scenes. Artistically, Klemperer's *Flute* is the opposite of Beecham's; but here again Legge produced, spreading more talent through his cast than even a festival could—Schwarzkopf, Ludwig, and Marga Höffgen as the Three Ladies, for instance. Legge's five principals are near-classic, Gundula Janowitz a seriously beautiful Pamina, Lucia Popp a headstrong Queen exploiting her naturally plangent timbre in the opening of her first aria, Nicolai Gedda an audacious Tamino, Walter Berry even more the *Gassenteufel* than for Böhm, though here he is somewhat subdued by the majesty of the Masonic court, embodied in the darkly stolid splendor of Gottlob Frick's Sarastro.

Some *Flutes* split the difference between the potential extremes, such as Karl Böhm's 1965 Berlin set (DG), hailed as near-ideal. It is certainly a contender, especially for Fritz Wunderlich's haunting Tamino and Fischer-Dieskau's touching Papageno; but Evelyn Lear's Pamina is more sensitive than sure and Roberta Peter's Queen expert rather than formidable. Note James King and Martti Talvela as the Armed Men.

Wolfgang Sawallisch's 1972 Angel set, one of the few operas released in quadrophonic sound before the industry retired it, is neither one thing nor another, the lovers (Anneliese Rothenberger and Peter Schreier) a bit more vital than usual but the Masons (Kurt Moll and Theo Adam) less imposing. The set has a few distinctions, in Edda Moser's superbly turbulent Queen and the best of Walter Berry's three Papagenos, with many fetching line readings. Mozarteans should investigate the album if only for a rare duet for Tamino and Papageno, attributed to the composer by the opera's librettist, producer, and original Papageno, Emmanuel Schikaneder (who used it to attract attention to a revival after Mozart's death), and otherwise unrecorded. In all, a good but unexemplary *Flute*, though it looks better and better as digital sound checks in with increasingly humdrum performances. Von Karajan's (DG) is bloodlessly excellent. Haitink's (Angel) is curiously stagnant, even with Popp graduated to Pamina, Edita Gruberova's confident Queen, and the imaginative Siegfried Jerusalem as Tamino. Davis's (Philips) is irrelevantly elegant, typified in Luciana Serra's instrumental handling of the Queen's arias, near flawless but lacking personality. (Philips's CDs, however, flourish the reading in a luminous soundscape, preferable even to von Karajan's *Flute* CDs). James Levine's Salzburg set (Victor), annoyingly promoted to four instead of the standard three LPs, offers some fine singing. But while all digital *Flutes* include more dialogue than most people will enjoy on repeated home listening, Victor seems to regard *Die Zauberflöte* as a play with incidental numbers. Thus the extra disc. This much dialogue would be unbearable in the theatre, let alone at home. At that, none of these modern sets rivals Beecham's for sheer love of life, or Klemperer's for love of Mozart.

Those were the good old days.

5

EARLY GERMAN
ROMANTICISM

❧

"Rot your Italianos! for my part, I loves a simple ballat!" So, in Byron's *Don Juan,* does an Englishwoman battle the colonialist expansion of the Italian style in opera. Only in France did native art subsume the foreigner. Everywhere else, native art was subsumed, as major theatres and talents concentrated on *opera seria* or *buffa*—on Italian plots, structures, melody. On *canto.* Frederick the Great of Prussia, so devoted a buff that he attended performances with the score of the night in his lap, took an active role in developing opera—for instance, urging composers to deemphasize the antidramatic *da capo* aria in favor of the shorter, more flexible cavatina. Frederick even wrote the libretto to Karl Heinrich Graun's *Montezuma*—but note that he wrote it (in French) to be translated, then set in . . . Italian. This rule of *canto* held true from Petersburg to London. Barring the various forms of musical comedy, musically helter-skelter and culturally disreputable, music theatre was Italian opera, whether by native sons or by maestros visiting from Venice or Naples.

We observe this phenomenon in highlights of two Baroque operas by Richard Bonynge's expert house team (London), a disc each of Giovanni Battista Bononcini's *Griselda* and this same *Montezuma:* one "Italiano" invading London and one German blithely surrendering Berlin to the conqueror. Joan Sutherland appears in both, as does mezzo

Monica Sinclair, taking over roles originally sung by castratos. But there is a great difference between the works themselves. *Griselda*, from 1722, reflects *opera seria*'s fatal obsession with the *da capo* aria, the three little duets on side two not just refreshing but lifesaving. *Montezuma*, from 1755, reflects not only Frederick's distaste for the repetitive *da capos* but the general exhaustion of the ABA aria as opera's exclusive expressive device. Montezuma's long solo in prison (handsomely done by Lauris Elms) is so ambitious in structure that it looks forward to Florestan's long solo at the opening of *Fidelio*'s second act—forward, one might say, from the discrete architecture of Classicism to the more variable, more personalized forms of Romanticism.

One of opera history's favorite tropes is the native "breakthrough" piece, the work designed to stimulate an indigenous repertory by creating an indigenous style: *The Abduction from the Seraglio*, *Ruslan and Lyudmila*, *The Bartered Bride*. For German opera, creating a German operatic style was not the first breakthrough. What was needed was an art beyond art, a work to capture the burgeoning Romantic spirit, making intelligible Germany's sense of character, of nation, of destiny. Germany, after all, was in 1800 a concept rather than an entity, for the territory itself was composed of a number of kingdoms, duchies, and city-states separated by cultural and political pressures. Yet there was a dream of unity, one that might be made true most profoundly in the theatres, at that time the absolute center of public life among the leadership classes.

Thus Carl Maria von Weber's *Der Freischütz* (The Free-Shooter), produced at Berlin in 1821, brought a feeling of ethnic affirmation that cut across the boundaries from Berlin to Dresden to Munich. One can catalogue the work's Romantic-nationalistic elements—the green-world setting, the demonic elements that spur the plot, the folkish strains and dances, the uniquely Teutonic gusto of Kilian's Mocking Song, even the title itself, so German that literal translation into any language makes no sense. But this is trivia. Mainly, *Der Freischütz* is German in story, song, and morale. What opera had been so before? It is this almost devotionally self-affirming temperament that we listen for on disc.

Undergrounds of Wilhelm Furtwängler's Salzburg Festival *Freischütz* in 1954 give us a zesty ethnicity; even the dialogue, mercilessly uncut for page after page, sounds vital. So does the cast—Elisabeth Grümmer, Rita Streich, Hans Hopf, Kurt Böhme. The chorus and orchestra are surprisingly scrappy. Still, it has the air of a very genial labor of love. And Böhme's villain is amazing—lurid, stamping, creeping, the very soul of Gothic grotesquerie.

This is not to underestimate Grümmer, the first choice as Agathe, and best heard on EMI's bright stereo set under Josef Keilberth (reissued on Seraphim with most of the dialogue cut), a *Freischütz* balanced between the lyrical and the theatrical. Grümmer is both at once, lovely and involved. In her first aria, she is touching at "Welch schöne Nacht!" (What a lovely night!), the famous moment in which she draws the curtain on a bewitching nighttime perspective. Yet a few pages later, she is rapturous in the *Allegro con fuoco*. Her second aria, "Und ob die Wolke," has an almost instrumental purity, and in the last scene she is winning on the line "Schiess' nicht, Max! *Ich* bin die Taube!" (Don't shoot—*I* am the dove!), when her free-shooting swain is about to let loose a fatal bullet. In the end, Grümmer's resolute lyricism embodies a key Romantic figure, the virginal, redemptive *Ewig–Weibliche*, Goethe's Gretchen untempted. Dramatic sopranos also sing Agathe, less aptly—Birgit Nilsson (Angel), for instance, in a generally big performance under Robert Heger with Nicolai Gedda and Walter Berry. Rafael Kubelik's set (London) with Hildegard Behrens (excellent) and René Kollo (unsteady on top) may be too lyrical—Peter Meven's Kaspar lacks demonic drive, weakening the macabre side of things and thus clouding the outline of the pure side.

By far the most comprehensive *Freischütz* is Carlos Kleiber's DG set (Janowitz, Mathis, Schreier, Adam), as much a sensation when it came out in 1973 as was Kleiber's Beethoven's Fifth, which is still considered by many to be the most intense of all. Kleiber brings out every element in Weber right from the start, in an overture of beauty, hesitation, and menace, the whole bound up in that fear of and fascination with emotional engulfment that gives Romantic art its rich paradoxes. This is a highly theatrical reading, the gunshots and ad libs of the opening suggesting the rise of the curtain; and Kleiber takes the first chorus at quite a clip, drawing us into his world. Then Günther Leib (Kilian) leads the contest kibitzers in the Mocking Song with biting *Witz*, the choristers perfectly synchronized and the Dresden Staatskapelle sounding like a village band. So Kleiber continues, in a fresh but utterly correct reading of a classic, the outdoor scenes hearty, the indoor scenes tidy, the Wolf's Glen terrifying through stereo effects and an echo-chamber Samiel. Janowitz is beautiful (if no Grümmer), Schreier fetching, Adam handsomely threatening, and Mathis a fine Aennchen: the essential set.

Undergrounds carry Weber's contemporary Heinrich Marschner, whose *Hans Heiling* and *Der Vampyr* (together in a four-disc MRF box), share some of *Der Freischütz*'s characteristics but little of its quality. No, it is Weber who clues us into the spirit of German opera as it was coming into its province, not least in *Euryanthe*, chivalrous where *Der Freischütz* deals with the woodsy bourgeoisie. Angel's fine set, made in Dresden under Marek Janowski, offers a *Lohengrin* cast: Jessye Norman, Rita Hunter, Nicolai Gedda, Tom Krause, and Siegfried Vogel. The performance splits the difference between the Classical and the Romantic, as the opera itself does, more picturesque than Gluck, less ecstatic than Wagner. Weber was a natural in this line of Romantic opera, far more than Schubert, who gives us a poorly tailored example in *Alfonso und Estrella*, with Edith Mathis, Peter Schreier, Fischer-Dieskau, and Hermann Prey (Angel). It looks like a Lieder evening, and sounds like one, too: no dramatic impetus. Schumann's *Genoveva*, with Edda Moser, Schreier, and Fischer-Dieskau (EMI, Arabesque), moves more decisively, but lacks Weber's flowing rhapsody. Traveling to London for a fairy rescue spectacle—a British *Magic Flute*, as it were—Weber created in *Oberon* a one-of-a-kind version of the era's most ordinary genre. DG's set under Rafael Kubelik in the German translation sings well but fails in style, Birgit Nilsson a grander soprano than Weber wrote for and Plácido Domingo trying to scale his lyric instrument to equal hers. True, big voices have long been the norm in these parts; but voices weren't that big in Weber's day. Nor does Kubelik have the sense of humor for what is essentially a heroic comedy. Worst of all, DG encumbered the set with a narrator (happily dropped in rerelease on Prestige, from three discs to two). Still, the music comes through. *Oberon* was Weber's last opera, but *Die Drei Pintos* was his "next"—the completed numbers filled out from sketches and obscure Weber material by Gustav Mahler. Victor (Popp, Hollweg, Prey; Gary Bertini) presents a delightful performance of a delightful composition.

Comedy is strategic in this chapter, for where *Der Freischütz* and *Hans Heiling* could audition new forms, comedy could more directly assert the anticolonialist revolution by overturning rules of *opera buffa*. Albert Lortzing is historians' choice as Most German Composer of Comic Operas; perhaps that's why Otto Nicolai's *Die Lustige Weiber von Windsor* (The Merry Wives of Windsor) has traveled the world more comfortably. London's Kubelik and DG's Bernhard Klee lead idiomatic, musical casts, skilled even in the spoken dialogue that German opera preferred to Italian recit. However, DG textures its dialogue with a narrator who keeps popping in to tell you what fun you're having. No matter—London's is the more vivacious performance, Helen Donath deliciously worldly in "Nun eilt herbei," with a most insinuating "Jedoch" (However . . .), and Karl Ridderbusch's Falstaff endlessly absurd. For starters, on his entrance he really plays with the repeated "Komm her," where DG's Kurt Moll just repeats it. A more operatic comedy may be heard in Peter Cornelius' *Der Barbier von Bagdad*, sung throughout. Note the title's teasing revision of Rossini. If Figaro is a deft troubleshooter, Cornelius's barber is an oaf who aggravates any problem he attacks. Eurodisc's stereo set (Geszty, Adalbert Kraus, Weikl, Ridderbusch; Hollreiser) is bright and cute, but it can't compete with Angel's mono classic (Schwarzkopf, Gedda, Prey, Oskar Czerwenka; Leinsdorf). Czerwenka is a natural comic, going for glory in what may be the longest cadenza in opera, on the name "Margiana"—Schwarzkopf at her most ravishing. Ridderbusch is much freer on top in the warmly grandiose "Salamaleikum!" finale, but his Eurodisc gang make it sound like Mendelssohn. On Angel, it sounds like champagne.

One opera above all dominates this field, more even than *Der Freischütz: Fidelio*. This work has become almost a sacramental exercise. Amid the *Manons* and *Toscas*, it recalls to us the cathartic and socializing effect of the ancient Greek stage. *Fidelio* is not a good opera for records, then: we need to *undergo* it live in the amphitheatre, experience the desperation of Florestan's solitary confinement and the persistence of his wife and savior, Leonore. Even the humdrum comings and goings of jailer Rocco, his daughter, and her boyfriend add to the event, by rooting the amazing heroism in a naturalistic environment.

Of course, Beethoven didn't add them in for that reason—didn't add them at all. Rocco, Marzelline, and Jacquino are part of the property, first a French *opéra comique* (supposedly based on a real-life adventure), then an unusual combination of *buffa* and *seria* by Ferdinando Paër, *Leonora*. Again we find the Italian style dominant in foreign parts. *Leonora* was written for Vienna in 1804; Beethoven heard it and decided to recompose it in German. Hear what inspired him on London (Koszut, Gruberova, Jerusalem, Brendel, Norbert Orth; Maag), an attractive performance. Paër gave Beethoven the basis for Leonore's "Abscheulicher!" solo, Florestan's scene alone in prison, the famous trumpet call. But Paër has no Prisoners' Chorus, no shattering democratic finale. As Maag suggests in his notes, *Leonora* is a love story, whereas *Fidelio* is a political event.

Thus carrying over the comic elements while expanding the heroic ones, Beethoven brought forth what is now—falsely—called *Leonore*: meaning the first of the three versions of *Fidelio*. In fact, though Beethoven wanted to name the opera after his heroine rather than her pseudonym, the piece was billed as *Fidelio* in 1805, 1806, and (at last successful in the form we are used to) 1814. To move from Paër to Beethoven is to realize that the development of German opera depended as much on spirit as on form. Even in its longer first version—well but not brilliantly served on EMI and reissued on Arabesque (Moser, Cassilly, Adam, Ridderbusch; Herbert Blomstedt), *Fidelio* remains a German interpretation of Italian opera, the *buffo* elements vital in Marzelline and Jacquino's quaint wrangling, or in Rocco's Gold Aria. Yet Beethoven's Leonore and Florestan are beyond what Italian opera had been able to create till then, so inspiring in their idealism that Richard Wagner liked to date his artistic epiphany from Wilhelmine Schröder-Devrient's fiery Leonore. Right singer, wrong opera, scholars tell us—Schröder was probably singing Agathe or Euryanthe. But the romance is persuasive, because Beethoven is.

Fidelio is festival opera, like *Don Giovanni.* How else but under festival conditions to serve its nobility and profundity while matching the heroes to the comics? The great *Fidelio* is held to be that of Furtwängler's 1950 Salzburg cast, on numerous undergrounds (Flagstad, Schwarzkopf, Patzak, Schoeffler), towering and wise. Three years later, Furtwängler taped a studio *Fidelio* with his Vienna cast (Victor, Seraphim mono: Mödl, Jurinac, Windgassen, Edelmann), vocally less satisfying, though the omission of the dialogue may appeal to some listeners. Rivaling Furtwängler is Bruno Walter, at the Met in 1941 (EJS) with a younger Flagstad, René Maison's passionate Florestan, and Alexander Kipnis's grand Rocco. Viewed as a conductor's opera, *Fidelio* is rich in stylistic choice, a work poised on the boundary between tradition and innovation, between the sturdy eighteenth century and the roiling nineteenth. Furtwängler looks back to Mozart, building from the *buffo* characters to the dazzling revolution of the heroes, while Walter treats the whole as an operatic Ninth Symphony. Otto Klemperer completes the trio of great *Fidelio* conductors with a Classical Romanticism, the *buffo* elements made weighty and the heroes less athletic, more archetypal. Melodram has Klemperer's 1961 Covent Garden performance, with Jurinac (graduated to Leonore), Vickers, and Hotter, Angel his studio classic in prime early stereo, with Ludwig and Berry flanking Vickers. Melodram has a more exciting Prison Scene, as well as the customary interpolation of the *Leonore* Overture Number Three, absent on Angel—two reasons why those who heard Klemperer in the theatre felt a little disappointed in his studio set. However, Klemperer did oblige those who wish to compare all four of the opera's overtures—unpretentious *Leonore* One, the virtual tone poems *Leonore* Two and Three, and *Fidelio,* last and directly between least and most—on Angel, mono and stereo remake with the Philharmonia.

Klemperer's is not the only studio *Fidelio* to disappoint expectations based on live performances. Toscanini's set (Victor mono), from the 1944 NBC broadcast, lacks the cast to compete with his Salzburg *Fidelios* with Lotte Lehmann in the 1930s. Von Karajan (Angel) has cast trouble, too, Helga Dernesch overparted and Vickers not as good as for Klemperer. Bernstein was the talk of Vienna for his *Fidelio*, but his set (DG) lacks something, even with Janowitz, Popp, Kollo, Sotin, Jungwirth, and Fischer-Dieskau as Don Fernando, a superb lineup. They deliver the dialogue better than any other group, and Kollo may well be the best Florestan on records. But we miss that sense of overwhelming release at the end, that feeling of having shared some of Florestan's idealism and Leonore's heroism that so marks, for instance, Klemperer's Angel set.

Solti's 1980 set with the Chicago Symphony (London) claims a bit of history as the first complete opera released in digital sound. His cast (Behrens, Hofmann, Adam, Sotin) is top of the line for 1980, but, after Furtwängler's and Klemperer's casts, not sufficiently distinguished. Obviously, the shortage of Wagner singers has struck *Fidelio* as well, since we think of Beethoven's opera as the Wagnerian matrix, just as Wagner insisted. After all, Furtwängler's *Fidelio* singers *were* Wagnerian, most of them the same artists we hear on his two Italian *Rings*. It's bad enough that we have trouble scaring up our *Tristans* and *Walküres*, but any age that cannot field a major *Fidelio* is in a lot of trouble.

6

ROSSINI

※

Rossini's relationship with the phonograph has been one of the most frustrating and enlightening in opera. The frustration came first, for till quite recently only his comedies were thought marketable, along with a "Bel raggio" here and a "Di tanti palpiti" there: thus supporting the assumption, common even in his lifetime, that Rossini's was a comic talent, dryly witty but lacking the nobility for serious work. The enlightenment came when record companies began to turn to the other Rossini—for, far from lacking nobility, Rossini revealed himself as a brilliant and affecting dramatist, the key man in the all-important transition between *opera seria* and the *melodramma* that served Bellini, Donizetti, and Verdi (till Verdi, in his turn, refined it for the next generation).

That Rossini was one of opera's towering masters was no secret to the composers who followed him in Italy, especially in the light of *Guillaume Tell*, which Bellini heard thirty times and whose second act Donizetti declared to have been written by God. But *Tell* faded from the scene along with Rossini's other French grand operas, and Verdi's *Otello* replaced Rossini's, and the rise of verismo thrust aside the delicate technique needed to sing Rossini's florid lines. The comedies stayed alive, especially in the hands of Conchita Supervia, whose 78 excerpts were regarded as hallmarks of the Rossinian style. Giulietta Simionato, Supervia's apparent successor, lacked the older singer's capering oomph, as we hear on Angel's early mono Scala set of *L'Italiana in Algeri* (The Italian Girl in Algiers) under Carlo Maria Giulini (Seraphim). Simionato is wry, agile, bold—but not delightful. London's stereo *Italiana* under Silvio Varviso (Berganza, Alva, Corena) is more complete but flavorless. Yet another specialist in Rossini's mezzo heroines, Lucia Valentini Terrani, recorded the opera twice. But we turn to Claudio Scimone's crew of Marilyn Horne, Ernesto Palacio, and Samuel Ramey (Victor digital) for the ideal *Italiana,* infectious fun crisply conducted according to a corrected text, with a sixth-side bonus of alternate arias interpolated into various stagings when the opera was new. Palacio brilliantly places the penetrating high notes we have come to expect from the Rossinian tenor, and Horne rivals Supervia in her vivid coloratura and relish of key phrases. Even the recits seem to dance.

With *Il Turco in Italia,* the Angel-Columbia comparison reverses itself, for while Columbia's digital set (Caballé, Ramey; Chailly) is complete in a restudied edition, Angel's mono Scala performance in a corrupt text under Gianandrea Gavazzeni (Callas, Rossi-Lemeni; reissued on Seraphim) has the dash. *Il Turco* is an unusual piece for *opera buffa,* a farce-within-a-farce urged on by a character called the Poet. On Angel, Mariano Stabile gives him a touch of mania, uttering amusingly ecstatic cries of "Turco!" (A Turk!) at the thickening of his plot. On Columbia, the moment goes for nothing.

La Cenerentola (Cinderella) is more romantic, the *buffo* characters upstaged by the love plot. Still, this is no excuse for the dully earnest sheen of Columbia's stereo set with Terrani. On the other hand, everyone in Victor's 1953 Glyndebourne set under Vittorio Gui sparkles—everyone but the pallid heroine, Marina de Gabarain. Nor is the Russian set (MK, Eclat) acceptable, despite Zara Dolukhanova's charming Cinderella and Evgeny Belov's amusing Dandini. Style runs wild here, with piano-accompanied recits, a nasally white tenor (Anatoly Orfenov), and a conductor who breaks the cardinal rule governing the celebrated "Rossini crescendo": get louder, *not* faster.

Unfortunately, the best *Cinderella* is so heavily cut that it amounts to highlights. This is Cetra's mono set under Mario Rossi with Simionato, Cesare Valletti, and Saturno Meletti, who give *buffo* its due while respecting the poignancy of the romance. Simionato remade the opera in stereo for London in a fuller text, but she was fresh out of voice by then. Luckily, Claudio Abbado's stereo set (DG) has many virtues, not least its corrected text, in Alberto Zedda's edition. The fun begins in the overture, when Abbado gives a lesson in the care and maintenance of a Rossini crescendo, taking the London Symphony down to *pianissimo moltissimo* in order to instate a wholly graduated *fortissimo* at the climax. The fun dampens a bit when Zedda's scholarship replaces "Vasto teatro," the often-cut solo of Alidoro (the fairy godfather figure), included on London, with an authentic Rossini piece. It's a clinker of a scene, and rather heavy for the work (if not the character) till its zippy second half. Anyway, Ugo Trama makes heavy weather of it. At that, Abbado's cast (Berganza, Alva, Capecchi) could use some of Cetra's zest, Berganza especially. But then this is a tricky role to bring off, a soulful dear trapped in a farce.

Il Barbiere di Siviglia has no such problems; this one is all comedy. No other of Rossini's operas demonstrates as well the growing interest in the purification of style, the purging of traditional corruptions. Going back to Victor's 1919 set under Carlo Sabajno, an odd conflation of ten- and twelve-inch discs, we find not only an assault on text but a perfunctory performance to boot. Ernesto Badini's Figaro, at least, is prime, the best till Tito Gobbi's, with a savvy chuckle when Rosina presents the letter on "Eccolo qua." But Malvina Pereira, a soprano Rosina, tootles without savor, and Edoardo Taliani's Almaviva is woefully inept in his divisions. Typically for the day, the Bartolo sings Pietro Romani's "Manca un foglio" instead of Rossini's "A un dottor"—but most shocking is the handling of the Lesson Scene, at the time an excuse for the soprano to pump in any showpiece of her fancy. At the end of side twenty-six, Taliani says, "Incominciate" (Let's begin), the cue for Rosina's solo. But, as side twenty-seven begins, Bartolo is crying, "Bella voce, bravissima!" (Lovely voice, excellent!). Not only don't we get the lesson song that Rossini wrote—God forbid—we don't even get the interpolation! Presumably, listeners were expected to slot in a showpiece of their fancy, by a soprano more nimble than Pereira.

Not till LP days did mezzos reclaim Rosina to instill the darker earth tones of Rossini's original casting. Victoria de los Angeles recorded the *Barber* twice, on Victor's blatant mono set, then, in stereo, with Angel's Glyndebourne group under Vittorio Gui, an admirable but not infectious reading. We still count our soprano Rosinas, as in Beverly Sills's sparkling turn under Levine (Angel), with a hefty group of Names: Nicolai Gedda, Sherrill Milnes, Renato Capecchi, Ruggero Raimondi, and Fedora Barbieri. It's a hefty performance, too; the finale sounds as if the Mormon Tabernacle Choir were sitting in. Once again, Marilyn Horne and a Zedda edition come to the rescue under Chailly (Columbia digital), with Leo Nucci's marvelous Figaro, the "Largo al Factotum" tossed off with tremendous brio. Horne, her big voice girlishly scaled down, is delicious, with an "Una voce poco fa" so keen she outshines Callas. Still, many will prefer Angel's 1957 set under Alceo Galliera for Callas's savagely elfin intriguer and Gobbi's detailed partnering. MRF preserves, live, their Scala failure of the preceding year, a production denounced for exaggeration of shtick. Toned down for the studio, Callas and Gobbi hit just the right note, even given Callas's soprano keys.

Purifying Rossinian comedy, however, is less important than revealing Rossinian drama in its influential expansion of *melodramma*'s trim package of solos, duets, and trios into the full-scale epics that set grand opera on its course. Note the almost simplistic structure of *Tancredi*, Rossini's first great success, in 1813, on Columbia with Horne in digital sound. Move on to *Otello*, of 1816, not longer or grander but more detailed, with a cast made up largely of tenors, who replaced the castrato when *opera seria* turned into *melodramma*. (For a while, conservative centers such as Vienna and Dresden resisted the new vocal types; Dresden even mounted *Tancredi* with a castrato replacing the mezzo lead.) Philips has a superb *Otello* with José Carreras and Frederica von Stade under Jesús López Cobos. Rossini provided an alternate happy ending for those who like their romance righter than their Shakespeare; Philips reinstates the tragic ending.

In 1823 we reach the more spacious *Semiramide*, filled out not with plot action but with the pageantry of rhetoric—a grander scale in the solos and ensembles, and increased participation from the chorus. The vocal casting, too, has altered, suggesting in its soprano, mezzo, tenor, and two bass leads what was to become a standard lineup, especially after Donizetti and Verdi developed the first bass into a dramatic baritone. London's fine *Semiramide* offers a Bonynge team led by Sutherland and Horne, as identified with this work as Flagstad and Melchior were with *Tristan und Isolde* in the late 1930s. The heroine's great solo, "Bel raggio lusinghier," popular as a 78 solo even when the opera itself had vanished, became even more popular when the opera became familiar, making *Semiramide*, like *Lakmé*, something of a famous aria surrounded by an opera. Callas recorded the solo, in the grand manner but failing voice. Frederica von Stade's more radiant reading (on her Columbia Italian recital) challenges Sutherland's cooler expertise.

Both Desdemona and Semiramide are "Colbran roles," written for Rossini's wife, Isabella Colbran. Like Maria Malibran, another Rossini specialist, Colbran was a coloratura mezzo with a free upper register, the tintype of the Rossinian prima donna who has only recently reclaimed her eminence. Some sopranos tackle Colbran roles without adjustment—Caballé, for instance, in Philips's elegant *Elisabetta, Regina d'Inghilterra*. Callas and Deutekom are heard in undergrounds of *Armida*, and Caballé (BJR) faces off the more naturally Colbranesque

Valentini Terrani (Columbia) in *La Donna del Lago,* one of the early Romantic era's many operatic gleanings from Sir Walter Scott. Along with the Rossinian mezzo, we require the Rossinian tenor, out of currency for so long that Callas's *Armida* in 1952 makes do with stand-ins of various styles for its six tenor parts, while Deutekom's, in 1970, fields an authentic (if variably successful) assortment.

The Neapolitan Rossini (1814–23) seems at times to be capably holding the fort, at other times to be making sorties—in form, in instrumentation, in expressive technology. Moving to Venice, less conservative than Naples, Rossini experimented further—*Semiramide,* written for Venice, might almost be an Italian stab at grand opera. Then Rossini moved to Paris, and there he attempted French versions of grand opera, integrating the Italian spirit with the resources of the French style. First, however, came *Il Viaggio a Rheims* (The Trip to Rheims), an all-star farrago of little merit. DG's digital set, even worse, is less than all-star. But then came *Le Siège de Corinthe,* a revision of the Neapolitan *Maometto II*—and, as both have been recorded, we can compare *melodramma* with grand opera.

The differences are many, both great and small, though it must be said that *Maometto II* was one of Rossini's more adventurous Neapolitan operas, a *melodramma* already edging out of the tight, aria-oriented form into the grander scheme typified in *Semiramide.* Still, we notice that *Maometto* has more florid vocal lines, a trouser role, a lax narrative drive, and simple orchestration, while *Le Siège de Corinthe* bows to the French taste for relatively clean lines, lets the tenor wear the pants, tightens up the scene plot, expands the wind scoring, and adds an overture. Philips's digital *Maometto* under Claudio Scimone delivers the piece in full true, with soprano June Anderson in the Colbran role, Samuel Ramey as the Moslem invader (her old boyfriend, alas, under an alias), and Ernesto Palacio as Anderson's father. Margherita Zimmermann is the latest addition to the ranks of the Rossinian mezzo, and very nearly challenges the unchallengeable Shirley Verrett on Angel's *L'Assedio di Corinto* (the Italian translation of *Le Siège*), based on the Met production with Sills, Harry Theyard, and Justino Díaz. The Met staging was based in turn on the 1969 Scala production, something of a conflation of *Maometto* and *Le Siège* and famous for its American contingent, Horne joining Sills and Díaz. (Franco Bonisolli played Sills's father.) Angel's set is fine, but MRF's relay of the Scala performance has a virtually historical excitement, pulling legend into life. And, of the three mezzos, only Horne delivers, in an amazing tour de force, the mezzo's big solos from *Maometto* and *Le Siège,* back to back. It was quite a night.

Rossini's next opera for Paris, *Moïse et Pharaon,* was similarly a revision, of *Mosè in Egitto,* on events leading up to the crossing of the Red Sea. Voce's French tape suffers from fuzzy sound and Joseph Rouleau's weak Moses, but Philips's old mono set of the revision's Italian translation under Serafin horribly typifies what Rossinian "style" was like in the 1950s. In the Colbran role we get Caterina Mancini, a rough-and-ready Verdian soprano. As Moses we get Nicola Rossi-Lemeni, a fine artist but no singer of coloratura. Giuseppe Taddei is an able Pharoah—Taddei never recorded anything incapably—but the tenor lead, rewritten for the suave Adolphe Nourrit, is given to Mario Filippeschi, a clumsy dramatic tenor. It's interesting, though, that the works that Rossini rewrote for Paris both deal with political oppression, for democratic resistance was to provide grand opera with its thematic matrix, from *Le Siège* (1826) and *Moïse* (1827) through Auber's *La Muette de Portici* (1828) up to *Guillaume Tell* (1829), the greatest of all grand operas till Verdi's *Don Carlos.*

Tell's politics, derived from Schiller's Romantically idealistic play, are less interesting than the music is: than how the score presents both a summit of Rossini's career and a challenge to his successors, how Rossini educated French voices with Italian eloquence, how the phonograph regarded a masterpiece so fallen into disuse that it was rarely heard by 1900. *Tell* 78s are common, and we note little participation by singers who would have graced *La Cenerentola* or *Otello.* The tenor, Arnold, has become dramatic; the soprano, Matilde, is a high lyric, not a Colbran mezzo. Above all, we hear power and ring in, say, Agustarello Affre's or Antonio Paoli's excerpts, especially in Paoli's fiercely keening line in the famous second-act trio in which he learns of his father's death. In Rossini's day, the high notes were taken in falsetto rather than in the penetrating chest voice we hear on these 78s and today; still, the very stock of the voice has been built up to carry dramatic weight in ensembles. In Naples, the Rossinian tenor was a charmer. In Paris, he's a hero. As for the soprano, Claudia Muzio's "Sombre forêt" (in Italian, however), beguilingly alarmed, looks forward to Puccini; perhaps Grete Forst, with Leo Slezak in a snippet of the duet that follows, suggests an authentic Matilde, albeit one who has sung a lot of Lortzing. The baritone, Tell, and bass, Walter, do refer back to what Rossini had been writing in Italy. But his notion of romantic casting has changed: the soprano is less gritty, more expansive, and the tenor has put on weight.

All of which may explain why Cetra's mono set of 1952—the first *Tell* ever—has an almost Verdian cast: Rosanna Carteri, Mario Filippeschi, Giuseppe Taddei, and Giorgio Tozzi under Mario Rossi: a team for *Luisa Miller, Rigoletto, Simon Boccanegra.* The Cetra catalogue was known to collectors of the mono years for its boxy sonics and brawling, provincial casts; and in the 1960s for its mass recirculation on the Everest label, in both the original mono and atrocious gimcrack "stereo," in packaging so shoddy that Leoncavallo's *La Bohème* came out with the libretto booklet all set for Puccini's. (Lately the Italian firm has reclaimed the best of its line.) Some listeners may avoid Cetra's *Tell,* then, on general principle—and, yes, in certain particulars it is unimpressive. The sound is flat mono, the singers are of local rather than international glamour, the reading is constantly hectored by cuts (usually, however, of repeats), and the Italian version obscures Rossini's vocal alchemy. But, in the larger view, this may be the best *Tell* of all.

It is surely the most committed. Conductor Rossi emphasizes the story's revolutionary energy, biting down on Tell's exhortations of the Swiss and defiance of the Austrians; and Taddei, thus roused, gives a gruff, officious Tell in the grand manner, truly astonishing in how much music he gets out of the recits. Carteri, too, responds, singing on the text as if she were being paid by the word. Even the wooden Filippeschi fits in, for his trumpeting top Cs and C sharps, crucial in this notoriously high part. Certainly, Filippeschi looks good in comparison with the helter-skelter Gianni Jaia on a pirate relay also under Rossi (MRF, Foyer). This performance shows what can go wrong in an Italian *Tell,* with the political confrontations edging into verismo and the love music strenuously sobbing. At least we get Dietrich Fischer-Dieskau's pensively greathearted Tell and Anita Cerquetti's gorgeous Mathilde.

What can go right in an Italian *Tell,* many will feel, are Milnes, Freni, and Pavarotti, on London under Chailly in bright, spacious stereo and an uncut text. Milnes is quite moving in the "apple" aria, "Sois immobile," adding in a cadenza that Rossini might have resented and everyone else of the time thought quite appropriate. Milnes is more likable than Taddei, but not political enough: moving but unmoved.

Angel's set under Gardelli shows what can go right, in an authentic *Guillaume Tell* in French. The leads (Bacquier, Caballé, Gedda) are French stylists, and the reading is not only complete but unveils a forgotten extra scene for Tell's son Jemmy, Mady Mesplé. (Jemmy comes off wonderfully on disc—Cetra has Graziella Sciutti and London Della Jones.) Perhaps only Gedda really hones in on the work, formidable in Arnold's nationalism as well in his music. But Caballé renders a beautiful Mathilde—who else today can so deftly smudge coloratura divisions?—and Bacquier is a sound if undistinguished Tell. Gardelli's Verdian conducting presses a bit on the work's majesty, but he is graceful in the awesome C Major finale in which Rossini tries a single theme over and over in contrasting harmonies, a stunning effect unthinkable in the straiter confines of the *melodramma* that Rossini had inherited. To hear *Tancredi* or *Armida*, then jump to *Guillaume Tell*, is to realize—in that flash of comprehension that the phonograph makes possible—how influential Rossini truly was in the development of opera. Not of comic opera.

Of opera.

7

GRAND OPERA

Building on Gluck's *tragédie lyrique,* two generations of expatriate Italian musicians developed grand opera in its heyday in the mid-1800s into the most respected—or perhaps simply respectable—form of music theatre. The development may be seen as an expansion of architecture, as two or three acts become five and pageantry multiplies. Or it may be seen in vocal phenomena, as the soprano lead breaks into two sopranos, lyric and dramatic, while the tenor grows in power and the baritone and bass explore their differences in timbre and assume greater importance as principals. Or consider the cultural evolution, from Gluck's strenuous Classicism to Rossini's political idealism . . . thence to Meyerbeer's tin-whistle spectacles.

Or so Meyerbeer's critics would say. There is another way to view this chapter: as a development away from opera as moralistic parable to opera as entertainment. If Gluck primarily needs great singing actors and Rossini needs great singers, Meyerbeer needs great singer personalities, those unique virtuosos who could leave their mark on a part more through joyful noise than through any concentration of character—Nellie Melba, for instance, presumed to be heard through the background road of a Mapleson cylinder onstage in a Met *Huguenots* and, though no actress, absolutely smashing.* Meyerbeer appreciated great character artists, too, He wrote Fidès in *Le Prophète* for Pauline

---

*The Melba *Huguenots* cylinder, of the cabaletta to "O beau pays," is legendary. However, scholars now take it to be not of Melba at all, but Suzanne Adams.

Viardot, a marvel of the age as well for her Orphée in Berlioz's 1859 revival of Gluck's first reform piece. But it is notable that when the unique virtuosos became rare, Meyerbeer did, too. As we shall see, much of grand opera's discography reveals the public's lack of interest in the generation of composers who followed Gluck in Paris—too serious—and performers' lack of ability in the composers who followed them—too difficult to sing.

First of all comes Luigi Cherubini, comparable to Gluck in tone but more dependent on fully developed musical structures. MRF troubled to fill out Cherubini's discography with a number of forgotten titles. However, in the end Cherubini centers his reputation on Médée, one of the few famous operas that has never been recorded. What has been recorded—three times commercially, and further privately—is Medea, a French opéra comique transposed into an Italian opera seria, with recit replacing the spoken dialogue. If Gwyneth Jones (London) is monotonous and Sylvia Sass (Hungaroton) passionately erratic, Maria Callas, in relays of her 1953 Scala Medea with Fedora Barbieri, Gino Penno, and Giuseppe Modesti under Leonard Bernstein, is simply stupendous. Her commercial recording of the role under Tullio Serafin (Mercury, Everest) was a poor job, in poor voice, though with admirable colleagues. But the live Callas in this, of all roles, proves how much more the musical singer can give—not the actress, the singer. Penno is sensitive, Barbieri solid, and, as Glauce, Maria Luisa Nache surprises with her vitality. But this is a title-role opera. In a single page of recit, at the start of Act Two, Callas finds more character, more music, than some singers find in their whole careers. Her sense of color, her flamboyance, her always startling chest register, the love and fury on which—not to put too fine a point on it—Callas lived . . . all this is here. If her discographer John Ardoin calls her Berlin Lucia the Callas record, and if the soprano herself singled out her second Gioconda, I would call this Medea basic, compleat Callas.

Gasparo Spontini, who came to Paris after Cherubini was established, exemplifies the expansion of Gluck's tragédie into Meyerbeer's grand opera. Spontini's best-known work, La Vestale, is early, Cherubinien, and almost compact: only the soprano and tenor have fully realized parts. The second soprano has but one short solo, and the bass and second tenor are little more than decor. As with most of Cherubini, La Vestale is admirable rather than enjoyable. Since Cetra's lackluster mono set, there have been only undergrounds. LR offers Montserrat Caballé and Nunzio Todisco under Carlo Felice Cillario in a sedate walkthrough from Barcelona in 1982. MRF's more gallant Leyla Gencer and Robleto Merolla under Fernando Previtali in Palermo, 1969, are more persuasive, Gencer, as always, both impressive and awkward, abusing the glottal attack but committed and musical.

Spontini's later works are more enjoyable but less admirable, so long out of fashion that all the sets are pirates. As with Cherubini, MRF has extended itself, to *Fernand Cortez, Olimpie,* and *Agnes von Hohenstaufen. Cortez,* with its piquant Aztec pastiche, points up what was to become a favorite grand-opera plot line: Romeo and Juliet against a background of political upheaval (like *Guillaume Tell's* Mathilde and Arnold, she of the Austrian tyrants and he of the native Swiss freedom fighters). MRF's 1974 RAI *Cortez* under Lovro von Matacic, in Italian, is decent, though sabotaged by the shaky Angeles Gulin. MRF's RAI *Olimpie,* suddenly, is in French, though filtered through the international slant of Yasuko Hayashi, Alexandrina Miltscheva, Werner Hollweg, Alexander Malta, and Alexander Zagrabelni under Gianandrea Gavazzeni. It's a poised but uncompelling performance, lacking the oomph of the 1966 Scala revival with Pilar Lorengar, Fiorenza Cossotto, Franco Tagliavini, and Giangiacomo Guelfi (Melodram). Again, the love plot is set in a political context, in this case the squabbles of the generation that succeeded Alexander the Great in Macedonia.

Agnes von Hohenstaufen is most interesting historically, as it marked the climax of Spontini's reign at Berlin's Royal Opera. There he attempted to popularize the French style, meanwhile demonstrating grand opera's paradoxical relationship with the European *ancien régime:* cultural-capital opera, in Paris and Berlin, was subject to royal authority, yet the operas' plots hammered away on the theme of democratic idealism. (The paradox becomes itself paradoxical when *L'Africaine* features a hero who defies Church and state—to further colonialist expansion.) As it was, Berlin's nobility and the opportunistic bourgeoisie supported Spontini, while the general public preferred the less pretentious subjects of Weber. MRF's *Agnes* (Caballé, Stella, Prevedi, Guelfi, Bruscantini; Muti; RAI, 1970) presents a good account of what may be Spontini's greatest opera. It is certainly his grandest, with much ceremony, huge act finales, and a cast so big it has three characters named Heinrich and two named Philip (one of the latter, forgivably, is mentioned but never appears). MRF knocks the whole thing down to three discs. The complete work is so long that the first act was presented by itself when *Agnes* was premiered in 1827.

The complete *Agnes* saw light in 1829, the year *Guillaume Tell* was first heard, and, somewhere between Spontini's royalist pageantry and Rossini's novel-sized *melodramma,* Meyerbeer pitched his camp. In imagination, even foresight, he was their worthy successor. He dared, for instance, to drop *L'Africaine*'s second-act curtain on an *a cappella* septet, the orchestra silent. This had never been done before. But in taste and feeling, Meyerbeer was a hack despite his best intentions, turning potentially intriguing scenes into formalities, the kind of things that get cut, to general relief, after the first performances. What is most interesting about Meyerbeer's four grand operas is how much they owe to Rossini's *comic* style: stray lines, even whole numbers, and much of the roles of Raimbault, Marcel, and Nélusko suggest a coarsened Rossinian brio, not only in melody but in scoring. Yet Rossini himself had retired this eccentric side by the time he came to Paris.

German by birth and culture, Meyerbeer, too, came to Paris from Italy. His last Italian work, *Il Crociato in Egitto* (The Crusade to Egypt), may be heard in relays of concerts. BJR's, with Janet Price, Patricia Kern, William McKinney, and Christian du Plessis under Roderick Brydon, is suave and in vastly better sound. Voce's, with Yvonne Kenney, Felicity Palmer, Rockwell Blake, and Justino Diaz under Gianfranco Masini, is more complete, and embellished to the nth— as contemporary performances would have been. Interesting, then, to jump to Meyerbeer's next opera, and flash Paris sensation, *Robert le Diable,* for we see how fully Meyerbeer dropped Italian *melodramma* and embraced Rossini's brand of French grand opera. Even *Robert*'s casting was *d'après Tell:* Laure Cinti-Damoreau, Adolphe Nourrit, and Nicholas Levasseur (as well as dancer Marie Taglioni) appeared in both premieres.

It is worth noting how Romantic grand opera had become, after Cherubini's Classical subjects (however, as in *Médée,* treated with Romantic fire) and Spontini's Classical poise. *Tell*'s revolutionary fervor and idyllic nature-painting marked a break with tradition, and *Robert le Diable* pursues this with a tale of demonism, chivalry, and debauchery. *Robert*'s vocal writing, especially the comic duet of bass and tenorino, is Rossinian. But there are original touches as well—in the use of the tenorino's Ballade and a martial timpani figure as *Leitmotive* for, respectively, hero Robert and his evil genius Bertram, say; or in the furious triplet figure that binds sections of the lovers' big Act Four duet. One can see why Meyerbeer was—at first—not only popular but admired, a composer who other composers thought had great potential.

Once again, the private labels bring history to life. MRF has it in Italian as *Roberto il Diavolo* from the 1968 Florence May Festival, with Renata Scotto, Stefania Malagù, Giorgio Merighi, and Boris Christoff under Nino Sanzogno. LR's relay from the Paris Opéra in 1985 features June Anderson, Michèle Lagrange, Alain Vanzo, and Samuel Ramey under Thomas Fulton. The Italian performance, cut to ribbons after a disastrously long dress rehearsal, is the more characterful, with Christoff's usual Shalyapin routine and Scotto's passionate Isabella, making the coloratura of the Tournament Scene a communication of irate despair. LR's set has about an hour's more music, but it is not—claims on the album to the contrary—complete. There are many internal cuts. The opening chorus is shredded, Raimbault's Ballade and Alice's first aria lose a verse each, the ballets are chopped up, the fourth-act finale is cut to a third, and so on. Still, it is in the right language and generally stylish, Ramey more tasteful than Christoff and June Anderson sensitive and generous with the added high notes that Meyerbeer would have loved. Lagrange's Alice, the falcon* part, comes over nicely, giving us some idea of why many golden-age prima donnas preferred this part to that of Isabella, *Robert*'s romantic lead. Vanzo sings with spirit as the vacillating, ultimately redeemed Robert. (Like Tell, *Robert* has the happy ending that grand opera would soon trade in for the tragic tableau, infinitely more Romantic.) But Vanzo lacks the trumpet power and the grace that Léon Escalais displays in his famous piano-accompanied Sicilienne of 1905, sung while Bertram goads Robert into gambling away everything he owns. Escalais takes the high C in chest; Vanzo does it in falsetto, as Nourrit would have done it in 1831, when *Robert* was new.

Notice the two Meyerbeers: French and Italian, not only in different languages, but absorbing different vocal traditions. Rossini, the Gallicized Italian, connected them. But singers in their turn disengaged them, the French favoring the narrative flow—as if Meyerbeer were Lully's immediate successor—and the Italians, above all, *singing*. One hears this in the oldest 78s—in, say, Agustarello Affre and Antoinette Laute-Brun's version of the climactic duet of Meyerbeer's second grand opera, *Les Huguenots*; as opposed to Fernando de Lucia and Anna de Angelis's version of the duet, *Gli Ugonotti*. The first pair seem to navigate around the words, at times to the pain of the notes.

---

*This is the dramatic soprano, or mezzo, built upon Gluck's Armide and Alceste, but, in Meyerbeer's Rossinian program, as embellished as *Tell*'s Mathilde, the model for grand opera's lyric soprano. From *Robert le Diable* on, grand operas generally had two heroines, and the dramatic soprano often had the more interesting role: Valentine in *Les Huguenots*, Eboli in *Don Carlos*. These are falcon parts, named for Meyerbeer's choice dramatic soprano, the original Valentine, Marie Cornélie Falcon. She also created roles in Halévy's *La Juive* and everybody's favorite as-yet-unrecorded grand opera, Auber's *Gustavus III*. She literally ran out of voice in six years.

The second pair float on the melody rather than the words—*feeling* the scene, as opposed to playing it. There was a German Meyerbeer style, too—as witness, pursuing the duet analogy, Emmy Destinn and Karl Jörn, superbly in voice yet characterful as well, though the vocal attack occasionally sounds a little prim.

In 1957 Westminster offered to reinstate the native approach in a two-disc *Huguenots* highlights under Jean Allain. After the "bouillon cube" versions the short 78 sides made necessary, it was refreshing to hear the big scenes in full bowl, so to speak. But the singing is atrocious, though such prominent singers as Renée Doria and Guy Fouché take part. As it happens, an RAI *Ugonotti* of the same era under Serafin (EJS, Cetra) featuring the by then insistently deathless veteran Giacomo Lauri-Volpi, was even worse. It was yet another *Ugonotti* that reclaimed this work from legend, and launched the Meyerbeer Revival.

This was the 1962 Scala production, legendary itself: Joan Sutherland, Giulietta Simionato, Fiorenza Cossotto, Franco Corelli, Nicolai Ghiaurov, and Giorgio Tozzi under Gavazzeni. It's a far cry from *Les Huguenots*, almost a verismo Meyerbeer, *Gli Ugonotti Rusticani*. It is also one of the most exciting performances in this repertory. Not only is everyone in voice; everyone has *the* voice for the part—accepting, that is, the revisionist delivery, urged on by Gavazzeni's fiery reading and heavy cutting, which turn a grand opera into fleet *melodramma*. Compare Simionato and Corelli's Act Four duet with the 78s mentioned above to see how opportunistically Meyerbeer adapts to different singing styles. At La Scala, the pressing weight of the voices; Simionato's contraltoish timbre, so unlike the bright sound of the falcon; the brazen ring of Corelli's high notes in the lyrical G flat section, "Tu l'as dit"; the almost uncouth splendor of the acting . . . all this is incorrect Meyerbeer. But it is unquestionably great opera.

What of *Les Huguenots?* London's 1970 set, based on an Albert Hall concert, is note-complete and in fine sound; MRF's set, from a 1971 Vienna concert, is sonically handicapped and considerably cut, but more persuasively performed. It is precisely where London is weakest that MRF is strongest: in Raoul, the opera's key role, for in French grand opera the tenor carried the weight of character that Italian *melodramma* most often entrusted to the soprano. Only Raoul, of *Les Huguenots*' six* principals, sings in every act. (Valentine, his sweetheart,

---

*In the golden age, gala castings of *Les Huguenots* were called "nights of the seven stars," because a seventh part could be assigned to a front-line baritone. However, the role is small, with a single solo, "Nobil dame," so short that in the 78 years only Mario Ancona recorded it, in Italian—and even Ancona can't find anything in it.

appears in each act, but is veiled and mute in the first.) London's Anastasios Vrenios is utterly swamped by Raoul's high line and energy. The Duel Septet, running up to a high C sharp—in 78 days a showpiece for the likes of Léon Escalais and Leo Slezak—finds Vrenios in such distress that his assailants could dispatch him with an encore, let alone the duel. MRF's Nicolai Gedda is virile and elegant, exactly right. Furthermore, where Martina Arroyo offers a beautiful but uninvolved Valentine, MRF's Enriquetta Tarres is very involved and vocally fetching, edging the Vienna group into a propulsive sense of story that London's set lacks. London has Bonynge's exciting and excited conducting, the relish of a connoisseur; and Bonynge has Sutherland repeating her Scala Marguerite. It is standard lore that she was in better voice earlier, but her "O beau pays" on her great London recital *The Art of the Prima Donna* is cut to bits, and the same aria at La Scala is not much more complete and not as musical. Only on the commercial set does Sutherland give us the entire scene (including a second verse of the first section, not in the standard vocal scores and never recorded elsewhere), with minute attention to Meyerbeer's markings, at that in her best voice. MRF's Rita Shane is in some ways more daring—*her* "O beau pays" sneaks up to a high F sharp, to Sutherland's mere D. But Shane's scene is as cut as Sutherland's was on the recital. In but one instance are London and MRF equal: in the role of the page, Urbain. Meyerbeer wrote it for a lyric soprano— MRF's Jeanette Scovotti, cute as the dickens. But Meyerbeer rewrote it for contralto Marietta Alboni, beefing it up with a rondo showpiece, "Non, non, non, vous n'avez jamais." London presents in Huguette Tourangeau this historical alternative, complete with the rondo. Armida Parsi-Pettinella's 1906 rondo, in Italian, is more sumptuous, but Tourangeau is a treat, though she does leave out four bars of decoration that Pettinella takes in stride. In short: students of grand opera, especially of Meyerbeer, must hear London to comprehend the form at its fullest, if in a flawed performance. Others should try Vienna for style, Scala for excitement.

Another possibility is Columbia's *Le Prophète,* the only other complete studio Meyerbeer and a much better performance than London's *Huguenots,* with Marilyn Horne, Renata Scotto, and James McCracken under Henry Lewis, all from the 1977 Met revival. This is a less typical grand opera than others, with its contralto protagonist—the opera is narrated from the tenor's viewpoint but most strongly felt from the mezzo's. Meyerbeer wrote Fidès for the remarkable Pauline Viardot; it is hard to imagine anyone but Horne filling Viardot's shoes today. As old-timers would say, "Oh, but I heard Alboni [or Parsi-Pettinella] in

that part," veterans of the future will have heard Horne. Before the
Met staging, Horne sang Fidès in an RAI broadcast under Lewis with
Margherita Rinaldi and Nicolai Gedda (BJR); Gedda has the velvet
that McCracken never quite puts on. But Scotto's over-the-top Berthe
gives Columbia the edge.

The paucity of complete recordings clouds our view of grand opera
as a form. Cuts offer a devolution of grand opera's essential quality,
majesty; they improve the works as theatre but ruin them as history.
Not that the Opéra itself didn't reduce the long evenings during a
work's run. Verdi not only had to strip music out of *Don Carlos* during
rehearsals, but was forced to make further cuts immediately after the
first night. Even *Guillaume Tell*, the cornerstone of full-fledged grand
opera, suffered slashes, till all that remained was a halfhearted Act
Two, on call to fill out evenings of ballet. *L'Africaine*, the last of
Meyerbeer's four grand operas, on the loves and work of Vasco da
Gama, raises the question of length, of where to cut and what is essential, for three recordings make different decisions.

All three are undergrounds. The sole commercial *Africaine*, Philips's
stereo disc of highlights, is well sung and acted by Denise Monteil,
Andrée Esposito, Tony Poncet, and Henri Peyrottes under Robert
Wagner. But grand opera has too many highlights for a single disc.
These are, strenuously, number operas, one *big* number after another.
Philips nervously jumps from one scene to the next, trying to sneak
in a swallow here, a taste there. Listening is a little like attending a
banquet while running for one's life.

A 1963 Naples revival in Italian (Stella, Rinaldi, Nicola Nicoloff,
Protti; Capuana; EJS) is but one disc longer, and suggests early Verdi
in its eager narrative tempo. Capuana is sensitive and everyone's in
form, yet none of them bothers to observe Meyerbeer's meticulous
markings. True, Protti's voice rings out vastly in "Holà, matelots"
(here, "All'erta, marinar"), Nélusko's *a cappella* call to the Portuguese
sailors, virtually a vocal fanfare. Even the immense Titta Ruffo's 78—
voice, voice, and voice—does not dishonor Protti. But this is only the
start of a great scene. Nélusko goes on to his Ballade telling of Ada-
mastor, ruinous king of the ocean. Apparently a big number for the
baritone, of no importance to the action, this is in fact an ironic
guignol in that Nélusko, supposedly guiding the Portuguese over a
treacherous course, is actually sending the ship to crash, whereupon
his people will swarm on board and murder the colonialists for the
third-act curtain. Here is an opportunity for a gifted singer: a vocal
showpiece with character and situation in it as well. Ruffo is a sly
devil in it, Riccardo Stracciari almost matter-of-fact. But Protti is en-

tirely at sea here. He can't even stay on the beat, throwing this most rhythmic of numbers out of sync. How can we speak of a Meyerbeer revival without Meyerbeerean singers to persuade us?

EJS later released Riccardo Muti's admirable 1971 Florence May Festival production, still *all'italiana,* but more beautifully tendered and more complete, taking in some of the grand-opera pageantry. Jessye Norman is the "African" of the title, lush and stylish; Mietta Sighele has, for a lyric, surprising fire; and Veriano Luchetti gives a decent Vasco. Giangiacomo Guelfi's Nélusko, on good days Ruffoesque, suffers a bad day here. Perhaps the set's best feature is the sixth-side filler, 78s from *L'Africana,* emphasizing the Giacomo in Monsieur Meyerbeer: the Vascos of de Lucia, Caruso, Gigli; Ponselle's restitutive trill; the Néluskos of Battistini, Ruffo, and Stracciari, the last two in the shipboard sequence and Battistini in the big solo from Act Two, shockingly uncut for an early acoustic and full of character but roughly pushed and pulled about. Granted, Nélusko acts like a bully; but he shouldn't sing like one.

Now, what of *L'Africaine?* Most complete, best performed, and in genuine stereo sound is OD's relay of San Francisco's 1972 staging under Jean Périsson, with Shirley Verrett, Evelyn Mandac, Plácido Domingo, and Norman Mittelmann. Périsson brings out the score's dignity, giving the pageantry dramatic weight, as if looking toward *Don Carlos* and *Aida.* His singers are superb, making this not just a revival but a vindication. OD even supplies a text booklet. One interesting note: at the first meeting of Vasco's two loves, the dark and the fair, Verrett changes "Qu'elle est blanche!" (How white she is!) to "Qu'elle est belle!" (How beautiful she is!), no doubt to correct conventional Empire racism but, incidentally, showing how important the *sense* of these parts can be to singers who don't just deliver but enact them. A few more such, and we really may have a Meyerbeer revival.

Meyerbeer's contemporaries in this field are even more neglected. Ambroise Thomas's *Hamlet* doesn't impress, albeit with Sutherland and Milnes under the energetically proslytizing Bonynge (London digital)—and lo, there are cuts. Refer to Ruffo for a truer Hamlet, to Melba, Callas, and a younger Sutherland (in *The Art of the Prima Donna*) for a defter reading of Ophélie's mad scene. Halévy's *La Juive* (The Jewess), on race relations in fifteenth-century Constance, seems to me one of the few really dull operas, dullest in its highlights—the tenor's turgid "Rachel, quand du Seigneur," the soprano's vapid "Il va venir," the bass's plodding "Si la rigueur." HRE's 1981 Vienna concert, under the dynamic Gerd Albrecht, is acceptable, international but in French: Ilona Tokody, Sona Ghazarian, José Carreras, Chris Merritt, Cesare Siepi. Carreras, in one of Caruso's favorite roles, sings beautifully but ducks the high notes; Merritt goes for them, not beautifully. Ghazarian, the lyric, is not up to her coloratura. Tokody, in the falcon role, is fine.

One grand opera keeps its falcon mute, Auber's *La Muette de Portici*, which assigns the more dramatic of the two women leads to an actress or dancer. (Berlioz's wife Harriet Smithson played it.) Famed for sparking a rebellion in Brussels that led to Belgium's separation from oppressive Holland, Auber's piece, also known as *Masaniello*, after its hero, typifies grand opera not only in liberal politics but in the highly rhythmic cut of its numbers, a kind of operatic pop music with plenty of barcarolles and marches. MRF presents a BBC broadcast, heavily cut but nicely performed, especially by Janet Price in the Mathilde role (though, truth to tell, *La Muette* precedes *Guillaume Tell* by a year).

To follow grand opera into its twilight, try Ernest Reyer's *Sigurd*, from 1884. By then the form had inspired too many composers superior to those above. Wagner co-opted its length, Verdi improved its vocal lineup, various nationalistic movements borrowed its politics, Offenbach savaged its heroics. *Sigurd* is one of the last of the line, very accessible to opera buffs in that its plot corresponds to *Siegfried*, Act Three, and all, more or less, of *Götterdämmerung*, with Brünnhilde as falcon: Brunehilde. Reyer thus combines the nineteenth century's two most antagonistic influences: the Opéra and Wagner. BJR's relay of a French broadcast takes four discs, but the performance suffers many internal cuts: all the scenes are here, but so scissored that the uninitiated may think he has discovered a streamlined grand opera. (No. that was not to come till Massenet's *Le Cid*, a year later, in 1885.) Manuel Rosenthal excellently conducts Andrea Guiot, Andrée Esposito, Guy Chauvet, Robert Massard, and Ernest Blanc, and all is well, in clean if not overly spacious sound. *Sigurd* is as hard to cast as *Siegfried*. Chauvet has guts, but in "Esprits gardiens" (Guardian spirits), Sigurd's solo before awakening Brunehilde, and a popular 78 title among French tenors, Chauvet lumbers where Leon Campagnola is ecstatic, César Vezzani regal, and Georges Thill poetic.

Perhaps this is the place to consider Saint-Saëns's *Samson et Dalila*, though it is no grand opera—technically not opera at all. Still, the Opéra eventually mounted it, and Opéra forces under Louis Forestier backed Hélène Bouvier, José Luccioni, and Paul Cabanel in the first complete and sole thoroughly French set (Columbia, EMI) in 1946. Luccioni has an authentic ring. His "Israël, romps ta chaîne" is awesome, and Bouvier and Cabanel conspire tellingly. Leaping into stereo, we meet Christa Ludwig, James King, and Bernd Weikl under Giuseppe Patané (Eurodisc, Victor), exciting but unstylish. True, they never quite try to sing in German, but next to the svelte Bouvier and the elegantly fuming Cabanel, Ludwig and Weikl sound heavy; and King is dull. Daniel Barenboim's reading (DG) has Domingo and Renato Bruson, both excellent, with French forces backing them; but he also has the outrée Elena Obraztsova. The big love duet typifies the set—Obraztsova simply ferocious, Domingo very touching, capping "Mon coeur" with a superbly judged B flat. Connoisseurs favor Angel's classic: Gorr, Vickers, and Blanc under Prêtre, perfect casting and all on form.

While grand opera immeasurably enriched Italian *melodramma,* from Rossini through Donizetti to Verdi and beyond, on the home stage it collapsed under its own rhetoric. It imploded. After *Sigurd* and *Le Cid,* grand opera survived exclusively in revival, while French composers sought refreshment in the intimacy, brevity, and comedy of neo-Classicism: *L'Heure Espagnole, Padmâvatî, Mârouf.* At that, grand opera had reached its apotheosis only two years after *L'Africaine*'s posthumous premiere. Typically, given grand opera's transmontane origins and development, from Lully to Rossini, the work was Italian by authorship, though French in textural rhythm, architecture, even sound. This was of course Verdi's *Don Carlos,* increasingly regarded as one of the masterpieces of the nineteenth century, though in its day it went unappreciated. Notably, the essential auteur of grand opera, Rossini, recognized Verdi's genius of entitlement in this genre. Writing to Verdi's publisher Giulio Ricordi after *Don Carlos*'s first night (a year before Rossini's death), Rossini said that Verdi "is the only composer capable of writing grand opera"—capable, that is, of using the form for enlightenment as well as entertainment.

8

BELLINI

❧❦

Bellini brings us to bel canto, the "beautiful singing" that opera buffs associate with the early middle 1800s, when Bellini and Donizetti wrote for such singers as the dramatically expressive Giuditta Pasta, the exquisite tenor Giovanni Battista Rubini, and the versatile bass Luigi Lablache. In fact, while the term "bel canto" was coined in the nineteenth century, it referred not to contemporary singing but to that of the earlier era of *opera seria*, when the art of the singer, it was thought, had been nobler, purer, and more accomplished. Rossini, who preceded Bellini and Donizetti by a demi-generation just as Verdi thus succeeded them, insisted that standards of virtuosity and musicianship had all but collapsed during his career.

They had collapsed again by the end of the nineteenth century, when the style of late Verdi and the rise of verismo put an emphasis on power and drama at the expense of nobility and purity. Much of the Bellini-Donizetti repertory had vanished, leaving only the most popular titles; and *Norma*, perhaps the central item in this field, began to slip out of reach, too pure, too noble, to sing. Even at La Scala, Italy's foremost house, Toscanini could attempt but not succeed with a *Norma*. Shattered by his failure to bring the classic to life, he canceled the revival halfway through the dress rehearsal.

The turning point in all this was the *riesumazione* (exhumation), the series of revivals in the 1950s that determined to reclaim the so-called bel canto repertory in faithful style, reintroducing forgotten works, rediscovering the decor and plastique of the old days, and reasserting the values of late bel canto—that is, the expressive power of the beautiful singing. Eventually the *riesumazione* became an international movement, but in its first seasons it took its energy from productions at La Scala staged by Luchino Visconti and Margherita Wallmann, conducted by Leonard Bernstein and Gianandrea Gavazzeni, and featuring Maria Callas. Altogether, this exhumation of the true Bellini revealed a far more resourceful composer than querulous *Normas* and halt *Puritanis* had suggested: a composer who, inheriting Rossinian *melodramma*, both expanded and tightened, partially dismantling the set aria form, for instance, to emphasize ensemble, and developing the characterological possibilities in recitative.

At the same time, the *riesumazione* touched off a controversy that takes in not only Bellini and Donizetti but Rossini (even Handel) and Verdi: are we to hear these operas in the manner in which they were originally performed, with all the virtuoso embellishments that bel canto counted on; or in the currently chic "do as written" approach, which ignores the fact that these embellishments are, when not written, understood to be? To forbid embellishments (especially in second verses, where they were *de rigueur*) that were not written down because they were supposed to be more or less extemporized is arrant nonsense.

Belatedly falling into step with the *riesumazione*, the phonograph has assembled a respectable Bellini discography. Five sopranos dominate it: Callas and Joan Sutherland in four titles each, and Beverly Sills, Montserrat Caballé, and Renata Scotto in three. The *riesumazione* is a soprano's arena. Historically, it is true, Bellini was as much associated with tenor expertise; but that sort of expertise is very rare today, and tenors come and go in this repertory without leaving much of a mark (though Luciano Pavarotti has implanted himself through his collaboration with Sutherland and Bonynge). Stage directors, as a Bellinian force, fell out of the picture after Visconti concluded his Scala partnership with Callas, and conductors have not convinced us that Bellini is a conductor's composer in the way that, say, Verdi is. Typically, it is the sopranos whose capabilities support Bellini revivals, even if the tenor be hit-or-miss and the conductor bored. The question is, then, how capable are these sopranos in each role and how good is their company?

Barring two apprentice works, all of Bellini's operas are on disc. They are:

Il Pirata	1827
La Straniera	1829

I Capuleti e i Montecchi	1830
La Sonnambula	1831
Norma	1831
Beatrice di Tenda	1933
I Puritani	1835

Let's start with *Il Pirata* (The Pirate), as this case illumines variables that typify Bellini's discography. For one thing, there is no 78 catalogue, a situation that obtains for virtually all but *Norma, La Sonnambula,* and *I Puritani.* As the word *"riesumazione"* explains, these other Bellini operas had to be not just revived but disinterred. For another thing, there is the question of the underground versus the commercial—or, the same comparison in different terms, the live as opposed to the studio performance. There is as well the question of cuts, for the first years of the *riesumazione* concentrated on production and vocal style, not on revealing complete texts, while from about 1962 on, cuts were opened up, especially on record. Last, there is the question of what kind of diva is best suited to this repertory: the vocally secure but dramatically questionable (Sutherland, Caballé) or the highly expressive but vocally controversial (Callas, Scotto, Sills)?

Il Pirata's two sets pit a cut Callas underground against the full score with Caballé on Angel. Neither set boasts a substantial tenor or baritone, but both conductors are adepts of late bel canto (forgiving, that is, a certain Verdian slant in their drive). Callas's Nicola Rescigno is so sharp at "stick technique" that, when at one point tenor Pier Miranda Ferraro goes off the beat, Rescigno drops half a measure on the spot to jump ahead and collect him. Caballé's Gavazzeni, with far more of the score at his survey, generally keeps things firm, not an easy task in Bellini's longest and structurally most challenging work. Occasionally Gavazzeni seems to lose interest, only to snap to on the next page.

Callas's performance has a sense of occasion Caballé inevitably misses, as this *Pirata,* a 1960 American Opera Society concert, marked Callas's return to New York for the first time since Rudolf Bing had fired her from the Met. The night *had* to be gala, a reproach of the impresario, an appeal to the public. And so it was. Caballé is stylish but uncommitted, her husband Bernabé Martí coarse. Callas spreads style through her evening, shows us how vital this writing is. When heroine and hero first meet after a long separation, and she explains that she had to marry the baritone to save her father—"Periva il genitore!" (My father would have perished!)—Caballé just sings it. Callas shows us how honor (of family) made her a traitor (of her lover), taking the high note on a cry of distress, the downward chromatic run on a moan, a one-woman *riesumazione.*

Yet how can we appreciate these works if they come off as diva vehicles? Undergrounds of the late *riesumazione,* after 1960, emphasize this problem—Scotto trying to pull off *La Straniera* (The Foreigner) in Palermo in inferior company to Nino Sanzogno's torpid beat (MRF), or Sutherland in surprisingly ordinary company at La Scala for a *Beatrice di Tenda* (Cetra), though the soprano did get to take the piece into the studio with Josephine Veasey and Luciano Pavarotti—one of London's most persuasive bel canto rediscoveries.

Of these less-well-known titles, *I Capuleti e i Montecchi* (The Capulets and the Montagues) has fared well, though MRF preserves Claudio Abbado's corrupt 1968 Scala version, with slashing cuts and no embellishments. Abbado cast Bellini's mezzo Romeo as a tenor, doing violence to Bellini's vocal line (here recomposed to avoid low notes) and to the gender psychology of the early Romantic period, when a lyric mezzo in tights was thought more sumptuously pathetic than a birthright male. However, Abbado does conduct an exciting performance, with Scotto a fetching Juliet and Pavarotti a dashing Tybalt. Only Giacomo Aragall disappoints for his unsteady Romeo.

Moving into commercials, Angel's first try, under Giuseppe Patanè, is not as thrilling as Abbado's, but it is complete and stylish, though only Sills embellishes. Her Romeo is the brilliant Janet Baker, their Tybalt an unusually fiery Nicolai Gedda. Angel's digital set, live from Covent Garden under Riccardo Muti, is faultless yet somehow never superior. On two discs (to Patanè's three), it is complete but for Capulet's bit of recit at the start of Act Two and the short outburst that Bellini added for Juliet as she drinks her sleeping potion. (Sills sings it.) Muti is an ideal conductor, so sensitive that, in a simple high violin line rising from C to C sharp, he can make the heart stand still. He even—unusual for him—allows his singers (Edita Gruberova, Agnes Baltsa, Dano Raffanti) to embellish *very* slightly on repeats. Still, Abbado's and Patanè's singers give us more. Muti's reading is admirable and even moving—trim, in the modern style that fears, above all, individuality. Too trim and too modern. Bellini's singers reportedly gave more of themselves: what holds Muti's back? Muti, of course.

Of all Bellini's operas, the one least applicable to the diva-vehicle syndrome is *I Puritani,* written for four of the greatest singers of its day: Grisi, Rubini, Tamburini, and Lablache, who became known as the *"Puritani* Quartet." Here we find roles for baritone and bass of unusual prominence for Bellini, who most often made do with the one or the other, at that in supplementary capacity; and the tenor line calls for the very sweet, very high (up to F above high C, though of course Rubini sang it in falsetto), and impeccably smooth line that Verdian or verismo tenors cannot manage, however often they may fake their way through *Norma*'s Pollione. In one way, at least, reinstituting a stylish *Puritani* was the *riesumazione*'s greatest challenge, for Callas alone isn't a *Puritani*—as her Mexico City underground (MRF) proves, with its squandering cuts and raffish colleagues. This is an important Callas opera, important as well to the bel canto revival, for it was as Elvira at Venice in 1949, after establishing a career in such dramatic roles as Gioconda, Turandot, and Isolde, that Callas first made her history. She herself was uncertain as to whether she should tackle Elvira—she was in Venice to sing the *Walküre* Brünnhilde when Margherita Carosio, the scheduled Elvira, became ill. Tullio Serafin urged Bellini upon Callas, together all three of them made the point that these late bel canto parts, so long the province of the feckless canary, more truly belonged to the dramatic coloratura.

Callas is in stronger company in her commercial *Puritani* (Angel), the first issue in the Scala series that introduced her to most listeners and that still most often gives the newcomer his taste of Callas. Designed by producer Walter Legge around a triumvirate of Callas–di Stefano–Gobbi, most often under Serafin, and buoyed by La Scala's reputation as Italy's finest house, the series—of some twenty-odd titles—misled many into taking them for virtual "cast albums" of Scala productions. In a very few cases they nearly were—the Scala *Sonnambula*, for instance, about which more shortly. But in general Angel's Scala sets were studio conceptions. Serafin never conducted at La Scala in those years, because of his distaste for its chief, Antonio Ghiringhelli. This *Puritani*, with di Stefano, Rolando Panerai, and Nicola Rossi-Lemeni along with Callas and Serafin, is in fact more representative of a Chicago Lyric Opera cast of the glorious mid-1950s seasons than of any Scala performance. Perhaps there are two *riesumaziones*: one in the theatre, where Visconti and Callas actually worked; and the other on the phonograph, where Callas took on a complementary crew, and where less thespian personalities could concentrate on their musical gifts. At that, Angel's *Puritani* is less than superb. True, Callas's desperation in her big second-act solo is one of the era's marvels, and Rossi-Lemeni, sometimes rough, is quite beautiful here. But di Stefano is stentorian rather than honeyed, and the score is riddled with internal cuts.

Moving into stereo, we gain complete texts, better tenors, and more spirited conducting. Muti (Angel: Caballé, Kraus, Manuguerra, Agostino Ferrin) renders a crisp Bellini. The thoughtfully martial horns in the main theme of the prelude warn us of a prudent performance, very musical but ascetic; the ensuing men's chorus, sure enough, is the best on disc, with all Bellini's markings carefully observed. But Muti doesn't let Caballé decorate the Polonaise, an out-and-out showpiece that Bellini added for Malibran; and Malibran decorated it. Caballé must stand there, grimly uttering it. Rudel (ABC, Angel: Sills, Gedda, Quilico, Plishka) is more stylish in such matters; his swinging ease in the Polonaise, and Sills's delightfully penny-foolish singing of it, notes spent by the hundreds, typify the set. Both performances fill out the quartet responsibly. (Perhaps Angel's Kraus has the edge for his telling way with words.) But London's 1975 quartet is overwhelming: Sutherland, Pavarotti, Piero Cappuccilli, and Nicolai Ghiaurov, all in fine voice under Richard Bonynge. Conductor and soprano had recorded *Puritani* in 1963 for London, dully. The remake is spectacular, the most complete reading yet (all cuts opened, with an extra solo for Elvira) for the greatest voices.

With *La Sonnambula* (The Sleepwalker) we come to Bellini's odd-opera-out, well known but not often performed, less attractive to divas than Norma or Elvira (Caballé and Sills steered clear of it), and of the unusual genre of *semiseria*, basically romantic opera with *buffo* elements and a happy ending. (Take Lisa and Alessio out of *La Sonnambula*, add to them a comic mime, and you'd have *La Serva Padrona* ready to play.) *La Sonnambula* inspired one of the key productions of the *riesumazione*: Callas, Visconti, and Bernstein at La Scala, so admirable an affidavit that it was toured as far afield as Edinburgh and Cologne. Undergrounds take us to all three places, along with Angel's official Scala set, and the casts for all four performances are so similar—Nicola Monti, Nicola Zaccaria, and the young Fiorenza Cossotto (as Callas's mother) traveled along with Callas—that parsing them is work fit for the most committed aficionado. Certainly Bernstein, live at La Scala, is preferable to the placid Antonino Votto elsewhere; and Bernstein has Cesare Valletti, superior to Monti. John Ardoin, Callas's exhaustive discographer, hears the truest magic in Cologne (in best sound on BJR). I don't find it that much better than the commercial set. However, many buffs second Ardoin's opinion—and it makes for interesting history that, while Angel's Votto-Monti casting misrepresented the production as it was first staged under Bernstein, it was in fact a document of the production in its revival, a rare case of Legge's studio-ideal albums bearing witness to live art.

All the Callas *Sonnambulas* are cut to emphasize the love plot and suppress the machinations of the heroine's rival Lisa. Typical *riesu-*

mazione: the movement rescues *La Sonnambula* from the limp, traditional approach, in Callas's extraordinary word-pointing and daredevil
embellishments, Bernstein's storytelling dynamics, and Visconti's nostalgic antiquing, all to overthrow the business-as-usual sort of *Sonnambula* typified by Cetra's 1952 set (Pagliughi, Tagliavini, Siepi). But
somehow no one thinks it important to bring back the entire opera.
If Callas was the mother of the *riesumazione*, Sutherland was its daughter, and *her* London *Sonnambulas* are complete. The first try is routine,
but the second, in digital sound, brings in Pavarotti and Ghiaurov,
and boasts truly fine work from the Lisa (Isobel Buchanan) and Teresa
(Della Jones), Buchanan making a treat of her tiny aria, "De' lieti
auguri," with plenty of embellishments. Bonynge finds the middle ground
between Bernstein and Votto, locating the theatricality in *morbidezza*,
in sentimental beauty for sentimental beauty's sake. Most interesting
of all, Pavarotti finds in Elvino one of his most convincing characters.
Next to him Monti and even Valletti seem uninvested.

This brings us to *Norma*, the *summum bonum* of bel canto, most
challenging to musicians and most stimulating to listeners. The skimpy
accompaniments make it the most Italian of operas, pure song—but
the overture and scene preludes give a conductor something to bite
on. This, in the postwar years of the Verdi revival, has led some
conductors to pull Bellini out of style into the outspoken power of his
successors. *Norma* is, more correctly, Classical in tone, looking back
to *Médée* and *La Vestale*, wherein poetry of utterance counts more
than brazen antagonism.

Looking back deep into the 78 years, we seek vainly for stylistic
roots. *Norma* had already undergone some reevaluation by 1900. Adalgisa, originally a lyric soprano in contrast to Norma's heavier tone,
was by then largely the province of the mezzo, throwing off the character balance of age and temperament. Giannina Russ recorded "Casta
diva" in 1906 and 1914, her cabaletta a mess, though she assumes
some authority in her duet sides with Virginia Guerrini. Celestina
Boninsegna, in her second "Casta diva," in 1909, displays a lovely
voice but the same roughness in coloratura. At least Armida Parsi-
Pettinella, a mezzo Adalgisa, charmingly lightens her naturally deep
tone for her 1907 "Sgombra è la sacra selva," and Ezio Pinza several
times managed a majestic "Ah! del Tebro."

Still, not till Rosa Ponselle do we encounter a fit heroine, and this
by the late 1920s, when *Norma* had slipped out of sync with itself.
Ponselle's "Mira, o Norma" with Marion Telva, her Met Adalgisa, is
brilliant, with an extremely lovable ritard on "Per ricovrarci insieme."
But we are hard pressed to find other colleagues worthy of Ponselle.

Surely Giannina Arangi-Lombardi's "Casta diva" is unremarkable, Claudia Muzio's almost dull till she wakes up at the climax; and Francesco Merli's Pollione is a swashbuckler in the modern style, sobby and strained. In such an atmosphere, Cetra's 1937 complete set is almost inevitably unsatisfying. Vittorio Gui conducts with a keen comprehension of the work's Classic-Romantic temper, dramatic but graceful, but only Tancredi Pasero (Oroveso) matches him. Giovanni Breviario (Pollione) is unimaginative, Ebe Stignani (Adalgisa) not at her best, and Gina Cigna has Norma's voice but not Norma's technique. Many of her pages are very appreciable; even the touches of verismo *Sprechstimme* are compelling. But overall the set is workmanlike when it isn't worse.

The next complete set hails from the *riesumazione,* and our search for a fair *Norma* begins: with Callas. The most driven of great singers would naturally make the hardest role her signature part, and her progress in it is well documented. We have, besides her two commercial sets, Callas's Norma unformed and too late, roughly partnered in Mexico City and nicely served in London, walking out halfway through in Rome and pleading for forgiveness in her Paris farewells. Buffs prefer her at Covent Garden, not least to tune in on the thoughts that might have been running through the head of her Clotilde, Joan Sutherland. But the two Angel sets, both under Serafin in mono and then stereo, are representative. Like Gui, Serafin places Bellini before Verdi, not during; Serafin's second-act prelude prepares for "Dormono entrambi" rather than overwhelms it. And this is Callas's great scene, too, the center of her portrayal, as it is a test of all Normas for its conflicted psychology. "Muoiano, sì" (They die), she declares, moving toward her children with the knife—but while the first word is resolute, the second concedes. Popular opinion holds that Angel's stereo remake finds her vocally embarrassed. No; and the company is distinguished, Franco Corelli an improvement on the mono's wooden Mario Filippeschi and Christa Ludwig more entrancing than Stignani.

Too bad Sutherland never sang Adalgisa to Callas's Norma, to give us a taste of the opera as it sounded in Bellini's time. At least Dame Joan has the splendid Adalgisa of Marilyn Horne in her *Norma* (Victor, London). Bonynge follows the Gui-Serafin line, and John Alexander is a poised Pollione. So far, so good. But, even better, Bonynge offers a restudied text, mostly in some variants in ensembles, but notably in the wonderfully pacific (and previously unrecorded) coda to the brutal "Guerra! Guerra!" chorus, anticipated in the overture, somewhat of a Schubertian Mozart—Andrew Porter likens it to Beethoven's Pastoral Symphony. As to Sutherland herself, she is unquestionably a great Norma, though she doesn't leave her mark on the score as Callas did, except perhaps in the singing of "Casta diva" in the original key of G Major, a whole tone higher than virtually anyone else; or in the spectacular high D with which she closes Act One. Callas doesn't try it.

After Callas and Sutherland there is little to enthuse about. Sills (ABC, Angel) is short on sheer instrument, and James Levine conducts Verdi's *Norma*. Caballé (Victor) has some of Callas's intensity and some of Sutherland's ease, but no true Norma splits the difference. We need both. Caballé has been more exciting as Norma onstage: BJR preserves her first try ever, in Barcelona in 1970. Throwing down the knife, Norma sings, "Son miei figli!" (They're my children!), and Caballé nearly shrieks. On Victor she croons it. Levine conducts again, for Scotto (Columbia). The soprano is resourceful, but the role defeats her, especially given the slashing orchestra. Bellini marked the big trio, "Oh! di qual sei tu vittima," as *Andante marcato.* Levine plays it as *Allegro carnevale.* Caballé and Scotto have worthy Adalgisas in Fiorenza Cossotto and Tatiana Troyanos, respectively. But we're getting too far from Bellini with these "Guerra! Guerra!" conductors and earth-mother Adalgisas. Bel canto, we must remember, was a nostalgia, a lost ideal romantically moribund by 1850. It does not look ahead, but behind.

9

DONIZETTI

꙼

Of all late bel canto operas, *Lucia di Lammermoor* best demonstrates the effects of the *riesumazione*, the "disinterment" of late bel canto. Extracts and complete sets till about 1960 reveal a highly dramatic composition debased into a canary's vehicle, the other roles cut to insignificance as the soprano aimlessly embellishes here and there as if bowing to formality rather than to the needs of the music. Melba's various Mad Scene 78s are serene, not mad, Tetrazzini's almost jocose. Urania's early mono LP set, unimportantly sung, was regarded as a curiosity because it opened up the standard cuts (including the Wolf's Glen Scene for the tenor and baritone, normally not shortened but omitted entirely). Victor's early stereo LP set (Peters, Peerce, Maero, Tozzi; Leinsdorf) is brusque and dull.

The *riesumazione* was, of course, a collaboration of singers, conductors, directors, designers, and even a few critics. But at the center of it was Maria Callas, as star of the most significant revivals, as reinvigorator of debilitated bel canto, as model for contemporaries and successors—even as focus for public assimilation of the movement. Callas's Lucia is even more essential to the *riesumazione* than her Norma, for Bellini's heroine had always been regarded as the highest challenge, whereas Lucia had become a carnival. The earlier of Callas's Angel *Lucia* sets is vastly preferable for Callas's distinguished colleagues Giuseppe di Stefano, Tito Gobbi, and Tullio Serafin. But the true Callas Lucia lies on various undergrounds of La Scala's legendary 1955 visit to Berlin: Callas, di Stefano, Rolando Panerai, Nicola Zaccaria, and Herbert von Karajan. This is *Lucia* still on the way to re-discovery: cuts abound, no Wolf's Glen, and von Karajan even grants the infatuated Berliners a historically correct but artistically reproach-able encore of the Sextet. But the singing is extraordinary. BJR has the best sound and, in the booklet (notes, no text), Robert Jacobson's helpful analysis of the performance.

It is ironic that Callas's productions and recordings observed cuts, for the *riesumazione* inspired the opera world to dispense with cuts, at least on disc. How can we give the old style a fair hearing if we don't, at least now and then, hear the operas in their entirety? Thus, most stereo *Lucias* are complete—Sutherland's two tries (London), for in-stance, the first in ravishing voice but dull company, the second less superbly giving but in the grand company of Pavarotti and Bonynge. Sills's set (ABC, Angel), with Carlo Bergonzi, Piero Cappuccilli, and Justino Díaz under Thomas Schippers, is very dramatic but almost per-functorily so, noisy, busy, overembellished. Still, it's worth hearing how much more character Sills gets out of her coloratura than Melba and Tetrazzini did. Another facet of the *riesumazione*, this—coloratura as a vehicle of dramatic expression.

Highly *riesumazione* in approach is Montserrat Caballé's set with José Carreras under Jesús López Cobos (Phillips). This is the conduc-tor's personal disinterment, from Donizetti's manuscript, with much of Lucia's music in slightly higher keys and no added high notes. The maestro states his case in the text booklet, and, one must admit, the Mad Scene's "Spargi d'amaro pianto," in F rather than the usual E flat, makes quite an effect—or, rather, Caballé does. One tone up-ward, and this former canary's warble becomes an actress's contention, real madness by its very sound. Comparably, Carreras goes up for what turns out to be a high E (E flat in the Ricardi score) at the end of "Verrano a te." Critics damned the album for a lack of oomph, show-ing how much more we expect from *Lucia* after Callas. Still, if dra-matically inefficient, Philips is gorgeous song, true bel canto.

Angel's digital set under Nicola Rescigno (Gruberova, Kraus, Bru-son, Lloyd) typifies the modern style, post-*riesumazione*. The reading is complete and the performance stylishly dramatic, Gruberova digging into the recits and Kraus not afraid to exploit accents and portamento. Gruberova's hard tone and wobbly top will annoy some, but she is lovely in the first duet, leaping up to take Kraus's climactic high note. One nuisance is the men's fear of coloratura. When these operas were new, *all* the singers embellished. Nowadays, the soprano invariably decorates, the tenor sometimes—but no one else. Note, incidentally, that Rescigno was one of Callas's pet conductors, an authentic veteran of the *riesumazione*.

Dramatic energy, whether from Callas or Gruberova, Visconti or Zeffirelli, Gavazzeni or Rescigno, was the *riesumazione's* most enlightening boon. Thus reinstructed, looking backward, we see Donizetti not so much as a transition between Rossini and Verdi, but as Verdi's major inspiration. As early as in *Anna Bolena*, Donizetti's first important success, we discern the pattern of early Verdian *melodramma* in its purest form, before Paris stimulated and challenged him. Of the two commercial sets, London's (Souliotis, Horne, Alexander, Ghiaurov; Varviso) is, but for the erratic Souliotis, richer in voice, ABC's (Sills, Verrett, Burrows, Plishka; Rudel) richer in theatre, and absolutely uncut. For the best performance, a telling document of the *riesumazione*, we turn to undergrounds of the 1957 Scala revival, a key Visconti production, planned to recapture not only the sound but also the look and atmosphere of Donizetti's day. The cast exemplifies *riesumazione* aesthetics: Callas, Simionato, Gianni Raimondi, and Nicola Rossi-Lemeni under Gavazzeni. True, the performance lacks the authenticity that we now take for granted. There are huge cuts; the two men not only don't embellish but ignore much of the coloratura that Donizetti himself wrote out; and Gavazzeni energizes tempos and volume unstylishly, even contradicting the composer's markings. It might almost be early-middle Verdi. But Callas brings us back to Donizetti in her insistence in acting on the music, singing on the story line. Hear, in Anna's great confrontation with her rival, Jane Seymour, how artfully Callas blends the meaning of the text with that of the music. Compared to Callas, Souliotis is unfocused, Sills unvoiced. Even Simionato seems underequipped next to Callas, too direct, uninflected, though she is in magnificent form. With three small words, mere interjections in Seymour's solo of repentent confession, Callas flashes Anna's character before us, bitter on "Ah!," pensive on "Ella!," rearing back majestically on "Dio!," building her arc of rage the better to set off her climactic act of forgiveness that leads into the duet's closing C major *più mosso*, the two voices thrillingly entwined. This is timeless art, archeology that rerouted the present. This is opera history: most immediately, and sensationally, when in the first-act finale Callas seems to hurl "Giudici! Ad Anna!" (Judges! Of *Anna!*) not at the accusing Henry but at the sometimes unappreciative Scala public.

Donizetti's other queens take us to Callas's successors and the *riesumazione's* effects. Cuts are opened, and bel canto's *morbidezza*—the sentimental plangency that distinguishes bel canto from the more energetic Verdian style—is emphasized. Of conductors, London's Bonynge is the most stylish, also the most enthusiastic, hunting down added or alternate material and observing the innate vivacity of Donizetti's rhythmic numbers. *Lucrezia Borgia's* famous Brindisi is a case in point. However much connoisseurs may savor Ernestine Schumann-Heink's old 78 (not to mention that of the incredibly deep-toned Clara Butt), Bonynge puts a real swing into it; and it doesn't hurt matters that he has Marilyn Horne as Orsini.

Of the singers, a representative sampling may be taken on Westminster's *Roberto Devereux* under Charles Mackerras, with Beverly Sills, Beverly Wolff, Robert Ilosfalvy, and Peter Glossop (Angel). Except for Sills, none is associated with bel canto, and all make solemn effort to find themselves in the style. But only Sills truly succeeds, hurling herself into Elizabeth's character, biting down on the highly inflected music. By comparison, MRF's preservation of the American Opera Society's 1965 concert under Carlo Felice Cillario with Caballé, Lili Chookasian, Juan Oncina, and Walter Alberti gives us style in disarray, Caballé lovely but generalizing the portrayal as if one line meant much the same as another, her colleagues gutsy where they should be graceful (sometimes even vice versa, which is absurd). Both sets, though, are historic, MRF recalling the greatest days of the AOS, created to reintroduce forgotten operas to New York using erratic casts composed of the latest international sensation and, at times, whoever else was willing to learn a relatively unmarketable role for one night's work. Westminster brings us back to New York City Opera's personal *riesumazione*, in a Donizetti series with Sills that revised Visconti's faded-postcard look for a contemporary design and upbeat staging. (Sills in *Roberto Devereux* recalled Bette Davis in *The Private Lives of Elizabeth and Essex.*)

Maria Stuarda affords us a champion comparison, not only of performances, but of texts: each recording offers a slightly different score. Bel canto composers often retailored roles to sanction the singer of the moment, and for the central rivalry of Mary Stuart and Elizabeth I we may choose among soprano versus mezzo (London), mezzo versus soprano (Angel), soprano versus soprano (ABC, Angel), and even, on undergrounds, soprano versus mezzo in soprano keys. London brings us the Bonynge team (Sutherland, Tourangeau, Pavarotti, Soyer), vocally the best even if Tourangeau's excellent Elizabeth has been reinflected downward, overexploiting her chest range. This gives us a strong contrast of tone between the two queens, but we lose the climactic power of Elizabeth's high-lying lines. ABC's Farrell-Sills rivalry offers too much contrast: between Farrell's huge instrument and Sills's petite one. In their confrontation Sills is forced to push chest notes, even— it appears—to resort to a gimmicked acoustic to hold her own. Yet her naturally plangent timbre suits Mary, a victim not just at the end but throughout: "da tutti abbandonata" (abandoned by all). ABC's set has the dramatic ring London misses. Pirates of Caballé with Verrett cannot compete despite the two stars' quality. But EMI's *Maria Stuarda* (digital) is unique because sung in English, live from the English National Opera in 1983. Charles Mackerras's Elizabeth, Rosalind Plowright, utters her lines with panache, but her voice is harsh and stringy. Nor do David Rendall, Alan Opie, and John Tomlinson importantly challenge their counterparts on London and ABC. In fact, the performance that Angel issued on disc is inferior to the published videotape, caught in the same series of performances. Still, Baker's is the richest Mary on record, combining Sills's intensity with Sutherland's instrumental depth.

One defect of the *riesumazione* was its inability to reinvigorate comedy. Cuts are opened, yes: but where is the exuberance, the vivacity? Take *L'Elisir d'Amore*. Before the *riesumazione* takes hold, we have Victor's mono set (Carosio, Monti, Gobbi, Melchiorre Luise; Santini), generally creditable, Gobbi's confidently nagging Belcore outstanding. After the *riesumazione* makes its points, we have Angel's stereo set (Carteri, Alva, Panerai, Taddei; Serafin), generally creditable, Taddei's antic Dulcamara outstanding. Comedy needs more. Columbia's 1977 Covent Garden set under John Pritchard improves the average, with a nice chemistry drawing Ileana Cotrubas to Plácido Domingo, and with Ingvar Wixell's suavely pompous Belcore. But the set is tasteful when it needs to be lilting, never funny, *brillante*. Here again, London's Bonynge, Sutherland, and Pavarotti take over. The Belcore (Dominic Cossa) and Dulcamara (Spiro Malas) are, again, just creditable. But the two leads are personable, in flawless voice; and Bonynge really pulls out the character in the score. Hear the swagger he finds in Belcore's entrance march, with just enough of the raucous in it to suggest the risible splendor of the barnyard rooster. For dessert, Bonynge gives us the showpiece finale that Charles de Beriot wrote for his wife Maria Malibran, "Nel dolce incanto." Adina needs it, not least its closing high E flat, after the tenor has won all ears with what Broadway calls "an eleven o'clock song": "Una furtiva lagrima." Pavarotti's, poised and touching, stands up to those of Fernando de Lucia, John McCormack, and Tito Schipa on 78s. However, no one rivals Enrico Caruso's 1904, piano-accompanied Victor ten-inchers (one verse per side), regarded as one of the finest tenor solos on disc. The aria has been ground into cliché by lachrymose tenors, taking their cue from the minor-key atmosphere that imbues the first line, "A furtive tear fell from her eyes." But the song is sensitive, not sorrowful. "M'ama!" (She loves me!), Nemorino cries, as the music expands into the major—and Caruso in particular sees this moment as the climax not only of the aria but of the opera, rising to a wonderfully virile cry that tells us why this was one of his most successful parts.

As with *L'Elisir*, London and the Bonynge house team ideally present *La Fille du Régiment* (The Daughter of the Regiment), Donizetti's blend of *buffa* and *comique*. Cesare Valletti, on Cetra's mono set of the Italian translation, sings the big Act Two aria, "Pour mon âme," in B Flat; Pavarotti takes it in C. And lo, an innocuous idyll becomes a startling showpiece with nine of the boldest high Cs ever recorded. Critics loathed the Bonynges' *Fille*, but audiences loved it, and the album remains a buff's favorite, especially for the bamboozling audacity of Sutherland in a rare tomboy turn.

Don Pasquale, pure Italian *buffa*, has been called the perfect comedy. The premise—old bachelor takes young wife—is stock matter, but Donizetti composed it for the second version of the celebrated *Puritani* Quartet—Grisi, Mario (replacing Rubini), Tamburini, and Lablache. Something unique, then: a thin farce suitable for the greatest singers in the world. You'd never guess it from the *Don Pasquale* recordings. The old HMV 78 set (Seraphim) has the lovable Tito Schipa and, as Pasquale, the lovably unlovable Ernesto Badini, but soprano Adelaide Saraceni is not lovable. Recently, Angel brought forth *Pasquales* under Sarah Caldwell (Sills, Kraus, Titus, Gramm) and, digitally, Muti (Freni, Gösta Winbergh, Nucci, Bruscantini), Muti's brighter and sweeter but humorless.

For a truer *Pasquale* we turn to the famous Scala revival of 1904, with Rosina Storchio (who created Butterfly that same year), Aristodemo Giorgini, Giuseppe de Luca (who created Sharpless), and Antonio Pini-Corsi, all caught, with various alternate singers, by G & T and Fonotipia. Perhaps the Rubini label will gather all the material, some thirty-three sides, in a two-disc set, to teach us this uniquely *buffo* bel canto in the effortless fun the players generate. The touches of Gallagher-Shean vaudeville in de Luca and Ferruccio Corradetti's patter duet will shock youngsters who know *Don Pasquale* only in the dainty modern style.

Like Verdi after him, Donizetti adapted to and learned from grand opera in his Paris commissions. The results are variable. *Les Martyrs*, originally composed as *Poliuto* for Naples, but banned and revised, seems more correct, more comfortable, as a *melodramma*. Various undergrounds preserve the coarse 1960 Scala revival, with the crowd furiously welcoming Callas in what was to be her last exhumation there; precarious high notes reveal that Callas is well into decline. At that, Franco Corelli and Ettore Bastianini have the meatier parts. Voce has a cleaner and more complete performance in better sound (Maliponte, Casellato-Lamberti, Bruson), tamely respectable. *Dom Sébastien,* Donizetti's last opera, is more naturally grand. Some of it suggests Auber's influence, not least in the baritone's barcarolle. The Florence May Festival, committed to exhumations even before the *riesumazione* proper began, revived it in Italian in 1953 with Fedora Barbieri, Gianni Poggi, Enzo Mascherini, and Giulio Neri under Giulini, but MRF's album of the production points out how much more Verdi got out of the form.

Certainly Donizetti made grand opera work for him in *La Favorite,* popular in Italy in translations as a *melodramma* but in complete form with ballet—a superior grand opera. It remained popular in France, too, lasting into the early twentieth century to count nearly as many French 78s as Italian. Pathé even gave it the complete treatment in 1912, with Ketty Lapeyrette, Robert Lassalle, and Henri Albers under François Rühlmann. The cuts are startling—most of the tenor's "Oui, ta voix m'inspire," the g minor *vivace* of the second-act finale and some of the succeeding G Major, and much of the C Major section of the third-act finale, as well as second verses of cabalettas, most of the ballet, and snips here and there. Nor is the ensemble work anything to admire. But we do get a taste of the French grand opera style before it grew moribund, with some real French voices taking rubato and breathing spaces for granted as part of the singing line itself. Mezzo Lapeyrette is enticing, tenor Lassalle no more than decent till he wakes up for the final duet, and Albers in rich voice, often taking higher options than an Italian baritone could stand. Bourg issued the set on LP in 1983, without a text booklet but in fine sound. I constantly spot-checked it for pitch fidelity, given the fluctuating speeds of the originals. It's absolutely faithful.

The Italian *La Favorita* is shorter, though nothing like the overhauling that Verdi gave *Don Carlos.* Too many promising discs fail to deliver: Columbia's 78 highlights with Giuseppina Zinetti and the lamb-voiced Cristy Solari; Cetra's and London's early mono complete sets with, respectively, Fedora Barbieri and Giulietta Simionato, even London's stereo box (Cossotto, Pavarotti, Bacquier, Ghiaurov; Bonynge), the orchestra distant and all but Pavarotti rough or perfunctory. Luckily, BJR released, complete with text booklet, Eve Queler's excellent 1975 concert with Shirley Verrett, Alfredo Kraus, Pablo Elvira, and James Morris. At times the performance reflects the elegance of the original French version, especially in Kraus's work, and in Barbara Hendricks's delightfully soubrettish Ines, a Dinorah who has wandered over from the Opéra-Comique to see what's doing. But we hear as well the more vigorous Italianate approach, not least in Queler's conducting. She lacks the big singing grandeur—at, for instance, the D Major tune of the third-act finale—that Toscanini or Serafin would have emphasized. And the overture is coarsely played. But the opera as a whole comes through better than on any other recording, perhaps because the singers seem to be listening to each other, as they surely aren't on Cetra or the two Londons. The audience cheers as if for the greatest of performances. That it isn't. But it is an exciting one, in celebration of our renewed appreciation for the long-undervalued theatre of late bel canto. We may be short in the singers it needs, but at least it is, once again, a true theatre.

10

BERLIOZ

❧

Perhaps more than any other composer, Berlioz proves the phonograph's enormous influence on the postwar expansion of the repertory. An ingeniously eccentric artist, one of music's most stimulating acquired tastes, Berlioz had been neglected for over a century, not benignly. His symphonies and overtures were of course favored, but, of his operas, *Benvenuto Cellini* was little more than a footnote, *Les Troyens* regarded as a last lump of Classical debris, and *Béatrice et Bénédict* unsung. Only *La Damnation de Faust* could be called popular, but this is a "dramatic symphony," concert theatre, the opera that isn't an opera.

It was the LP that revived Berlioz—at that, without a full complement of stylish French artists to match Bolshoi Musorksky, Scala Verdi, or London's Britten campaigners. The French are notorious wasters of their artistic heritage, and the Berlioz revival became perforce an international movement, counting heavily on English performing forces working with a Dutch recording company. Nor is this an entirely recent development. *Les Troyens* was first given complete not in France but in Germany, and many years after Berlioz's death; the composer himself warned that *Béatrice et Bénédict* was "not music for Paris."

He was right. Berlioz's first opera, *Benvenuto Cellini* was a success in Berlioz's lifetime not in Paris but in Franz Liszt's Weimar. Quickly neglected after its London failure shortly thereafter, it was brought back to life in the postwar era by England's Carl Rosa Company and BBC, at the Holland Festival, Geneva, and Covent Garden. The last three productions featured Nicolai Gedda, further emphasizing the polyethnic character of modern Berlioz style, and Gedda thus becomes, with conductor Colin Davis, historically official in Philips's stupendous four-disc set, essential in any Berlioz collection.

Pursuing its integral Berlioz cycle, Philips did not simply master a valid *Benvenuto Cellini* (in 1972) and proceed to more promising titles, but made an all-out effort on this bizarrely farcical, violent, satiric, and moving opera, a unique masterpiece in a unique output. Even now, amid the reappreciation of Berlioz in all his moods, *Cellini* is overshadowed by *Les Troyens*, unarguably the greater opera. But it may be that only by complementing *Les Troyens'* epic grandeur with the more confidential, more richly textured *Cellini* can one comprehend Berlioz's irony.

With *Les Troyens*, Philips had only *(only!)* to cast, record, and release. With *Cellini*, however, a question of text had to be answered, for there are basically three possibilities: the rather lengthy *opéra comique* Berlioz originally wrote; the same with recits instead of spoken dialogue that constitutes the opera's original performing text (at the Opéra); and the vastly shortened version of the latter that was given at Weimar and London.* In addition, numbers were pruned, dropped, reordered. Following the Covent Garden revival of 1966, Philips decided on an authentic but also complete text, reinstating rather than cutting. This raised another question: record the largely British Covent Garden cast of Gedda, Elizabeth Vaughan, Yvonne Minton, Robert Massard, Napoléon Bisson, and David Ward (with Davis replacing John Pritchard) or track in more French natives?

In the event, the new French cast—Christiane Eda-Pierre, Jane Berbié, Jules Bastin, and Roger Soyer joining Gedda and Massard—is not only stylish but winning. One wishes that Berbié had a more serviceable high B for Ascanio's first song (in Geneva [EJS] the Ascanio is a tenor; he ducks the note entirely), but Berbié brings plenty of humor to her second number and generally sings with elegance. And yes, Gedda is not in quite the dashing voice he had brought to the Geneva performances six years earlier. Then, in the first-act trio, he sang the high D flat in full voice—as, surely, did the original Cellini, Gilbert Duprez, who introduced this bold manner of tackling high

---

*This shorter *Cellini*, hacked about by Hans von Bülow, Liszt's assistant at Weimar, was approved by Berlioz, but should not be taken as his final thoughts. The fuller version failed dismally in Paris, while the abridged, at Weimar, succeeded—and Berlioz may have thought it expedient to accede to *force majeure*. It would have been one of the few times in his stormy life that he did so.

notes—whereas for Philips Gedda pulls off a suave but less thrilling falsetto.

Still, here is the great, perhaps the only Cellini of the day, under the ranking Berlioz conductor, in a reclamation of a virtually lost opera, and, topping it off, brilliant stereo separation for the intricate Roman Carnival ensembles. The three other operas in this chapter reveal some of Berlioz's most characteristic passions—Goethe's *Faust*, the Classical world, Shakespeare. But in *Cellini* he set his most personal tale, that of an artist at odds with the authorities, with the bourgeoisie, with the opinion makers. He disarms the first, fools the second, and humiliates the third, and all in a form, *opéra comique*, that from its informal beginnings at the market fairs aimed to tell only of happy lovers outwitting scoundrelly opponents. Amazingly, Berlioz retains this historic basis: but what an epic he builds upon it.

Berlioz's *Faust* actually predates *Benvenuto Cellini* as *Huit Scènes de Faust*. But, expanded into a full evening in revision, *La Damnation de Faust* follows *Cellini* as Berlioz's second . . . opera? Opera-ballet? Stageable cantata? In a way, the fuller version remains *Scenes from Faust*: excerpts from Goethe, but so cinematically episodic, so open to expressionistic presentation, that it has become the rock video of opera. Debussy thought one *Faust* staging "a cross between a conjuring act and some of the attractions of the Folies-Bergère," but the temptation to give this piece utterly to the theatre has proved irresistible. In a sense, all Berlioz is theatre, for his sense of drama, of description and narrative, is as palpable as that of Verdi or Britten—or of Beethoven, who wrote one opera but a great deal of more or less theatrical music.

On records, *La Damnation de Faust* loses the stimulating theatricality that has been applied to it from outside; we concentrate instead on the work's natural theatricality, on the performers' sense of character. *Faust* is exposed on records as few operas are, then, and few of the many sets are outstanding. Columbia's 1948 album under Jean Fournet with Mona Laurena, Georges Jouatte, and Paul Cabanel is dull (Jouatte's Faust shows passion but little voice), Charles Munch's Victor mono is stylish but lackluster, and Igor Markevitch's DG mono suffers cuts to fit two discs. Later, in stereo, we have Seiji Ozawa's Tanglewood concert (DG) with Edith Mathis, Stuart Burrows, and Donald McIntyre, an intelligent group well served by the Boston Symphony. Nothing's wrong; it's all quite correct. But Berlioz's inflamed genius—that eccentricity again—defies the acceptable.

Perhaps this is why Angel's early stereo set under Georges Prêtre with Janet Baker, Nicolai Gedda, and Gabriel Bacquier is so disappointing. Everyone involved is French or a fellow traveler, but the result is sloppy and aimless. Baker is excellent—naïve, distracted, nonplused, she expresses Marguerite's bourgeois tragedy with simple grandeur. Bacquier is a lively devil, subtle in the Serenade. But nothing else takes hold; and stereo, useful in the soldiers-students counterpoint or the Ride to Hell, is hardly touched upon.

Daniel Barenboim has been challenging Colin Davis and Philips with his own Berlioz cycle on DG, but Barenboim's *Faust*, better than Prêtre's, shows the same failure to wire together the work's many strands of sensuality and asceticism, innocence and ambition, naturalism and fantasy. Some things are excellent, especially Dietrich Fischer-Dieskau's devil, with a spirited Song of the Flea—delivered, for once, as if he is truly *telling* a story. Yvonne Minton is fine, though no Baker in this part; and Plácido Domingo, in good voice, lacks the daring to find in Faust the Tonio Kröger–turned–Don Giovanni—the Goethe becoming Goethe, really—that distinguishes Berlioz's *Faust* from, for instance, Gounod's. The sonics are clean but imaginative, as is Barenboim's conducting.

Two *Fausts* seem to me to capture Berlioz's energy and poetry, Georg Solti's digital set on London and Colin Davis's on Philips. Solti's Kenneth Riegel is a rare thinking man's Faust, with a vivacious sense of suspicion when he asks the devil to prove his identity. Riegel isn't approaching Berlioz from Puccini, as many do, but from Goethe. The top C sharp gives him trouble, but otherwise he has the ring of the part as well as its feelings. Frederica von Stade is lovely and José van Dam a gleaming devil, their recits especially vivid.

Oddly, Davis's set, mere stereo, sounds yet more brilliant than Solti's—and his cast is as good. Gedda is at last in the right voice for Faust, right up to the high C sharp, and Jules Bastin presents the most flamboyant of devils. They play well together. Josephine Veasey never quite establishes Marguerite's character, but sings ravishingly; for all that, has anyone but Baker truly brought this character to life on disc?

With *Les Troyens* we come to a key work in opera's discography, perhaps the greatest work that the fewest number of people have actually heard in the theatre. Philips's complete set, like the Toscanini *Otello*, the Fürtwangler *Tristan*, and the Solti *Rheingold*, has been taken into history. In the 1950s, music journalists who couldn't read the sheet music of "Que sera, sera" were describing *Les Troyens* as a monster, a failure, a bore; and nonmusicians had little evidence to go on. Besides the ever-excerptable "Royal Hunt and Storm," there were Marie

Delna's piano-accompanied 1903 78 of "Chers Tyriens," Georges Thill's 1934 sides of Énee's big solo, and an underground of Beecham's broadcast of the Carthage "part," * a ghastly performance in miserable sound. Is that not Beecham himself angrily correcting when the Hylas goes badly off in his solo?

In 1952 came Hermann Scherchen's three-disc set of *Les Troyens à Carthage* (Westminster). This is a small-scale performance, not only mono but shallow and shrill. The first statement of Dido's triumphal march will sound like a crawl to those raised on Davis—but how jubilantly Scherchen builds it. Arda Mandikian's voice will suggest a surprisingly modest Dido to those used to international power, but—despite occasional slips in her French—she captures wonderfully the conflict of majesty and vulnerability that this section of the opera turns on.

A set, then, of some interest. However, the Aeneas, Jean Giraudoux, is a disaster, as he had been for Beecham, his tiny tenor absurd in "Reine! Je suis Énee!," the great moment in which the hero first steps forward in Carthage, to offer his services as warrior when Dido is threatened. Aeneas is not a role we merely prefer a heroic sound in, like Manrico or Parsifal. Aeneas is *the* hero, like Otello or Siegfried, of a ring absolute. The rest of the cast is all French but variable in effect, with a fine Anna and Narbal. Scherchen, really, is the great thing, lively, forceful, piquant—as eccentric, his legend tells us, as Berlioz himself. He leaves the impression that "Italie!" impells him as much as it does Aeneas.

Nineteen sixty-five brought Angel's stopgap reply to growing interest in the work, two discs of highlights with Régine Crespin, Guy Chauvet, and Opéra forces under Georges Prêtre. It's skimpy pickings, for surely we did not need another reading of the Royal Hunt instead of a vocal number; at that, the sides are not filled. More's the pity, as it's a fine performance, Crespin among the most entitled of Cassandres and Didos, Chauvet a surprisingly able, even tender Énee (he takes the optional high C in his aria), and Prêtre and his assistants excel-

---

* Because *Les Troyens* was broken into two sections, *La Prise de Troie* and *Les Troyens à Carthage*, published thus and often performed separately, many operagoers think of them as two parts, even two operas. However Berlioz insisted that *Les Troyens* is one work, one night, a single adventure in which a hero (Aeneas) is presented with and despatches, after dallying, an epic task (to refound Troy in Italy). Berlioz added to the confusion by composing a prelude for use when the second section is given alone. As if he knew that, too frequently, it would be, the music sounds dispirited, inappropriate as an introduction to Aeneas' inspiring task.

lent. But they *are* assistants, no more, for this is virtually *Crespin Sings Troyens' Greatest Hits:* the few scenes included are actually cut to favor her lines.

Five years later came Philips's five-disc box, and *Les Troyens* was home. Based on Covent Garden's 1969 staging, Davis's set is international rather than French: Josephine Veasey as Dido, Berit Lindholm as Cassandre, Heather Begg as Anna, Jon Vickers as Énee, Peter Glossop as Chorèbe, Roger Soyer as Narbal. "Les gretch ont disparu!" Lindholm observes on her entrance, putting a northern spin on "grecs." Still, she sings with great aplomb. Indeed, this is generally a great performance, not just a valid one useful in energizing a work's reputation till the ultimate reading comes along.

Davis's *Troyens,* like his *Cellini,* may well *be* the ultimate reading. Some deplored Philips's failure to enlist Janet Baker's Dido. (She recorded the final scenes with Alexander Gibson and Scottish Opera forces in 1972 on Angel, magnificently.) Baker did, in fact, sing Dido at Covent Garden in an emergency for two nights, her clean English vying intriguingly with her colleagues' not always natural French. Still, Veasey was the Dido of the production (Lindholm replaces Anja Silja, whose French was even less apt), and she is superb, wonderfully haughty, for instance, in "Son insolence est vaine" (His insolence is fruitless), when referring to "le farouche Iarbas" and his unlovable proposal of marriage. Vickers's Aeneas is beyond faulting. Here is a "Je suis Énee!" Berlioz would have liked, and the portrayal is in all perhaps the best in Vickers's gallery.

Of Davis's secondary singers, the Carthaginians impress more than the Trojans, Glossop too stolid even for the stolid Chorèbe. Anna and Narbal, however, come to life, and the D Flat Major quintet, as it pulses on, truly suggests "all conspiring to vanquish Dido's remorse," with her suite gloating over her attraction to Aeneas. Best of all, the sonics are tremendous, with all the clarity and grand dimensions that stereo had been promising for fifteen years. Here Philips delivers, as in the enhanced perspectives for the ghosts in Aeneas' big solo scene; then we hear him running about the harbor as he musters his troops for the last voyage. It is said that Barenboim's DG cycle is hesitant about proceeding to *Les Troyens* without a suitable successor to Vickers's Aeneas. But surely it is Philips's achievement as a whole that gives DG pause: Davis's *Troyens* is not likely to be bettered.

Les Troyens' Romantic temper with a Classical frame, its purifying nobility as the grand opera meant to reform grand opera, and its failure to establish itself for a century—all this seems typical Berlioz, typical of his paradoxes and headlong despairs. So it is surprising to realize that *Les Troyens* is not the summit of the man's opera, not the ultimate work: the tidy little *Béatrice et Bénédict* followed *Les Troyens* almost immediately. It is Berlioz's least unusual major work, turning the outlines of the plot of *Much Ado About Nothing* into an *opéra comique*, and it also his most successful on disc, with three excellent stereo sets.

The oldest, Colin Davis's of 1962 (Oiseau-Lyre), offers Josephine Veasey and John Mitchinson (Goodall's Tristan) as spirited battlers in the title roles, though Veasey gets a touch Classically Poised in her big aria. April Cantelo's Hero is delightful, if not as agile as some in the runs and cadenza (here cut down) of her solo. Helen Watts's Ursule is amusingly Clara Butt in style, *mezzo profundo*—not entirely wrong for this rather square, Liederesque character.

Pursuing his Philips series, Davis tried again seventeen years later in brighter sound (too bright at times), with Janet Baker, Christiane Eda-Pierre, Watts again, Robert Tear, and Thomas Allen. This is the most Shakespearean of the three sets, the richest in character, especially in Baker and Tear's sparring—their "Quelle menace" (What fury) is wonderfully nuanced. Of all Benedicts, only Tear has the dash; of all Beatrices, only Baker is ingenious, as in the increasingly impassioned "Je t'aime" she utters in the aria, suggesting that only then, that moment, is she realizing that, indeed, she loves after all.

Barenboim's DG set of 1981 may have the best voices: Yvonne Minton, Ileana Cotrubas, Nadine Denize, Plácido Domingo, Roger Soyer, and, as the pedantic Somarone, Dietrich Fischer-Dieskau. But the comedy's mercurial glitter eludes the two leads, Barenboim lacks Davis's expert grasp, and Domingo's French (for example, "orgay" for *orgueil*) is chancy. At least Cotrubas presents the best of all Heros, as a kind of valiant virgin, and only DG troubled to take its troops to Paris. Still, where's the quirky atmosphere that Berlioz found so sympathetic in Shakespeare? Each of the three sets finds a different solution to the problem of recording the dialogue; this may influence purchasers most of all. Oiseau-Lyre records only the music, Philips retains enough of the script to connect the numbers, and DG substitutes a French narrator.

11

OPÉRA COMIQUE

☙❧

If grand opera was French by osmosis, from Lully through Gluck and Spontini to Rossini and Meyerbeer, *opéra comique* was the native form, derived from the old fairground "vaudevilles" (comedies with song, usually old tunes adapted to new lyrics in the style of ballad opera) and developed almost entirely by French artists. As a theatre experience, however, the difference between grand opera and *opéra comique* lay not in who wrote them as much as in who *performed* them. Grand opera was, as the term suggests, gala and expensive, noble in subject and designed for the most expansive voices, a rhetoric of the *ancien régime*. *Opéra comique* was modest, bourgeois, a place for less formidable singers who suited less heroic storylines. There was a great deal of crossover activity: most composers wrote in both forms, and some *opéras comiques* were revised, with inflationary emendations, into grand operas. But the essential division between the two forms lay in what kind of voices composers wrote them for. The greater singers belonged to grand opera, the greater entertainers to *opéra comique*. To distinguish French opera's two main genres by the old rule that grand opera set recit between the numbers, and *opéra comique* spoken dialogue, is to miss the point entirely. Grand opera was *grand*: ambitious, however silly. *Opéra comique* was cute: sweet diversion.

A good starting point in early *opéra comique* is André Grétry's *Zémire et Azor* (EMI, Arabesque), *Beauty and the Beast* in a Persian setting. The rough vitality of the old vaudeville—what Offenbach was to term "le genre primitif et gai"—has been soothed to favor love and magic, though some comic energy remains in the servant Ali. Here is sweet music, sweetly sung by Mady Mesplé (beauty), Roland Bufkens (the beast), and Jean-Claude Orliac (Ali) under Edgard Doneux.

Pursue the history with Auber's *Manon Lescaut* (EMI, Arabesque), coy and worldly where Grétry is demure, comely. *Opéra comique* is becoming Parisian: the boulevards are lending an air, and Eugène Scribe, the "libretto factory" of the day, as glib with the oaths and loyalties of grand opera as with the disguises and pranks of *opéra comique*, has entered the scene. *Manon Lescaut* has more coloratura than *Zémire et Azor*, a stronger sense of rhythm, even an immortal aria, the Letter Song, "C'est l'histoire amoureuse," which Galli-Curci recorded, no better than she should have. EMI's Jean-Pierre Marty leads a delightful performance, though Manon Mesplé and her chevalier Orliac are far livelier in the dialogue than in the music.

By now, *opéra comique*'s aesthetic should be clear: unsophisticated musical structures, light voices never forced, middle-class or fantastic characters playing essentially romantic comedies in an exotic or historical setting. Grétry represents the late 1700s, Auber the early-middle 1800s. Let us consider *opéra comique* in its prime, the latter half of the 1800s, in Léo Delibes's *Lakmé*.

The recipe holds firm: the composition is simple, basically a series of tunes with a slight touch of *Leitmotiv*. The Indian heroine is a lyric soprano who must turn coloratura for the Bell Song; the English soldier who loves her against political odds is a lyric tenor; her Anglophobe father is a *basse chantante*, cultivating honeyed tones for his imprecations against the colonials; and the other characters would be comfortable in an operetta troupe. The romance is tenderly portrayed, the heroine's death pathetic rather than imposing, by poisoned blossom (as in *L'Africaine*). There is comedy, supplied by the English governess, Mistress Bentson, another of the many French roles defined not by vocal range but by the name of the unique artist whose performing style the composer had in mind.* Of course the setting couldn't be more exotic, with plenty of Hindu pastiche and a ballet to empha-

---

*French opera dotes on these classifications: the baryton-Martin (after Jean-Blaise Martin, light in texture but capable of reaching into the tenor range), the Trial (after Antoine Trial, one of the first of the acting, as well as singing, tenors), and of course the Falcon we know from grand opera. Mistress Bentson is a Dugazon, after Louise Dugazon, whose tradition is so rich she inspired two types, Dugazon-*mère* and Dugazon-*fille* ("mother" and "daughter": basically, for those who know Gilbert and Sullivan, a Little Buttercup or an Iolanthe). To take the classifications a step further, if, say, *Kiss Me, Kate* had been written in the 1930s, Cole Porter might have dubbed his leads a King, Segal, Whiting, and Velez (for Dennis King, Vivienne Segal, Jack Whiting, and Lupe Velez).

size the air of wonderland on display. The drama—especially the heroine's part—lacks bite. But the music has charm, and the pseudo-Indian material is piquant, reminding us that *opéra comique* feeds as much on oddity and surprise as on dear romance.

The oldest *Lakmé* is a relay of a Met broadcast from the Edward Johnson years, a spirited, graceful performance under Wilfred Pelletier and built around Lily Pons's Lakmé, a fixture of that era. One hears why. Other sopranos lower the high notes; Pons raises them. She seems a little vague about what's happening in the story scenes but sings a great Bell Song, clear, bright, and fast. (Milton Cross, another fixture of the day, and one of opera's few figures who can truly be called beloved, catches a sense of the time when he crows, "Lily Pons and her famous Bell Song!," and breaks in just after it to observe, "That was singing Es with ease.") Pelletier reminds us how strong the Met was then in *répétiteurs*—seldom inspired but always sound. The cast has a Broadway feel—Ezio Pinza, Irra Petina, and Annamary Dickey all subsequently appeared in musicals, reminding us of America's hunger for real voices on its popular musical stage. (Petina, who would play a marvelous Dugazon-*mère* part as the Old Lady in the original *Candide,* is not Mistress Bentson, but Mallika, Lakmé's confidante, and not even a Dugazon-*fille.*) Pinza's French is execrable, but he rolls out the notes with full tone, and only Armand Tokatyan's labored tenor and the absence of the ballet mar the event. Not a great *Lakmé:* but an attractive supplement.

More authoritative but less interesting is London's early mono set (with ballet) featuring Mado Robin and Opéra-Comique forces under Georges Sebastian. Robin's otherworldly timbre suits the part, but her relentlessly uncolored delivery dulls the ear. Like Pons, she darts up on high whenever no one's looking, reaching a high G sharp in the cadenza to the Bell Song's first verse. But, except for her intrepid trill, the whole scene seems perfunctory. London's stereo remake offers an international cast, with an assured Joan Sutherland, a masterful Gabriel Bacquier (though the higher lines frustrate him), and, most telling, Monica Sinclair as Mistress Bentson, Buttercup *à la française* and a true Dugazon-*mère.*

Opéra comique is too French for internationals—which is why EMI's set (Seraphim), with less fetching voices, catches the tale more truly. The original European pressing, in gorgeous sound, featured alert stereo separation—as when Hadji actually seems to run "onstage" when Lakmé spots her spying English admirer and calls for help. Mady Mesplé and Charles Burles emphasize *opéra comique*'s sentimental heart, most effectively in the caressing phrases, least at climaxes. Roger Soyer's father cleans the character of stock villainy, giving us a true sense of the loving parent and committed patriot—and his "Lakmé, ton doux regard" betters Pinza's. Conductor Alain Lombard errs on the suave side; his Market Scene lacks Pelletier's wonderful energy. But Lombard's is a very musical *Lakmé*. The Bell Song, for once, is quite haunting.

Perhaps we should lay history aside for a moment and consider this aria, so popular that it was thought the sole reason for *Lakmé*'s survival. At first look it seems an intrusion, a showpiece of no aid to the story. But it does alter the plot in that, after the applause, Lakmé's father demands a reprise, hoping to use it to unmask Lakmé's alien lover. It does intrude vocally in that the rest of the role calls for *legato, espressivo*, not coloratura fireworks. This explains why Pons and Sutherland are right only for the Bell Song, and why Mesplé, best of Lakmés, does not dazzle there.

As a recital item the aria is ideal. On 78s, Galli-Curci's is the most famous, cut and in Italian, but a classic of the American parlor. Callas, also in Italian on an Angel LP, gets the most from the piece dramatically and sensually. Rita Streich (DG) fails her French test and omits the trickiest runs, but emphasizes the piece as music. Sutherland's earlier version, in *The Art of the Prima Donna* (London), is spectacular. Edita Gruberova (Angel), however, rivals her. Some of the runs are yodeled, but the voice is ravishing.

Lakmé recalls *Zémire et Azor*: gentle romance in a foreign clime, with a taste of servent slapstick (from Ali; from Mistress Bentson). Let us factor *opéra comique* into its constituent parts, sampling them work by work. First, comedy. Try Auber's *Fra Diavolo* (EMI digital), with Mesplé, Jane Berbié, Nicolai Gedda, Thierry Dran, and Remi Corazza under Marc Soustrol. Gedda's a bandit, Mesplé a servant with a bedtime undressing scene (one hundred fifty-five years ago, Mendelssohn was scandalized), and Berbié and Corazza are British travelers, Berbié exploiting the Dugazon-*mère*'s gift for contentious fun. EMI's performance eradicates several ham-handed German-language sets, and reinstates the original ending, in which Brother Devil is apprehended. But as a whole it lacks zing.

Next, junior grand opera: *opéra comique* as a smaller version of the big form. Lalo's *Le Roi d'Ys* (Angel, EMI) fills in well. Though its lengthy overture promises broad structures, and it does have grand opera's noble characters and busy choruses, now setting scenes and now being outraged for a big ensemble finale, the opera is fleet and tight, just two discs, albeit of boxy mono. The love-triangle-and-revenge plot may be old business, but it comes dressed in the coloring of

Brittany. (Lalo specialized in ethnic pastiche; he also wrote a Russian Concerto, a Norwegian Rhapsody, and a Spanish Symphony.) Most interesting is the Noce Bretonne (Breton nuptials), a choral scene that explains the oddly plunking accompaniment to the score's popular aria, "Vainement, ma bien aimée": the entire sequence is set to this lutelike gavotte, meant to suggest a rustic musicale as the boys feign symbolic attack on the bride's door and the girls resist. Angel's cast is the one you'd expect for the time: Janine Micheau a pallid heroine, Rita Gorr vivid as her jealous sister, Henri Legay as the man they love (Gedda vastly betters him in the aria, on an Angel recital), Jean Borthayre as the villain—who, amusingly, bears the name of Johnny Carson's spiritualist wag, Karnac.

Most characteristic of all is the sentimental piece, usually an adaptation from a novel or play, with something romantic here, something quirky there, and something atmospheric drawing both together: Ambroise Thomas's *Mignon,* for instance. The source is Goethe's *The Adventures of Wilhelm Meister,* which was, in the year of *Mignon's* debut, 1866, extremely reputable. But the real point of the work is not literary transfusion but the mezzo heroine's pathetically yearning solos, the tenor's exuberant entrance aria (as romantic dandy) and later soothing arias in *mezza voce* (as poet: the young Goethe), the coloratura's dashing Polonaise, the passing touches of gypsy and Italian color, the general air of *fatigue du nord. Mignon* is neglected, even in France, but Columbia offers an excellent stereo performance, unfortunately not of *Mignon:* rather, of some grand opera on the same subject. The sonics frame too broad a perspective, as if addressing an audience of ten thousand. The crowd noises suggest a Hollywood cocaine orgy. And Marilyn Horne is ferociously gala for the role of a hapless waif. London's ancient mono set, made at Brussels' Monnaie with Geneviève Moizan, Janine Micheau, and Libero de Luca (Richmond), is more faithful and theatrical. Musically, however, Columbia still holds the ace, Ruth Welting, Frederica von Stade, Alain Vanzo, and Nicola Zaccaria assisting Horne, under Antonio de Almeida. Moreover, Columbia offers a complete text (London observes theatre cuts) and an appendix of alternate and extra numbers. Both albums use recit rather than the original spoken dialogue; BJR offers a fine, cut live performance (Tourangeau, Noelle Rogers, Henri Wilden; Bonynge) with the dialogue, as stylish as London and better sung.

Let us consider one composer in particular, one who was to *opéra comique* as Meyerbeer was to grand opera: Charles Gounod. True, Gounod wrote for the Opéra. Yet just as Meyerbeer was at his least inspired in *opéra comique*—as competent readings of *Dinorah* (Opera

Rara) and *L'Étoile du Nord* (MRF) report—so was Gounod most comfortable in the more intimate form. We can analyze this at our ease in an MRF box of Gounod's first and third operas, both from the 1850s, the full-scale *Sapho* and the small *Le Médecin Malgré Lui*, after Molière. *Sapho,* slightly cut in a commendable 1979 French radio broadcast (also on Rodolphe) headed by Katherine Ciesinski, Eliane Lublin, and Alain Vanzo, clearly does not want to be a self-important public event; all the rhetorical flourishes sound hollow, abashed, while the central romance comes off well. With the Molière, however, Gounod seems at ease and surprisingly Classical in style, almost Mozartean. MRF's tape of second-line French singers drops the dialogue.

Faust was Gounod's fourth opera—and here, you say, Gounod surely encompassed the larger form, writing big for the principals and imitating, in such numbers as the Soldiers' Chorus and the Duel Trio, the brio of Meyerbeer exploiting his genres. (The Duel Trio even sounds like Meyerbeer.) However, *Faust* was first performed as an *opéra comique,* with somewhat less music than we are used to—Valentine's "Avant de quitter ces lieux," for instance, and Siebel's "Si le bonheur," both added for London performances. It is a hallmark of grand opera that the lead singers get at least one big solo besides their duets and trios—the reason why grand opera had to be not only composed for great stars but, forever after, cast with them. Yet Gounod did not compose *Faust* thus, with obligatory scenes that would, first on a few off nights and then generally, be cut. Even the expanded *Faust* doesn't have the flab of Meyerbeer or Halévy. "Si le bonheur" is dull, true. But to snip Marguerite's Spinning Song or the Walpurgisnacht is to omit the work's most telling links with Goethe. This proves Gounod's lack of sympathy with grand opera. *Faust* has no diversions. *Faust* has integrity.

Its discography reflects its ancient popularity and recent decline: countless 78 extracts but vastly fewer LP sets than *Carmen, La Bohème, Der Rosenkavalier.* Essential are the twenty-one Victor 78 sides that Geraldine Farrar, Enrico Caruso, Antonio Scotti (Pasquale Amato on one cut), and Marcel Journet made in 1910, commemorating the Met in its "Faustspielhaus" days. A previous LP transcription was incomplete and badly turned; perhaps Rubini, Preiser, or Opal will address the task, for, as Gounod remarked at one performance, "Voilà mon *Faust!*" Journet, suave rather than tactless in the Shalyapin manner, is the best in general, but Caruso is superb in the Duel Trio, and Farrar, anything but a grand opera voice and everything in a *comique* personality, is a magical Marguerite. The 1908 German set with Emmy Destinn, Karl Jörn, and Paul Knüpfer (Discophilia), despite

Destinn's excellence, is in completeness and sound erased by the two electric sets, both Victors: under Henri Busser and Thomas Beecham. Busser has the edge in voice, with César Vezzani's very forceful hero and Journet, still in form after forty years onstage (he adds a high F at "un vrai gentilhomme" at his entrance). But Beecham's set, though almost every writer has disdained it, seems to me as stylish and more interesting. As early as the prelude, we hear Beecham digging in, making *music*, in the "Avant de quitter" melody; and the introduction to the Garden Scene presents the conflict of naïveté and stealth that Gounod wrote into it. Beecham's singers, too, have a lot of character: Georges Noué a virile and forward hero, Roger Rico another velvety devil, Huguette Saint-Arnaud a delightful Siebel. Geori-Boué, a famed beauty, always lacked something on record: a decent voice. Yet her intelligent plangence makes her Jewel Song unique, "Est-ce toi?" (Is it you?) not a question but a plea. We lose the Walpurgisnacht (and, through some halfhearted authenticity, "Avant de quitter"), yet we gain, first of all thus far, a theatre *Faust*—and one that puts it forth in persuasive *comique* proportions, with charm more than power.

Columbia's early mono *Faust*, with Eleanor Steber, Eugene Conley, and Cesare Siepi under Fausto Cleva, offers a cowboy Faust and Casanova devil, though Steber is lovely. Victoria de los Angeles, Nicolai Gedda, and Boris Christoff remade their Victor mono for Angel in stereo; only a student bucking for a Ph.D. could tell which is the duller, or where the interpretations differ. At least these two sets offered (except for Christoff) French stylists. But the stereo era brought back the international cast, at the opposite end of Beecham's crew: lots of voice and little personality.

London's Bonynge set, in a rather live acoustic, suggests a golden-age *Faust* in London or New York, in which one might have heard a Christine Nilsson, a Melba, a de Reszke—no one French. At least in those days the French style was *lingua franca*. Melba coached with Gounod and Saint-Saëns, Jean de Reszke with Massenet. Perhaps Joan Sutherland, Franco Corelli, and Nicolai Ghiaurov are less well grounded, and, counting in Margreta Elkins's Siebel, we have only Robert Massard's Valentin for the home team. This given, it is a pleasurable album, a very grand *Faust*, for everyone's in voice and Bonynge supplies the vitality for "Vin ou bière," the solemnity for the Sword Chorus, to support the ambitious architecture that, this one time, Gounod raised. And if Sutherland gets nothing out of "Il ne revient pas," Gounod's "Grettchen am Spinnrade"; if Corelli's French is appalling; and if Ghiaurov breaks up the line in recits in the Shalyapin manner: still the set is notable for the booklet's detailed historical notes, outlining places where more music apparently exists—unpublished, with-held by Gounod's heirs. Bonynge was able to add in a few incidental pages that no other set includes, but he omits Faust's Walpurgisnacht Drinking Song, "Vains remords."

Half a generation later, Angel offered a more youthful international cast under Georges Prêtre and Paris Opéra forces. The sonics are sen-sible, and the conductor has thought the piece through. *Faust* as a conductor's opera? But Prêtre is pensively slow in the prelude, truly *drawing* us into Faust's study, and he gentles the *Allegro ben marcato* of "À moi les plaisirs" as if edging from dotage into youth. Notice, too, in the Thulé ballad, how he seizes the paradoxical air of *Moderato maestoso* that Gounod requests, beautifully framing Mirella Freni's de-livery. Seldom does this aria come off well—even Farrar and Callas find little in it. It is a mood piece, something to see, not record. Yet here, for once, it sings. It helps that Freni really gives herself to Mar-guerite, acting as well as singing the Jewel Song, and very vivid in the Church Scene, where so many lyric sopranos come to grief. (Dramatic sopranos, conversely, thrive in it but sound absurd in other scenes: Gina Cigna, big enough for Turandot and Gioconda, recorded the Church Scene with Nazzareno de Angelis in mid-electric years, most impressively.) Alas, only Freni and Thomas Allen's Valentin rescue Angel's set from routine, for Ghiaurov is now badly labored, and Plá-cido Domingo, though fresh in tone, is not remotely the weary phi-losopher of the first act or the rejuvenated idealist of the rest. He does, at least, perform the Drinking Song, which Prêtre rushes coarsely. This solo fills out the Walpurgisnacht when the ballet is cut, so Angel set the dance music by itself on side eight. Tradition holds that Léo Delibes composed the ballet music, but it seems to be true Gounod, so Prêtre vies with Bonynge for most complete (with a more Gallic) *Faust.*

There is no one certain *Faust,* then. Nor is there one great *Roméo et Juliette,* perhaps the only grand opera consisting largely of soprano-tenor duets. Angel's highlights disc with Gedda and Rosanna Carteri could dispense with a chorus and not feel inessential—and surely An-gel's Freni-Corelli stereo set counts less on its Paris Opéra backing under Alain Lombard than on the two stars. It's a charismatic pairing, though already, in their first scene together, the Madrigal, Freni is graceful and Corelli coarse. His diminuendo on the high B flat at the climax of "Ah! lève-toi, soleil!" raised a controversy: did engineers finesse it? Angel persevered in a digital entry in 1985 with Catherine Malfitano and Alfredo Kraus under Plasson. Here, style is not a prob-lem, and a lively performance attempts to balance the lovers' music with the rest of the piece. Ann Murray's vivacious Stephano is useful here, especially as Gabriel Bacquier's Capulet is too tired to get the opening ball scene off to a gala start. As for the lovers, Kraus sounds senior next to Malfitano's youthful timbre, but he's in smart voice, ringing out the B flat in "Ah! léve toi, soleil!" and adding in a few Cs in later scenes.

This is a cast that would also do well by *Faust* and *Mireille*. All Gounod's persuasive operas center on virtually the same set of characters—the sensitively passionate tenor, the demure soprano, the menacing bass-baritone, the sprightly trouser kid, with baritone dandy Mercutio and contralto beldame Taven (in *Mireille*) varying the texture. Certainly, when Gounod strayed out of this essentially *comique* realm of lyric voices and arias of character rather than of gesture, he did second-rate work, as in, say, *La Reine de Saba*, like *Roméo* written for the Opéra and unique in its failure to make anything of a character as enticing as the Queen of Sheba herself. Where *Roméo et Juliette* largely dispensed with grand opera's accessory numbers, *Le Reine de Saba* tried to revel in them; it seems nothing but processionals and revenge trios, as we can hear on a fatuous performance under Plasson (MRF, taken live in the theatre with Suzanne Sarocca and Gilbert Py). Yet Gounod wrote one of his very best pieces for the tenor's big solo, a classic instance of defiantly questioning recit and resolute aria, "Inspirez-moi, race divine!," caught on an electric 78 by César Vezzani in dazzling voice.

It is the *opéras comiques* as wholes, the intimately focused operas, that find Gounod at his best, as in *Mireille*, too often regarded as a third fiddle to *Faust* and *Roméo*, but equally tuneful and, in its Provençal setting, more colorful, with its native argot and the driving drums of the Farandole, an opportunity that Gounod seizes delightfully. In truth, he takes us on a tour of France's fiery south from the first moments of his opera's prelude, quirkily rustic woodwinds dancing against held strings. Angel's mono set under Cluytens, from a staging at the Aix-en-Provence Festival, respected the opera's ethnic flavor enough to include a lavish booklet explaining the terms and customs concerned. Janette Vivalda's sweetness is vivid, and Gedda's command increases as the sides turn, but Angel's stereo version with Freni and Vanzo under Plasson is more theatrical, Vanzo more intense than Gedda and Freni in great voice (if not great French), a bit shrill on top but always touching. Perhaps Cluytens caught the rough Provençal *colorito* better than Plasson. In the Farandole, Plasson is crisp and amiable, Cluytens joyous and noisy. He has a further advantage, giving as an encore the familiar waltz that Gounod wrote to replace the original sad ending with a glad one.

This question of alternate endings to soothe the public's feelings crops up often in *opéra comique*—another difference from grand opera, whose more worldly public expected at least one heroic and possibly violent death (though such influential grand operas as *La Vestale*, *Guillaume Tell*, and *Robert le Diable* end happily, and no one is sure how *Don Carlos* ends). *Opéra comique*, again, was sentimental, quaint. Georges Bizet, writing of a savage tribe in *Les Pêcheurs de Perles*, was expected to indicate—at most—the savagery and emphasize the triangle of two blood brothers parted by their love for a priestess. Angel must love this opera, having released three editions. The mono set with Marthe Angelici, Henri Legay, and Michel Dens under Cluytens suggests a typical night at the Opéra-Comique, with competent song and sloppy orchestra. The stereo set under Pierre Dervaux offers a better night at the same house, with Gedda guesting to present his famous white semifalsetto in "Je crois entendre encore," a Gedda specialty. Janine Micheau is as pallid as Angelici; but Ernest Blanc, alone of Angel's Zurgas, takes the optional high A in the priestess's swearing-in. Both sets used a corrupt text that includes music not by Bizet. On its third try, in 1978, Angel set Ileana Cotrubas, Alain Vanzo, and Guillermo Sarabia before Opéra staff under Prêtre in a spacious acoustic and a corrected text. This is the liveliest of the three, and the most careful. The Brotherhood Duet, for once, begins in the requested hush, the two men suggesting a rapt narration—which it is—instead of a Big Tune. Note also how Vanzo holds the last sustained E in his aria, letting the clarinet finish the melody, a piquant effect seldom heard elsewhere.

Bizet brings us to the least typical of *opéras comiques*, the one that offended the establishment (less so the curious public) with its earthy violence: *Carmen*. The romantically exotic setting and Micaëla's rustic innocence were pure *comique*. But Bizet's source, Prosper Merimée's naturalistic novel, led the composer to what was, for the time and the form, an excess of honesty. Merimée's protagonist, Don José, is psychotically violent; he was toned down, except for the final scene. But Merimée's gypsy came through as perhaps the first unapologetically sensual woman since the days of Cavalli. She seduces and abandons, acts that opera forgives only in male characters. Even George Bernard Shaw, sympathetic to gender equality and himself the creator of many strong women, was horrified.

The opera caught on after its first faltering run and quickly became

standard—but in recits cooked up after Bizet's death by Ernest Guiraud. The last two decades have welcomed a return to the original
spoken dialogue; at the same time, musicologist Fritz Oeser prepared
a more complete score, taking in music cut during rehearsals. It's a
controversial edition, offering more Bizet but denounced by some Bizet
experts. Thus, a search for a great *Carmen* observes two different ideals, the great performance and the great text.

The heroine's many solos and duets fit nicely on 78 sides, and over
the years three very different kinds of Carmen developed. Geraldine
Farrar exemplifies the dashing, vastly enacted Carmen, almost raucous
in the Gypsy Song and biting off "La mort!" (Death!) in the Card
Song; Conchita Supervia presents the sensual charmer; and Gabriela
Besanzoni, on Victor's complete set in Italian, relies on a booming
voice occasionally lightened by what Besanzoni hopes is devil-may-
care laughter. Note also that the three offer, respectively, a soprano's,
a lyric mezzo's, and a near-contralto's Carmen. There is a fourth Carmen type, most basic and yet least often encountered—cool, unclut-
tered, and very French. This is the Carmen that Lucy Perelli sang in
an old Victor set with Yvonne Brothier, José de Trevi, and Louis
Musy under Piero Coppola. Unfortunately, its only LP reissue, on
Camden, was thoughtlessly taped a half-tone sharp.

Columbia's 1950 LP set under Cluytens, from the Opéra-Comique,
was a shock: dialogue instead of recit, fifteen years before Oeser. The
reading is perfunctorily brisk but theatrical (the crowd's cries during
Carmen's interrogation might have been caught at Les Halles), and
the cast—Solange Michel, Marthe Angelici, Raoul Jobin, and Michel
Dens—is respectable, Jobin a little less so in his singing and more so
in his portrayal. Certainly Columbia is preferable to Fritz Reiner's
hopelessly international grouping (Stevens, Albanese, Peerce, Merrill)
of a year later. Beecham's very stylish early stereo set (Angel) with
the Supervian de los Angeles was the first excellent *Carmen*, despite
variable contributions from Micheau, Gedda, and Blanc.

Oeser's reinstitution of the original *Carmen* set Beecham somewhat
to the side—but spoken dialogue and gleanings from Oeser's reclamation do not a *Carmen* make. Leonard Bernstein's Met reading with
Marilyn Horne (DG) is much too overpowering—it seems to take place
in a bull ring—and Rafael Frühbeck de Burgos's Angel set (Bumbry,
Freni, Vickers, Paskalis) is marred by a cast of actors piped in from
remote parts for the dialogue. Worse yet, the performance is lifeless,
except for Vickers, who develops José so well that by the finale he
sounds like a man who hasn't slept in weeks. Solti's set (London)

boasts his thoughtful consideration of Oeser's addenda, laid out in the booklet; but Tatiana Troyanos, Kiri Te Kanawa, Plácido Domingo, and José van Dam are better at singing their parts than making them live.

Carmen may be, like *Don Giovanni,* too ideal to realize ideally. Erato's digital sound track of Francesco Rosi's movie counts in Lorin Maazel and Julia Migenes-Johnson excellent interpreters, but Faith Esham, Domingo, and Ruggero Raimondi offer little more than support. Too bad: for Maazel is so atmospheric that he follows Bizet's markings in the Gypsy Song to start slow and build to a frenzy. As for Migenes, whose career had taken in Broadway (she was one of the "Matchmaker, Matchmaker" daughters in *Fiddler on the Roof*) and German operetta before she made international stardom in the film, here is a special Carmen, out of the traditions. Listen to the brusquely matter-of-fact "C'est certain!" just before the Habañera; the correctly "pp et léger" she observes in the Séguidille (not to mention the flawless top B at the end); the vibrant confidence of "Là-bas dans les montagnes."

Another special Carmen was better set off than Migenes, albeit in the discredited Guiraud version: Angel's Callas. Here, as rarely, is the woman Micaëla describes as "dangereuse" and "belle," combining, as it were, the Farrar and Supervia approaches. Callas's Carmen is very performed, yet very natural—barely threatening in a blithe Habañera, momentously insinuating in the interrogation, confidential in the Séguidille (with a perfect top B), spontaneously calculated in the Act Two duet, Carmen as gambler and manipulator at once.

And this is a mezzo Carmen, avoiding the traditional soprano's higher options we hear from Leontyne Price (Victor), if not quite as comfortable on the lowest notes as Teresa Berganza (DG). Callas truly fails the challenge at one spot, in the big fourth-act duet, on "Non, je ne te céderai pas!", where the notes lack tone. Otherwise, this work is entirely in place, Prêtre solid, Gedda excellent (if he lacks Vickers's concentration, he does fix the role in vocal style, showing, more than he did for Beecham, how Bizet edged the *comique* lyric tenor into a dramatic one, halfway to the Arnolds and Raouls of grand opera), and Massard gaming at his torero's bluster with a light touch. Andrea Guiot's Micaëla is the best on disc, surprisingly energetic, making her duet with José not a convention of *comique* but a significant element in the narrative. Unlike the usual placid kid—Micheau, or Sutherland, or Freni—Guiot offers José a persuasive alternative to the life he will lead if he lives for love of Carmen. Nor does Guiot center her third-act aria on delicate fear, as so many do; she is refreshingly avid in the middle section. If there is no outstanding album of this most unusual *opéra comique*, this one is at least unusual itself, subtle where others are heavy, and energetic where others make do.

The most *usual* of *opéras comiques*—speaking historically—is Offenbach's *Les Contes d'Hoffmann*, a work with roots in the raucous gaiety of the fairground vaudevilles. In *Hoffmann*, much of what *comique* lost in its fancy for exotic settings and less and less narrative librettos, Offenbach reclaimed. And his source, E. T. A. Hoffmann, provided the grotesquerie and irony that such works as *Lakmé* and *Mignon* retired. Offenbach added his natural element—that of the spoof—and came up with the century's unique work in the form, almost a handbook of *comique* genres and characters. Opera legend has it that Offenbach longed all his life to rise above his *boulevardier* musical comedies with a real opera, did so in his last work—and died too soon to see it staged. In fact, he had been stabbing at the grander musical forms throughout his career. Sample an excellent example in Opera Rara's *Robinson Crusoé* (unfortunately in Don White's infantile English translation): a sizable theatre piece built on *comique* tropes but constantly seizing occasions to expand the musical communication. *Hoffmann* is even more musical, and if it leans back to recall the zest of its most primitive compositions, before it was ensconced in Salle Favart and went respectable, it does rely almost entirely on the available *comique* voices. However, Offenbach did die too soon, leaving the work to make its way, like *Carmen*, in a corrupt edition.

All but one of the recordings honor the ersatz *Hoffmann*, either in all-star gatherings that sometimes create a grand-opera atmosphere alien to Offenbach's lean theatricality, or in "stunt casts" in which all *Hoffmann*'s lovers and nemeses are sung, respectively, by a single soprano and a single baritone: a convention that, nonetheless, calls for trick voices. As well, the four *bouffe* clowns—the most certain homage to *comique*'s antiquity—are given to one man (sometimes a nonsinging comic with a lot of nerve), and Nicklausse and the Muse double up, in all trying to homogenize what is on paper a scattered and episodic evening. Too, the premiere at the Opéra-Comique introduced the one singer–many parts concept, so there is a historical precedent. However, that first *Hoffmann* was not Offenbach, but Offenbach-Guiraud, omitting the Venice act (the one that gives Olympia-Antonia the most trouble, and lies high for many a Lindorf-Coppélius-Miracle) and geared to the particular singers of the production. An authentically Offenbachien performance, then, is not to be found in the sparkless "City Opera" *Hoffmann* (ABC, Angel) under Rudel, with Beverly Sills and Norman Treigle, badly extended by their eight parts; or in Angel's night-of-a-thousand-stars set with Gianna D'Angelo, Elisabeth Schwarzkopf, Victoria de los Angeles as Hoffmann's loves, Nicola Giuselev, George London, Ernest Blanc, and London again as the four heavies, Jean-Christophe Benoit usurping Nicklausse's trousers (but Christine Gayraud steps into the Barcarolle for him, for harmony's sake), and Nicolai Gedda doing the entire role of Hoffmann—almost surprisingly, in this context—by himself; all under Cluytens. Gedda is fine and Schwarzkopf plays marvelously with Blanc in Venice; but this is the Meyerbeer version.

Those who want the all-star approach, but in a more appropriate *boulevardier* version, should investigate Columbia's late 78 set, also under Cluytens, but this time featuring most of the great performers of post-Vichy French opera: Renée Doria, Vina Bovy, the winningly pallid Geori-Boué; Raoul Jobin as a passionate Hoffmann; Louis Musy, the quietly sinister André Pernet, Charles Soix, Roger Bourdin; Bourvil as the incomparable droll; and, to vouch for the excellence of the casting, the noted Pelléas, Camille Maurane, in a small role in the Prologue. The Nicklausse, Fanély Revoil, was once dubbed "notre Réjane lyrique" (not unlike "opera's Meryl Streep"), a testament to the set's theatrical grip. Here, as not on Angel, Cluytens is light, frisky, keen, and Opéra-Comique forces entered the studio as if still in the house, as when the students laugh in relief when Hoffmann aborts his romantic reverie to return to the Kleinzach song, or in Coppélius's laughter, ringing out *after* the end of Act One. If some singing is unsteady, still the event is stylish and dramatic.

This is also true of London's stereo entry under Bonynge, an attempt to reconstruct Offenbach's original. The casting of Sutherland, Domingo, and Bacquier may suggest the usual international compromises, but the set is flavorful, Bacquier in good voice and up to the mischief. Some of the major singers, for instance Hughes Cuénod, suggest by their excellence that more thought went into the stylistic tact of a single scene herein than in all six sides of the lumbering Beecham sound track (London mono—and Beecham himself tried to suppress the album in court).

Style is everything in *opéra comique*. The weight of voices, the delivery of text, the very size of the orchestra . . . all this can elate the intimacy or shatter it. Think light, fleet, keen. A great evening of grand opera is, above all, well sung. A great evening of *opéra comique* is well *meant*.

12

VERDI

꧁꧂

Verdi not only developed the structure of Italian opera: he also developed its vocal architecture. How different are *La Forza del Destino*, *Otello*, *Falstaff* from the *melodramma* that Verdi inherited from Bellini and Donizetti, we say. But how different, also, the singers who thrive in the above works from those suited to *La Sonnambula* or *Lucia di Lammermoor*.

True, the 1880s saw no great division of vocal kind. Singers of the early 78 era merrily moved from Verdi to bel canto and back; the very lyric Patti and Tetrazzini sang Aida (not, unfortunately, into the recording horn). But it is also true that Verdi's career, which spanned the last two-thirds of this century—from Rossini to Puccini—saw opera's voices grow in volume and dramatic intensity. In the 1900s, as bel canto fell away to a few favorite titles and the early (and somewhat bel canto–flavored) Verdi went largely unheard, the difference between the mature Verdi's vocal casting and that of his predecessors became more noticeable: the transitional matter had dropped away.

Like all Italian composers—like virtually all theatre composers of the day but Wagner—Verdi wrote for the voices at hand. Still, he had ideals in mind. One can trace the development of his voices partly through his response to stimulating singers and partly through his exposure to the French style in opera, which led Verdi to expand the more limited Italian approach. The Verdian tenor, increasingly strengthened till in *Otello* he is literally the biggest voice in Italian opera, was influenced by Gaetano Fraschini, the heroic "tenore della maledizione" (for his stirring delivery of Edgardo's "curse" of Lucia in Act Two), who created six roles for Verdi. The Verdi baritone can be traced first to Giorgio Ronconi, whose forceful personality led Donizetti to investigate this hitherto unexploited voice in four roles, including the hero of *Maria Padilla*—very unusual in the soprano-and-tenor-oriented Italian theatre. Ronconi sang the first Nabucco, and was succeeded by Felice Varesi, the first Macbeth and Rigoletto—again, a baritone hero outsizing the tenor.

There is no one Verdian soprano. As late as in the 1850s, in his so-called middle period, more or less launched by *Rigoletto, Il Trovatore,* and *La Traviata,* Verdi is working in the mode of the coloratura soprano of lyric weight, though *Il Trovatore's* Leonora at times points toward a more dramatic singer, one with power as well as flexibility—a Norma, even. By the time of *Don Carlos,* the Gildas and Violettas—the Lucias, going back to a model—have been banned, and thus the Verdian soprano is a full-fledged dramatic, with some flexibility, not for coloratura, but for the sinuous Verdian line.

Sifting through the early 78 years, mere years after Verdi's death, we find ideals for these essential Verdian voices in the discs of Enrico Caruso, Mattia Battistini, and Rosa Ponselle. Originally a bit light for an all-around Verdian tenor, Caruso developed into one over the years, his instrument darkening in color and building in power—from Alfredo, say, into Radames. Hear Battistini's aptness in his five 1906 sides of *Ernani,* grouped on a Rubini recital. The force of "Lo vedremo," balanced by the grace of "Vieni meco" and the almost absurd ease of the highest lines in "O sommo Carlo," easily obscure Battistini's one fault, a dead space on the lowest notes. As for Ponselle, her command of the nineteenth-century Italian repertory, from *La Vestale* to *Aida,* is an article of faith among aficionados. The evenly purchased registers, from chest voice up through the *passaggio* to the top notes; the weight supporting the brilliance; the astonishing fluency in difficult coloratura—all this defines the Verdian soprano retrospectively, looking back to Spontini, Bellini, and Donizetti even as it surges forward to a new bel canto, streamlined and energized. At her best, Ponselle rises effortlessly to the difficult high phrases, dips grandly to the low ones. Put simply, she sings as if music were her first language. She is not always at her best, however. She recorded "Ernani, involami"—recit, aria, and cabaletta—twice for Victor, in 1924 and 1928. The acoustic surely presents a great voice, but not a great performer; not till 1928, in the improved technology of the electric era, does Ponselle truly interpret the scene. But then, Caruso fluffed the odd note on his discs; Battistini thrashed out many a line in the name of "drama." Performances vary; what we seek in Verdi for starters is rightness of instrument.

For instance, *Nabucco,* Verdi's third opera and first success, needs a Ponselle and Battistini. Caterina Mancini and Paolo Silveri (Cetra mono) are correct but scrappy, and Callas, on undergrounds from Naples with Gino Bechi under Vittorio Gui, is superb but lost in dim sound. Stereo brought forth Elena Souliotis and Tito Gobbi under Lamberto Gardelli, a generally exciting performance, even if Souliotis seems to be rousing an insecure instrument to a Callas imitation, while Gobbi lets art fill out what was always an imperfectly defined tone. He is a touching Nabucco more than a hardy one, a tragic hero on the wrong side. Angel's more imposingly cast album under Riccardo Muti offers in Renata Scotto Abigaille's perfect interpreter—but Scotto's voice itself is perfect for other parts. In her big solo, her recit is thrilling, her legato in the cavatina inevitable and expansive, her cabaletta properly dire. But her low notes are forced, her top wavers, and her power thanks will more than nature. In her duet with Nabucco, Matteo Manuguerra, her voice spreads under the pressure of maintaining a solid line at forte. He is rock-solid, but impersonal, in the modern style. Muti likes it neat, orderly. (One wonders how he would have worked with the impetuous Battistini.) Manuguerra's "Ahi, misero!" (I'm wretched!) is hard to believe, musical but unstressed.

Yet another of the contemporary baton despots, Giuseppe Sinopoli, gives us the best *Nabucco* (DG digital), in sonics that provide a theatre perspective—even more so on CD, where Sinopoli's brash dynamics come through with an alarming thrill. Forces of Berlin's Deutsche Oper back up a very strong cast, Piero Cappuccilli's Nabucco very pathetic in his collapse, Evgeny Nesterenko's Zaccaria rolling out in cantabile or leaping in fury—what a swing he, Sinopoli, and the chorus put into the third-act finale! The rich casting takes in Lucia Valentini Terrani and Plácido Domingo in the smallish parts of the lovers, but interest centers on Ghena Dimitrova, latest (along with Aprile Millo) of the "new" Verdian sopranos. Actually, Dimitrova had been plying her trade for some time before bursting upon the international scene, and her Abigaille is a sensation, the hard-edged timbre the very sound of explosive ambition. She easily hurdles the role's great intervallic jumps, and her high Cs lambaste or soothe, as called for. Next to the other sets, with their tentative singing or insufficient portrayals, DG's *Nabucco* reveals Verdi in full true.

Ernani, two operas after *Nabucco,* claims no comparable set, though there are good things in most of them. Victor's early stereo try (Price, Bergonzi, Sereni, Flagello; Schippers) suggests a Met performance of the time, especially in the general lack of involvement. Price is in wonderful voice, but not quite up to the coloratura of a role that, like Abigaille, looks back to Norma rather than forward to Aida. "Tutto sprezzo che d'Ernani," the cabaletta to "Ernani, involami," is smudged, and we lose the accents on "Ah, l'amor vostro, o Sire" in the duet with Carlo—a surprisingly mellifluous Sereni, by the way. On the other hand, Hungaroton's digital *Ernani* under Gardelli (Sass, Lamberti, Lajos Miller, Kolos Kováts) suggests, if not a night in Budapest, something less than utter rightness of approach. There's something endearing in a text booklet that gives notes and libretto in Italian, English, French, German, Russian, and Hungarian (which yields, for the opening chorus, "Eljen! Igyunk! Igyunk!"). But the singing is erratic, unfocused, sluggish.

Best of the commercial *Ernani*s is Angel's digital set, which not only suggests but records a night at La Scala, with Mirella Freni, Plácido Domingo, Renato Bruson, and Nicolai Ghiaurov under Riccardo Muti. Ghiaurov sounds woolly and Freni a little overparted, especially in the coloratura. But Domingo sustains a winsome zeal and Bruson excels, taking the cadenza to "O dei verd'anni miei" *a piacere*, as marked. Perhaps it's not the specific contributions but the correct *feeling* of the whole—or that it's a live performance.

Ten years before, this performance would have had to come out as an underground; nowadays, the big labels make "undergrounds" themselves. There are older, pirate *Ernani*s from the Met (MRF) and San Francisco (BJR). The Met reading (Milanov, del Monaco, Warren, Siepi) is cut and sloppy, but it does reveal what an astonishing Verdian Dimitri Mitropoulos was. The sheer *singing* of the big string tune in the prelude is fiercely beautiful, Toscaninian. BJR's set (Caballé, Prevedi, Glossop, Christoff; Gavazzeni), of more recent vintage, is not great Verdi but it is good opera, Caballé alone holding vocal entitlement to her part, though the men at least play the show with great spirit.

We come now to the less-well-charted area of that great terrain known, somewhat condescendingly, as "early Verdi," the bulk of which many non-Italian operagoers seldom if ever experience. But, again, the phonograph seized the opportunity that theatres miss, in Philips's stereo series of early-Verdi exhumations, all with stylish international casts and complete texts. Philips's *I Masnadieri* (The Bandits) is typical: Caballé, Bergonzi, Cappuccilli, and Raimondi with the New Philharmonia under Gardelli. This is "corrected" Verdi of the "do as written" type, so Bergonzi closes his first scene, a fiery cabaletta in B Flat, going *down* for the last note (as written) rather than *up* for it (as, surely, intended; or at least approved), leaving a dull impression on a vital scene. Similarly, Caballé avoids embellishments. Even a cadenza *a piacere* finds her doing, however gorgeously, as little as possible. But *I Masnadieri* was written for Jenny Lind and Luigi Lablache, singers of a style given to plenty of *a piacere*. Thus, London's digital set under Richard Bonynge (Sutherland, Bonisolli, Manuguerra, Ramey) outdoes Philips in authenticity. Bonisolli, virile if unsubtle, interpolates high C's and C sharps at the ends of most of his numbers, and Manuguerra matches him, capping his first solo with a high A flat. All this is mere icing on the cake, no doubt, but it tells something of the spirit of the performance, of the musicians' attitude toward the archeology. *I Masnadieri*, rather sharply telescoped from Schiller's *Die Räuber*, is not a dead piece struggling to live again; it's all ready to go—and Bonynge's energy doesn't hurt, either. Sutherland takes time to warm up, but she's superb by her second aria, turning the cabaletta into a showpiece, our Jenny Lind. True, Sutherland has no feeling for words. She delivers "Ti scosta, o malnato!" (Back, you bastard!) and "Lo sguardo avea degli angeli" (He had an angelic look) in the same tone of voice. Nevertheless, the overall feeling on London is one of brawling invigoration, whereas Philips gives us a neat little reenactment.

Before Philips undertook the early Verdi project, the undergrounds were covering this territory; and here, too, the competition is keen. Philips's *I Lombardi* (Deutekom, Domingo, Raimondi) pales next to BJR's relay of a live performance (Scotto, Pavarotti, Raimondi), despite Philips's stereo advantage. However, MRF's promising transcription of *Il Corsaro* (Gulin, Ricciarelli, Casellato-Lamberti, Bruson; López-Cobos)—from an audience tape, not a broadcast—turns out to be noisy and messy, where Philips's (Caballé, Norman, Carreras, Mastromei) is even better than it looks on paper. True, Gardelli is still holding his singers to the notes in the Ricordi score; but what singers! Carreras is a little underpowered, but Lamberti could use some of Carreras's elegance; and Gulin should have borrowed one of Caballé's high D flats for her interpolation on the last page. The most telling comparison lies in the delineation of ensemble, MRF's crew falling apart in the big second-act finale and Philips's gang much more on the beam (though Carreras and Mastromei still generalize a bit on the double-dotting in their parts). Now that we have discovered what beauty and vitality lie in Verdi's early works, we want more than the mere reviving of them: we want to hear the details of atmosphere and character that Verdi poured into them. How ordinary Gulnara's first scene sounds on MRF. Then, on Philips, we hear Gardelli carefully tending the piquant woodwind turns of the introduction, and the music takes on color and shape.

Perhaps the best of Philips's resuscitations, and a strong work itself, is *I Due Foscari* (Ricciarelli, Carreras, Cappuccilli, Ramey). Ricciarelli's struggle to master the florid late bel canto lines of early Verdi is as touching a modern opera saga as her struggle to encompass the heroic volume of late Verdi; she sounds at times like a lyric who won't behave. But here she is in fine form, if stuttering on the coloratura. Carreras is at his very best, rising superbly to the intense declamation of his scene in prison, a very Verdian moment, mixing arioso and fierce recit. Both Ramey and Cappuccilli could use a bit more force (till Cappuccilli explodes impressively in the last scene), and Gardelli seems less engaged here. Still, the set is never less than acceptable and often nearly brilliant, arguing a sound case for the widening of the living repertory through studio productions.

Other labels have taken part in the Verdi Revival, perhaps most successfully Angel in *Giovanna d'Arco*, with Caballé, Domingo, and Milnes under Levine. Caballé's studio performances sometimes have an assembly-line air, but as Schiller's Joan of Arc she is supreme, sensitively listening to the words. In her first-act duet with Domingo, for instance, he has only to play the imploring lover, she the more complex situation of a saintly warrior torn between her simple country life and the love of a king, all the while haunted by conflicting heavenly voices. Sure enough, if Domingo remains Domingo, Caballé meets every point. Verdi's Joan must mix a certain alchemy in somewhat staid singers, for it also lured the very best out of Tebaldi, in Venice in 1951 with Bergonzi and Panerai (MRF), a legendary reading. Besides preserving such events, the Verdi undergrounds offer alternate versions of operas that the big labels record only in their most familiar state. Thus, to hear how heavily Verdi revised *I Lombardi* for the Paris Opéra as *Jérusalem*, we apply to BJR's relay from Turin in 1975 (Ricciarelli, Carreras, Nimsgern; Gavazzeni), in excellent sound but for a few overloaded climaxes. I worry about the polish of this reading; it suggests the lapidary glitter of the studio rather than the vitality of the theatre, as if our staged performances were trying to sound like von Karajan recordings. At least we do get to hear, in French, Verdi's first try at grand opera—more specifically, his first exposure to a more able chorus and orchestra and a more sophisticated format than were available in Italian houses. MRF has *Gerusalemme*, the same revision now translated into Italian, again under Gavazzeni with Leyla Gencer, Giacomo Aragall, and Giangiacomo Guelfi, a rougher performance than BJR's but enjoyable. Indeed, it's a good chance for doubters to sample the Turkish Gencer, perhaps the essential "underground" personality in that she never appeared on a commercial set, despite having been very active in Italian theatres in the 1960s and 1970s.

Not all of early Verdi is curiosities in need of attention, for *Macbeth* figures in this period, too. Dating from 1847, just before *I Masnadieri* and *Il Corsaro*, it was revised in 1865, between the premieres of *La Forza del Destino* and *Don Carlos*, making *Macbeth* a sort of improved early Verdi—though many of the opera's best pages, such as the muttered duet for the Macbeths during Duncan's murder, date from the original score. *Macbeth* is also unusual in its vocal casting, for here the leads are soprano and baritone, supported by an important bass role; the tenor is a problem, being too small for a star but too strategic for most comprimarios. At that, Lady Macbeth calls for something near to a "character" voice, not for the heroine timbre that we enjoy in Ponselle or Price. Good casting joins with good history in Voce's recording of a 1978 Albert Hall concert of the 1847 *Macbeth*, for Rita Hunter and Peter Glossop sound so apt in sheer timbre that Shakespeare might have hired them, she rigidly grasping and he hollowly wheezing. They are not, however, the best singers as such of these roles. Undergrounds with Callas at La Scala (best on BJR) and Gobbi at Covent Garden (Melodram) convey a more fulfilled theatre. And, as it happens, there is no shortage of fine commercial *Macbeths*.

Barring Urania's wartime broadcast in German, Victor's 1959 set (Rysanek, Warren; Leinsdorf), based on a Met production, was the first *Macbeth*. It has its moments, but one might take exception to Leinsdorf's insensitive haste, to Rysanek's unsteady middle voice (a crucial register in this part), or to the manipulated sonics, which constantly shunt singers from the distance into a close-up. Certainly, London's 1964 set (Nilsson, Taddei; Schippers), despite cutting even in untraditional places and Nilsson's less than natural Verdian style, was preferable, and Giuseppe Sinopoli (Philips digital) corrects Schippers's mediocre rendition in the abruptly dynamic approach that enlightens Sinopoli's *Nabucco*, with perhaps the most correct casting thus far in Maria Zampieri's masked tone and Renato Bruson's haunted cantabile. CDs improve the listening, heightening the contrasts in dynamics that Sinopoli lures out of his team, now whispering, now trumpeting.

However, two sets of 1976 featuring mezzo Ladys are generally thought of as the best. Claudio Abbado (DG) has Shirley Verrett and Piero Cappuccilli; Riccardo Muti (Angel) has Fiorenza Cossotto and Sherrill Milnes. Following Victor's lead in giving Macduff to Carlo Bergonzi, all LP *Macbeth*s utilize important names in this part—Bruno Prevedi with Schippers, and Pavarotti wasted on the ghastly Souliotis–Fischer-Dieskau set (London). Now Domingo (DG) and Carreras (Angel) join the group. With Ghiaurov (DG) and Raimondi (Angel) as Banquo, we have the most secure performances in good sound, though no Verdian should be without Callas's absorbing Lady, led by the fiercely brilliant Victor de Sabata.

It is often the conductor who makes the difference between a mediocre and an excellent *Macbeth*, for this opera, above all other early Verdi, demands imposing gifts in coloration, pace, and narrative wisdom. *Macbeth* is High Maestro Opera, so if Verrett outacts Cossotto or Cossotto outsings Verrett, and if Milnes gives less textual shaping than the vocally smaller-scaled Cappuccilli, it is far more decisive that Muti draws a more telling theatre from his people than Abbado does. Muti seems to hear Shakespeare's imagery of tumultuous nature and brooding, occult darkness better than Abbado. In the first witches' scene, Abbado's *Allegro brillante* is fleet, but Muti's is breathless; when Banquo cries out, "È morto assassinato il re Duncano!" (King Duncan has been murdered!), and the orchestra spills upward into the great chorus that closes Act One, Abbado is formidable, but Muti is shattering. Angel has one more advantage in a sixth-side appendix of 1847 arias deleted in the 1865 version.

Macbeth is an honorary middle-Verdi piece, more comparable to the later *Rigoletto* or *La Forza del Destino* than the earlier *Ernani* or *Il Corsaro* in terms of compositional finesse. One other early work, however, has been increasingly viewed in this light, *Luisa Miller*. It foreshadows middle Verdi in a number of ways: in its six principals (early Verdi usually observes late bel canto's fondness for two or three leads, while late works treat more complex situations), in the heroine's almost schizophrenic vocal portrayal (she starts Act One as an old-fashioned lyric coloratura but ends the opera as a slimmed-down semidramatic), and in the emphasis on confrontational ensembles over aria scenes (suggesting the fluid narrative of, say, *Un Ballo in Maschera* rather than the more soloistic outlines of most of the early works, or even of *Il Trovatore*, middle period but a throwback). *Luisa Miller* needed no Philips exhumation, as there are three big-name stereo sets. Victor's, the oldest, with Anna Moffo, Bergonzi, and MacNeil under Fausto Cleva, is disqualified by the others, one vocally richer and the other theatrically richer—respectively London's (Caballé, Pavarotti, Milnes; Maag) and DG's (Ricciarelli, Domingo, Bruson; Maazel). London suffers from too much studio polish. The grainier DG team, which also includes Elena Obraztsova, Gwynne Howell, and Vladimiro Ganzarolli, hails from a Covent Garden *Luisa* and thus creates theatre in the studio. This is one of the erratic Ricciarelli's best performances, balancing moments of caressing simplicity with a thrilling *slancio* in the confrontations—but Caballé nevertheless has more of that Verdian power needed for the final act. Then, all at once, London's three leads come alive, while DG's lose their commitment. Bruson ignores Verdi's *Con molto passione* on "Andrem ramminghi e poveri" (as, by the way, does Milnes), and Ricciarelli's repeated E flats at the tune's reprise lack Caballé's floating grace. When the tenor enters and the duet turns trio, Pavarotti brings more personality to the scene than Domingo, and by then even Milnes has taken fire.

Toscanini seems to have seen Gilda as another Luisa Miller, for his 1944 broadcast of *Rigoletto's* Act Four (Victor, Victrola) casts a dramatic soprano in the part. Zinka Milanov might well have sounded odd in "Caro nome," but she certainly rides the top lines of the storm trio. The Rigoletto of this concert, Leonard Warren, recorded the whole opera for Victor at the very start of the LP era with Toscanini's Duke and Maddalena, Jan Peerce and Nan Merriman, and the coolly infantile Erna Berger, Beecham's Queen of the Night, as Gilda. For many years this was a standard set, not least for Warren's giant-toned jester. However, Rodolfo Celletti, discussing one of the phonograph's earliest Rigolettos, noted, "He was a baritone not only of beautiful voice, but technically and stylistically masterly: clear and fluent of timbre, easy and full on the high notes, able to sing at half voice with sweetness almost like a tenor's, impeccably smooth of line. Without all this, no one can portray to the utmost a character like Rigoletto."

The baritone when Celletti cited was Giuseppe Danise, on HMV's 1917 set under Carlo Sabajno, and, yes, Danise's subtly acted yet always absolutely *sung* portrayal shames Warren's bluff reading. On the other hand, Danise's cohort takes in a sloppy Duke, two ordinary Gildas spelling each other worse for worst, and a co-Rigoletto: Ernesto Badini alternates with Danise in some of the scenes, a procedure not uncommon on HMV's Wagner discs but unusual in the Italian operas that the firm recorded in Milan throughout the 78 years. By hap, Bongiovanni has gathered Danise's scenes on one LP; and while I can't agree with Celletti that Danise is "probably the best Rigoletto in record history," certainly Danise's very lyrical approach puts the admirably sturdy but legato-starved Riccardo Stracciari (on Columbia's 1930 set) in a critical context. Carrying the comparison onto LP, we wonder if even the resourceful Giuseppe Taddei (Cetra mono) needs more of that Celletti-Danise sweetness, to show us the doting father as well as the savage zany of a licentious court.

In fact, all three of *Rigoletto*'s principals are more interesting characters than we're used to hearing in *Rigoletto* performances, especially in all-star packages such as London's Bonynge set (Sutherland, Pavarotti, Milnes), which gives little more than a sad girl, a happy Duke, and a loud baritone. Gilda *is* a sort of Luisa Miller, as a sheltered child whose romance hurls her into the power of cynical grownups not unwilling to destroy her; and the Duke, unusually for Verdi, is a debonair charmer who remains completely outside the impulse of the story. Here, the baritone is the protagonist, the soprano the "flaw" in his defenses, and the bass and mezzo are the agents of the act of tragedy. Even Monterone, perhaps the smallest lead role in opera, figures more importantly than the Duke, by framing the tragedy in a curse from father to father. The tenor just sings love songs. The common view that *Rigoletto* launched Verdi's middle period is no mere convenience, but an appreciation of the work's sophisticated personality.

Surely, then, London's early mono set under Alberto Erede (Richmond) is sinfully incorrect, with Hilde Gueden's emptily pleasant Gilda and Aldo Protti's humdrum Rigoletto edging respectfully around del Monaco's braying Duke. Smarter casting marks Mercury's stereo set under Gavazzeni, the first to include the Duke's "Possente amor," the ungainly cabaletta to "Parmi veder le lagrime." Gavazzeni's driving reading suits Ettore Bastianini's big-scale approach, and urges along the Gilda of Renata Scotto (then between her lyrical youth and dramatic maturity, a perfect Gilda) and the Duke of Alfredo Kraus. With Fiorenza Cossotto and Ivo Vinco as the assassins, this set is very "voice," correct if not brilliant.

Strong conducting lends brilliance. Carlo Maria Giulini's Vienna set (DG) is promising: Ileana Cotrubas, Elena Obraztsova, Domingo, Cappuccilli, and Ghiaurov, in a note-complete text (without, however, any of the usual added high notes). Somehow the performance never comes to life, except in Giulini's conducting, reproduced in an ample dynamic range. No other conductor—in a tally of over thirty complete sets—gets as much out of the work as Giulini, as an entity and in details, as in the slithery brass snarls at the climax of the "In furia è montato!" ensemble in Act One just before Monterone's entrance, an effect written into the score but never quite achieved on other discs. Guiseppe Sinopoli (Philips digital), similarly banning the high notes, has a comparable cast (Bruson, Gruberora, Shicoff, Fassbaender, Lloyd) and slightly better luck, especially in the way the three leads relate to each other. Rafael Kubelik's Scala album (DG) has its admirers. On its release in 1963, more than a few critics praised it as the best till then, and truly Dietrich Fischer-Dieskau articulates

Rigoletto's vulnerability as well as any. But the role's brutal side eludes him.

The most unusual *Rigoletto* is Angel's digital recording of the famous English National Opera production that reset the tale in New York's Italian community, the tenor now "The Duke" in an underworld sense and James Fenton's 'English translation, according to John Steane, suggesting "Margaret Rutherford dressed as James Cagney." The many photographs in the text booklet do reveal a provocative production—the tenor launched "La donna è mobile" by giving a jukebox a kick, cueing in the orchestra as if for an impromptu singalong. Despite this veneer of naturalistic contemporaneity, the performance is better sung than acted, by Helen Field, Arthur Davies, and John Rawnsley. (Norman Bailey sings Monterone.) But it is *very* well sung, complete (with "Possente amor," as "The power of love") on two LPs, and a neat bit of opera history—a document of notable production.

My choice for the best *Rigoletto* is a piece of false history—another of Walter Legge's Scala sets that "preserved" nonexistent productions. But if Callas, di Stefano, and Gobbi never sang *Rigoletto* at La Scala under Tullio Serafin, they should have. Anyway, here on Angel is *Rigoletto*'s personality brought to life, especially in the delicate chemistry between Gobbi and Callas in that most basic of Verdian combinations, father and daughter. Their two scenes together have no match elsewhere on disc, and many a line stands out in the memory, such as Gobbi's "Solo, diforme, lurido" (Alone, deformed, ugly), delivered apologetically, pleading, as if he is still not sure how his daughter reacts to him. (Gobbi's "Pari siamo" monologue, strangely, does not equal his famous 78 of it, made but five years before, apparently on one of those singer's miracle days whereon everything—instrument, imagination, and morale—feels utmost liberty.) The Duke is a natural for the happy-go-lucky di Stefano, even if he is unable to master the syncopated line in the "In furia è montato!" ensemble. At that, there are cuts, plain mono sonics, unimposing secondary singers, and a tame chorus. But the set's virtues overwhelm criticism.

If *Rigoletto* calls for very strict character casting, *Il Trovatore* simply calls for "the four greatest singers in the world," in Caruso's judgment, if not that of record companies. The trouble is, the four greatest singers of any given era may be somewhat less than the four greatest performers—and this concisely expansive, logically coincidental monster show needs interpreters who can smooth out the paradoxes and address the emotional core of the action. Thus Victor's classic mono set with Zinka Milanov, Fedora Barbieri, Jussi Björling, and Leonard Warren under Renato Cellini is eloquent song but incoherent theatre—even if Milanov's "D'amor sull'ali rosee" is a demonstration cut in Verdian style. Similarly, London's Bonynge set (Sutherland, Horne, Pavarotti, Wixell) fails in its limp return to golden-age singer power, despite Horne's arresting "Condotta ell'era in ceppi," unlike any other (and admitting Bonynge's appreciable conducting of the seldom-heard ballet, built largely on themes from the Anvil Chorus). Characterless singing of such dynamic characters is the "dog ate my homework" school of operatic art.

Or take those *Trovatores* of thespian ambition but humiliated vocalism. Philips's digital set with Covent Garden forces under Colin Davis will do. Some if not all of Katia Ricciarelli, Stefania Toczyska, José Carreras, and Yuri Mazurok may be the greatest singers in the world, but some of them don't seem so here some of the time. Davis churns up an exciting show, but Toczyska is barely there in "Condotta," an account of how her mother was burned alive. *Barely there.* When, at the end, Carreras exclaims, "Quale orror!" (What horror!), one wonders how he can tell. Ricciarelli, in perverse spirits, is dull in Act One but beautifully commands the big ensemble closing Act Three. Mazurok, in great voice, misses every chance to illustrate the text or even follow Verdi's markings; perhaps the language inhibited him. Only Carreras finds his way back to Verdi, as vivid in recit as in song. When Verdi stipulates *Con espressione* on "Ah sì, ben mio," that's how Carreras sings it. He also sings "Di quella pira" in C, complete with the top note.

The chemistry of the four stars has persisted, as in DG's Scala quartet (Stella, Cossotto, Bergonzi, Bastianini) under Serafin, pure Italian; or in Victor's mostly American gang (Price, Cossotto, Domingo, Milnes) under Mehta. Both are well sung. But perhaps there's a bit more sheer story, sheer *presence* (not to mention sheer opera) in Cetra's mono set under Fernando Previtali. Caterina Mancini, the Leonora, cannot touch Stella or Price for beauty of timbre, and her explosive chest register suggests Verdi-Mascagni. But she has the part in measure in every way and phrases quite beautifully. Miriam Pirazzini's Azucena is mediocre, Carlo Tagliabue's di Luna over the hill, and, as Manrico, at fifty-nine Giacomo Lauri-Volpi is, as Shakespeare put it, staying on the order of his going, especially in his insistently clarion top notes, so resonant that Cetra's grooves buzz. A genuinely exciting artist in his youth, Lauri-Volpi is here a caricature of himself. Why does the set, with all these faults, convince as many others don't? Von Karajan has four more or less great singers in his Berlin set (Angel: Price, Obraztsova, Bonisolli, Cappuccilli), and they all have their moments, Obraztsova through guts if nothing else, Bonisolli in a kind of lunkheaded grace. But we end up with a sort of Festival Provincial, an aimless attack—whereas Cetra's ragtag gang delivers *Il Trovatore.*

Von Karajan was better off back in mono on Angel with Callas, Barbieri, di Stefano, and Panerai: a bel canto Leonora, a bloodcurdling Azucena (Barbieri vastly better here than on Victor), an overparted but engaging Manrico, and a resourceful but light-toned di Luna—a kind of imperfect perfection. There are flaws, but it's absolutely right. Compare Callas with Milanov on "D'amore." Callas's atrocious high notes are ludicrous next to Milanov's, silk flying on the breeze. But hear Callas's dashing authority in the recit on "Presta è la mia difesa," the magical hush in which she launches the aria, the plangent legato on the decoration in "Conforta l'egra mente." Or compare von Karajan with anyone. Caught between his experimenting youth and his maturity of the excruciated tempi and the end-of-the-world dynamics, he just jumps in and plays it—as in the "motor rhythm" accompaniment to "Mira, d'acerbe lagrime." Most conductors (von Karajan himself, later in the Berlin set) fear its vulgarity and try to ease it down. Here, von Karajan *emphasizes* it, whacks it out, and it loses vulgarity to become driving, taut. This is Cetra's energy with a bit more voice and finesse.

Riccardo Muti, restudying these early-middle Verdi operas, noted with surprise the recurring pianos and pianissimos—"much more *notturno,*" he found them. More than what? Perhaps more than Toscanini's bombastic *La Traviata* (Victor mono: Albanese, Peerce, Merrill), so fast that it feels like a trailer for the movie. We may counter Toscanini with, say, Serafin's set (Angel mono: Stella, di Stefano, Gobbi), underlining the intimacy of the subject. This was, for Verdi, a contemporary opera above all, set in parlors and bedrooms, and so Serafin plays it. He got a feud for his trouble, with Callas, who considered the Angel Scala sets her preserve and resented Serafin for making "her" *Traviata* without her. Callas's studio *Traviata* (Cetra), released three years earlier, contractually disqualified her; but she had grown considerably as Violetta, one of her pet roles, and ached for a second chance, especially as Cetra gave her mediocre company and di Stefano, as Angel reveals, was in glory then. Antonietta Stella is not an adequate substitute for Callas, but she is more than recommendable—accomplished. A similar sense of intimacy pervades Pierre Monteux's Victor set (Carteri, Valletti, Warren), made back to back with Serafin's in the summer of 1956. If Gobbi seems somewhat reticent in his big scene with Stella, his explosive talent constrained by the character's lack of scope, Warren counters Carteri's delicacy with an untoward boom, Rigoletto in a frock coat. But otherwise Monteux keeps this romance of bourgeois bohemia light and true.

Few conductors do. Muti (Angel digital) grandstands, the guests' exit in Act One suggesting a flight of disaster victims, the Card Scene boorishly rushed, and everything, in general, far from *notturno*. Aldo Ceccato (Angel) at least lets his singers drop in a high note or two, but his lumbering power tortures Beverly Sills's tenderly detailed portrayal, not to mention Gedda and Panerai, a convincing son and father.

Along with the big *Traviatas*, there are the "voice" *Traviatas*, casual as theatre but pleasing listening—Victor's with Caballé, Bergonzi, and Milnes, say, or Sutherland's digital remake (London), with none of that Muti *roba* about embellishing cabalettas or capping your "Sempre libera" with a high E flat. (Both sets, too, are note-complete.) Then there is the English *Traviata* (EMI) under Mackerras, another ENO job, clean and musical, fitting both men's cabalettas in on the two discs. Or there is the historic *Traviata*—Met, 1935—with Ponselle's fascinatingly agitated Violetta, different from all others, a kind of Tallulah Bankhead cut with Luise Rainer. At "Qual figlia m'abbraciate" (Embrace me as a daughter), Violetta's plea to Germont, Ponselle is vivacious, like a champ runner revving up for the hurdles. At Alfredo's denunciation, most Violettas cringe; Ponselle laughs. At "È tardi!" (It's late!), after the reading of the letter, Violettas wearily empty the voice of color; Ponselle rages. Ponselle is of course of the heroic class of Traviatas, with the instrument that would seem to up the stakes in volume—consider, for instance, Ponselle's volume (density, really)—in comparison with Carteri's. Yet, for Violetta Verdi originally wanted Rosina Penco, who created the *Trovatore* Leonora. Surely great Leonoras—Mancini, Milanov, Price—are not what we want as Violetta. But vocal casting was less typable in Verdi's day. In the 1800s, a Milanov might well have sung Violetta, even if an Ileana Cotrubas, as touching as Sills in a more pleasing timbre (DG), would make an unlikely Leonora in any age. Various undergrounds carry Ponselle's Violetta, but beware the Pearl album: the entire performance runs a half-tone high.

There is no all-around "best" *Traviata*, but there is Callas. The buffs prefer her at La Scala with di Stefano and Bastianini for Giulini's inspiring conducting. I prefer, as a whole, Angel's relay of the "Lisbon Traviata" (long a tape collector's legend, celebrated in Terrence McNally's play), with Kraus and Sereni under Franco Ghione. Here admittedly, Callas is in less agile voice, the conducting is routine, and the incessant prompter even cues Callas in on the "Oh!" that follows Alfredo's intrusion into "Sempre libera," a virtually unflubbable line. But Lisbon's is a fuller *Traviata*. Kraus (then thirty-one) is far more the ardent, foolish young man than di Stefano (who blemishes the Scala tape with a number of wrong entrances), and Sereni is at least as good as Bastianini. At Milan, we can hear Giulini goading his singers, framing the tale. Ghione plods. But *La Traviata*, as work, comes through more evenly in Lisbon.

The growing enthusiasm for *Don Carlos* has bounced some light onto *Les Vêpres Siciliennes*, the second of Verdi's three grand operas, and it is the English, instrumental in the reinstitution of the later title, who give us the original French *Vêpres*, in a 1969 BBC concert under Mario Rossi (Voce). The performance, bedeviled by cuts small and large (no ballet) and by an erratic (but French) cast, does at least support critics' contention that the somewhat different melodic shape of the original French has greater ring than the Italian accommodations.

Still, *I Vespri Siciliani* is the work we usually hear. Victor's set, despite Levine's galvanizing leadership, is flabby. Two undergrounds, both drawn from the Florence May Festival, give us a firmer Verdi. From 1951 comes Erich Kleiber's revival (MRF, Cetra) with the entire ballet, but other pages missing, including Procida's cabaletta, some of the third-act finale, and the chorus that opens Act Five. At that, the chorus is sloppy, its entry on "O splendida feste" way off rhythmically for the first four phrases. Otherwise, however, Kleiber leads a very fine performance, one that finds even mediocre talents heroically reaching beyond their gifts. Enzo Mascherini, a baritone given to gallery-flattering volume, makes something touching of Monfort, and, as his son, Giorgio Kokolios sounds like a brute stimulated by Kleiber—and the Elena of Maria Callas—to try a little tenderness. By Act Two, in duet with Callas, he is, however raw, genuinely involved and even musical, and after her deliriously impeccable Siciliana (barring a misfired attack on the penultimate high E), Kokolios braces himself for something almost like a falsetto on the line that climaxes on a high D. Indeed, Arrigo— Henri, more properly—was written not for an Italian voice, but for the more flexible lyric-dramatic French grand-opera hero, though, back on Voce, Jean Bonhomme gives us the pale French timbre without the free French top. (Only Victor's Domingo really pulls off the role, albeit vocally rather than characterologically.) In the second Florence underground, from 1978 under Riccardo Muti, tenor Veriano Luchetti is creditable till the last act, when that tricky solo with the high D totally undoes him, despite the fleet tempo that Muti adopts to sweep him along.

However, this later performance (LR) is uncut, in excellent sound (no text booklet), and runs on Muti's energy to tell the story, as Kleiber's crew does but fitfully and Levine's hardly at all. It is also, for once, an all-Italian *Vespri*, with Scotto (superb until a strangely lumpy Siciliana), Bruson, and Raimondi almost matching Boris Christoff's towering Procida for Kleiber. After Kleiber and Levine, we are not weak in great *Vespri* conductors. But Muti is especially in tune with his cast, driving, broadening, turning on a hairpin, yet never losing contact with the stage. For just one instance, he breathes so naturally with Bruson in Monforte's third-act aria that it sounds, as rarely, like a major solo; the audience really erupts after it.

Simon Boccanegra, like *Macbeth*, was revised long after the premiere. Voce has the original, and various undergrounds carry Met performances of the 1930s with Elisabeth Rethberg, Giovanni Martinelli, Lawrence Tibbett, and Ezio Pinza—all great Verdians, but the sound is dim and the cuts are irritating. Two modern sets are near-classics, Capitol's mono reading under Santini (Angel, Seraphim) and DG's stereo Scala set under Abbado. With Cappuccilli, Freni, Carreras, and Ghiaurov, Abbado has a distinct edge, finding more lyricism in this dark work than most conductors do. But Capitol has Victoria de los Angeles (offbeat and very successful casting), another of Christoff's massive heavies-with-a-heart, and, most notably, Tito Gobbi's extraordinary Simone, better even than his Rigoletto, perhaps his greatest portrayal on disc. His cry of "Figlia!" (Daughter!) at the close of the second-act duet will echo for quite some time to come.

With *Un Ballo in Maschera* (A Masked Ball) we come to another unique piece, like *Macbeth* and *Rigoletto* treating characters rare in Italian opera: a frivolous king (tenor) and his madcap page (soprano). The soprano, mezzo, and baritone might suit any Leonora, Azucena, or di Luna; but the two high livers feed an odd note into the whole. Ordinary performances—Muti's (Angel) and Abbado's (DB), say—are insufficient. Admirable bits here and there—Price and Bergonzi's love duet (Victor) or Fedora Barbieri's Ulrica on the only 78 set (Victor, Seraphim)—are pleasures in passing, as is London's digital set under Solti (Margaret Price, Ludwig, Battle, Pavarotti, Bruson), in gorgeous sound but unique only in Price's Amelia. One senses that this distinguished cast might have made more of the piece but for Solti's High Maestro approach, the Toscanini-Mahler formula that imposed discipline on an unruly art but has knocked a lot of personality out of the show. Battle, for instance, should make a superbly frolicsome Oscar. In the event, she is excellent, but plain, *abstinent*. What might she have done with the character if Solti had permitted her to embellish the lines, as Oscars invariably did right into the 1930s? After all, the part is written for coloratura soprano but lacks coloratura. Most 78s of Oscar's solo in the last scene, "Saper vorreste," are embellished, some quite heavily, and the flighty decorations, heard against a worry of impending murder, make a marvelous effect. Hear Luisa Tetrazzini, Selma Kurz, or—best of all, I think—Adele Kern (albeit in German; on a Preiser recital or in Seraphim's *The Record of Singing*, Volume III) to consider what an opportunity our Battles are losing in this scene.

Star voices and embellishments are not the only route into the unmasking of *Ballo*'s hidden riches, as witness the famous Glyndebourne-at-Edinburgh performance of 1949 (Melodram): Ljuba Welitsch, Alda Noni, Jean Watson, Mirto Picchi, and Paolo Silveri under Vittorio Gui. This is no one's idea of international glitter, even with Welitsch. Yet the opera plays wonderfully, as a mixture of the passionate (Welitsch), the self-delighting (Picchi, Noni), and the stolid (Silveri—invariably stolid throughout his career, so this is doubtless biology rather than portrayal). Gui points up the work's quirky nature, underlining the antithesis of capricious king and unbending councilor that makes their bond so touching and the fatal misunderstanding all the more lamentable. We prize Gui especially on hearing Angel's mono Scala set, Callas, di Stefano, and Gobbi more or less conducting themselves under Votto's baton. (Undergrounds have Callas and di Stefano live at La Scala in 1957 with Bastianini under Gavazzeni, a more decisive narrator.)

Colin Davis (Philips), leading Covent Garden forces, argues in favor of the star cast, at any rate the international grouping. His crew fields not a single Italian: Caballé, Sona Ghazarian, Patricia Payne, José Carreras, and Ingvar Wixell. Yet, as with Gui's cast, we actually follow the story, bouncing from Carreras's zest to Caballé's sensitivity and, thus sobered, dreading Wixell's revenge. It's a spontaneous performance, and spontaneity this opera above all needs. Ordering his page to get him a fisherman's outfit for the jaunt to Ulrica's cave, Carreras sings "E tu m'appronta un abito" thoughtfully, weighing the caprice. Then, as if it just came to him, he concludes, with a chuckle, "da pescator."

What works for Gui and Davis is their rapport with game casts. Yet Toscanini's *Ballo* (Victor mono) works almost in spite of its cast; his spark fires the ordinary. One feels an authoritative narrative presence, a Verdi surrogate, shading the whole, and the tactless perfection that rushes Toscanini's *Traviata* somehow does not mar the roomier *Ballo*. On the contrary, Toscanini's energy lightens many a moment that other conductors make turgid—the chorus that closes the first scene, for instance, with the jagged intrusion of the 'cellos running up to a D flat just after "alle tre." Votto, completely thrown, loses the rhythm, and even Muti and Solti find it tricky to sing over the gap, so to speak. But Toscanini nails it and sails over it at once, and by the time the ensemble joins the tenor the number is rolling with an elation no other recording shares.

When exactly Verdi's third and last period begins is debatable. Certainly, by now he has reached his seniority, especially in the merging of the most stimulating elements of *melodramma* and grand opera: *canto* and theatre, to put it naïvely, or perhaps let's say expression and architecture. *La Forza del Destino* is a kind of Verdi filled out with grand-opera genre scenes. Its cast—soprano, high mezzo, tenor, baritone, bass, and comic—suggests Meyerbeer. Voce, again, carries a BBC concert of an original version, this from Petersburg in 1862, very different from the familiar *Forza*, not as much in major points as in details. John Matheson leads an erratic performance, now sung well, now acted well—seldom both at once. With, most noticeably, a fuller overture and a tenderized finale, *Forza* started life all over again at La Scala in 1869, ending Verdi's long feud with that theatre. Angel's mono set (Seraphim) celebrates the truce in one of the best of its Scala series (Callas, Elena Nicolai, Tucker, Tagliabue, Rossi-Lemeni, Capecchi; Serafin), an extremely Italianate performance despite the heavy foreign participation. On three discs, it snips here and there, though it does include the "Sleale!" duet for tenor and baritone, omitted on the four-LP Cetra set, under Gino Marinuzzi, taken over from 78s. Cetra almost mirrors Angel: unsteady but committed soprano (Maria Caniglia), cool mezzo (Ebe Stignani), unpredictable tenor (Galliano Masini), correct baritone (Tagliabue in both cases), paternal singing bass (Tancredi Pasero), Rossinian comic bass (Saturno Meletti), and scrupulously un-"interpretive" conductor (Gino Marinuzzi). Cetra is rougher in feel yet, at its best moments, superior, as in the highly evocative genre scenes, or in Caniglia's very sensitive launching of "Madre, pietosa Vergine." Victor and Angel put out complete stereo readings of greater security than these two sets, Victor with American Verdi champs Price, Verrett, Tucker again, Merrill, and Tozzi, Angel with Martina Arroyo (also on Voce) greeting Italiani Bergonzi, Cappuccilli, and Raimondi. Yet the stereo casts, axiomatically temperate and smoothed-out in the modern manner, could use some of the individualistic intensity of the older sets.

We see this conflict of energy and polish most tellingly in two *For-zas*, by nearly the same company yet totally different in execution. London's 1955 set under Molinari-Pradelli offered a standard front-line cast of the time: Tebaldi, Simionato, del Monaco, Bastianini, Siepi, Corena. As it opened Cetra's and Angel's cuts, was taped in stereo (and, once marketing caught up to technology, thus rere-leased), and found world-class voices *in* voice, London's was generally regarded as the best *Forza*, especially after Victor's 1959 set, similarly complete and in stereo but catching Milanov too late and di Stefano overparted in a generally routine reading under Previtali.

However, it happens that London's cast (with Barbieri in for Sim-ionato, Aldo Protti for Bastianini, and Capecchi for Corena) had sung *Forza* at the Florence May Festival under Dimitri Mitropoulos two years before, and by all reports it was one of the greatest events in postwar Italian opera. Mitropoulos's excitingly depictive *Toscaninismo* (as they term it in Italy) would naturally rouse the performers more than Pradelli's humdrum vigor. Yet can virtually the same cast give a performance that passed into legend, then march into the studio for a mere stereotype? Perhaps the legend was exaggeration. In the wake of the Italian law freeing live performances after twenty years, Cetra is-sued the Florence *Forza* . . . and the legend held. This is a stupen-dous reading, Mitropoulos's awesome grasp of tempo shaping action, goading character, surrounding the composition to liberate it: *Tosca-ninismo*. And Tebaldi, merely creditable on London, is so exciting here that at last we understand why Callas was so threatened by their rivalry, why the hunting of Tebaldi from La Scala was Callas's proof that she had made *soprano assolutissimo*.

Don Carlos is the aficionado's Verdi, the caviar masterpiece that, till recently, was the relish of elite tastes. Now that it has made its way into the repertory, the aficionado still holds a peculiar claim on it, preferring to hear it, as we seldom do, in the form Verdi gave it: as a five-act French grand opera.

There are a number of ways to count the versions *Don Carlos* has appeared in. Essentially, there are three: the uncut original (here termed version one), a four-act Italian *melodramma*, not only cut down but in places wholly recomposed (version two), and this same *melodramma* preceded by the original "Fontainebleau Act," translated into Italian (version three). Version one contains scenes only recently rediscov-ered (by Andrew Porter), abandoned in a dusty back room of the Opéra, music cut before the premiere. Again, Voce brings it to us, in a 1973 BBC broadcast with Edith Tremblay, Michèle Vilma, André Turp, Robert Savoie, and Joseph Rouleau under John Matheson. It's a generally good performance, troubled by some hair-raisingly misfired top notes from the tenor and baritone but illuminated by beautiful conducting. Philips's digital set of 1985, supposedly of the complete version one, counters with stronger singing (Ricciarelli, Valentini Terrani, Domingo, Nucci, Raimondi; Abbado). However, this is in fact version three, with the restored scenes grouped separately in an appendix. Moreover, Voce's cast is not merely singing in French but *feeling* it; Philips's Italian crew is only variably comfortable with the French text, letting key scenes float out of their grasp. Voce excells, for instance, in the King's interview with the Grand Inquisitor, superbly brought off by Richard van Allan. This smallish role is very central, as the opera turns on conflicts of church versus state and love versus power. We need to take in more than the two love triangles, Elisabeth-Carlos-Eboli and Philip-Elisabeth-Carlos: with which, along with a bit of spectacle, ordinary performances make do.

This is why I profess a fondness for the old Cetra set, version two (and cut, at that). In boxy mono, the reading is vocally rugged. Maria Caniglia and Ebe Stignani are past their prime. Paolo Silveri makes a woolly Posa, Nicola Rossi-Lemeni a grainy Philip. Previtali conducts just well enough. Yet it's a fiery, importunate, meaningful show, great Verdi: even great Schiller. It typifies the set that the Carlos, Mirto Picchi, with far less tonal distinction than his successors Bergonzi, Domingo, or Carreras, activates the plot—as Carlos should—through musicianship and textual vitality.

Three stereo sets offer first-rate performances by the world's top voices. London's finds Solti in charge of Tebaldi, Bumbry, Bergonzi, Fischer-Dieskau (outstanding for good and bad reasons: he's a most sympathetic Posa but a rather Germanic one in this company), and Ghiaurov. Even more than *Les Huguenots*, *Don Carlos* is a potential "night of the seven stars," in that besides the five principals and the Grand Inquisitor, there is the unnamed Friar, crucial in the two church scenes and especially at the climax, when he more or less turns out to be Charles V. Angel inadvertently underlines this on the Giulini set (Caballé, Verrett, Domingo, Milnes, Raimondi), for the Friar, Simon Estes, was a youngster at the time of taping but is a star today. Von Karajan, wouldn't you know it, makes it a "night of the *nine* stars," for besides José van Dam's Friar, he has Edita Gruberova's Page and Barbara Hendricks as the Heavenly Voice—not to mention Freni, Baltsa, Carreras, Cappuccilli, Ghiaurov, Raimondi, and the Berlin Philharmonic, all on Angel.

Listeners will doubtless prefer the set with their favorite singers, but there are other variables. Von Karajan chose version two, giving less music than Solti and Giulini, both with version three. Von Karajan also has the most intensely sung of all *Don Carloses*, emphasizing the personal dilemmas, whereas the other two comprehend the political panorama. Solti has the best sound, with a full bass, Giulini the loveliest voices. Perhaps the ideal *Don Carlos* would be Giulini's cast singing Voce's edition with Cetra's elation of involvement.

Aida is not unlike an Italian *Don Carlos*, a leaner version of a similar story in Opératique architecture. If *Il Trovatore* calls for the four greatest singers, *Aida* needs the four greatest Verdians—five counting the conductor. Certainly any specialist in Verdi stakes art and reputation on these parts, though sheer entitlement of instrument will not serve *Aida* as it might *Il Trovatore*. Victor proved this in its 1928 Scala set under Carlo Sabajno (rereleased, for some reason, on the Czech label, Supraphon). Most of Victor and Columbia's Scala sets of this era made do with second-line stars in at least some of the lead roles, but this *Aida* offers an unusually important cast, at that from one of Toscanini's golden-age regimes: Dusolina Giannini, Irene Minghini-Cattaneo, Aureliano Pertile, and Giovanni Inghilleri. The performance, all the same, is unsatisfying. No one seems to be truly playing to anyone else. Inghilleri's grandiose "Pensa che un popolo," sobby showboating though it is, would have roused a cheer in the house (as Toscanini scowled). Yet otherwise Inghilleri does little to bring Amonasro to life. Cattaneo is in superb temperament, but Giannini's on an off day. Most disappointing of all is Pertile, Toscanini's favorite tenor, and rather avant-garde for the day in his forward projection and clean-cut accenting. An intelligent tenor, professional, musicianly. The perfect voice and style for Radames. But somehow Pertile never quite delivers the part, never connects with the story. Not that the set is bad Verdi: it is very good Verdi. It just isn't *Aida*.

The work may be harder than it looks. Even Caniglia, Stignani, Gigli, and Gino Bechi under Serafin (Victor, Seraphim) can't pull it together, though the set is better than it's often said to be. Toscanini (Victor) at his rightest suffers weak casting, though as always one notices certain moments—the announcement of Radames as *duce* in the first choral scene is one—that *no one else* can play, as Toscanini does, *exactly* as Verdi wrote them. In 1955 came two starry lineups, from Angel at la Scala (Callas, Barbieri, Tucker, Gobbi; Serafin) and Victor in Rome (Milanov, Barbieri, Björling, Warren; Jonel Perlea). Victor's cast is more entitled vocally than Angel's, Angel's more alive than Victor's—but, again, neither reading works as a whole. For Callas's Aida, one refers to the pirates, for the second of two Mexico City seasons, with Oralia Domìnguez, del Monaco, and Taddei, an exemplary case of the superiority of the theatre performance over the studio rendering. There is, too, the historic high E flat with which Callas caps the Triumphal Scene, first tried the year before to scorn an arrogant tenor, then repeated out of sportsmanship and latterly a Mexico City tradition, no matter who's singing.

Clearly, all-star casts are no cure-all in *Aida*. In stereo years, both von Karajan (Angel) and Abbado (DG) give us "nights of the seven stars," with, respectively, Lucia Valentini Terrani and Katia Ricciarelli as the Priestess, a cute touch. Abbado's *Aida* is merely okay, and von Karajan's ferociously majestic conducting of an essentially lyric cast (Freni, Baltsa, Carreras, Cappuccilli) throws the piece out of sync with itself. On the other hand, *Aida* of all operas is unthinkable without stars. Muti (Angel) proves the efficacy of the studio event, with Caballé, Cossotto, Domingo, and Cappuccilli, all velvet in sound and passionately interacting. This was Muti's first complete opera recording, and Angel, anticipating decades of similar outings, took great care with it. There is none of the assembly-line approach, the "if it's Tuesday, this must be Verdi" feeling that dulls many of today's big-star studio sets. The chemistry that the old Sabajno 78s lack, Muti's singers enjoy.

Only one *Aida* is superior to Muti's, and it's a classic: Solti's (Victor, London) with Leontyne Price, Rita Gorr, Jon Vickers, and Robert Merrill (plus a hint of "seven stars" in the assistance of Giorgio Tozzi and Plinio Clabassi, with the young Mietta Sighele as the Priestess). Merrill hardly stands up to Gobbi and Taddei in ingenuity, but if ever a baritone had instrumental entitlement in Verdi, Merrill did. It is the other three principals who carry the action, along with Solti's very pictorial conducting, as in the way he accents Radames's "Nè le mie forti braccia smuoverti potranno, o fatal pietra!" (Nor can my strong arms move you, o fatal stone!) in the Tomb Scene, as if making the exertion along with him. Vickers's Radames, too, is all one with Solti's dynamic approach, banging out the syllables in "Io son disonorato" with a querulous despair; and Gorr's sledgehammer mezzo fits in well. She can lighten up for "Ah, vieni" at the start of Act Two, a woman in love, but she is at her best in the confrontations, stressing the set's dramatic bent. In fact, the constant surge of sound, both vocal and orchestral, sets off Price's lyric heroine most sympathetically in a kind of timbre theatre, Price's very tone that of the overwhelmed beauty.

Solti's *Aida* stands comparison to the holiest of golden-age 78s. Johanna Gadski's acoustics of Aida's two arias give us that old-time religion of stand-and-deliver *canto* (albeit with some pitch trouble). But

Price is more polished, and, in "O patria mia," far more interpretive. In 1909, Elena Ruszkowska, a magical soprano, laid down "Fuggiam gli ardori inospiti" with tenor Carlo Barera (whose timbre suggests Giovanni Martinelli without his concentration). Set next to Price and Vickers, the two are hedging. Victor's famous Nile Scene, an early electric with Elisabeth Rethberg, Giacomo Lauri-Volpi, and Giuseppe de Luca, gives us pause for its lavish voices, and a verismo version of the scene's first half with Lina Bruna-Rasaa and Carlo Galeffi fetches us emotionally. Yet Solti's crew are still ahead: vocally and dramatically most apt. Surely the Tomb Scene, then, will humble these stereo moderns. (It is, by hap, not Solti's strongest band.) No. Though Vickers lacks the Latin warmth of Miguel Fleta (with Florence Austral), and though Price's voice lacks the decisive reach of Rosa Ponselle's (with Martinelli at his most honeyed), still Vickers outdoes Fleta in illustrating the nostalgia, desperation, and resignation that the scene turns on, and Price's smoky sweetness yields something Ponselle never quite projected: vulnerability.

After *Aida*, Verdi was more than ready to retire, and we too should pause, momentarily, to consider Verdi's Italian contemporaries in the time when this one man dominated what had been a competitive field. Not only was Verdi popular beyond rivalry; in Italy, he was universally influential. When he began, Rossini, Bellini, and Donizetti were composers' main points of inspiration, along with the alluring heterogeneity of French grand opera. By the time of *Aida's* premiere in 1871 (in Cairo, followed a year later by the Italian premiere at La Scala), Verdi *was* Italian opera: Verdi, who by then contained Rossini, Bellini, Donizetti, and the best aspects of Opéra style. Amilcare Ponchielli's *La Gioconda*, which arrived five years after *Aida*, is like Frenchified *melodramma* with a *Trovatore* cast (plus an extra mezzo), and even mirrors *Trovatore's* convivially idiotic contrivances of plot. Columbia's 1930 Scala set (OASI) is, indeed, very Verdian in sound, though made at the climax of the verismo era. Conductor Lorenzo Molajoli, usually quite good, outdoes himself here, but his cast disappoints: Giannina Arangi-Lombardi distinctive but vocally rocky, Ebe Stignani under her par, and Alessandro Granda a ringing but sobby Enzo, as if trying to cross Verdi with *Andrea Chenier*.

We get much more from London's first of three tries in modern sound. The Gioconda, Anita Cerquetti, came onto the scene in 1951 in an Italy sorely in need of her dramatic-coloratura voice, a kind of fiery Milanov, and she enjoyed a sensational seven-year career before suddenly retiring, a legend. This is her only complete commercial opera (there are also a London recital and a number of undergrounds), and she holds her own with such experts as Simionato, del Monaco, Bastianini, and Siepi, blazing so truly with Simionato in their second-act confrontation that even Gina Cigna and Cloe Elmo's justly famous 78 is shadowed. Best of all, del Monaco is at his least raucous here. His second cry of "Laura!" when Simionato reappears after her presumed death, is actually ravishing.

Next to this cast, Victor's stereo entry with Milanov and di Stefano sounds exhausted, and London's second stereo entry (Tebaldi, Horne, Bergonzi, Merrill, Ghiuselev; Gardelli) is spotty despite Horne's splendid Laura. London recovered on its digital remake, under Bruno Bartoletti, most Verdian so far, with a touch of nostalgic late bel canto elegance. Caballé does overdo the verismo chest tones, especially on the last side, but her "Enzo! Ah, come t'amo!" rises to a delicious high B flat with a deft portamento for the descent to the lower octave rather than the lunging noise that many Giocondas inadvertently give up on. This is an international *Gioconda,* with Agnes Baltsa and Alfreda Hodgson as Laura and La Cieca, Pavarotti's Enzo, Milnes's excellently sneaky Barnaba, and Ghiaurov as Alvise.

And there is Callas, especially compelling in this opera. Her Cetra mono set suffers from some rough colleagues, but her 1959 stereo reading (Angel) is, many feel, one of her two or three greatest recordings. Callas thought so, too: "It's all there," she said, "for anyone who . . . wishes to know what I was about." By this time she was running out of voice and morale, but somehow these Scala sessions under Votto found her in a last wonderful moment. Note, too, how she integrates the role's frenzies of love and hatred, rooting *Gioconda* in its time, not in that of Tosca and Santuzza. Her colleagues—Cossotto, Pier Miranda Ferraro, Cappuccilli, and Vinco—are not up to her level, but all are good, and one hears them here and there taking fire from Callas's spark.

It is one of opera's favorite curiosities that *La Gioconda*'s risible libretto was the work (pseudonymously) of Arrigo Boito, Verdi's brilliant collaborator in his post-*Aida* years. A composer as well, Boito stands out for *Mefistofele,* outstanding itself for its blustery bass protagonist, more like Musorksky than Verdi; for its oddly reflective tenor Faust; and for its two essences of woman, lyrical (Margherita) and dramatic (Elena; Helen, in fact, of Troy). What Verdi opera could be regarded as a vehicle for the bass? Victor's mono *Mefistofele* under Gui is so centered on Boris Christoff that the entire Greek act is deleted. A better idea is Columbia's 78 set, complete yet anchored in the formidable devil of Nazzareno de Angelis. Here is an Italian Shalyapin, with a sturdy instrument, an amazing array of vocal tricks, and certain liberal tendencies regarding textual fidelity. Though Antonio Melandri, Mafalda Favero, and Arangi-Lombardi all fail us here and there vocally, they have the measure of these characters, putting London's digital set (Ghiaurov, Pavarotti, Freni, Caballé; de Fabritiis) into relief as colorless and, except for Pavarotti and Caballé, not particularly well sung. (The set's best portrayal is that of the world globe, which gives a shattering smash at the climax of "Ecco il mondo.")

Only one *Mefistofele* brings the piece wholly to life: Angel's under Julius Rudel, a celebration of Norman Treigle's much-admired devil but strongly limned as well by Domingo's pensive, poetic Faust, Caballé's touching Margherita (very special with Domingo and Rudel in "Lontano, lontano"), and Thomas Allen and Delia Wallis in small roles. Not everyone will take to Treigle's eccentric Mefistofele as New Yorkers did, when the City Opera production was hot ticket; he lacks the grandeur of voice that de Angelis and Christoff lend to the Prologue, for instance. But Treigle's vast personality carries him along, and the resonant, open sonics give air and color to the crowd scenes. Angel holds the ace.

Boito's only other opera, *Nerone*, is more ambitious, even less like Verdi's form than *Mefistofele* is. It took so long to complete that its posthumous Scala premiere under Toscanini in 1924 made it an antique amid Pizzetti and Zandonai, Verdian if only by comparison. *Nerone* never was, in fact, completed, for Boito did not set his Pirandellian fifth act, wherein the matricide Nero plays Orestes with a chorus of thespian—or real?—Furies, as Rome burns. There is something desperately touching in the care with which Toscanini mounted *Nerone*, with some of the finest singers available (Rosa Raisa, Aureliano Pertile, Carlo Galeffi, Marcel Journet, and Ezio Pinza) and the faculties of Italy's greatest opera house commandeered to the nth. Perhaps Toscanini regarded *Nerone* as a last link with the living Verdi; Boito, after all, had been the great man's confidant for twenty years. Or perhaps Toscanini simply admired the work. Few others do. It has an extraordinary libretto—the composer's own, of course—and the copious grip of epic. But the music, as music, lacks melody. Eterna put out an LP of 78 extracts, poorly transferred but counting two of the original team, Pertile and Journet, the latter spectacular in Simon Mago's séance act, "Nell'antro ov'io m'ascondo."

Today's recorded repertory is so wide of reach that we have no fewer than three complete *Nerones*, one of them a studio project on a commercial label. This, for an opera scarcely heard even in Italy, is remarkable. Least worthy of the trio is Cetra's, live at Naples's San

Carlo in 1957 under Franco Capuana, an untidy performance in boxy sound, spread out to four discs and without a text booklet, notable only for Mirto Picchi's resourceful Nero. MRF's RAI broadcast under Gavazzeni, in good sound on three discs, is better, though an often ordinary reading (Prevedi, Ligabue, Baldani) of an extraordinary opera. One appreciates Journet's magician all the more, noting Agostino Ferrin's difficulties with Simon's high range; Ferrin slips down to lower options on lines meant to ring out charismatically. All credit, however, to MRF's fine presentation, taking in not only the libretto and introductory notes but extensive annotations on Boito's linguistic and cultural excavations and the text of the fascinating fifth act. The commercial *Nerone,* picturesquely enough, comes from Hungaroton with János B. Nagy, Ilona Tokody, Klára Tákacs, Lajos Miller, and Jószef Dene under our own Eve Queler. This is an excellent, very characterful performance in rich digital sound, and the style is more Italianate than one might expect, barring an occasional "Gvarda" for "Guarda." Again, however, the Simon, Dene, fails to ride the high climaxes, somewhat embarrassingly at that.

Boito, of course, ushers us into Verdi's last period, that of opera's absolute master, tackling Shakespeare in structures so finely honed down from nineteenth-century tradition that *Falstaff* is in effect an opera without arias. *Otello,* of course, presents numerous solo scenes and duets, and even a quartet. It's an excerptable work, as its lively 78 history proves. Yet only in the context of a complete performance do they truly make their effect. The quartet, especially—a crucial scene, in which Iago takes possession of the fatal handerkerchief, and the only time we see him with his wife, Emilia—seems almost pointless on its own, whereas *Rigoletto's* quartet made a dandy cut right from the start of the 78 era. Then, too, if *Otello* offers archetypes of Verdi's vocal development in the aggrandized dramatic tenor, the pliantly sturdy soprano, and the high dramatic baritone, the three don't really "tell" except in interrelation over the course of the work, as Iago exercises Otello's jealousy and the romance crumbles to bits.

Otello is one of the few nineteenth-century operas claiming original-cast cuts, by Francesco Tamagno and Victor Maurel. Recorded in 1903–1905, some fifteen years after the premiere, the discs say little, for the dead studio ambiance, the piano backup, and the primitive technology cannot convey what these men were like in the theatre. Tamagno's trumpet, if sounded full out, would have exploded the acoustic horn, jumped the needle out of its grooves. Yet we get a taste of his disciplined intensity. Tamagno left us "Esultate!," "Ora e per sempre addio" (twice, two years apart), and "Niun mi tema." Maurel made only "Era la notte," an ideal excerpt under these conditions for its wispy intimacy. It's a strangely undernourished reading from the man who, in Verdi's last years, was Verdi's favorite baritone, the original Falstaff as well as Iago. A great Otello of the following generation, Giovanni Zenatello, has the advantage of electrical sound for his excerpts taken down live at Covent Garden in 1926 with Giuseppe Noto's Iago under Vincenzo Bellezza (collected on EMI's three-disc Covent Garden anthology). Here is an Otello more suggestive of our modern-day Otellos, lacking in *squillo*—the burnished ring that Tamagno, Léon Escalais, and certain other tenors of the late 1800s developed—but stalwart and passionate, with a bright top and a tendency to scant the written notes in the fervor of performing.

The most famous exemplar of this approach is Giovanni Martinelli, heard live at the Met in 1941 with Stella Roman and Lawrence Tibbett under Ettore Panizza (Pearl). In all, this is a respectable *Otello*—Roman better than one might imagine and Tibbett less good than his reputation warrants—but for cuts in the chorus to Desdemona and in the Act Three finale. Martinelli's intensity made him legendary in this part, and it often drives him beyond the bounds of the score. (Perversely, he is fastidious, and very moving, in "Dio! mi potevi scagliar," the monologue in Act Three, made largely of repeated A flats, in which even disciplined Otellos tend to edit Verdi's setting.) Martinelli starts the evening in shaky voice, not to reach form till the high B on "Amore e gelosia vadan dispersi insieme" in Act Two. But there is no denying the fullness of the portrayal, the concentration but also the abandon. In Act Three, when Iago is about to lay his handkerchief trap for Cassio and Otello cries out, "Oh, gioia!," Martinelli delivers it so savagely that the audience breaks into applause—unusual flattery from the torpid Met public of the Johnson years. Interestingly, Victor's 78 highlights of Martinelli's Otello, with Tibbett and Helen Jepson (Victrola), were universally denounced as a pale souvenir of the real thing: an early warning that theatre opera and phonograph opera were two different things.

Of Desdemonas, Mirella Freni (Angel), Margaret Price (London), and Renata Scotto (Victor) point in various ways toward the ideal; interestingly, none recalls the sound or style of our prototypal Verdian, Rosa Ponselle. Freni is the softest, Price the firmest, Scotto the most imaginative. Listeners will be swayed by the companies involved, for Freni sings for von Karajan in his *vieillard terrible* phase, unbearably dainty in the hush of the love duet, then clobbering his Iago, Peter Glossop, with the octaves in the Credo. (And why the cut in the Act

Three ensemble?) Price, teamed with Carlo Cossutta and Gabriel Bacquier for Solti's Vienna forces, may have the edge. Scotto is heard
with the incisive Levine, but Domingo and Milnes treat the roles too
generally, moving scene by scene rather than line by line. True, Cossutta is a "clean" Otello, correct, but without Zenatello's or Martinelli's strenuous sensitivity. Thus Bacquier has little to play to. But the
smaller roles are richly filled. For once, we have an important singer,
Peter Dvorský, as Cassio, almost invariably a comprimario even on
record. And should not Cassio claim a threatening glamorous tone, to
sound worthy of Otello's jealousy?

To see how crucial a good Iago is, play, back to back, two early
stereo *Otellos*: von Karajan's first try (London) and Serafin's (Victor,
London). Vocally, von Karajan has the advantage in del Monaco—
here is *squillo*—and Tebaldi, interpetively pallid but a joy to hear for
the clarity of her *canto*. Serafin's Vickers and Rysanek are not in their
best voice, though even without a true Italian ring Vickers makes a
fascinatingly intellectual Otello, all the more pitiable because his Moor
is too intelligent to be manipulated. Here is where the Iago comes in,
for von Karajan's Aldo Protti is about as manipulative as jello, while
Serafin's Tito Gobbi is atrociously clever, every line a gambit, a snare.
He is short on sheer instrument compared to Tibbett or Glossop, but
one scarcely notices. Note, by the bye, the typical completeness of
the early stereo years: von Karajan and Serafin not only play the whole
opera but add in the ballet (written for Paris), piquantly Eastern pastiche just long enough to build suspense for Otello's public humiliation of Desdemona.

This is a conductor's opera, too, as Toscanini (Victor mono) proves
in one of the few all-time great recordings made without great singers.
But the lack of attractive talents, however much it mars Toscanini's
Aida, seems of small moment in the context of the conductor's shattering precision, though his Aida and Amonasro sing Desdemona and
Iago. Perhaps Ramon Vinay makes the difference, for he was a noted
Otello, with a portrayal of great dignity and power. One cannot help
wondering what this set might have sounded like with Freni and Gobbi.
But, as it is, it overwhelms today as in 1947, when the broadcast was
first aired. Vinay sings again for Wilhelm Furtwängler at Salzburg in
1951 (MRF, Melodram), even more vitally but surprisingly faithful to
the details of score even in the heat of live theatre. Vinay is in better
company here, with Carla Martinis's erratic but lively Desdemona and
Paul Schoeffler's superb Iago, most purely evil of all on disc. Anton
Dermota's lyrical Cassio is another boon. However, as with Toscanini,
Furtwängler provokes us more than his cast does. He is more overtly

indicative than Toscanini, underlining every weighted line—and there are many in Boito's libretto, which often follows close upon Shakespeare's original, expanding the opera buff's Italian vocabulary as da Ponte and Piave never do. Toscanini seems more intent on conserving a savor of form—the quartet stands out as an important piece as in no other performance.

EMI's digital *Otello*, recorded live at the ENO in 1983, is somewhat *hors de concours*, as it is sung in English (in Andrew Porter's translation). It is a very English performance in voice as well, Charles Craig, Rosalind Plowright, and Neil Howlett (under Mark Elder) all lacking the fluency of *canto* we expect from our Verdian archetypes Caruso, Ponselle, and Battistini. The ENO crew works in drier terms, fearing the vibrato, portamento, tenuto, and other "effects" that were a campaigner's artillery in Verdi's lifetime. Plowright holds up best, with Craig a kind of Martinelli with spread-tone problems. But the translation brings home scenes that we may miss in Italian, such as Iago's "Era la notte," here "Darkness had fallen." On two discs it's a bargain, though the sound is poor for digital, constricting badly at climaxes.

I seem to be the only one to think so, but Angel's 1968 set under John Barbirolli with James McCracken, Gwyneth Jones, and Dietrich Fischer-Dieskau is the best *Otello* in modern sound. Like Toscanini a 'cellist, Barbirolli was active in opera in the 1930s—it is he who leads Eva Turner's Covent Garden *Turandot* highlights. But he concentrated on symphony just as the LP generation of conductors was divvying up assignments, and thus Barbirolli recorded few operas. This is a great loss, for like Toscanini Barbirolli has a unique approach, slow tempos framing strong legato architecture. It works beautifully in *Otello*, especially with this cast. Jones is an unreliable recording artist, but this time she is in gorgeous voice; and while Fischer-Dieskau is, as always in Verdi, too generous with his phrasing finesse, this does suit the fastidiously scheming Iago. McCracken, of course, made history in this part when he abandoned his Met comprimario career, made a reputation as the Moor in Europe, and came proudly home to illustrate how blithely Rudolf Bing's Met undervalued young American singers. History aside, McCracken's portrayal vindicates its fame in a unique reading. Here is the most humiliated of husbands, the most shaken of warriors, "Dio mi potevi scagliar" the outburst of a wounded beast. Martinelli and Toscanini each give a more exciting show, Solti yields prettier voices, Levine tends a more Italianate sound. But Barbirolli has a stronger cast than Martinelli or Toscanini, shapes finer music than Solti, and frames surer theatre than Levine.

As with Wagner's last opera, *Parsifal*, Verdi's—the autumnal, wisely self-mocking *Falstaff*—seems a most fit farewell. It is an ideal phonograph work, because home listening with text in hand gives us the chance to savor Boito's astonishing poetry, perhaps the most sophisticated libretto in Italian opera. Moreover, *Falstaff* has proved particularly successful on disc, every set creditable. Choosing among them depends on one's personal priorities. Those who like state-of-the-art sonics will pass up, to their loss, Columbia's 1930 set with Giacomo Rimini, a fantastical *buffo* with a big, dark sound, and, after Mariano Stabile, the ranking Falstaff of his generation. The young lovers come off uncharmingly in zippy tempos, but Aurora Buades's Quickly makes amends with her ruthlessly fruity contralto, a Shakespearean Arnalta. Stabile himself, after forty-two years of active singing, graces a classic live Scala performance of 1952 (Cetra, Turnabout) under Victor de Sabata, and Cetra's mono studio cast, sloppy and delightful, boasts Guiseppe Taddei's incomparable Sir John. Then there is Toscanini (Victor mono). Some think *Falstaff* the greatest achievement of his opera broadcasts, but the low glamour profile of his cast mars it. He does, however, share with de Sabata the spectacular Quickly of Cloe Elmo.

The stereo years brought in more refulgent casts, as in Angel's Gobbi, Schwarzkopf, Anna Moffo, Nan Merriman, Fedora Barbieri, Luigi Alva, and Rolando Panerai, the *Grand Hotel* of opera casts. But Solti's more naturally Italianate crew (Victor, London), led by Geraint Evans and taking in Mirella Freni and Giulietta Simionato, presents a breezier comedy. Note, though, how Solti and Evans build the great Tavern monologue in Act Three to a shattering climax. This is probably the most passionate *Falstaff*. Over on Columbia, Vienna forces under Leonard Bernstein offer duller singing but sharper characters, backing up the implausible but nevertheless persuasive Fischer-Dieskau, bracing his earnestly intimate timbre with gasbag ceremonial. It almost works.

Digital hardliners have only Giulini (DG), in a somewhat controversial live performance that may be called subtle (if you like it) or bloodless (if you don't). Renato Bruson, a bit straitened by Giulini's conception, renders a more naturalized figure than Stabile or Taddei, less antic and "performed." Nor is Bruson Shakespearean in the Gobbi manner, as if having coached the play. Bruson is least classic, but most warmly human, of all. Yea, Giulini's may be the most beautifully sung set, and the most youthful—Ricciarelli, Hendricks, Valentini-Terrani, and Nucci are also on hand. Von Karajan still holds the swank if not the sonics (Giulini gets even more edge on CD, brighter and firmer than the LPs), and de Sabata and Bernstein have the most fun. But many listeners find Giulini's album the most honest rendering of the piece, especially next to von Karajan's all-star parade and Bernstein's officiously festive set. Here, after all the blood and thunder, is a confidential Verdi, the artist beyond art.

Much more *notturno*.

13

WAGNER

❧

Like Verdi, Wagner needs a chronological chapter, one following a steady development from the derivative to the unique. But where Verdi began firmly in his native tradition, gradually bending its conventions to suit himself, Wagner began by shopping around the international scene.

His first completed opera, *Die Feen* (The Fairies), points the way to mature Wagner. In genre it recalls the old fairytale rescue opera; in sound it claims strains of Weber and Marschner. But the tying together of separate scenes is avant-garde for the day (1834): the long narrative monologues that slow the opera's first scenes suggest the *Ring* or *Parsifal;* and the heroine's great solo, "Weh mir, so nah die fürchterliche Stunde" (Alas, the fearful moment approaches)—a big concert aria in the line of *Oberon*'s "Ocean, thou mighty monster" and *Fidelio*'s "Abscheulicher!"—contains the theme that caps the meeting of Senta and the Dutchman in *Der Fliegende Holländer*. One could go on citing correspondences, especially in the test of a lover's loyalty, an obsession of Wagner's, as he himself was the most treacherous of lovers. In brief, *Die Feen,* despite its highly Italian derivation from the *commedia dell'arte* of Carlo Gozzi, is something like *Lohengrin* and *Die Frau Ohne Schatten* arbitrated by Euryanthe.

Orfeo's digital relay of a live performance in Munich (where *Die Feen* had a belated premiere in 1888) is excellent, Linda Esther Gray solid at both extremes of her role's range and John Alexander a nice surprise in the current dearth of good Wagnerian tenors. Moreover,

147

the composition itself is suprisingly good for entry-level work, tuneful and, once the narratives are over, amusingly fleet for Wagner. However, his second opera, *Das Liebesverbot* (The Ban on Love), dismally recasts Shakespeare's *Measure for Measure* in an Italian style that is not only artificial but clumsy and often boring. Melodram has a rough-and-ready broadcast relay, better acted than sung by Hilde Zadek, Hanny Steffek, Anton Dermota, and Kurt Equiluz under Robert Heger.

In his third opera, *Rienzi*, Wagner brought off his most successful co-option of available styles, perhaps because by 1842 he was already finding his own. *Rienzi* is, in structure, a grand opera—wags dubbed it "Meyerbeer's masterpiece." Yet while observing convention Wagner adapts it, making *Rienzi* one of the few grand operas that never stray—well, hardly ever—into *divertissement*. It is Wagner's only overtly political opera, following *Guillaume Tell* and *La Muette de Portici* in its treatment of the people rising against oppression, here that of the corrupt aristocrats of medieval Rome, challenged by Cola di Rienzo, one of Wagner's few heroes to belong to history rather than to folklore.

Rienzi is a long opera; for years Wagner buffs had to content themselves with a tape of a 1960 Vienna concert (Anne Lund Christiansen, Christa Ludwig, Set Svanholm, and Walter Berry under Josef Krips) that lacked well over an hour of the score. As proof of the undergrounds' determination to widen opera's discography, the Penzance label expanded Krips's performance by deftly splicing in bits of five other readings (including two in Italian) and preceding the whole with Guido Cantelli's superb reading of the Overture. Yet some music was still missing, including most of the ballet; and not all the singers in this omnibus shared Ludwig's beauty or Svanholm's authority.

Angel's five-disc set of 1976 is not quite complete—oddly, as some sides are rather short. Nor is it a first-rate performance. René Kollo tries hard as Rienzi, but the part is a killer, sitting on the notes at the top of the staff. As his sister Irene, Siv Wennberg is similarly taxed, and, as Adriano, the noble torn between class loyalty and love for Irene, Janis Martin is no more than acceptable in the opera's most interesting part—Wilhelmine Schröder-Devrient, the Leonore of the age as well as Wagner's first Senta and Venus, created the role. But Sawallisch gives a good reading in the city of *Rienzi*'s birth, Dresden; and the sonics are warm and handsome. There's an instructive novelty, too, in hearing Martin's soprano timbre in a role that has belonged to mezzos for seventy-five years—though, as with Adalgisa, it was composed for the higher voice.

Best of all, *Rienzi* is truly listenable, a study in genre: for surely, if

Meyerbeer had had Wagner's genius, *Rienzi* is what he might have hoped to produce. *Rienzi* was Wagner's first success, still popular when his later, more uniquely Wagnerian works had begun to catch on, and the implied reproach of *Rienzi's* compact with the routines of fashion exasperated the composer. Would *Rienzi* never die? Cities that had scarcely tasted *Tristan* were gorging on *Rienzi*! It even had a trouser role, Wagner forbid! (This, by the way, is the reason the Wagner family later gave for banning *Rienzi* from the Festspielhaus in Bayreuth.) At any rate, here is one's only chance to hear how Wagner handled conventional ballet music (*Tannhäuser's* Bacchanale is dramatically involving, ballet of the future), though Angel drops the first half, a pantomime on the rape of Lucretia.

Starting with *Der Fliegende Holländer* (The Flying Dutchman), we encounter a truer Wagner: in his all-basic theme of the sinner seeking redemption through love, in the generous use of *Leitmotive,** and in the tentative withdrawal from conservative musical architecture into a more fluid texture, each utterance leading on to the next. We also encounter Wagner's unusual relationship with the gramophone in the many recordings made at Bayreuth, the family theatre—the sole instance of a nineteenth-century composer reaching into modern times with a legacy of performing traditions. (Of innovations as well: after World War II, Wagner's grandchildren Wieland and Wolfgang put forth a new Wagner in their casting and coaching as well as in their avant-garde staging. But till then, under Wagner's widow, then son, then daughter-in-law, Bayreuth was *passéiste,* devoted to preserving the way of the Master and binding each new generation to that way. Thus, the recordings of *Parsifal* made at Bayreuth in 1927 are—forty-five years after the premiere—something of a replica of what Wagner's fastidious premiere was like.)

So London's Bayreuth *Holländer,* taped in 1955 complete with the famous Bayreuth trumpets caroling the public into the auditorium with *Leitmotive,* is disappointing: a good performance, no more. The sound (originally mono, stereo on the Richmond reissue) is better than in many studio sets of the era, and Hermann Uhde's Dutchman is brilliant. But Astrid Varnay's singing is oddly erratic, now secure, now shaky. Nor is Josef Keilberth's conducting competitive with that of the energetic Antal Dorati (Victor) or the profound Otto Klemperer (Angel)—using, as few do, the original Dresden version of the opera's overture and finale, which both close in a brusque iteration of the

---

* "Leading theme," a musical cell to be replicated or evolved over the course of a work. In this case, themes symbolize the Dutchman, his curse, his redemption, the ocean in storm, and Daland's sailors—all nicely interwoven in the overture.

Dutchman theme. (Only later did Wagner realize that the opera's subject is not the Dutchman's curse but Senta's lifting of it; whereupon he wrote the transfigured ending we commonly hear today.) Dorati and Klemperer suffer insufficient singers. Where is the Senta with the solidity and grace of Emmy Bettendorf, famed for her two-sided 78 of the Ballade? Where the Dutchman who can match Friedrich Schorr's 1929 "Die Frist ist um" for anguished majesty?

They are not in Herbert von Karajan's 1984 digital reading (Angel), though José van Dam and Kurt Moll make a fine Dutchman and Daland, and though the at-first unsteady Dunja Vejzovic improves almost by the note, becoming wonderfully rapt in her interjections during Erik's dream. Even Peter Hofmann, the Erik, is in, for him, good voice. Von Karajan is at his best, not afraid to take an unmarked but thrilling *ritardando* in the big E Major tune as he glides from Act Two to Act Three. (Like almost all recordings and few theatre readings, this one takes the work in one act, as Wagner requests, not in—as he allows for—three.) What really ruins this set is the absurdly inflated sonics, the climaxes unbearable and the quiet parts simply dropping out. At a sensible volume setting: (1) the second subject of the Overture (Senta's theme), (2) the opening of "Die Frist ist um," (3) the first bars of the spinning music, (4) the start of "Wie aus der Ferne," and many other pages literally aren't there. (This is much less of a problem on the CDs, where the quiet passages come through even at a low volume setting.)

As it happens, Angel had already presented the ideal *Holländer* in plain stereo in 1959, with Marianne Schech, Sieglinde Wagner, Rudolf Schock, Fritz Wunderlich, Dietrich Fischer-Dieskau, and Gottlob Frick under Franz Konwitschny. Here, perhaps, we do find the equals of Bettendorf and Schorr. Schech is an old-fashioned Wagnerian (as Bettendorf, for her day, was also), pouring out lovely sound in great diction with an expert's knowledge of what Senta knows and wants. Fischer-Dieskau even betters Schorr in launching "Die Frist ist um" as if he had just stepped onto land after seven years at sea. Of course the music suggests this, in its woozy, rolling gait—but how many singers have done so? Adding in the virtues of a truly fine cast, we have a *Dutchman* as intent on action as it is beautiful to hear—exactly what Wagner aimed at when he broke away from opera's existing forms: music theatre.

Tannhäuser comes to us in two versions, the original Dresden setting of 1845 and the Paris version of 1861, which completely reconceives Venus's influence on the action, in the added Bacchanale and in a vastly sensualized recomposition of Venus's music. In Dresden,

Venus is a hausfrau; in Paris, a goddess of love. But then, between Dresden and Paris Wagner had written *Tristan und Isolde,* and completely changed the texture of love music in opera. It is a cliché of criticism that the renovated Parisian Venus doesn't suit the style of the rest of the opera—but she *shouldn't* suit it. Venus must stand out. *Tannhäuser* is not simply a man's struggle between sensuality and chastity, for the man, Tannhäuser, is a poet: his opera shows, rather, his struggle between hedonism and creativity. Elisabeth inspires poetry; Venus inspires nothing, saps one's vitality. You can be a lover or a poet, Wagner warns us, though he himself managed to be both.

It seems to me that Dresden *Tannhäuser*s are handicapped from the start, though companies favored it almost as a rule till quite recently. We hear a Dresden stolidity reining in Annie Krull, Fritz Vogelstrom, Hermann Weil, and Léon Rains in Odeon's 1909 set of Act Two (beautifully transferred onto one disc by Preiser), for though that act was scarcely altered by the Paris revision, still everyone sings beautifully but too prudently, unknowingly. Just as we want an erotic Venus, we want a radiant Elisabeth and real horror from the court when they learn where Tannhäuser has been.

All this we do get in Columbia's 1930 Bayreuth set, with Maria Müller, Ruth Jost-Arden, Sigismund Pilinsky, Herbert Janssen, and Ivar Andrésen. (Erna Berger sings the Shepherd.) One reason for this album's excellence is the surprising use of the Paris text; the other reason is Toscanini. The maestro, a key figure at Bayreuth in these years, prepared and conducted this production, but his Victor contract kept him off the discs, and Karl Elmendorff esentially beat time for a cast inspired by Toscanini. Only Janssen and Andrésen were truly first-rate, yet everyone offers an outstanding portrayal. No doubt Toscanini, a devoted artist and a tireless seducer, explained Tannhäuser's dilemma to them with great clarity. Cuts in Act Two deny us half of Andrésen's Landgrave, and Act Three claims only highlights. Still, the spirit of the work comes through as on few note-complete sets, especially in the almost rhapsodic quality of the scenes dealing with the power of music. Remember, most of *Tannhäuser*'s principals serve a court whose activity revolves around a song contest.

Strangely, most *Tannhäuser* LP sets went back to Dresden, often in casts that have trouble just singing the music, let alone playing the struggle of hedonism and creativity. Angel's early stereo set under Franz Konwitschny is vocally unsteady and dramatically dreary despite Elisabeth Grümmer's enchanting Elisabeth. DG's offering of Birgit Nilsson as both Venus and Elisabeth is thematically apt, but vocally Nilsson lacks the one's erotic provocation and the other's exhilarating sensitivity. Angel's digital box under Bernhard Haitink, though a bargain on three discs, offers in Klaus König a Tannhäuser so graceless he might as well give into hedonism. Even Melodram's relay of a 1961 Bayreuth performance under Wolfgang Sawallisch—with Victoria de los Angeles, Grace Bumbry, Wolfgang Windgassen, Dietrich Fischer-Dieskau, and Josef Greindl—offers Dresden with the Paris Bacchanale spliced in. Bumbry is brilliant in the role that launched her internationally—"the black Venus!" newspapers raved, shocked and glad, it appeared, at once—and de los Angeles leads an expert court. This is the choice in Dresden *Tannhäusers*. But most choice of all is Solti's Paris version with Helga Dernesch, Christa Ludwig, René Kollo, Victor Braun, and Hans Sotin (London), vividly realized in singing, portrayal, and sonics. Here, as on the Bayreuth 78s, we feel each character's commitment to what he represents—not just Venus's sensuality, but her belief that life *is* sensuality; not just Elisabeth's purity, but her idealism—"Doch welch ein seltsam neues Leben," she tells Tannhäuser, "rief Euer Lied mir in die Brust!" (But what a rare new life your music called up in my heart). All the men are excellent, making the song contest, for once, spontaneous. Even London's use of the Vienna Choirboys as the Shepherd and the four Pages is, though technically out of style, a correct—a realistic—touch.

Lohengrin is easier than *Tannhäuser*: two good guys, two bad guys, two officials, and lots of chorus. London's 1953 relay from Bayreuth, like its *Holländer* in surprisingly good sound (and of course a true theatre acoustic, even if local technicians kept switching around the "foreigners'" microphones), presents Eleanor Steber, Astrid Varnay, Wolfgang Windgassen (a bit unsteady), Hermann Uhde (a brilliant Telramund), Hans Braun, and Josef Greindl, all notable Wagnerians but for Steber, an enchanting Elsa. Conductor Keilberth rises to what is clearly an event—this was, for instance, the production in which Varnay was disclosed at the start of Act Two not "sitting on the cathedral steps" in defeat, as Wagner requests, but standing against the wall, arms spread out in confident defiance. And this is how she sounds.

Surely such a performance can't be bettered. Victor set out to better it with some opera news: Leontyne Price's Elsa, the Boston Symphony under Leinsdorf, and a rare section of Lohengrin's final narrative, seldom performed and never before recorded. But Price bowed out of what was already an uneven cast. Nor is von Karajan (Angel) competitive, though the conductor is at his best in sensible sonics. The halt delicacy of Elsa's entrance, the choral precision of Lohengrin's arrival, the biting strings at Telramund's defiance of Lohengrin before the duel, and the immense building of the Prayer—just to keep to Act

One—testify to von Karajan's intensity. But if Anna Tomowa-Sintow is a lovely Elsa and Siegmund Nimsgern a vivid Telramund, uniquely hurt by his shame, Dunja Vejzovic is a rough Ortrud and René Kollo a very wobbly hero.

But Bayreuth *was* bettered: by Rudolf Kempe's early stereo grouping of Grümmer, Ludwig, Jess Thomas, Fischer-Dieskau, Otto Wiener, and Gottlob Frick with the Vienna Philharmonic (Angel), one of the greatest recordings ever. The casting is utterly right, and more than that, Kempe is extraordinary. Take that wonderful moment in the Act One finale when Lohengrin reaffirms his incognito and turns to Elsa, expecting her supportive and finding her uncertain. Wagner wrote the awkwardness into the score (on 'cello; Ernest Newman termed the theme "Ortrud's Machinations"), and Kempe brings it out as no one else does. Then the following ensemble sets a standard in precision and musical fullness, not letting the drama collapse but rather expanding it. A Wagnerian's essential set.

Lohengrin brings us to the end of Wagner's second period. First came the three auditions, then the three truly Wagnerian operas. Now come *Tristan und Isolde, Die Meistersinger von Nürnberg, Der Ring des Nibelungen,* and *Parsifal:* not "operas" (music of dilenttantes, the bourgeoisie, the past) but music drama (music of devoted revolutionaries, the future, unfettered by company routine, singers' options, or spectators' gloating). These later works are somewhat less excerptable than their predecessors—*Tristan,* particularly. Ironically, it eventually proved an ideal phonograph opera, so much easier to bring off in the studio than live that one of the greatest *Tristan* recordings boasts two leads who almost certainly wouldn't dare it in the theatre.

In the acoustic years, *Tristan* cuts were relatively rare, and, at that, more remote from the theatre experience than most 78s: how to accommodate that vast orchestra, those giant voices? Let's take a sampling. In 1903, Pelagie Greef-Andriessen tackled "Dein Werk?" from the confrontational second-act duet with Brangäne. The reading is majestic (at times majestically off pitch), but quaint against a mere piano, and the soprano sings Brangäne's lines as well, not unlike trying to play Oliver and Hardy at once. In 1909, Johanna Gadski tried the same passage with a chamber orchestra, in flawless voice, wisely skipping over Brangäne's part, but the "shave-and-a-haircut, two-bit" concert ending jars miserably.

Not till the late 1920s, safe in the charge of the electric microphone, did 78 excerpts suggest the true *Tristan,* with full orchestra and singers approximating theatre energy and power: Margarete Bäumer's and Frida Leider's Narrations, Bäumer lovely and vital, Leider

too rushed to do her best and strapped for the climactic high Bs; Leider and Lauritz Melchior's Love Duet, taking the "night and day" cut
(named after its symbolistic images of intrusive day and soothing night)
but singing magnificently under Albert Coates; Meta Seinemeyer's
breathtaking Liebestod. Meanwhile, Columbia's 1928 Bayreuth albums, with Nanny Larsen-Todsen, Anny Helm, Gunnar Graarud, Rudolf Bockelmann, and Ivar Andrésen under Karl Elmendorff, marked
the first attempt at a "complete" reading, with small cuts in Acts One
and Two (the "night and day" chunk stands intact) but Act Three
shredded away to nearly nothing. It's an excellent performance, for if
the conductor and two leads make more of the work's beauty, less of
its passion, the rest of the cast is superb. Helm is impetuously involved
in her mistress's fate, Bockelmann the best Kurwenal on disc, and
Andrésen rises above an absurd cut right at the climax of his big solo
to deliver a very touching Marke. It's notable, too, how much sheer
sound fit onto the early electrical disc. The prelude isn't as clear as it
might be, but—at least on the correct equipment—the voice of the
young sailor (Gustaf Rodin) rings out with shocking fidelity. Larsen-
Todsen went on so impressively as Bayreuth's Isolde (under Toscanini)
that the Met tapped her, but she canceled, and, in straits, the house
gambled on a rather lyric soprano who was about to retire to family
life . . . Kirsten Flagstad.

This brings us to the 1930s and '40s, the era of Flagstad and Melchior—and, alternatively, Helen Traubel. Too bad for history that the
Scandinavians took all the glory, for the St. Louis Woman Traubel
enacted the titanic Isolde that Flagstad could deliver only through lung
power. An Odyssey LP combines Traubel's stupendous Narration and
Liebestod with Melchior's third-act 78s, but it is the Flagstad-Melchior
Covent Garden undergrounds that the buffs favor, one set under Fritz
Reiner (1936) and another under Thomas Beecham (1937). The Reiner set catches Flagstad just a bit more in form and the Beecham set
is slightly more complete* (and collated from two different evenings;
Discocorp's box contains both versions of Act Two). Either set finds
these two titans in their element, she gaining in beauty as she grows
in recognition and he saving up for a strenuous third act.

Both Reiner and Beecham performances survive because of HMV's
attempt to take down *Tristan* for a commercial issue that didn't come
off. Melchior never went into the studio for a complete set, but Flagstad did, when she was nearing retirement. She was not pleased when

---

* The cuts reflect standard procedure at the time in non-German-speaking countries.
The Love Duet's "night and day" cut, for instance, is observed just as in the Leider-
Melchior 78s.

word got out that Elisabeth Schwarzkopf had supplied the high Cs and Bs for Flagstad's 1952 reading with Ludwig Suthaus under Wilhelm Furtwängler (Victor, Angel, Seraphim), long an unquestioned classic. Still, I question it. The sound is a bit backward for the time, voices and orchestra overfiltered into soup (the CDs clean this up considerably), and Furtwängler makes one of his few wrong judgment calls—but a crucial one—in ignoring the Narration's many sudden fluctuations in tempo. These are essential to the situation, for the Narration marks Isolde's first utterance after weeks of humiliated silence. It was Tristan she saved, Tristan she forgave, Tristan she loved: and now it is Tristan leading her like booty to his uncle! Burning with shame and rage, she hurls the story at Brangäne, citing insult upon insult, to her nation (Ireland) and herself, and Wagner marked it to sound like an outburst, constantly shifting in tone and tempo. Perhaps Furtwängler was trying to accommodate the rigid Flagstad (Beecham didn't—his Narration observes the markings). But much of the set seems a bit smoothed out compared with two live sets of the time, one from Munich under Knappertsbusch (Movimento Musica) with Helena Braun, Margarete Klose, Günther Treptow, Paul Schoeffler, and Ferdinand Frantz; and one from Bayreuth under von Karajan (Melodram) with Martha Mödl, Ira Malaniuk, Ramon Vinay, Hans Hotter, and Ludwig Weber. The Munich set, in cloudy sound, reveals a fine but never unique performance—the kind of *Tristan* one used to take for granted—while Bayreuth is striking, the two leads so resourceful that such an unbeloved moment as Isolde's first confrontation with Tristan becomes a highlight. Like Furtwängler's Suthaus, Treptow and Vinay mark the shift away from vocally splendid Tristans (like Graarud and Melchior) to more dramatic but slightly harsh or dry ones.

Birgit Nilsson's Isolde is so well documented that one may follow her artistic progress: from the aimlessly stentorian, at the 1957 Florence May Festival under the brilliant Artur Rodzinski, hampered by greedy cuts for the restless audience; to the emerging Valkyrie under Solti on London, a loud and vulgar presentation in general; to the supreme Isolde of her day (after coaching with Wieland Wagner) at Bayreuth in 1966 in grand company (Ludwig, Windgassen, Wächter, Talvela) under the hasty but exciting Karl Böhm (DG). This is a classic performance, long favored as a *Tristan* for the "average" taste: clear rather than gimmicked sound, intent performers with fine voices (Ludwig joins Helm and Klose as immortal Brangänes), and a forthright, unidiosyncratic conductor. Windgassen, in poor voice with Nilsson at Florence, really takes over the role here with a compelling third act.

Von Karajan made his studio *Tristan* in 1972, with perhaps the last truly distinguished group of natural-born Wagnerians. At that, Helga Dernesch, though a lovely, vital Isolde, does not rival either the great voice Isoldes like Flagstad or the great interpreters like Mödl. But Jon Vickers, Walter Berry, Karl Ridderbusch, and Ludwig again are the goods, Vickers in particular. He is the most intelligent of Tristans with many unexpected line readings, such as his prompt, crisp "Fragt die Sitte!" (So custom demands!), defending his neglect of Isolde on the voyage to Cornwall. Vickers's third act is astonishing. No other Tristan is so wounded, so delirious, then so refreshed when Isolde's ship is sighted. Even more remarkable than the performance is the extraordinary sound, beautiful in itself, a resonance shimmering about the myth. The Berlin Philharmonic, von Karajan's accordion, is too closely miked, often masking the singers. But how intensely it plays! When Isolde tells Brangäne of dropping the sword with which she meant to kill Tristan, the strings' *pizzicato* hits out so closely that one looks at the floor to see where the weapon landed. The Love Duet in particular is an equipment tester, a trio for soprano, tenor, and the Berlin Philharmonic. Some decry this *Tristan* as von Karajan's valentine to himself. Others call it the unique recording of one of the four or five greatest operas. Controversial, then, but essential.

By the digital 1980s, all the likely Isoldes and Tristans had checked in, leaving Reginald Goodall (London), Carlos Kleiber (DG), and Leonard Bernstein (Philips) to make some compromise in casting expectations. Goodall's is the most sensible, using the leads of his English National Opera *Tristan*, Linda Esther Gray and John Mitchinson, world-class talents if not stars. Kleiber's is the most daring, equalizing the somewhat lyrical Margaret Price and René Kollo through the powers of the microphone. Bernstein got what was left, Hildegard Behrens and Peter Hofmann.

The results are, vocally, very variable. Goodall's all-British team, backing Gray and Mitchinson with Anne Wilkens, Phillip Joll, and Gwynne Howell with Welsh National Opera forces, offers a respectable performance, but Mitchinson presents an intelligent hero in the Suthaus manner and Gray is stupendous. She is the biting sort of Isolde, like Mödl and Nilsson, who may lack absolute beauty in the Love Duet but delivers a smashing first act. Gray's "Seines Elendes jammerte mich" (His torment moved me) cuts right to the core of Isolde's tragedy of honor: she loves the man she loathes. At "Seinen Ohm" (His *uncle*) her disgust is chilling. And the high B that climaxes the Narration caps a towering rage.

Kleiber's Brigitte Fassbaender, Dietrich Fischer-Dieskau, and Kurt

Moll came by their parts naturally; Price and Kollo lack the vocal physique for a theatre performance. At the mike, however, they make a blazing, beautiful pair, goaded by Kleiber's ferocious approach. Like Dernesch, Price is that rare Isolde who combines loveliness of tone with command of character, and Kollo, sometimes unsteady in Wagner, is solid enough to bring to life not only Tristan's feelings but also his public self, his shining reputation (Tristan's "day" half, in the opera's central metaphor) that, inspiring Melot's jealousy, destroys the lovers.

Bernstein has a wonderful Brangäne in Yvonne Minton and a fine Marke in Hans Sotin. But Behrens and Hofmann are inadequate, Behrens but half-formed dramatically and constantly swamped by the orchestra, Hofmann toneless and dull. Granted, these two are parish favorites: Behrens regularly presents Wagnerian heroines to the world's most exacting audiences, and Hofmann sings nothing *but* Wagner, save Florestan and rock. But these are perhaps Wagner's most exacting parts, most hazardous and most vulnerable in times of vocal exhaustion. Brünnhilde and Siegfried are as dangerous; but *Rings* go on with second-rate singers in those roles. A *Tristan* with second-raters would cause a scandal. Besides, what other five-disc opera depends so heavily on just two people? What else is there in *Tristan und Isolde* but the title parts?

There is the conducting. Here, all three digital *Tristans* repay investigation. Goodall's is a reading in the classical mold, long-lined, deliberately building to the titanic, as in the way he takes the prelude in one great swelling to the climactic statement of the *Tristan* chord, pulling back magnificently just as he reaches it. The effect is of time itself shuddering almost to stillness. Every so often one worries that Goodall is too deliberate, will lose the swelling tension—as his most comparable predecessor, Furtwängler, never did. Nor does Goodall oppose the *Leitmotiv* strands in Tristan's delirium as fiercely as Furtwängler, as if madness were literally ripping Tristan's mind into bits. Kleiber, on the other hand, is fast and electrifying, the holder of the black belt in baton karate. He also has the best orchestra of the three—the Dresden Staatskapelle—and the best sonics. However, on the LP, DG attempted a unique approach to side breaks: each next disc starts at a point *before* the last one ended. A jarring effect, though nothing dims Kleiber's energy. Oddly, LR's relay of a 1976 Vienna performance with the undistinguished Catarina Ligendza and Spas Wenkoff finds Kleiber way off form, even haphazard. But then, unlike Knappertsbusch and Klemperer, never at their best out of the theatre, Kleiber thrives in the big-budget workshop of the recording studio. As for Bernstein, his inferior cast unfortunately mars one of the great readings. He presents the Sailor's Song with a space-shaping melancholy that aptly launches the drama, and closes Act Two in overpowering despair—the final chord is a shock. This is a unique *Tristan*, with many conductor's choices in tempo and in bringing out inner voices that will surprise the longtime buff. The Bavarian Radio Orchestra, moreover, follows Bernstein with a marvelous cohesion. (The recording was prepared around broadcast performances, an act at a time.) Most flagrantly, and stunningly, and immortally, Bernstein conducts the last utterance of the all-basic *Sehnsucht* (yearning) *Motiv* at the opera's close as one has always dreamed of hearing it: as a placeless, ageless need falling out of the lovers' abhorred day into blissful night, as if the four notes were magically playing themselves, an autonomous *envoi*.

Die Meistersinger von Nürnberg reverses the terms of *Tristan*'s day and night, as comedy must: the sun shines on pranks and township festival, and the moon looks down on riot, not all that dangerously, though it disturbs Hans Sachs all the same. *Die Meistersinger* further turns *Tristan*'s casting qualifications inside out: *Tristan* needs the biggest voices and monumental commitment, while *Die Meistersinger* wants lighter instruments but great versatility of character. Tristan, Isolde, and Marke are mythological archetypes brought to life. *Die Meistersinger*'s psychology is more dense, allowing for latitude of interpretation. There are gruff Sachses, kindly Sachses, intellectual or plain-man Sachses. Is Eva innocent or shrewd, Walther arrogant or conventionally knightly, Pogner thoughtful or plodding? Beckmesser is especially questionable, for his music styles him as a caricature, Wagner's lampoon of all his visionless critics, not least the critic Eduard Hanslick. (Beckmesser, a pedantic scribe, was originally called Veit Hanslich.) To sing the part in caricature overloads the joke and tests credibility: would Pogner consider as a son-in-law a man utterly without dignity?

The 78 years, concentrating on the big solos, avoided the issue, though the fifteen HMV sides cut from 1927 to 1931 and built around Friedrich Schorr's warmly poetic Sachs (with such colleagues as Elisabeth Schumann, Göta Ljungberg, Lauritz Melchior, and Rudolf Laubenthal, mostly under Albert Coates and Leo Blech), transferred to LP (Angel, Seraphim), make a potent highlights disc. This is, of course, a conductor's opera as well as a singers'. Two of the greatest *Meister* offer their conceptions under festival conditions, Toscanini at Salzburg in 1937 (FWR) and Furtwängler at Bayreuth in 1943 (EMI). Both sets suffer technical drawbacks, Toscanini's in coarse sonics and Furtwängler's in chunks missing from the master tape, the Act Three quintet among them. Furtwängler is burdened, too, with a forgettable cast; but Toscanini has Hans Hermann Nissen's excellent Sachs, Maria Reining's very winning Eva, and Heink Noort's strong Walther. Toscanini's Salzburg *Meistersingers* were legendary. The master himself, overcome by the perfection of his second act, staggered to his dressing room murmuring, "Like a dream . . . a dream." It's a passionate reading, with the most thrilling riot fugue, faster yet more precise than any other.

It was up to LP to give us *Die Meistersinger* complete; this longest of Wagner's operas would have made an impractical armful of 78s. There was, at least, Karl Böhm's 1936 Dresden album of Act Three (Victor), uncut, proving the value of a company ensemble in the nicely dovetailed playing of Margarethe Teschemacher (Eva), Torsten Ralf (Walther), Eugen Fuchs (Beckmesser), and, *als Gast* from Munich, Toscanini's Sachs, Nissen. The set is notable for its exuberance—the chorus breaks into wonderful shouts of joy as Pogner leads Eva into the third-act song contest.

LP was scarcely launched before London (Richmond) issued a complete *Meistersinger* act by act (on a total of seven discs, reduced to a box of six), made in Vienna under Hans Knappertsbusch, a sort of Hans Sachs as conductor, reflective but slyly humorous, an artist who takes his time. He has a superb Sachs in Paul Schoeffler and a lovely Eva in Hilde Gueden. However, Günther Treptow's Walther sounds so tired that his scene with David (the amused and amusing Anton Dermota) suggests not two youngsters but a generational saga, and Karl Dönch is clearly rehearsing for the absurdly overplayed Beckmesser he made famous at the Met in the 1960s. At least his scenes with Schoeffler are tensely motivated. Much of the rest of the album feels . . . well, a bit unfeeling. Listen for a famous mark of changing times, after fifty years of direct-to-disc recording: tape has become the medium, and it leaves its trace in a violently clumsy splice just as the overture slides into Act One.

Lack of feeling is definitely not the problem in Angel's late mono Berlin set under Rudolf Kempe with Ferdinand Frantz, Elisabeth Grümmer, Rudolf Schock, Benno Kusche, and Gottlob Frick, for Kempe gets an astonishing swing into this music that carries his entire cast along. One senses that Kempe loves not only this opera but everyone in it. This is a classic, a conservative *Meistersinger*, marred by Shock's labored high register (shouldn't Walther of all people be a flawless singer?) but brightened by Kusche's Beckmesser, punctilious in diction to emphasize the town pedant. Kusche is so vivid that we actually hear him turning to spot Walther just before "Wer ist der Mensch?" (Who is that man?). Angel's mono sound is full and clear, at least partly because Kempe is. But this opera demands stereo, to bring out the contrapuntàl textures: in the overture, for instance, when Wagner plays the masters' theme, the guild march, and the Preislied at the same time; or in the blocks of choral harmony in the hymns and anthems; or in the riot.

The first stereo set (Eurodisc, Victor), taped live in Munich, where the world's first *Meistersinger* production had held the stage with little alteration for a century, preserves Munich's second production, but Otto Wiener, Claire Watson, and Jess Thomas under Josef Keilberth are not of centenary standard. Nineteen seventy-six saw in two imposing versions, George Solti's (London) and Eugen Jochum's (DG). Solti's Vienna team counts Norman Bailey's famous Sachs; Jochum's Berlin group has Fischer-Dieskau's novel Sachs—light in tone and above all nice, truly Nürnberg's "theurer Mann," as Eva puts it—and the refreshing jolt of Plácido Domingo's Walther. On balance, Solti's set is merely competent and Bailey especially disappointing, his rhythm sloppy and high notes forced, while Jochum's, recorded in conjunction with a Deutsche Oper production, is uniquely sensitive, very aware of the text. Jochum also has the most believable Beckmesser in Roland Hermann, who actually makes the man almost attractive; and Jochum's Lene is Christa Ludwig, rich casting in this ungrateful part.

Of all conductors, two seem to me to present the richest *Meistersinger*, and both of them are Herbert von Karajan, first in his 1951 Bayreuth relay (Columbia, Seraphim), then, nineteen years later, in studio stereo (Angel). Obviously, Angel has the better sound, warm and clear in a sensible dynamic range where the Bayreuth is good late-middle broadcast, listenable but shallow in ensembles. However, von Karajan's Bayreuthers are not only live onstage but possibly the best *Meistersinger* cast on disc. Otto Edelmann was not known for vitality of portrayal, but his Sachs is very fully rounded, as a plain man almost angrily confounded by his artistic and intellectual sides; and his fellow masters are cogently drawn, giving us, with Gerhard Unger's vital David and Erich Kunz's dizzy Beckmesser, a strong sense of Nürnberg itself, as a historical setting and a nostalgic idealization of German culture. Hans Hopf is no great Walther, true. Like a number of Heldentenors active in the 1950s, he was sturdy rather than interesting. But in Elisabeth Schwarzkopf's Eva we meet the greatest single performance in all *Meistersinger* recordings, vocally resplendent and textually daring, as in her fierce "Euch oder *keinen!*" (You or no one!) to Walther in their first duet, or her officiously reassuring "Ei, was! zu alt?" (What, too old?) in Act Two when Sachs tells her he is too old to wed again.

If von Karajan gives us beauty of personality at Bayreuth, in the studio he switches to beauty of tone. His Angel set, made in Dresden, is suddenly lighter, wittier. Typically, its best scene is David's coaching of Walther; as Peter Schreier and von Karajan present it, it has the spontaneity of a precarious cram session. Typically also, the set suffers from Theo Adam's less than profound Sachs and Helen Donath's idly pretty Eva, almost a Gretel. But Geraint Evans is an agile Beckmesser, Karl Ridderbusch a marvelous Pogner, and René Kollo a Walther as ardent revolutionary to challenge the stolid masters. Kollo was to sing Walther again for Solti, but in troubled voice. Here he is ideal, less sure than Jochum's Domingo but more aware of his role in the evolution of art. If von Karajan's Bayreuth show centers on Edelmann's penetrating Sachs, a king of Wagner-as-advisor, this Angel set leans toward Kollo's bracing Walther, Wagner as iconoclast.

With the *Ring* we step into a different world altogether, one with numerous staging problems that the earlier works lack; one so imbued with the eloquence of the *Leitmotiv* that by *Götterdämmerung* the composition almost entirely consists of *Motive*; and one that is essentially the saga of two families, Wotan's and Alberich's. Almost everyone in the *Ring* is a parent, a child, or a sibling, and *Walküre*'s great chain of duets is at heart the communication of brother and sister, husband and wife, and father and daughter.

All of this suggests the *Ring* as an ideal phonograph opera, as there are no staging problems on disc; one can follow the narration of the *Leitmotive* through handbooks; and the domestic intimacy of the character relationships comes through as not in the theatre. Yet there was little *Ring* on disc for thirty years. Some of the greatest Wagnerians left appreciable marks—Ernestine Schumann-Heink's 1907 "Weiche, Wotan, weiche," Anton van Rooy's 1902 "Abendlich strahlt," Jacques Urlus's 1909 "Ein Schwert verhiess mir der Vater," Lilli Lehmann's 1907 and Johanna Gadski's 1913 takes of "Du bist der Lenz," Ottilie Metzger's 1910 Waltraute Narration—all with a highly vocal panache we seldom hear in Wagner today, using free tempos, portamento, and unexpected pianissimos: singing, in short, more than acting, but singing expressively.

The adoption of the microphone in 1925 and the vastly increased fidelity of orchestral reproduction brought on the first significant attempts to record the *Ring* in more than bits, to capture whole scenes, even acts. (HMV took the lead and virtually retained the monopoly to the present day, on reissues through its various affiliates, especially Germany's Electrola, Britain's EMI and America's Angel and Seraphim.) Luckily, this was in the late 1920s and '30s, when a new generation of singers had come into prominence to set standards that, for many, have yet to be surpassed: Kirsten Flagstad, Frida Leider, Lotte Lehmann, Florence Austral, Lauritz Melchior, Friedrich Schorr, Ivar Andrésen. Some of their predecessors' innate musicality, intoning *Ring* melody more than *Ring* libretto, was lost. Some of the voices seemed less solid as sheer sound. But their dramatic intensity swept all criticism aside.

A few of these huge *Ring* albums have become major classics, especially the first act of *Die Walküre* with Lehmann and Melchior under Bruno Walter and Melchior's *Siegfried* selections, made, as many early Wagner albums were, with bemusing changes of cast and conductor from side to side. (Wotan is sung by Schorr, Emil Schipper, and Rudolf Bockelmann, each to an act.) There was no attempt to forge *Das Rheingold,* however, and the sixteen *Götterdämmerung* discs, featuring Austral, Walter Widdop, and Rudolf Laubenthal under no fewer than four conductors (all great Wagnerians: Albert Coates, Lawrance Collingwood, Leo Blech, and Karl Muck) somehow fell out of important memory, though Austral is perhaps the greatest of all Brünnhildes, emotionally available yet a titanic fury when betrayed. Even by 1948, on the eve of the LP era, the closest thing to a complete *Ring* opera was a multicast *Walküre:* the Walter Act One, the slightly cut Walter-Seidler-Winkler Act Two (made in 1938 in both Berlin and Vienna because Walter's share of the cast had fled Nazi Germany), and Columbia's Helen Traubel–Herbert Janssen Act Three with the New York Philharmonic under Artur Rodzinski.

Clearly, only the LP would bring the *Ring* home—literally home, where the buff could play and replay and accustom himself to the details of one of opera's few genuine epics. In an early stab at piracy, Allegro-Elite issued Bayreuth tapes from 1953 under Josef Keilberth— the first complete *Ring.* But the sound, like the legalities, was questionable. The lack of a cast list and the crediting of one "Fritz Schreiber" as conductor made the boxes seem a hoax, and Regina Resnik, the Sieglinde, put the kibosh on the matter when she heard the *Walküre* in a store and asked her lawyer for his opinion on the state of the art of *Ring* recordings.

It was producer John Culshaw of London Records, of course, who made the history, daringly launching his cycle with *Das Rheingold* when no one could forsee a good sale even for a *Walküre*—or a time, as of this writing, when eleven complete cycles would have appeared. As it happened, London's *Rheingold* was a superb performance, taking in what might be called nostalgic innovation in Kirsten Flagstad's Fricka (her first new Wagner role in twenty years; and her last of all). Moreover, it was also the opera set that revolutionized the recording of opera. Heretofore, opera-on-disc was supposed to supplement opera-in-theatre, as discreetly as possible. But this *Rheingold* arrived in 1958, at the start of the stereo turnover, and its inventive sonics proposed opera recording as a thing-in-itself, rivaling rather than complementing live performances, creatively exploiting technology—even supplying special effects beyond theatre resources. Culshaw's *Rheingold* became a demonstration item, the first opera set everyone bought to test his new stereo system, not least on the Nibelheim anvils and Donner's hammerblow.

Culshaw's *Ring,* which eventually took in Birgit Nilsson, Régine Crespin, Christa Ludwig, Wolfgang Windgassen, and Gottlob Frick (along with Gustav Neidlinger's Alberich from the *Rheingold* plus Joan Sutherland, *als Gast* as Siegfried's Woodbird), is of course Solti's *Ring,* with the Vienna Philharmonic. Solti's reading—nervous, dynamic, and monumental, crashing out through London's extremely clarified sound—has become the modern measure by which other conductors' readings are discussed. Thus, Böhm is fast: faster than Solti. Von Karajan is light: because Solti is heavier. Goodall is dense . . . and so on. Perhaps this is because Solti's cycle embodies a new average in performance tactics, his orchestra fleet and direct after the Furtwängler-Knappertsbusch generation of *Ring* mystics and his cast neither just vocal angels nor barking actors. It is an influential set, the one that many learned the *Ring* from, and its great virtue is that it has scarcely any weak links. Solti's Wotan,* Hans Hotter, at the end of his career and tether, is better encountered in Cetra's Bayreuth relays under Knappertsbusch, and James King is a leaden Siegmund. But everyone else is top, and a few are the best of kind. (Some object to the prominence of the orchestra, emphasized on the CDs.)

After *Das Rheingold,* Solti's *Ring* operas came out at intervals, *Siegfried* four years later in 1962, *Götterdämmerung* in 1964, and *Die Walküre* in 1966. Rightfully, *Götterdämmerung* marked the climax of Culshaw's project, not only in his stereo-as-theatre (in the atmospheric prelude, the vibrant horns of Hagen's Call, the spatial texture of the massing of the Gibichungs, and the overpowering dynamics of Siegfried's Funeral March—not to mention the technical manipulation of Siegfried into Gunther in the Tarnhelm scene), but in the masterly vocalism of the cast: Nilsson's Brünnhilde, Windgassen's Siegfried, Frick's Hagen, Dietrich Fischer-Dieskau's Gunther, Ludwig's Waltraute, Claire Watson's Gutrune, and Neidlinger's Alberich. At the

---

*George London, in better voice than Hotter but less characterful, sings Wotan in Solti's *Das Rheingold.*

time this ensemble was superior; today it seems fabulous. Note the versatility of Solti's cast—Nilsson sensitive as well as powerful, Windgassen intelligently heroic, Fischer-Dieskau a lyrical villain, Ludwig opulent and epic in the all-important duet of Valkyries, and Neidlinger keeping the Wotan-Alberich relationship alive even without a Wotan, through sheer force of personality.

Von Karajan's *Ring* (DG), geared to his Salzburg Easter Festival productions with the Berlin Philharmonic, came out—like Solti's, piecemeal, at intervals—in the late 1960s, in what appeared to be an air of challenge. Solti had veterans, speed, and volume. Von Karajan used a young, lithe cast, took his time with the tempos, and dared a more intimate approach. Even today the sonics, though in too broad a range, are the most attractive of any *Ring;* and the youthful voices make sense, as Siegmund, Sieglinde, Siegfried, Hagen, Gunther, and Gutrune are all about twenty or so. (With Brünnhilde it's hard to tell.) True, Wotan shouldn't sound quite so young, and true also that young voices suffer under Wagnerian pressure, even under studio conditions. Furthermore, von Karajan's quasi-chamber style sometimes fails in power where Solti excels—as in the prelude to *Siegfried's* Act Three, wherein Wagner puts a few *Leitmotive* together to build a picture of Wotan striding through the sky to his climactic meeting with a mortal—his grandson Siegfried—that signals the final acts of the epic, the listener's ears ringing with melodic concepts of heavenly morality, natural order, and the end of the world. Solti is in his element here. Von Karajan has to bend his aesthetic a bit to instill a sense of climax.

Yet von Karajan holds the edge in sheer storytelling. Solti is more overtly "dramatic," but von Karajan's records tell the tale with greater detail and color—as in the shouts of the terrified Nibelungs as Alberich outlines his plan to rule the world. Solti gives us the yelps of children. Von Karajan gives us the screaming of grown men, a chilling effect. And von Karajan's grouping of Helga Dernesch, Gundula Janowitz, Josephine Veasey, Helge Brilioth, Zoltan Kélémen, and Karl Ridderbusch (amusingly comradely just before murdering Siegfried) rivals Solti's. Moreover, von Karajan has in Régine Crespin's Sieglinde, Jon Vickers's Siegmund, and Thomas Stewart's Wotan three of the outstanding Wagner portrayals of the era.

Though Allegro's bootleg cycle was never reissued, Bayreuth was of course heard from, in cycles led by Knappertsbusch in 1957 (Cetra) and Karl Böhm in 1966–67 (Philips). These performances feature singers heard elsewhere, but Knappertsbusch, despite an almost unbearably deliberate reading, does have Hotter and Varnay in their prime, essential study for Wagner buffs. Böhm has an extra advantage in the CD

transfer, which emphasizes the theatrical acoustic, thereby adding excitement to an already dynamic reading. Böhm also takes fewer CDs
than Solti.

Adopting the new tradition of recording *Rings* live on stage, the
English National Opera had its say—in Andrew Porter's wonderful
translation—in Reginald Goodall's weighty reading, an article of faith
among certain Wagnerians. So are Rita Hunter's womanly Brünnhilde,
Alberto Remedios's almost lyrically valiant Siegmund and Siegfried,
and Norman Bailey's Wotan, rasping out each mention of the ring in
his great *Walküre* monologue in direst agony. Indeed, some buffs take
these three for the Leider, Melchior, and Schorr of our day. Too many
of the smaller parts are given to inadequate voices, but Anne Collins
delivers a superb Erda, balancing her epic role with a sense of character; Katharine Pring's Waltraute sounds, for once, like Brünnhilde's
sister; and Derek Hammond Stroud is such a fascinating Alberich that
he makes his scene with Wotan at the start of Siegfried's second act a
highlight of the cycle.

Best of all, Hammond Stroud's diction is very, very clear. As that
Siegfried scene proceeds, Bailey starts to improve in *his* diction, as if
reproached by his colleague's clarity—for this *Ring* cycle's unique feature (the eloquence of an English text) is its unique defect (few of the
singers are intelligible). Then, too, the stereo sound distances the voices
in favor of the orchestra, for the London Coliseum, where the ENO
plays, is a great barn of a place, built as a music hall and later host to
big American musicals. By comparison, Bayreuth, built by Wagner for
his operas, has the famous covered pit, specifically designed to protect
the singers from Wagner's contentious orchestrations.

As it happens, the orchestra is the feature of the English *Ring*—or,
rather, Reginald Goodall's conducting. Storytelling is his forte, and
next to him Solti seems tyrannical and von Karajan self-absorbed. In
Goodall's *Siegfried*, the Act Three prelude is less pictorial than Solti's
but more topical, thematic, as if Goodall were hurling *Leitmotive* at us
retrospectively, considering the characters and events and even the
very shape of the epic as he conducts it.

Goodall's *Siegfried* (EMI) is by far the great achievement of his *Ring*.
The *Rheingold* (Angel) is a bit *too* well integrated into his cycle, too
preparatory; on four discs as opposed to the usual three, it warns of
the grandeur of Goodall's pacing. *Die Walküre* (Angel) suffers from an
insufficient Sieglinde, and though *Götterdämmerung* (Angel) retrieves
Siegfried's tension—and presents Rita Hunter's most glorious moment
in the Revenge Trio—it never recalls *Siegfried*'s concentration. Still,
Goodall's is far preferable to the succeeding live cycle, Pierre Boulez's

(Philips digital) in Patrice Chéreau's questionable production for Bayreuth's centennial, marred by a number of poor principals and by Boulez's deadpan reading.

Eurodisc made a digital *Ring* in the studio, available domestically only on CDs expensively spread out—Eurodisc's *Götterdämmerung* takes six CDs, as opposed to Philip's four. This is basically Solti-style conducting with von Karajan–style voices. Marek Janowski leads the Dresden Staatskapelle expertly, though expertise is not enough in face of Solti, von Karajan, and Goodall. However, some of the casting is very competitive. Jessye Norman's Sieglinde has Lehmann's dash but a lot more voice; Siegfried Jerusalem refreshes some of Siegmund's most familiar lines; Yvonne Minton makes Fricka *reasonable,* almost persuasive; René Kollo is the sweetest of all Siegfrieds (except on the highest notes) and, better yet, a sensitive hero, with a marvelous death scene; Matti Salminen offers a truly black Hagen; and—like Neidlinger and Hammond Stroud—Siegmund Nimsgern finds Alberich a singing actor's exhibit. Well and good: but Theo Adam's Wotan suffers advanced wobble, Peter Schreier makes Mime the whining screamer that Gerhard Stolze popularized for Solti and von Karajan; the Waltraute is almost terrible—what a difference a Ludwig or Pring makes in that scene!—and the Brünnhilde, Jeannine Altmeyer, simply does not have the power. Surprisingly, for a digital *Ring,* sonics are perfunctory; Wotan's scene with the Valkyries and the big chorus in *Götterdämmerung* get no play. One effect Eurodisc does give us: Kollo as Siegfried-as-Gunther is very effective—an *hommage* to Culshaw? It both sounds like him and doesn't, exactly right for a man magically disguised.

Essential to any Ring discography are the two Furtwängler cycles, live from La Scala in 1950 and in a RAI broadcast in 1953, legendary not only because of the performances themselves but because they were tantalizingly heard of, but not heard, for years. The tape underground passed them around, then EJS issued the Scala cycle, MRF issued the RAI cycle, and Murray Hill—daringly, over the counter—put out the Scala set. But the sonics in all three cases were inferior to what authorities held in the vaults. Rumor long had it that EMI was attempting to get the rights to release the RAI tapes, an arduous process involving contacting all the singers and orchestra personnel (or their heirs) who took part. At length EMI issued the RAI *Ring* in quite listenable sound, and, generously, on Seraphim instead of a full-priced label. Then Cetra released one great box of the Scala performances, now in superb sound. Finally, EMI digitally remastered the RAI tapes, now on fourteen instead of the original eighteen LPs. And lo, the legend held. For, beyond the glamour of the Furtwängler mystique and the excitement of reclaiming the great Wagnerian past, there is, for many, the feeling that these are beyond question the greatest performances of the *Ring* that anyone knows of. The majesty of Furtwängler's conception is almost shocking. Not a bar goes slack, not a page fails to add to the flow of story. Furtwängler's reading shifts in feeling as the *Ring* shifts, from brutality to recklessness to joy to despair. None of the other conductors quite pulls this off: Solti always tends to the energetic, von Karajan to the beautiful, Goodall to the stentorian. They lose the nuances. Above all, Furtwängler is best at keeping the sense of heroic doom within consciousness at all times, so *his* prelude to *Siegfried*'s third act is most momentous of all. Listening, one knows that world is about to break apart. Some discs later, during *Siegfried*'s Funeral March, one hears it shatter.

The other attraction of Furtwängler's *Rings* is his casting, for he drafted the greatest Wagnerians of the time—two different helpings' worth, with a little doubling. Most notable of all is Kirsten Flagstad in glorious voice, a Brünnhilde of amazing stamina (she was fifty-five) in the Scala set. Her RAI counterpart, Martha Mödl, was more interesting but far less radiant. On the other hand, the Scala's two Siegfrieds, Set Svanholm and Max Lorenz, sound effortful, Svanholm going wildly off in *Siegfried* at the end of Act One and, as Act Three closes, making truly wretched noises. The RAI's Ludwig Suthaus is much better, one of the few Siegfrieds who can darken their timbre to sound like Gunther in the Tarnhelm scene. As for Wotan, we get Ferdinand Frantz in both cases (except in the Scala *Siegfried*), and while Frantz lacks Schorr's inward authority or Stewart's emotional vitality, Frantz's very sound seems most authentic. Note the gravely humorous tone of his "Heil dir, weiser Schmied" as he strides into the RAI *Siegfried*.

One could go on balancing the players: the Scala's superior Hagen (Ludwig Weber), the RAI's superior Mime (Julius Patzak). There are the orchestras as well, received opinion holding that the Scala outdoes the RAI. True, the Scala crew has the advantage, with a fuller string tone and more secure horns. But both groups make the same amount of flubs (in different places). In the end, I see no absolute primacy in either of the two cycles. Those who demand the better sonics, or who prefer Flagstad, will want Cetra's Scala box. Those who need a more involved Brünnhilde—and remember, the action turns on her rebellion, then love, then jealousy—or who are new to the work will want Seraphim's RAI set for Mödl and the text booklets.

Comparing *Rings* too often comes down to the matching of sword-in-tree duets, or Rhine Journeys, or Immolation Scenes, sifting Albert

Coates's dash alongside Otto Klemperer's splendor, or Austral's passion alongside Leider's beauty. This sweepstakes approach undervalues the integration of scenes, the way each new narration of foregoing events supports the epic architecture, keeps the action (which after all covers many decades) immediate. The stronger these structural elements are, the more stimulating is the whole. When I compare *Rings* I audition two scenes from *Götterdämmerung;* the Norns' trio and the Alberich-Hagen dream that opens Act Two. Perverse? But remember that the *Ring* is Wotan and Alberich's struggle for power. The Norns, daughters of Erda, Wotan's extralegal mate, are Wotan's people, though philosophically neutral. Hagen, Alberich's son, represents the other side. And, after all, Alberich holds the title role in the saga: he is the Nibelung whose ring Wotan steals. As Wotan does not appear in *Götterdämmerung,* his war with Alberich is affirmed, by proxy, in the Norns' scene, which also serves as a What Has Happened to remind the listener of the great events that have led up to world's end. The Norns' trio is not meant to fill in newcomers on doings in Valhalla, earth, and Nibelheim: Wagner never intended anyone to have access to *Ring* operas separately. Rather, the trio pins down the sensations of idealism, fortune, and greed that impel the action of the cycle's conclusion.

In this context, the Norns' scene and Alberich's address of Hagen become all-basic, to strengthen or sabotage a *Ring.* Von Karajan's Norns sing with great beauty, Solti's trio have presence, and Goodall's suffer a weak link. But Furtwängler's RAI group of Margarete Klose, Hilde Rössl-Majdan, and Sena Jurinac are vocally top and more involved than all other Norns, narrating as if what follows wouldn't make sense without their analysis. Consider Klose's "Trüben Sinnen ward mein Gesang" (Darkly felt was my song). How pensively she phrases, weighing the odds, telling us the game is still unclaimed.

Von Karajan's prelude to the Alberich-Hagen duet is spectacular but lovely. Should the villains be so well set off? His Alberich, Kélémen, saves the scene by sheer talent. Janowski, too, has great singers in Nimsgern and Salminen, the only pair that sound like father and son. But Janowski's prelude is flabby, suggestive of a rained-out Sunday bake sale, not a parley between the dark lord and his surrogate. Goodall's prelude is enticing, but the scene itself goes for little, and Böhm derives urgency simply by conducting too fast.

What is the best, the cheapest, the classic? All *Rings* have drawbacks. Furtwängler lacks sonics, Solti has in Hotter a ruined Wotan, Goodall forgives dowdy voices, von Karajan encourages weak ones. Perhaps Böhm's *Ring* is the only unflawed one (except by Böhm: if you like an unfolding rather than a ramrodding *Ring*). My choice is Furtwängler RAI for majesty and Solti for thrills and chills in great sound—remembering, too, that Furtwängler has veterans of the twilight of the Wagnerian golden age, and that Solti has the best of those who saw that age to its finish. Those who prefer to take the operas separately, to sample the variety of Ring performance, might try von Karajan's *Rheingold,* Furtwängler's Victor *Walküre* (more or less his RAI cast, with the Vienna Philharmonic in much better sound, reissued on Seraphim), Goodall's *Siegfried,* and Solti's *Götterdämmerung:* each of which finds conductors and cast at their best.

If the *Ring* depends on singers as well as conductors, *Parsifal* has been a conductor's opera from the start, when Wagner, in a burst of selfish magnanimity, allowed the Jewish Hermann Levi to conduct the first *Parsifals*—magnanimous Wagner, because the choice was so controversial in so Christian a work, but selfish Wagner (as always), because he believed Levi was the best there was. Levi's successor at Bayreuth as the essential Parsifalian, Karl Muck, made in Berlin in 1928 a complete Act Three for HMV with Gotthelf Pistor, Cornelis Bronsgeest, and Ludwig Hofmann, reissued, minus the first two sides to fit a single LP, on Preiser. This is a must for Wagnerians, imbued with the unique sense of a miracle play at once inward and outgoing that marks the great *Parsifals*, and glorying in Pistor's sensitive vigor. His slightly nasal delivery is attractive, and he leaves his mark on many a line.

Muck also made Bayreuth discs of some of the choral scenes, to be found on Odeon's two-record *One Hundred Years of Parsifal,* along with Furtwängler's Prelude, Frida Leider's "Ich sah das Kind," Melchior's first (of three) "Amfortas! Die Wunde!," the splendid Good Friday Scene by Fritz Wolff and Alexander Kipnis under the composer's son Siegfried, and other bits equally enticing. Some nearly forgotten voices reclaim eminence—Theodor Scheidl, very poignant in one of Amfortas's outbursts—and the engineers were ingenious in splicing different performances into whole scenes. Another must.

Muck's successor, Hans Knappertsbusch, introduced *Parsifal* to the LP era in a reading taken down at Bayreuth in 1951 (London, Richmond). The first complete *Parsifal,* it is conclusive, one of the greatest of all opera recordings. The cast—Mödl, Windgassen, London, Uhde, and Weber—are Wagner experts or about to become such, and everyone is inspired. Windgassen was at the start of his career, always a tricky time in Wagner, but in this role it helps; and Mödl, perhaps the only major singer who seems never to have sung a performance in good voice, makes Kundry fascinating, if never quite sensual. Hermann Uhde's Klingsor is stupendous, but then Uhde always was, in Wagner. There are flaws (sour Flower Maidens, a lessening of tension at the Good Friday Scene) and unexpected virtues (especially in the firm, clear sound). Still, it is not the elements that impress, but rather the whole. Like Muck, Knappertsbusch comprehends *Parsifal* as a blend of lurid theatricality and stark ritual, of glamour and candor. This sets the work apart from the rest of Wagner: not its passion (*Tristan* is passionate), nor its profundity (the *Ring* is profound), but its humility. Other Knappertsbusch Bayreuth *Parsifal*s have been issued; it would appear that a change of cast in a single Flower Maiden is enough to induce Melodram to publish the tape as historically vital. Still, of them all this one remains the great one, perhaps because of its sense of occasion: this was the first opera given under the new regime of grandsons Wieland and Wolfgang, the Festival having reopened the night before with Beethoven's Ninth under Furtwängler.

Pierre Boulez, unlike Knappertsbusch, misses out on the work's ec-static innocence, though Boulez's 1970 Bayreuth *Parsifal* (DG) is nonetheless valiant, with the voluptuous Gwyneth Jones (whose screams, groans, and manic laughter win the Kundry Special Effects Award), the sturdy James King, and the wonderfully detailed Thomas Stewart, an Amfortas who simply overpowers his wooden savior. Von Karajan's digital entry (DG) fails in the other direction, with too much gauzy wonder, though he has the best Klingsor in the wryly bitter Siegmund Nimsgern.

Solti's *Parsifal* (London) is generally thought the great stereo set. The cast is superb: Ludwig, Kollo, Fischer-Dieskau, Kélémen, and Frick (Hotter plays Titurel). Ludwig is virtually the only Kundry who com-mands beauty of voice and intelligence of portrayal, combining Leider and Mödl, but it is wrong to "star" any one aspect of the recording, except Solti's conducting, perhaps—for this is his supreme achieve-ment in Wagner. Solti's *Ring* has rivals, even conquerors. But even Knappertsbusch's *Parsifal* is not truly superior to Solti's. It is certainly different, more spiritual. But Solti's dramatic approach contains the spiritual as well. He builds the work disc by disc, giving the temple scenes an inviolable purity and the Flower Maidens a lascivious opu-lence, till by the third act (wherein Solti delivers the four big brass chords as no one else does) one is utterly caught up in this bizarre salute to the sinner's fun, viewed from within the saint's preserve. *Parsifal* is a lie, for Wagner was a sinner: hypocrite, bigot, opportunist, adulterer. Yet he was a saint of musical history, as a prophet who would not compromise with the conventional. If the grand-opera approach was indeed a corruption, it was Wagner who forced the music world to recognize it as such.

Saints swell the avant-garde in any age. Had he lived today, Wagner would probably be making opera on film—such as Hans-Jürgen Syberberg's *Parsifal* movie, a rare case of the director, not conductor, as auteur of the production. Erato's sound track reveals a performance dignified only by its Kundry (Yvonne Minton) and Gurnemanz (Robert Lloyd, emphasizing the character's childlike innocence). Sadly, Reginald Goodall's (Angel), with Welsh National forces, is even less worthy. It has digital sound; it also has Goodall's slogging, aimless conducting. At least Warren Ellsworth's odd timbre and flawed German do not sabotage a vital hero, and Waltraud Meier, rising above the Venus she recorded at this time, gives a gala Kundry. Her "Ich sah das Kind" has the air of an impromptu report.

A few *Parsifal* issues have centered on singers—Victor's 1940 Flagstad-Melchior Act Two duet, most obviously. Melchior outdoes his matronly partner till about the fourth side, when she remembers that this is a seduction rather than a recital of Dørumsgaard songs, and wakes up. Maria Callas, a Wagnerian early in her career, sang Kundry with the Rome RAI under Vittorio Gui, available both complete and, for Callas browsers, on a single disc of Act Two, by far the bulk of Kundry's role. Callas's *Parsifal,* Africo Baldelli, is not a major artist, but he is not uninteresting, and Callas is in fine voice. Most notable is Gui's Italianate view of the score, always more lyrical and less excruciated than we're used to. German conductors emphasize the solo violin at "Ja! Diese Stimme!" in the Love Duet as a foretaste of Schoenberg. Gui mutes it as interference. Leonie Rysanek, with Siegfried Jerusalem under the speedy Janowski, claims two discs, her (nearly) complete Kundry, plus other scenes (HRE). Was this the day someone in the house cried "Thank you!" after Act Two?

The notion of singers as the essential Wagnerians (albeit in a *Gesamtkunstwerk,* all arts integrated into one) seemed reasonable on 78s, as director and designers were excluded and conductors hobbled by sonics and hastened by side lengths. (Albert Coates's tempo for Austral and Widdop's "Zu neuen Taten" suggests that Siegfried will make his Rhine Journey on the *Super Chief.*) Seraphim's seven-disc *Wagner on Record* collects many of the greatest cuts made in the electric era, when technology allowed voices and orchestra to come through with a fidelity unknown in the acoustic years. Most of the 78s mentioned in this chapter are represented—Leider, Lehmann, Seinemeyer, Melchior, Andrésen, Bettendorf's Senta, Schorr's Wotan and Sachs, and, yes, Albert Coates's diesel-powered Rhine duet. The set is organized chronologically, title by title, from *Rienzi* to *Parsifal,* with most of the operas highlighted on one or two LP sides. The transfers are excellent, and texts and translations are included. Flagstad is missing, but otherwise this is an ideal introduction, either to the performers (for those who know only stereo-era Wagner) or to the material itself (for newcomers). Strongly recommended: some of these performances have never been equaled.

14

CZECH OPERA

⊱⊰

Of all well-known opera files, that of the Czechs is the most isolated from the West. Its language is as difficult as Russian, yet it has no *Boris Godunof* or *Yevgyeni Onyegin* with which to drive a wedge between the *Traviatas* and *Carmens*. *The Bartered Bride,* the most popular Czech opera, has often been performed and even recorded in German or English, making it more accessible but less authentic.

However, the Czechs are an extraordinarily musical people, with a wonderful opera tradition emphasizing history, folk subjects, and studies of village life. "Kterýpak Čech by hudbu neměl rád!" says the bass Beneš in Smetana's *Dalibor,* to a raptly solemn swelling of strings: "What Czech doesn't love music?" Thus, Czech opera recordings on the nation's sole label, Supraphon, are almost invariably excellent, for, where the voices aren't exceptional, the intensity and dedication are. Most of these performances stem from Czech opera houses, especially the Prague National Theatre, which seems to have maintained a glorious standard, at least in the 1950s and '60s, when most of these discs were made. The mono can sound shallow and the early stereo overly reverberant, but there is little of the shrillness that afflicted Russian recordings of the day, and libretto booklets are a given.

The best place to start is with Bedřich Smetana, as his operas virtually founded Czech music theatre, starting in the mid-1860s, when the native culture was throwing off the effects of German colonialism. (Smetana himself spoke German, and had to master Czech to set his librettos.) Needing originality—one doesn't launch a national opera derivatively—Smetana and his librettists ended up with an unusual *oeuvre* in which the serious works giggle and some of the comedies worry. *Braniboři v Čechách* (The Brandenburgers in Bohemia), first of them all, shows Supraphon at less than its best, though Milada Šubrtová is marvellous, and *Tajemství* (The Secret) never quite recovers from Václav Neumann's surprisingly zipless reading of the overture, though Smetana's odd use of woodblocks playing in 6/8 against the 4/4 of the chorus in the first scene, suggesting the labor of threshers in the field, is an earful. A late stereo reading of *Dve Vdovy* (The Two Widows) is delightful despite a vocally erratic cast, for here Smetana drew on the spirit of rustic energy that made *Prodaná Nevěsta* (The Bartered Bride) Czech opera's ambassador to the world repertory.

Originally a musical comedy, *The Bartered Bride* went through four revisions, gradually picking up arias to elaborate the love plot, dances to invigorate the setting, and recit to redefine genre. The result was the most Bohemian of operas. Even in its ecumenical success, however, *The Bartered Bride* proves Czech opera's isolation, for authentic performances by native specialists are lost to us on the stages of Prague, Brno, Bratislava—while Western *Brides* must be given in translation, which not only deprives us of veteran experts but forces English and German words onto melodies that do not flatter Germanic stresses. A rare attempt to reconcile the cultural differences only proves how supreme those differences are—as when Sarah Caldwell imported her Jeník and Kecal from Prague to assist in a Boston *Bride* in English. At the height of their duet, the lure of authenticity overcame the two Czechs and they lapsed—or ascended?—into the original text, infinitely improving their command of the scene but cutting the Bostonians out of the action.

Oddly, none of the many native recordings of the *Bride* is outstanding. Victor's 1933 set, from the Prague National Theatre under Otakar Ostrcil, keeps sounding as if about to become special, but the magic never happens. Supraphon's first stereo try, under the sensitive Zdeněk Chalabala, is similarly underpowered, and in crowded sonics. Reaching digital technology in a sound track from television, Supraphon gave the excellent Zdeněk Košler the Czech Philharmonic, the top orchestra in the most musical of countries. Košler's lovers, Gabriela Beňačková and Peter Dvorský, are quite fine. But the Kecal, Richard Novák, upholds the Czech tradition that the marriage broker, really the villain of the piece, be sung by a wobbly veteran past his great days.

What these Czech sets lack is a sense of the playful. When *The Bartered Bride* isn't sentimental, it's usually silly, especially when the circus comics come into play. Here, Angel's 1963 set—in German—holds the palm, with Rudolf Kempe conducting Pilar Lorengar, Fritz Wunderlich, the ingeniously stuttering Karl-Ernst Mercker, and Gottlob Frick, best of all Kecals, for his magisterial bass roots the plot's macguffin, the marriage contract, in the authority of village folkways. If we need lyricism from the sweethearts and energy from the circus gang, we look to Kecal for the resonance of tribalism that excites a folk opera's sense of mission.

Having tried history and comedy, Smetana next turned to legend in *Dalibor*, easily his finest opera. It has been called the Czech *Fidelio* for a resemblance not only in plot but in vocal casting. However, there is none of Beethoven's encompassing striving for liberty. Dalibor, like Florestan, is a hero, but there is no Pizarro counterpart, no tyrant—the Rocco figure, jailer Beneš, is the troublemaker who directly brings on the death of hero and heroine.

Still, Smetana rendered homage to Beethoven by giving Milada, *Dalibor*'s Leonore, a recit and aria not unlike "Abscheulicher!", and a *Fidelio* cast could virtually double into *Dalibor*—virtually, as the "Marzelline," Jitka, is not a lyric but a spinto. Supraphon's first *Dalibor*, in rough mono, bears this out with a helplessly overpowered Jitka, who sounds like Mimì attempting *Turandot*. Supraphon remade *Dalibor* twice, in stereo, first at Prague under Krombholc, then at Brno under Smetáček, both with Vilém Přibyl as Dalibor, vocally big enough but not as interesting a character as Beno Blachut had been in mono. Smetáček has a distinct edge sonically, and the more confident cast—Přibyl and Eva Děpoltová tackle the optional high C at the end of the second-act duet; no other pair does. Yet Krombholc offers the more exciting reading, especially in Naděžda Kniplová's Milada, as direly majestic in her opening attack on Dalibor as moving in her succeeding defense of him, her feelings changed by the sight of his noble style. Kniplová has a dangerous top, unsteady but exciting. If it adds a suspense to her scenes that Smetana didn't plan on, still her sense of involvement is astonishing. And in *Dalibor*—as in *Fidelio*—urgency is a basic element.

Antonín Dvořák took up where Smetana left off, but while Smetana was still active: Dvořák's *Jakobín* (The Democrat) is an opera that Smetana might have written, somewhat comic despite the tense title. (The liberal hero's family are landowners, thus the work's conflict.) Supraphon's *Jakobín*, under Jiří Pinkas, which for some reason bears an English-only text booklet, is delightful despite sopranos wobbly (Marcela Machotková) and shrill (Daniela Sounová). Even better, indeed one of Supraphon's best stereo entries, is Dvořák's altogether

comic *Čert a Kača* (The Devil and Kate), one of the nineteenth century's few *opere senza amore*—no love plot—and full of charming evocations of village music, even more informal than those in *The Bartered
Bride*. Anna Barová (Kate), Miloš Ježel (the shepherd who rescues her
from hell), and Richard Novák (the devil) are hardly singers of world
reputation. But there is no limit to what able native artists can do
when set free in the realm of evocative native art. For if Smetana was
Czech opera's socialist, pursuing native subjects on a kind of program—so much history, so much patriotism, so much local color—
Dvořák was Czech opera's ecumenical schoolmaster, traveling to
America in 1892 to serve for three years as head of the National Conservatory of Music (a private institution, despite the federal title, in
New York) and diplomatically composing a "New World" Symphony
that manages to sound American to Americans and Bohemian to
Czechs.

Rusalka, Dvořák's best-known opera, is actually a twentieth-century
work, premiered in 1901. But it looks back on the nineteenth-century
Romantic's choice trope of the mermaid who enchants and thus dooms
a mortal. Here, for once, the comic and sensitive elements are segre-
gated by character, all the quaint and farcical scenes going to two
minor functionaries; and the eternal Czech village is banned for the
more passionately invested magic forest and royal palace. Urania's
heavily cut, German-language mono performance under Josef Keilberth suffers a distant orchestra but boasts Gottlob Frick's tender Water
Sprite and Elfriede Trötschel's winning heroine, working with a leaner
and more focused voice than Czech sopranos tend toward. Supraphon's 1963 stereo album, back in the original language, is not quite
complete—surprising, on four discs—and overcrowds the sonics at climaxes. Nor is the singing all it should be, what with Eduard Haken's
labored Water Sprite and Milada Šubrtová's edgy heroine. Ivo Žídek's
Prince, at least, is excellent, and surely Šubrtová's very strongly felt
performance eventually overcomes her vocal problems, though aficionados will refer to Zinka Milanov's famous Victor cut of Rusalka's
Song to the Moon. What makes this set important is Zdeněk Chalabala's conducting, little less than stupendous.

With Leoš Janáček, we more thoroughly enter the twentieth century, in his often one-of-a-kind librettos; his heavily verbal melodic
lines, as if the music were trying to speak; and his use of ceaselessly
evolving musical germs that serve not only as *Leitmotive* but as the
very fabric of the composition. One senses a distinct break with Smetana and Dvořák, for though Janáček retains his predecessors' habit of
setting many lines twice over, so that characters end up constantly

repeating themselves, and though *Jenůfa* observes the rites of village life (including some delightfully rhythmic folkish choruses), the following five works in Janáček's major repertory draw away from the traditions; into bizarre fantasy, adaptations of plays, and, at the last, in *From the House of the Dead,* a view of life in a Siberian prison camp.

We also break with Supraphon's informal monopoly, for London's Janáček cycle, made with the Vienna Philharmonic under Charles Mackerras, offers superior performances and sonics—and, most important, textual authenticity. Mackerras' digital *Jenůfa,* with Elisabeth Söderström, Eva Randová, Wieslav Ochman, and Peter Dvorský, is a case in point; the sole recording, after three from Supraphon, to reclaim the overture (which the composer cut from the opera to float on its own as *Jealousy*), reinstate the Kostelnička's oft-deleted entrance solo, open up the many niggling cuts imposed on Janáček by Prague's intendant Karel Kovařovič, and clean the score of Kovařovič's "improvements." (As encore, Mackerras gives us Kovařovič's version of the rapturous final duet, so the curious may compare.) It was worth the trouble. From the first moment, the music sounds different: the rattling xylophone returns to the lower pitch Janáček wanted, more a rhythmic sensation than a sound. It doesn't hurt that the performance is superb. Naděžda Kniplová, under Bohumil Gregor on Supraphon's first stereo *Jenůfa* (released here on Angel), was a towering Kostelnička, but London's Randová equals her, albeit in a voice too beautiful for the role; she sounds as young as Jenůfa, her foster daughter. As a sample of transcultural transformation, try LR's relay of the 1974 La Scala *Jenůfa* with Grace Bumbry, Magda Olivero, Robleto Merolla, and Renato Cioni under Jerzy Semkov, Janáček *rusticana.* Coarse sound dimly reveals the Italians' misconstruction of the original's mingling of tenderness and brutality, of love and anger. Verismo bans nuances. Bumbry, in good voice, offers a darker Jenůfa than usual, a mezzo heroine, but she wanders dramatically; and Merolla's lachrymose Laca reduces his scenes to Kovařovič-Cilèa. Olivero, most *verista* of all, is also, interestingly, very on top of her music, often difficult for Italians. Her big solo in Act Two, wherein she foresees her humiliation—"Look at her! The Kostelnička!"—is hair-raising.

Jenůfa, on small-town love and betrayal—*jealousy,* as London's restored Overture reminds us—is conventional in action and accessible in melody, thus the most popular of Janáček's big six. *Výlety Páně Broučkovy* (The Adventures of Mr. Brouček) asserts Janáček's breakaway from typical opera plots, in a picaresque fantasy involving trips to the moon and into the past. Mackerras's version has yet to appear at this writing, but Supraphon's 1962 cast is ingenious, juggling several roles each and an astonishing number of tricky high notes, a feature of Janáček's style but especially exploited here. (Even the chorus bears the freight, the first tenors at one point sustaining a line sitting on high B, A, and C.) Václav Neumann conducts with an apt whimsey, and Bohumír Vich's Brouček captures the essential Czech babbitt, mystified by high-flown lunar art and cowardly in the fifteenth-century Siege of Prague. Other fine cast members will be known to buffs of Czech opera, Libuše Domanínská and Ivo Žídek in particular. But Beno Blachut disappoints in his cameo as Svatopluk Čech, a real-life author, creator of Mr. Brouček, and here a patriot exhorting his people to fight for liberty. A rapt moment, a steal-the-show part—yet Blachut merely utters it.

With *Kát'a Kabanová*, not unlike *Jenůfa* in plot but more conversational in Janáček's still-evolving song-recit, Supraphon's very theatrical stereo reading under Jaroslav Krombholc is quite superseded by Mackerras's team of Söderström, Kniplová, and Dvorský. With *Příhody Lišky Bystroušky* (Adventures of the Vixen Sharp-Ears), generally called *The Cunning Little Vixen*, every set has something to offer. Supraphon's mono, under Václav Neumann, is the most rhythmically invigorated and in Hana Bohmová presents the most characterful heroine, almost too worldly, but most effective in the big narrative scene with the Fox, the spirited Libuše Domanínská. The voices are delightfully close, adding to the confidential quality of this most personal yet most epic of Janáček's operas: all the world of animals and men brought forth in a few vignettes. Supraphon's stereo, under the sensitive Bohumil Gregor, is panoramic; the animals are most humanoid, the humans most caricatured. Helena Tattermuschová's girlish timbre creates a unique Vixen, and the many character roles are managed with zest— hear how the Forester's Wife rips into "O bestio!" (You beast!) at the end of Act One, how the Owl cackles in Act Two, how Harašta's song in Act Three has the air of a bellowed improvisation. However, in the foxy duet at the center of the work, Eva Zikmundová's discomfort in the Fox's high lines robs the scene of magic. Mackerras and his Vienna forces offer a somewhat suave reading, smoothing over a few of Janáček's eccentric but characteristic tight corners. Perhaps that's too suave. But London's digital sonics yield a wondrous clarity, and the cast—Lucia Popp, Eva Randová, Dalibor Jedlička, and Beno Blachut (another cameo, as the Innkeeper)—is excellent. The text booklet bears reproductions of the newspaper cartoons that inspired Rudolf Těsnohlídek's tale, Janáček's source. Lastly, let newcomers sample the piece in Andrew Davis's Columbia disc of the suite arranged by Vaclav Smetáček—a notable last name, combining the first and the greatest of Czech opera composers. Janáček's tone poem *Taras Bulba* is on the flip.

Janáček's last two operas, *Věc Makropulos* (The Makropulos Business) and *Z Mrtvého Domů* (From the House of the Dead), complete the aesthetic transition from Smetana and Dvořák's nationalist comedy and romance into sophisticated forms of humanist rather than patriotic intent. This is the "difficult" Janáček. It is instructive that the voice-rich Sena Jurinac was celebrated as the Jenůfa of her generation, while the vocally erratic but immensely artistic Marie Collier made her name as Emilia Marty, née Makropulos, three hundred forty-two years old and now seeking the elixir she needs to prolong her loveless life. Supraphon's stereo set under Gregor plays *Věc Makropulos* as a subtle horror thriller, with a monstrous heroine (Libuše Prylová), a fiercely drawn tenor lead (Ivo Žídek), and grotesque character parts. Mackerras sees it as a tense comedy of manners, his heroine (Söderström) poignant, his tenor (Peter Dvorský) elegant.

From the House of the Dead, after Dostoyefsky's Siberian novel, is another instance in which Mackerras's squad is not altogether superior to the competition, though again his is a purified text, the opera Janáček wrote—albeit in a virtually unreadable hand that kept editors guessing, after his death, just what it was he *did* write. Supraphon's 1964 set (Epic) under Gregor, however, features more imaginative stereo direction, and has in Přemysl Kočí the best Šiškov, a particular value, as his lengthy monologue all but contains the final act. Supraphon's 1979 remake is the most characterful of these three sets, the most barbaric, as in the interogation of Petrov, the Petersburg idealist, an early scene defining the brutality of prison-camp life. Indeed, amid the many bits and diversions, it is Petrov who roots the opera, centers our sympathies from his arrival at the opera's start to his release at its end. Yet he has little to sing. It is the others—Skuratov, for instance, sung by Ivo Žídek in all three sets—who keep the piece moving.

Toward the end of Janáček's career, a younger colleague confronted Janáček's almost Debussyan manner with an old-fashioned, nationalistic number opera in the Smetana-Dvořák style. This is Jaromír Weinberger's *Švanda Dudák* (Shvanda the Bagpiper), a flash success of the late 1920s. The wandering hero, goaded by a rogue and chased by a faithful wife, is a modern Orpheus whose piping bans all trouble, unfreezing the heart of the Ice Queen and even infecting the citizens of Hell with the delights of the dance. The famous Polka and Fugue, from the scene in Hell, was for decades the only note heard of this wonderfully tuneful fairytale, for the Jewish Weinberger was swept out of German culture by the Nazis, and *Shvanda* had virtually become a

German opera, sung everywhere in German by German artists. (Met performances, under Artur Bodanzky, featured Maria Müller, Rudolf Laubenthal, and Friedrich Schorr.) Strangely, Supraphon never got to *Shvanda*, though the catalogue took in such less importunate titles as Eugen Suchoň's *Svátopluk* and *Krútňava*.

Columbia recorded *Shvanda* in 1981, using the German translation and thus requiring the assistance of German singers—the sole instance, other than German *Bartered Bride* casts, in which a Czech opera has been taped by voices of the international midway. The recording, under Heinz Wallberg and in spanking bright sound, is smashing. Hermann Prey delivers a briskly winsome Shvanda, a modern Papageno; Lucia Popp (the one Czech on hand) as his wife underlines the poignancy of love and hearth in jeopardy; and Siegfried Jerusalem as the rogue Babinský prods with wanderlust, facile and seductive, his best portrayal on disc. This much is basic folk myth: man, wife, bad companion. As the magical cohort, Gwendoleyn Killebrew, Alexander Malta, and Siegmund Nimsgern provide the wonderful menace of great singing. I defy any opera buff to sample the squealing fanfares of the overture—the sound of a thousand bagpipes tuning up—and not stay on for all three discs. A rare thing in opera: the perfect recording.

15

RUSSIAN OPERA

≥⌐≤

Russian opera, in its pre-Soviet golden age of Musorksky, Borodin, Tchaikofsky, and Rimsky-Korsakof, is addictive. Once one samples these robustly tuneful works, one wants to survey the entire set. But there are problems. Even assuming that the language is no barrier, few of the operas have been recorded in the West, leaving virtually the entire repertory to Soviet companies. The problems, then, are availability and sonics, the first because the national Soviet label, Myezhdunarodnaya Kniga, is scarcely available here, the second because, till relatively recently, MK's engineering fell woefully behind Western standards.

There is not much to do about the sound except brace oneself and bear the muffled, sometimes shrill quality of the mono and the garish iron of the early stereo, which becomes quite listenable by about 1965. Availability, however, depends on which company has licensed MK's tapes for domestic release. Here again sonics are a troublesome factor, for MKs were domestically available in the 1950s on a bewildering array of labels, each with its own solutions to the sound situation, ranging from the sensible Westminster through the fumbling Ultraphone to the atrocious Period and Colosseum. Not till Angel in the 1960s and Columbia in the 1970s took charge (with a line dubbed, in both cases, Melodiya) could one count on clear, full reproduction. Lately, as the Melodiya albums have gradually been withdrawn, Chant du Monde, which retailed MK records in France, has brought back many of the old mono sets and some of the stereos in fine sound, with libretto booklets in French only.

About the MK performances themselves, there was never a problem. Even allowing for varying success in casting and the occasional shrill soprano or stringy, whining tenor, they are generally stupendous, conducted with a panache and ring that are nothing short of zealous, and sung with a thrilling sense of character. Soviet singers deal in the libertarian technique of the old golden age, with lots of portamento, ritenuto, and coloring, as if Russian vocal technique had stopped developing when Russia was cut off from the West in 1917.

This was a break for Russian opera, because these singers are never "instrumental" in their approach, never see opera as pure music, as too many singers do today. Russian singers are storytellers, actors. The basses in particular exploit this, relishing the larger-than-life parts Russian opera lavishes on them. Other nations offer basses the occasional great thespian role—the devils in *Robert le Diable, Faust,* and *Mefistofele,* for instance, or *Don Carlos*'s Philip. But rare is the Russian opera that gives the bass no main chance, whether as hero, villain, or comedian—as we note, most thrillingly, in Fyodor Shalyapin's various recordings of scenes from *Boris Godunof,* made both in the studio and live onstage at Covent Garden. Granted, Shalyapin was so cavalier about notes, meter, and even lines that his Boris constitutes virtually an edition of Musorksky, but the poignant intensity of his singing is always amazing, not only dramatic but technically adept. This is a rich Boris, with a bitter laugh socked into the most tender passages, a startling legato soothing the most brutal moments. As it was Musorksky's intention to naturalize opera, deliver it from happy noises into the sounds of Russian life, Shalyapin's highly realistic portrayal is all the more Musorksyan even as it wanders from the letter of the script.

The MK sets of the 1950s have no Shalyapin, perhaps, but many great names in Russian music are accounted for, among them Evgenia Smolenskaya, Galina Vishnevskaya, Georgi Nelepp, Sergei Lemeshev, Ivan Kozlovsky, Pavel Lisitsian, Mark Reizen, and Alexander Pirogov, in the care of such conductors as Alexander Melik-Pashayev and Nicolai Golovanov; and stereo ushered in such names as Irina Archipova, Elena Obraztsova, Vladimir Atlantov, Yuri Mazurok, and Evgeny Nesterenko. These are Bolshoi artists, as MK most often recorded Bolshoi productions, which partly explains the vivid theatricality: these are cast albums. Another boon is the general (but not absolute) distaste for cuts—this at a time when Western recordings routinely observed all traditional opera-house cuts. One drawback, particularly sorry in this unusual repertory, is the lack of text booklets. MK, assuming a Russian-speaking audience and counting on the extraordinarily clear diction of its singers, includes notes and a detailed synopsis. Fine—for Russia. But many of the Western releases included a translation of these same notes—no libretto.* Westminster troubled to prepare full texts—Cyrillic, a transliteration, and the English—and both Angel and Columbia followed suit in their Melodiya boxes.

One other series of Russian operas is of note, London's mono-era sets made with the National Opera of Belgrade. As these were readily available here, and in fine sound, they edged out MK in many collections. The performances feature such singers as Valeria Heybalova, Melanie Bugarinovich, Biserka Tzveych (the only one known for a career in the West, including a few seasons at Bing's Met), Dushan Popovich, Zharko Tzveych, and Miro Changalovich. They are competent, but lack the resonant authority of the Soviet singers. The accents, too, vary alarmingly. Sticking to classic repertory—Musorksky, Tchaikofsky, Rimsky-Korsakof, plus *A Life for the Tsar* and *Prince Igor,* and including full three-way text booklets—London's Belgrade series served as a stopgap till the Melodiya sets reinstituted Russian-made recordings in superb performances and fine sound.

There has been the odd Western foray into this arena, as in Capitol's *A Life for the Tsar* (mono, recently reissued on EMI). Actually, Glinka's original title, *Zhizn za Tsarya* (literally, *Life for the Tsar*) means *Saving the Tsar's Life,* in this case from a Polish invasion, the bass hero being a peasant who detours the Polish army into a forest, preferring death to dishonor. Little else happens in the piece, the first major Russian opera to sound truly Russian rather than like an Italian opera in translation. Capitol took Teresa Stitch-Randall, Nicolai Gedda, Boris Christoff, and conductor Igor Markevitch to Belgrade in 1957 to get a more beautiful performance than the home team had given London. Capitol succeeded. Christoff is unusually subdued here as the heroic peasant; and note Belgrade's own Melanie Bugarinovich, sounding much better than she does for London—the Markevitch effect, perhaps? London's version, by chance, follows the Soviet revision—same music, new text, no tsar—generally known as *Ivan Susanin.*

Glinka really made his history with *Ruslan i Lyudmila,* which somewhat devised the pattern for the "opera legends" that Rimsky-Korsakof later exploited: a picaresque adventure touched with sorcery and spec-

---

*The notes and translations often come through in fractured English. Ultraphone's *Sadko,* listing the opera's various productions, cites a 1930 Met staging in which the tenor hero was sung by one "E. Dzhonson": Edward Johnson, later the Met's General Manager in the pre-Bing years.

tacle, with plenty of chorus and a goodly measure of dance. If little happens in *A Life for the Tsar*, *Ruslan* scurries wildly over the terrain of fantasy—from a wedding feast to a cave, a desert littered with armor and dominated by a giant head (sung by the men's chorus), an enchanted castle, and the devil's magic gardens, all closing, evil defeated and love triumphant, in a gala, whirlwind ensemble. This brings up another problem some Westerners have with Russian operas—their length. Westminster's mono Bolshoi *Ruslan* (Vera Firsova, Ivan Petrov; Kiril Kondrashin) runs to four discs, the average in this repertory. (Some of London's Belgrade sets run to five.) HMV Melodiya squeezed *its* Bolshoi *Ruslan* tape (Bella Rudenko, Evgeny Nesterenko; Yuri Simonov) onto three discs in bright stereo. Each set mirrors the other's virtues: strong conducting and a vital Ruslan. (Note that the knightly hero is a bass, something virtually no Western opera would have attempted in 1842, when *Ruslan* was new.) HMV's sonic advantage obviously recommends it. Perhaps it is the more colorful performance, too, holding to a higher average in the many secondary principals—for instance, Tamara Sinyavskaya's Ratmir, a trouser role written for a sensual contralto. Sinyavskaya fills the bill, plummy and personable even in the absurd scene in which Ratmir is surrounded by a mob of waltzing ballerinas who, the score requests, "with their dancing drive Ratmir to voluptuous fascination."

Let us get a fix on the different sources of recordings using Alyeksandr Borodin's *Knyaz Igor* (Prince Igor), a uniquely Russian opera by possibly the most un-Western of the *moguchaya kuchka*, the "mighty grouplet," known in America as The Five and committed to creating Russian forms for Russian music. Borodin's form in his only opera is original but faulty, yielding something of a sloppy grand opera, the love plot overshadowed by the historical background of war between Russians and Mongols, and the two most interesting characters—the typical roughneck basses—dropped just when we want more from them. Worse yet, Borodin left the work incomplete at his death. Rimsky-Korsakof and Glazunof did the honors; but, as the third act was reconstructed from sketches, it is sometimes omitted, jeopardizing an already precarious story line. MK's superb mono Bolshoi performance under Melik-Pashayev errs here—not only is the third act cut, but, contrary to Russian practice, bits here and there are missing. London's Belgrade set, at least, is complete (and, alone of this series, in stereo). Zharko Tzveych doubles the bass leads, Galitzky and the Mongol Khan, a traditional usage designed to make one star part out of two parts too short for a star. Boris Christoff makes a good deal more of this combination on Angel's stereo set, made in Sofia in the bright, comprehensive sound we seldom hear on Russian recordings. Angel's is a satisfying—at least, a vigorous—performance, taking its cue from Christoff's burly approach. Again, Act Three is missing. Angel's Melodiya Bolshoi set under Mark Ermler, however, yields a full text. Better yet, it takes in some of the biggest names of the time, 1969: Elena Obraztsova, Vladimir Atlantov, Ivan Petrov, Alexander Vedernikov, and Artur Eizen. Unfortunately, they seem to have picked up bad habits from Western singers, losing much of the characteristic Russian intensity and delicacy. On the mono Bolshoi set, Sergei Lemeshev sings young Prince Valdimir's cavatina, a lover's nocturne, with fascinating tact. Atlantov delivers it like a Russian Franco Corelli, not pulling back for a *pianissimo* till the very end, by which time all sense of nocturne has burned away in the starry spotlight. Moreover, the singers are so closely miked (typical of MK right through the LP era) that the set takes on a repellent socko quality that undoes the fine work of Ermler and his rapt chorus. Here is a rare case, then, where the outstanding Russian recording (Pashayev's) is incomplete, and where the best set in good sound (Christoff's) comes from Bulgaria rather than from a Russian home team.

Borodin and his search for a Russian solution to the opera problem leads us to the rest of The Five. Rimsky-Korsakof was the grouplet's most tireless composer of (and editor of other men's) operas. But Musorksky takes pride of place for *Boris Godunof*, by far the most popular Russian opera. We meet Rimsky here, too, for Boris entered the international repertory in Rimsky's adaptation of Musorksky, correcting what was thought to be a primitive, even a bungled composition, full of "wrong" notes and "strange" scoring choices. Rimsky switched scenes around, even cut one (the St. Basil's scene), trying to reestablish Boris as an opera about a tragic hero rather than—as Musorksky wrote it— an opera about Russian history. Worse yet, to conservatives, was Musorksky's shockingly naturalistic approach, his greasy hanger-on characters, abrupt interruptions, colloquial text, cynical choristers, his very tunes themselves—"too Slavic" for opera. Boris's first scene of Muscovites begging Boris to become tsar might have slipped out of a grand opera but for the explicit revelation that the chorus sings not out of conviction but under duress. "If we must howl, might as well howl in the Kremlin," they observe—an idea so antithetic to the way operas were written (till then) that Rimsky cut the line entirely.

Boris is more like a novel in music than an opera, at that an oddly structured novel. Has it *two* heroes, Boris and the pretender Dmitri? Boris dominates, and he is the bass, a signal of importance in Russian music. But Dmitri, the tenor, gets the love plot; though, on the other hand, Musorksky added the romance with Marina—the Polish act—only to placate opera-house drudges. In the end, what makes *Boris* unusual is what makes it appealing. Like *Fidelio, Les Troyens, Carmen,* and *Ariadne auf Naxos,* it is unique, stimulating, refreshing, its own opera. Compare the Shalyapin scenes described above with the 78 highlights of Alexander Kipnis (Victor, Victrola) and Ezio Pinza (Columbia). Each album counts five twelve-inch discs but makes some variation of choice, Kipnis tackling Varlaam's song of the siege of Kazan and the scene with Shuisky, Pinza doubling on Pimen's second scene and throwing in the Polonaise. Pinza is far more disciplined than Shalyapin, Boris *cantante,* but less formidable, life-size where Shalyapin is gigantic. Kipnis splits the difference between the two, stopping short of Shalyapin's quasi-auteurist liberties but richly creating the figure Pinza merely sketches.

Grand-scaled *Borises* have become the rule in Russia as elsewhere, almost invariably in the Rimsky version. MK's first set, based on the Bolshoi's production of 1948, is spectacular. Not only Pirogov's Boris and Nelepp's Dmitri, but most of the characters come alive vividly, tenaciously, the strength of casting extending even to the Simpleton—Lemeshev in a portrayal of unearthly honesty. Maksakova's shrill Marina is a flaw, as is the loss of the first half of the Polish act. But we get the St. Basil's scene; and Golovanov's conducting is essential listening, an Ossia-on-Pelion of excitement. He lashes the Coronation choruses into a frenzy. His cymbal crashes in the Polonaise suggest the Second Coming. It is too much for Soviet mono to take in, perhaps, but it does assert a very Musorkskyan ferocity, especially in the last act, moving from the Kremlin to the Kromy forest. Rimsky reversed the order of these final scenes, keeping the work protagonistic and perhaps fearing that any Boris who could pull off a great death scene would render whatever followed anticlimactic. Indeed, Golovanov and Pirogov present a shattering death. But Golovanov and the Bolshoi still rise to a true theatre climax in the forest scene. We move from the death of a king to the death of a nation.

After this set, most *Borises* seem competent rather than distinctive, even if Christoff plays Pimen and Varlaam as well as Boris, first for Issay Dobrowen (HMV, Capitol, Seraphim mono), then for André Cluytens (Angel stereo), the latter set preferable for its beefy sonics, though Dobrowen's Nicolai Gedda is a far finer Dmitri than Cluytens's Dimiter Uzunov. MK's stereo remake has a statistical distinction in that George London is the only American—I think even the only Westerner—to have sung for the Soviet label, his scenes plonked into the existing Petrov recording under Pashayev. Von Karajan (London) is the least distinctive of all. His all-points-East cast (Ghiaurov, Spiess, Vishnevskaya), gathered in Vienna, boasts a marvelous Rangoni in Zoltan Kélémen. But what Musorkskyan bite Rimsky left in, von Karajan takes out.

What, now, of *Boris Godunof* in Musorksky's own version—or versions, the 1869 original and the 1872 revision with the interpolated Polish romance? Purists may skip the Polish act on Angel's 1977 set under Jerzy Semkow; they may want to skip the set altogether, made in Poland with Martti Talvela, Gedda again, and Božena Kinasz, all fine. But what a gloomy, interior performance! Luckily, MK finally took on the original—1872 again—with Vedernikov, Vladislav Piavko, and Archipova, under Vladimir Fedoseyev (Philips). Here is a performance to rival Golovanov's, less individual but wonderfully sung— Yuri Mazurok plays Rangoni. In fact, the Polish act is the set's highlight, the love duet superior to all others. I imagine that anyone introduced to *Boris* in this recording would then find the Rimsky sets a kind of Disney version. Another piece of statistical trivia; it took MK from 1978 to 1983 to record this *Boris*, a record among records.

Rimsky also prepared the standard edition of Musorksky's *Khovanshchina*—no, more than standard, for, unlike the authentic Boris, the ur-*Khovanshchina* is never heard. Nor is the opera truly popular. As long as *Boris*, it lacks its vitality; almost all of it is *Andante* or *Adagio*. It, too, is an opera whose principal is Russian history, set in Moscow during the political and religious upheavals of the late 1600s. The virtually untranslatable title refers to the faction led by the Khovanskys, just as today's Russians use *Stalinshchina* to mean "the age of Stalin," with a nuance of "the quality of life in that time." *Khovanshchina* is a splendid follow-up for any *Boris* fan who would like more of Musorsky's art, and by hap it has come off well on disc, though MK's 1946 set, from Leningrad instead of Moscow, drops a splendid performance into the void of primitive sonics. London's Belgrade set, reissued in stereo on Richmond, is outstanding, the same folks who trudge through *Boris Godunof* and *Yevgyeni Onyegin* suddenly turning into a troupe of singing actors. Angel's Melodiya set, however, is overpowering, especially in the Marfa of Archipova and the conducting of Boris Khaikin, who had led the Leningrad set. Then, to see how Musorksky's beery opulence takes to comedy, try Moscow Radio's excellent *Sorochinskaya Yarmaka* (Sorochinsky Fair) under Yuri Aronovich (Angel, Eurodisc). This look at Gogolian village life was left in pieces, here joined by Vissarion Shebalin—one of numerous composers who have tried to reassemble the opera's parts: almost everyone, in fact, but Rimsky-Korsakof.

Rimsky has been reproached for tampering with Musorksky, especially as his own operass are traditional in form and prefer glitter to brutality. Musorksky makes opera adapt to life; Rimsky sets everything in an operatic framework, in magical, patriotic epics that dovetail the heroic with the comic. *Snyegurochka* (The Snow Maiden) is representative, the usual tale of the sprite who loves a mortal man, made unusual by the expansive village setting, the evocative nature painting, and the detail of characterization. Most fetching is Rimsky's unflagging melodic gift, though it sometimes overruns the action, as when, in Act One, everything stops dead as Lyel, the trouser mezzo, delivers two songs hymning the woodland life. London's set is ordinary. MK's Bolshoi album, in mono under Evgeni Svetlanov, suffers Vera Firsova's fluttery heroine, though Vishnevskaya is also on hand as Snyegurochka's bombastic rival for the village Lothario. MK's stereo set (Columbia) under Fedoseyev loses the Bolshoi backing but gains in vocal oomph, especially in Archipova's Lyel and Vedernikov's Jack Frost, blustery and musical in the Shalyapin manner (though in fact Rimsky exploits the bass *Fach* far less than his compatriot predecessors, and the role is small). Most interesting, and highly Russian, is the Tsar of Yuri Yelnikov, singing a romantic role in a character tenor's voice (as does Svetlanov's Kozlovsky in the same part). It's not a sound one would welcome as Dmitri or Sadko, but in lyric roles it's common casting in Russia, and it does have its advantages, as when Yelnikov floats up to a ravishing falsetto high B at the end of his first cavatina.

Rimsky is a composer whom the phonograph makes most welcome, as his works are rare onstage in the West. DG released a fine Moscow Radio performance of *Maiskaya Noch* (May Night) under Fedoseyev; the cast is not well known, though the tenor, Konstantin Lisovsky, sounds remarkably like Plácido Domingo. *May Night* is early Rimsky, almost short (three discs), but *Sadko* gives us the mature practitioner of the "opera legend" (this one about the medieval sailor hero of Novgorod), so grandiose of proportion that Rimsky halts his show at the midpoint for a gala. Sadko is wondering where to aim his voyage of fortune, and three foreign "guests" step forth from the crowd at the harbor to argue for their respective homelands. MK's sole recording, in mono under the passionate Golovanov, rises to the occasion with three star cameos: Reizen, furiously blackhearted as the Viking; Kozlovsky, mesmerizing with rubato as the Indian; and Lisitsian, suave in the Venetian's barcarolle, "Gorod pryekrasni!" (Excellent city!). Chant du Monde reissued this *Sadko,* and also MK's brilliant (if in tubby mono) *Kityezh.* More properly, this is *Skazaniye o Nyevidimom*

Gradye Kityezhe i Dyevye Fyevronii (The Tale of the Invisible City Kityezh and the Maiden Fyevronia). Rimsky's most penetrating epic, it is a kind of synthesis of all that had preceded it in Russian opera. In Glinka, nationalism is festive; in Musorksky, it is violent. In *Kityezh*, it is ecstatic. Yet Rimsky's last work, *Zolotoy Pyetushok* (The Golden Cock), often called by the French title, *Le Coq d'Or*, turns the natural energies of Russian opera back upon themselves in a satirically antinationalistsic, pseudo-fantastic, and un-Pushkin-like adaptation from Pushkin with some of the strangest vocal writing in Russian opera, including a tenor who rises to high E, and not in falsetto. Everything is highs and lows in *The Golden Cock*, one reason why it proved a dandy vehicle for Beverly Sills and Norman Treigle at the New York City Opera. MK (Chant du Monde) has a suitably piquant if vocally erratic performance; BJR preserves the Sills-Treigle chemistry, in English: the only complete Russian opera recorded in our language. (Victor issued an abridged Met *Boris* with Giorgio Tozzi and Nell Rankin.) Little of the translation comes through, but one can enjoy Enrico di Giuseppe's high Es.

"To refuse to write opera is a form of heroism," Tchaikofsky said. Fortunately, "I am not that kind of hero, however, and the stage with all its shabby glitter attracts me all the same." It's important to remember that Tchaikofsky was not one of The Five. Unlike Glinka, Borodin, and Rimsky-Korsakof, he was cosmopolitan in his approach, favoring Russian subjects but Western techniques. He poured the dramatic power of his symphonies and the tuneful vivacity of his ballets into his opera scores, further distancing himself from the nationalists. Yet Stravinsky said Tchaikofsky is "the most Russian of us all." In attitude, perhaps? In feeling? Simply in the shape of his melodies? Lenski's nostalgic solo before the duel with Onyegin or Polina's piano-accompanied song in the second scene of *Pikovaya Dama* may well "feel" more essential as Russian melody than anything in *Boris* or *Sadko*. Yet *Orleanskaya Dyeva* (The Maid of Orleans)—a showcase for the astonishing Archipova (Columbia)—is virtually a French grand opera put into Russian. *Charodyeka* (The Enchantress) has the sensory overload and characters of 1840s *melodramma* pumped up with the "local color" *divertissements* of *opéra comique*. MK's mono set under Samosud is exciting, the stereo under Gennady Provatorov just competent, though Columbia gave it Western circulation.

Tchaikofsky joins with The Five in creating his own form in *Iolanta*, a one-act fairytale designed to accompany *The Nutcracker*. Erato caught it live in Paris with Vishnevskaya and Gedda under Rostropovich, but Columbia's Bolshoi box with Tamara Sorokina, Atlantov, Mazurok, and Nesterenko is almost embarrassingly beautiful. The structural organization of the "well-made" opera—the Western kind—is especially apparent in Tchaikofsky's most popular operas, *Pikovaya Dama* (The Queen of Spades) and *Yevgyeni Onyegin,* especially when one hears them next to, say, *Khovanshchina* or *Prince Igor.* Gone are the brawling choruses, the bracingly coarse basses, the barbaric opulence of Russian history. These Tchaikofsky operas are, above all, intimate and lyrical.

Pique Dame (as *The Queen of Spades* is called here) does have its many choral set pieces designed to color in the francophile culture of late-eighteenth-century Petersburg. Without them, the whole suffers—as on Urania's mono abridgment in German, despite a promising cast including Elisabeth Grümmer and Margarete Klose. *Pique Dame* is a "place" opera, music with a geography, and this is very Russian. The two stereo Bolshoi sets, under Khaikin (Angel) and Ermler (Columbia), are pretty good, Khaikin's brightened by secondary people—Archipova's Polina, Mazurok's Yelyetsky—and Ermler's more intense in better sound. But neither set compares to MK's mono Bolshoi reading (Smolenskaya, Verbitskaya, Nelepp; Melik-Pashayev) or Rostropovich's stereo set (DG), made in Paris with Vishnevskaya, Regina Resnik, and Peter Gougaloff, a rare international cast for Russian opera. Creative sonics add to the atmosphere, crucial in this ghostly tale, and if Vishnevskaya is vocally flawed, Gougaloff's heroic Ghyerman is very much in control of a difficult part and Resnik arresting in the Countess's eerie recollection of her Parisian youth. Only London's Melanie Bugarinovich rivals her in the scene.

It's fair to say that only those who haven't read Pushkin's *Yevgyeni Onyegin* can enjoy Tchaikofsky's. The adaptation loses not only the satirical, Byronesque tone of Pushkin's "novel in verse," but also its nuances of character. Pushkin's Yevgyeni and Tatiana are personalities that opera seldom deals with: the professional Romantic hero and the helpless Romantic victim, he materializing in drawing rooms "like Childe Harold, gloomy and languid," she keeping beneath her pillow Richardson's tales of women seduced by charismatic men. Such details help us understand how the man could so casually kill his best friend, how the woman can love, all her life, a man she had met but twice in her youth. Other than Madame Larina's sigh of "Oh, Richardson!" in the first scene, we get almost nothing of the atmospheric decor that enlightens *Pique Dame,* leaving the characters conventional Western operatic types who happen to communicate in Russian.

All the more reason to admire the principals of MK's mono Bolshoi set (Westminster), Vishnevskaya and Evgeniy Belov, for their individualistic intensity, not forgetting the beautiful phrasing of Lemeshev's

Lyenski. These are, however, distinctly Slavic voices, and many listeners prefer Solti's stereo gathering of Teresa Kubiak, Bernd Weikl,
and Stuart Burrows (London), though this must be the most Wester-
nized of Russian opera recordings, in respectable accents but without
the eloquence of the birthright speaker. Back we turn to the natives
for the most vivid of all *Onyegins*: Angel's Bolshoi set (Vishnevskaya,
Mazurok, Atlantov) under Rostropovich. Some fault the conducting
for eccentricity—but this, given the eccentric characters that Pushkin
created, seems to me to be the set's greatest advantage. Rostropovich
brings out the naïve passion of the Letter Scene and the worldly awkwardness of the final duet better than anyone else. The cast, too, is
outstanding, Vishnevskaya matronly compared to the nervous maiden
she sang for Khaikin, but still a comprehensive Tatiana.

After Tchaikofsky, Russian opera's Western popularity closes down,
as operas of the Soviet era have been politically hounded over there
and simply neglected over here. Those works that are available on
disc in the West, moreover, turn against the aesthetics of The Five,
as if Russian opera stopped dead at about 1910 and started up again
on entirely new principles. The nearest thing to a "traditional" piece
is Dmitri Kabalyefsky's tuneful *Colas Breugnon*, delightfully served
(Columbia) by the cast of the 1970 production at Moscow's Stanislaf-
sky and Nyemirovich-Danchenko Theatre, smaller and bolder than
the Bolshoi, maintaining the thespian mandates laid down by its two
eponymous founders.

Dmitri Shostakovich's two operas illustrate the age's political developments. His pseudo-expressionistic lampoon *Nos* (The Nose) appeared in 1930, when the Soviet regime, busy with other matters, let
the arts run their own course. But his sensualistic tragedy *Lyedy Mac-
byet Mtsenskowo Uyezda* (The Lady Macbeth of Mtsensk) arrived in
1934, by which time Stalin was an operagoer; the work was banned
and Shostakovich put on warning. Columbia's superb *Nos*, by the
Moscow Chamber Opera, unfortunately lacks a libretto, an unforgiv-
able marketing error in this vivaciously verbal adventure, after Gogol,
in which a nose, deserting its post on the face of a Major, runs around
Petersburg disguised as a civil servant. Angel issued MK's *Lady Macbeth* in the chastened revision called *Katyerina Izmailova*, but Rostropovich recorded the original version, also for Angel, Vishnevskaya
and Gedda heading the most international cast ever assembled (in
London) for Russian opera, counting principals from England, Sweden, Denmark, Finland, Poland, Bulgaria, Switzerland, Austria, and
even Russia. This is a vastly better performance than that of *Katyerina*, in more sophisticated sonics.

Syergyey Prokofyef points up the complex, contradictory nature of Russian opera, fearing but needing proved operatic techniques, admiring yet neglecting its own traditions. In *Igrok* (The Gambler), after Dostoyefsky's autobiographical tale of obsessive gaming, we have the unique, reckless genius, *enfant terrible* for life; in *Povyest o Nastoyashchem Chelovyeke* (The Story of a Real Man) we have the subservient mediocrity, placating the commissars with a piece of socialist realism about a crippled flier. Westminster released the dispirited *Real Man*— a Bolshoi reading under Ermler—with a historical essay by one "Lionel Garamond, retired French baritone" that blithely ignored, even disguised the oppression that forced Prokofyef to compose the piece. Anyway, most listeners will gravitate to *The Gambler* for the volatile Soviet Radio performance under Gennady Rozhdestvensky (Columbia), with Vladimir Makhov and Nina Polyakova compelling as the gambler and his fellow addict.

At least several decades of political upheaval separate *The Gambler* and the *Real Man*. What then of the comparably contrasting *Lyubof k Tryem Apyelsinam* (The Love for Three Oranges) and *Ognyeniy Angyel* (The Flaming Angel), both composed in the early 1920s, the first an urbane neo-Classical comedy-within-comedy after Gozzi's black romance, the second a Romantic tragedy? Angel's excellent Moscow Radio set of *The Love for Three Oranges* gives us Makhov and Polyakova again, now as the absurd Prince and his nemesis Fata Morgana, who enchants him with the titular obsession for the oranges—which, opened, each give forth a Princess. Two of them die of thrist, this being black; but, this being romance as well, the Prince marries the third. From here, jump to the directly emotional *Flaming Angel,* in a French performance from the Opéra (Westminster) under Charles Bruck, committed but strangely un-Russian for such Russian music. One yearns for Vishnevskaya.

Only in one opera did Prokofyef seem to reconnect his art to that of Russian opera's founders, but it was a big one: *Voina i Mir* (War and Peace). Chant du Monde released MK's 1982 performance, but the prize goes to the earlier set (Columbia), based on the Bolshoi's 1959 production, an all-star lineup right down to the smallest of the thirty-five roles. Melik-Pashayev conducts Vishnevskaya (Natasha), Archipova (Yelyena), Vladimir Petrov (Pierre), Yevgeny Kibkalo (Andryey), Lisitsian (Napoleon), Alexei Krivchenya (General Kutuzof), and such old friends as Evgeniy Belov (Vishnevskaya's first Onyegin) in a bit as Doctor Métivier. Here one senses something of Musorksky's episodic structure and historical-patriotic pageant, right from the startling opening of the entire cast hurling forth invocation to the ecstatic chorus of victory as Napoleon retreats, defeated. The perfor-mance itself is one of the Bolshoi's best, Vishnevskaya's fluttery young girl her foremost characterization on disc and everyone else so persua-sive that Tolstoy himself might have coached them. MGM (Heliodor) issued a cut version with an American cast in the early stereo era. But, once again, it is the Russians who best bring their operas to life, showing us, in their musicality, verbal awareness, and dramatic pun-gency, the clarity of music theatre as cultural affirmation.

16

THE VERISMO ERA

❧

Vocal standards fell during the nineteenth century. Bel canto's ideals of faultless legato and vivacity of embellishment began to give way to the new dramatic approach fostered by certain composers and singers. Wilhelmine Schröder-Devrient, Wagner's ideal Leonore and creator of roles in *Rienzi*, *Der Fliegende Holländer*, and *Tannhäuser*, was said to be acting her way through parts on a dubious instrument. The Parisian furor over tenors' high notes shrilled from the chest threatened the survival of bel canto's elegant falsetto, to Rossini's disgust. Verdi, as we have seen, pushed the baritone's range upward, gaining force but losing dexterity. Such operas as *Mefistofele* and *La Gioconda* seemed to thrust the principals upon the public, emphasizing volume and expressive intensity, causing overextended singers to declaim and shout and even mime in default of being able simply to sing.

To certain ears, all this found its completion in verismo ("realism"), generally dated from the premieres of Pietro Mascagni's *Cavalleria Rusticana* in 1890 and Ruggero Leoncavallo's *Pagliacci* in 1892. What in Rossini's day had been regarded as aberration or, at best, a field expedient for a troubled voice or incompetent technique suddenly became instituted as a style. In fact, verismo as an opera genre had a rather short life. It was "verismo" as a performing style that lived on.

In part a revolt against grand opera, but also a reflection of the new realism of the spoken stage, verismo opera was terse and intense. It had to be intense in order to capture a sense of "real" life: so it had to be terse, to stay intense. There would be none of grand opera's big choral finales and *divertissements*—and none of its chivalric characters and period costumes: verismo favored peasants or the working class in a contemporary setting. Thus, Mascagni's chivalry is rustic, a duel of knives in a Sicilian orchard; and *Pagliacci*'s people are villagers and vagabonds in one of Italy's poorest provinces, Calabria. Many of the titles associated with these two are not pure verismo. Francesco Cilèa's *Adriana Lecouvreur*, for example, with its fashionable, antique Paris, its salons and wigs, is not really a verismo piece. But then the name of the genre quickly became confused with the style of vocal composition and performance that the genre created: the dramatically overstating approach that signaled the official end of bel canto.

While Italy's post-Verdian composers generally wrote but one opera each in the short, violent, modern-dress form and otherwise continued to paint on the expansive canvas of *melodramma* as developed by Verdi, all their operas are called "verismo." The word loses meaning when applied to Mascagni's tender *L'Amico Fritz*; or Italo Montemezzi's symbolist medieval romance *L'Amore dei Tre Re*; or Ermanno Wolf-Ferrari's *Il Segreto di Susanna*, a reconstitution of the old Neapolitan comic *intermedio*. But verismo *as a vocal style* dominated this era in every type of opera. Consider Puccini's *Turandot*. What could be less realistic, less socialistic, for all its speed and violence? Verismo was above all contemporary, not adapted from the heritage of *commedia dell'arte*. *Turandot* is not verismo. But Turandot herself is, for her high-flying power, beyond what any Italian composer had asked of a soprano till then; and Calaf is, for the spinto attack that stimulates even his most sensual phrases; and Liù is, for the plangency that marks her role virtually line by line.

What is verismo singing, exactly? If the well-schooled singing of Adelina Patti's day—the 1870s and '80s—demanded a pure legato, neatly placed high notes, judicious use of vibrato, portamento, and rubato, along with a sense of decorum in the assertion of character, verismo countered in each particular. The legato was jarred by sobs and rages. High notes were assaulted. Vibrato, portamento, and rubato were often abused. And characterization became the first need, edging out pure song. Moreover, verismo singers ground out certain lines in *Sprechstimme* (roughly, "spoken song") to celebrate the theatricality of the new school. Some of them became so carried away onstage that they would contribute to the libretto, as in the exclamations with which Rosetta Pampanini would decorate her Butterfly, or the repeated "Infamia!" that Beniamino Gigli used after "Vesti la giubba," as if addressing the scene to all the husbands in the audience.

It sounds artificial rather than artistic. Yet it impressed—both singers used these outbursts in their complete recordings of the operas.

Connoisseurs shook their heads. But there was worse news: *veristo* singing was bad for the voice. Overworked sopranos would sound like crones while still in their thirties. Tenors would quickly lose their low notes, curdle their top ones. Baritones were loud, not elegant. But composers actively encouraged the new style, for it gave opera a passion, a textual clarity, and a sentimental languor it had lacked when Patti ruled.

Puccini's favorite soprano, Gilda dalla Rizza, might be taken as the exponential verismo singer; listening to her is a cautionary experience. By 1931, when dalla Rizza recorded a complete *Fedora* at the age of thirty-nine, her voice was entirely ruined through *veristo* excesses. There is no denying dalla Rizza's artistry, her commitment. But listening is a chore. She sounds even stranger in scenes from *La Traviata*, collected on an Odeon LP. (Verismo performers customarily invaded Verdi—even Mozart and Cherubini—revisionistically, as if in editions prepared by Giordano.) Dalla Rizza's "Sempre Libera" is a disaster, and in her duet with Germont her young baritone partner sounds as if he's singing with his grandmother.

While verismo became thoroughly acculturated in Italy, elsewhere critics and public found the sometimes gritty tone and nonstop Interpretation irritating. At Covent Garden and the Met, dalla Rizza had no hope of rivaling a singer of the old no-nonsense school—Nellie Melba, say. Melba's Violetta, preserved on a number of singles, collected in an EMI box, lacks dalla Rizza's compulsion. But Melba's sound is pure, clean and lovely. Nor did the descendants of Melba's fans ever make peace with those of dalla Rizza. A *verista* cynosure of the succeeding generation, Maria Caniglia, was, in Italy, thought supreme as Santuzza, Tosca, Maddalena. At the Met, the buffs preferred Zinka Milanov in those parts. One did not need to be a verismo singer to sing verismo opera.

We may view a kind of history of verismo singing by following the fortunes of the founding work, *Cavalleria Rusticana,* on records. Central to this tour is "Voi lo sapete," Santuzza's narrative lament to Mamma Lucia, plentifully recorded because appealing to both sopranos and mezzos. We hear the original Santuzza, Gemma Bellincioni, in 1903, to piano accompaniment; but our enthusiasm at the closeness of history dims at Bellincioni's sloppy diction, intrusive vibrato, and helter-skelter rubato. Bellincioni was celebrated as a singing actress, and she supports the reputation with some lovely portamentos and her overall vitality. But, at heart, she is less singing than sobbing. For a more musical performance of the aria, we turn to Giuseppina Baldassare-Tedeschi, a generation later. We hear a beautiful instrument, fine diction, secure rhythm. Barring some chesty sobs at the very end, this is grand singing. Is this verismo's choice; to act it or to sing it? Does one forbid the other?

Cavalleria's first complete sets reflect this problem—in the third-rate voices firing noisily away in Victor's 1916 Italian set on one hand and the somewhat reticent approach of Columbia's 1927 British cast on the other. Later 78 albums feature native stylists and better voices, especially Victor's 1940 Scala set (Seraphim), conducted with surprising gravity by the composer. Beniamino Gigli is splendid and Lina Bruna-Rasa so demented that it is easy to believe the legend that she attended recording sessions on leave from a mental home. On the whole, this is a clean verismo, strongly felt and strongly sung.

Thus far, the *Cavalleria* scene is largely Italian. But the LP era saw the internationalizing of verismo, with Yugoslavian, Romanian, and Spanish Santuzzas, Swedish and Spanish Turiddus, and a Hungarian-French Mamma Lucia who was born in Stockholm, raised in America, and made her career in the German repertory (Astrid Varnay). Even Italians seemed intent on reforming verismo, breaking its worst habits—making it, perhaps, a little too palatable. These operas want guts as well as musicianship. Victor's mono set (Victrola) with Zinka Milanov and Jussi Björling under Renato Cellini is a case in point. Milanov sings beautifully, of course, including phrases that lesser voices simply scream; and Björling presents a lively Turiddu, very much the village Lothario. But there is little sense of confrontation, and this opera is made of confrontations: Lola's with her lover and her rival, Alfio's with Turiddu, and Santuzza's with—literally—everybody, one after another.

Angel's mono Scala set offers a uniquely elegant verismo, thanks to Tullio Serafin's subtle conducting, Giuseppe di Stefano's lyric buoyancy, and Maria Callas's very inward intensity, Santuzza as Giuditta Pasta. Callas's stylistic grip is remarkable. Even her glottal gulps—one of verismo's most exasperating corruptions—are classy; she makes them Bellinian. And she brings out phrases such as the aria's repeated "Me l'ha rapita" (She stole him from me) with accents that are at once grandiose and judicious. Hear, too, her wonderfully aggressive attack as Turiddu enters the square for their big duet. This is a kind of reconstructed verismo, no less theatrical yet more musical than the thud-and-blunder procedures exemplified in those same years on Cetra and London (Richmond).

Moving into the stereo age, we note that Herbert von Karajan's

Scala set (DG) is even more silken than Serafin's, yet unfailingly *italiano*. An almost implausibly radiant opening suggests less Sicily than Switzerland, even Liechtenstein. But Fiorenza Cossotto and Carlo Bergonzi show fine form, Bergonzi in particular overmatching the more celebrated Mario del Monaco (London) and Franco Corelli (Angel) in steel and warmth. Cossotto can't get through "Voi lo sapete" without that touch of *veristo* grouching, but the big duet has breadth and polish, as if verismo were rising above itself. Is this the genre's fate—to be *tamed*? *Cavalleria*'s most recent recordings suggest as much—in, say, the neatness of Luciano Pavarotti's Siciliana and the poise of Julia Varady's "Voi lo sapete," on London under Gianandrea Gavazzeni. True, Varady unbridles a bit for the duet, and once it gets going Pavarotti heats up as well. Still, this is a careful rendering, much better disciplined than Bellincioni's creator disc but much less interesting.

Victor's latest try, with Renata Scotto and Plácido Domingo under James Levine (a rare bargain on a single disc), is also careful. But here we get the bite of theatre as well, in that elusive "performance atmosphere" that verismo opera especially needs when it sets up shop in the studio. Serafin has atmosphere, Cellini doesn't—and this is why Serafin's set is still great and Cellini's never was even good. Levine's has it to spare. Nowhere else on records does Lola's offstage interruption of Santuzza and Turiddu sound so accidental as here; Isola Jones's "Oh!" as she enters sounds really surprised. Finest of all is Scotto in her best voice. She can balance verismo's fury with its pathos, spitting out "Assai più bella è Lola," yet is ravishing in "No, no, Turiddu." This richness of personality is what we miss in Riccardo Muti's reading with Montserrat Caballé and José Carreras. Yet this performance is genuine verismo in its own way. Muti lays it out on the grand scale, with a wonderful swing for the opening choruses; and if Carreras's Siciliana is not as big in voice as some, it has the passionate insinuation of a mean-streets serenade. Caballé partners him well, and Muti balances all out, splitting the difference between the old-time fire and modern ice. Verismo, then, is adaptable. Tamed, it still soars, still moves and startles us. Certainly, Angel's wide dynamic range startles, at least on my German EMI pressing. No matter how high your volume setting, you'll have to turn it way up to hear the Siciliana—and if you don't turn it back down before Muti crashes in after Carreras's last note, your house will explode.

Pagliacci's discography affirms verismo's stylistic development from rough, Italianate intensity to an ennobled international beauty that, at its best, is yet intensely Italian—from HMV's 1907 set under Carlo Sabajno, cast entirely with front-line singers and supervised by Leoncavallo himself, on to Muti's 1980 Angel set with a cast that might have been drawn from a United Nations council. To instruct us, Opal has rereleased the 1907 album, in correct pitch and preserving the original side breaks in spacing bands. The set is a document of how quickly traditions of cuts and showboating high notes may be set— and this with the composer in attendance. However, he must have liked the performance, edged down from theatre size for the fragile technology, but nonetheless superior to most complete sets of the era. Indeed, this was one of the very first. Antonio Paoli shows us how hard Canios had to work, oversinging relentlessly on "Ridi, Pagliaccio" (though the transposition of the repeat of "A ventitre ore" to the upper octave apparently hadn't come into fashion yet). Paoli's Nedda, Giuseppina Huguet, matches him for verismo cultism, with a ton of chest voice and plenty of glottal gulping. She is a fine artist, taking the Ballatella with a rhythmic swing many a more polished soprano could use; yet she disfigures it with shtick. Francesco Cigada, the Tonio, is the most disciplined of the three, yet, once the drama overtakes him, he too cuts loose. At least we get a telling picture of Italian opera when Italian opera was *contemporary*—and a taste of primitive recording technology in the acoustic horn's failure to capture the sound of the timpani. (*Pagliacci* has plenty of drumming, and each blow sounds like the crash landing of a small flying saucer.) Of course Muti reproves the contentions of tradition: the added high notes are banned, the cut in the love duet is opened, and Tonio, not Canio, delivers "La commedia è finita," all as written. But can Muti be more authoritative than the author?

Pagliacci has fared more unevenly on disc than *Cavalleria*, but more interestingly, for its characters have more to do. *Cavalleria*'s people tend to the elemental: Alfio is gruff, Mamma Lucia worried, Lola sly. Only Santuzza and, to a lesser extent, Turiddu have a rounded vitality. More happens in *Pagliacci*, and thus casting is more vulnerable to weak elements. Victor's Gigli (Seraphim), for instance, is the very model of a great singer in a great role, arresting in his dialogues and thrilling in "No! Pagliaccio non son!" But his Nedda, Iva Pacetti, has an unpopular voice; Toscanini once called her a sheep. Montserrat Caballé, opposite Domingo on Victor, is gorgeous in the love duet but keeps dropping words, and certainly makes no attempt to sound like the kind of woman who would go on the stage. Teresa Stratas (Philips) is just the opposite, a colorful personality vocally out of sorts. Domingo is here as well, better than for Victor, no doubt through his work with Franco Zeffirelli—Philips's album is in fact the sound track to Zeffirelli's film.

Then there is von Karajan, of the chaste—better, the sumptuous—verismo. His *Pagliacci* (DG) is even more exquisite than his *Cavalleria*. Surely *Pagliacci* cannot come off well thus. Yet it does, partly through the commitment of a fine cast—Bergonzi, Taddei, and, for a delightful change in major-label cliché casting, Joan Carlyle—and partly through the conductor's agile musicality. This is bel canto verismo. For a more correctly styled *Pagliacci*, listeners should sample the two early-electric 78 sets, both now on OASI, Victor's (at least for Apollo Granforte's grand-scale Tonio) and, generally preferable, Columbia's with the earnest Francesco Merli, the demonic Carlo Galeffi, and the enticing Rosetta Pampanini, an ideal Nedda. Returning to our stereo-era corrector of verismo traditions, Riccardo Muti (Angel), we find a good compromise with Scotto, Carreras, and Kari Nurmela, something between sharp and beautiful. And of course the flip sides bear Muti's *Cavalleria* with Caballé's Santuzza, something between beautiful and beautiful. For those who want opera's favorite double bill in one box, Angel's Callas–di Stefano–Serafin set is the mono choice. Those who want more vivid sonics and fear von Karajan's ultra-smooth readings can hardly do better than Muti.

Seeking out the rest of Mascagni and Leoncavallo, we apply to the undergrounds, especially MRF's transcriptions of Italian performances, theatre and concert. MRF seems especially fond of Mascagni, having released the moodily Romantic *Guglielmo Ratcliff*, the zesty *commedia dell'arte* replica *Le Maschere* (The Masks), the chevaleresque *Isabeau* (a sort of Italian *Lady Godiva*), the Puccinian *Lodoletta*, and the weighty *Parisina*, weighted, unfortunately, with almost nonstop recitative. Besides revealing how much variety lies in Mascagni—in verismo generally—MRF includes extensive notes and appreciations along with the text booklets. For instance, MRF's pairing of two of Mascagni's shorter works, *Silvano* and *Zanetto*, takes in not only bits of other Mascagni as filler but a bonus disc of a second *Zanetto* performance to complement the main one (Carteri, Simionato; Votto), compelling but in dubious sound. MRF's sets vary greatly in quality, but there is no denying the artistry, and *veristo* entitlement, of Magda Olivero in Mascagni's *Iris*, so essential to the verismo repertory that MRF put out two different Olivero *Irises*, the second, with Amsterdam's Concertgebouw Orchestra under Fulvio Vernizzi, the stronger reading in vastly better sound. Of all of Mascagni's little-known titles, *Iris* most repays investigation: a tunefully symbolistic Japanese tale in which art (soprano Iris), romance (tenor Osaka), and commerce (baritone Kyoto) play out a conflict on the role of poetry in a brutal world.

Some of Mascagni's lesser-known titles have made it onto commercial discs. *L'Amico Fritz* claims a venerable Cetra box with Pia Tassinari and Ferruccio Tagliavini, disappointingly humdrum even in the sumptuous Cherry Duet (done to a turn on a two-sided Victor 78 by Dusolina Gianinni and Tito Schipa). Angel wins, with the youthful Mirella Freni and Luciano Pavarotti in a zestier *Fritz*. But it was up to Cetra to catch *Il Piccolo Marat*, Mascagni's look at French Revolutionary terror to a outstanding libretto by Giovacchino Forzano. The collaborator as well of Leoncavallo, Giordano, Puccini, and Wolf-Ferrari, and a stage director at La Scala, Forzano is one of the few verismo personalities who is neither composer nor singer. Forzano, typical *veristo*, exploited the theatre of contrasts, as in the clammy calm of *Cavalleria*'s Intermezzo amid the suspense, or in *Pagliacci*'s farce disrupted by murder. There is plenty of violence, too. "Do not look for melody," Mascagni warned. "Do not look for culture. In *Marat* there is only blood!" Indeed, Forzano pulls many a surprise. Alas, Mascagni doesn't, and Cetra's set affirms his failure with a horribly erratic cast—the superb Virginia Zeani, the monotonous Giuseppe Gismondo, the forgivably troubled Afro Poli, and the blustery Nicola Rossi-Lemeni. There is, at least, an interesting love duet, a popular item on 78s in the early 1920s, when the opera was new. Most start at "Va nella tua stanzetta," about halfway into the scene, where the tenor has all the best lines. Ettore Bergamaschi makes the most of them, leaving Maria Zamboni to twitter helplessly; Luigi Abrate and Giuseppina Baldassare-Tedeschi are much better, clean and musical. The most famous version tackled the entire duet on four sides in electrical sound, Hipolito Lazaro trumpeting out his famous high notes and Maria de Voltri very touching, the two of them reaching a passionate climax. Rubini included the duet on a Lazaro recital. Hear it to sample an authentic document of verismo at its best—and Lazaro created the "little Marat," so we taste history here.

Leoncavallo's recorded library raises another of verismo's problems: its fondness for adapting stage works written as vehicles for gala actresses. In their heyday, no doubt Bernhardt, Réjane, and others gave these leaden melodramas wings. But such plays don't need music—scarcely deserve it, even. Leoncavallo's *Zazà*, a backstage tearjerker that achieved ultimate completion as a Paramount film vehicle for Claudette Colbert, is typical, the kind of thing even verismo buffs cannot champion. Cetra's Clara Petrella, Giuseppe Campora, and Tito Turtura do their best. One cannot say as much for the gang squalling through Cetra's reading of Leoncavallo's *La Bohème*, like Puccini's from Henri Murger's novel but closer to the source. Leoncavallo, who usually wrote his own librettos, included more of the novel's reckless fun than Puccini did, and closes on a note of bitter despair. "A merry life," Murger observed, "and a terrible one." Alas, Leoncavallo also included about four good tunes and hours of fill. Still, Puccini veterans may enjoy encountering a tenor Marcello, a baritone Rodolfo, and a mezzo Musetta. Orfeo has a splendid performance in digital sound with a most unexpected cast: Lucia Popp, Alexandrina Milcheva, Franco Bonisolli (how did he get in there?), and Bernd Weikl under Heinz Wallberg. Verismo browsers should also take note of the fourth side of Victor's Caballé-Domingo-Milnes *Pagliacci*, a sampler of arias from *Zazà*, *La Bohème*, and *Chatterton* by the three stars: a chance to hear most unusual material sung by the most pleasantly usual voices.

It was the verismo generation's curse to be known outside Italy as "one-opera composers"—for one was all we'd ever hear. Italo Montemezzi is a classic case. Few operagoers have seen *L'Amore dei Tre Re* (The Love of Three Kings), much less could name other Montemezzi titles. *L'Amore* counts two very different readings, Cetra's by verismo experts (Petrella, Amadeo Berdini, Capecchi, Bruscantini; Basile) and Victor's smoother international crew (Moffo, Domingo, Pablo Elvira, Siepi; Santi). Cetra's is so atmospheric a performance that even in mono we feel as if we were looking out on Italy from a castle window; Victor's is perfunctory, though Elvira makes something of his part and Domingo, perfectly cast, is superb in killing voice. It happens, however, that the Met vaults hold a tape of a Saturday broadcast from 1941 conducted by the composer with Grace Moore, Charles Kullman, Richard Bonelli, and Ezio Pinza. It is amazing. Moore was not the most secure of sopranos, and of the men only Pinza fielded an important instrument. Montemezzi must have been some coach, then, for the performance ignites from the first bars and never flickers. The end of Act Two, in which the blind old Archibaldo slowly stalks offstage carrying the body of the strangled Fiora (another of the shocking curtain-pictures that versimo cultivated), is utterly hair-raising.

Francesco Cilèa is another one-opera man. He also wrote *L'Arlesiana*, which Cetra recorded with Tassinari and Tagliavini. But he mainly wrote *Adriana Lecouvreur*—not for Magda Olivero, though he might as well have, as she came to own the part, at Cilèa's own admission. Live, at Naples in 1959 (MRF, Cetra) with Giulietta Simionato, Franco Corelli, and Ettore Bastianini, Olivero uniquely demonstrates verismo's procedures—its grand gestures, vocal niceties, cries and whispers, all, admittedly, through a voice that is anything but pretty. MRF's Olivero *Irises* suffer uneven company, but this *Adriana* is famous for fullness of casting. Simionato is not only vocally imposing but subtle (a rare quality in this repertory), and while Corelli isn't, he is in splendid voice. Bastianini is the weak link, trying to sing his way through a part that calls above all for picturesqueness of character, as the harried theatre director who loves and understands Adriana better than the tenor but must settle for being her most supportive fan.

Simionato also made a commercial *Adriana,* with Renata Tebaldi and Mario del Monaco (London), an underrated set enlightened by a surprisingly textured del Monaco, less consistently burly here than in many of his Tebaldi partnerships. (A spacious acoustic helps, in keeping him somewhat distant from the microphone.) This was Tebaldi's favorite role, and one of her loveliest recordings. Perhaps Franco Capuana's unimpassioned conducting undermined the set's popularity; Mario Rossi, in the Naples tape, is similarly underwhelming. But conducting is not the problem over at Columbia, where James Levine truly *discovers* the piece for us, exploiting its many orchestral spotlights—the touching peroration to "No, la mia fronte," for instance, beautifully realized. Capuana just plays it. Better yet, Levine bends Renata Scotto, Elena Obraztsova, Plácido Domingo, and Sherrill Milnes into a confidentially storytelling quartet. It is, however, a somewhat husky cast, one superb *verista,* one Princess Igor, one valid tenor, and one Rigoletto trying not to be clumsy. At moments, one misses the all-out, smash-and-grab, take-no-prisoners verismorama of the Naples gang; but this is, in all, a beautiful rendition in ravishing sound.

Umberto Giordano holds a more important position than Montemezzi and Cilèa—or, rather, his *Andrea Chenier* does. This may well be the most popular verismo opera after *Cav* and *Pag* (of course excluding Puccini), with a classic triangle of sensitive heroine, rebellious hero, and menacing baritone: the *Tosca* Syndrome. Columbia's 1931 set has Mascagni's electrifying Santuzza, Lina Bruna-Rasa, unfortunately with the bleating and sobbing Luigi Marini and the blustering Carlo Galeffi. At that, Bruna-Rasa's single of "La mamma morta" (on an OASI recital) sings more truly than her reading on the complete set. No matter: for Victor's 1941 album (Seraphim) is the 78 classic, with Gigli at his most inspired. Here was a tenor, born to what many claim was the century's most beautiful voice, who increasingly disappointed his supporters with overbearingly demonstrative performances in lyric roles or unimpressive assaults on heroic ones. In *Andrea Chenier* we find Gigli at the midpoint, his sound strengthened, not yet grown pushy, and his imagination stimulated, not yet exhausted. As with Maria Callas's Tosca, or Jon Vickers's Énée, or Beverly Sills's Manon, the phonograph caught the singer at the perfect time in the perfect role. With Maria Caniglia and Gino Bechi (as well the young

Giulietta Simionato, Giuseppe Taddei, and Italo Tajo in small parts) under Oliviero de Fabritiis, this is verismo of such presence that stereo versions pale by comparison, such as those by the stentorian del Monaco and the dignified Tebaldi (London), or by Franco Corelli (Angel), outdoing Gigli in power but not musicality, and saddled with the schoolmarmish Antonietta Stella under the immobile Gabriele Santini. Nor has the latest generation, Victor's Domingo and London's Pavarotti, successfully defied Gigli.

Chenier is a poet obsessed by ideals of beauty, liberty, and honor, and unless we sense this commitment the opera makes no sense: or why would Chenier stay in Paris, denounced, to meet Maddalena? Why would he lead her jubilantly to death? Those who favor good sonics should consider London's digital set, despite Pavarotti's slack involvement, for Chailly's conducting and some good singing here and there. The enlistment of Astrid Varnay as the Countess and Christa Ludwig as Madelon is commercially impressive but stylistically irrelevant—Varnay sounds like a witch trying to fit in at a Tupperware party. But Chailly is masterly, churning up a real riot for Act Two's tumbril parade and painting a lovely calm in the E Major interlude before the act's big duet. And we do have Caballé as Maddalena, merely checking in till a stupendous "La mamma morta."

Giordano may be verismo's two-opera man, as *Fedora* hangs on, especially in London's set with Olivero, del Monaco, and Gobbi under Gardelli. Tebaldi was to have led this set, but illness forced her cancellation, and London's producer Terence McEwen, a longtime Olivero fan, slipped the unusual diva into her first complete commercial recording in thirty years, her only one in fine studio sound. An important debut, this, for Absolute Verismo in an age that loves pretty, not expressive, voices. London's *Fedora* is not a great performance; but then, this is not a great opera. Olivero and Gobbi, lightening up for what is virtually a *buffo* role, are quite fine, but del Monaco is crude, shouting his way through "Amor ti vieta." Fernando de Lucia takes it, on an ancient 78, in a near-croon with blissful ritardandos—excessive but more stylish. Strangely, Gardelli deletes Olga's aria, making this secondary role, Gobbi's foil, virtually that of a comprimaria. Gilda dalla Rizza's old 78 set included it. Pirate *Fedora*s give us Tebaldi and di Stefano (MRF) and Virginia Zeani and Domingo (LR), neither set very taking, though Domingo is excellent. MRF went on to more Giordano, most successfully in *La Cena delle Beffe* (The Dinner of Jests), from Sem Benelli's play, set in Medici Florence, about a feud played out in gruesome jokes. The Barrymore brothers made the original a great hit in New York; MRF's cast is less distinguished, but listenable.

Verismo also claims its no-opera men, at least as far as their international reputations run. Franco Alfano is exemplary, known to opera buffs as the man who completed *Turandot*, but not for any of his own titles. MRF's 1979 RAI broadcast of *Sakùntala* tells us why Toscanini favored Alfano for the thankless task of composing Puccini, for this Indian tale shares some of *Turandot's* quaint *colorito*. It's a nice reading, under Ottavio Ziino, with Celestina Casapietra and—an old friend to New York City Opera buffs—Michele Molese. Ottorino Respighi is another of verismo's mystery men, though Eve Queler presented his *Belfagor* to New York in concert, revealing not the contorted pathos of *Pagliacci* or *Tosca* but charming comedy with a tender puppy-love plot. BJR preserves Queler's *Belfagor*, excellently sung by Americans— Nancy Shade, James McCray, and Chester Ludgin—whom the big labels sadly neglect.

Verismo contains more comedy than most people are aware of, as witness Ermanno Wolf-Ferrari, who submitted his hot-blooded, proletarian *I Gioielli della Madonna* (The Jewels of the Madonna) and then concentrated on lyrical farces based on the work of Carlo Goldoni, the "purifier" of Venetian *commedia dell'arte* (as opposed to Carlo Gozzi, Venetian *commedia's* stimulator). It would not be unfair to see Wolf-Ferrari and Puccini as antipodes of verismo, just as, in the eighteenth century, Goldoni and Gozzi were antipodes of *commedia*. MRF preserves a vital *Gioielli* under Alberto Erede with Pauline Tinsley, André Turp, and Peter Glossop. It's short on voice—Tinsley's wiry instrument fails to connect with Maliella's first-act showpiece, the Canzone di Cannetella—but electric with character. MRF also carries the truer Wolf-Ferrari of the Goldoni comedies, ideally in *Il Campiello* (The Square), one day in the life of a Venetian neighborhood. The RAI broadcast under Ettore Gracis is very pleasant; more important, the opera is most illustrative of this subsector of verismo in its lagoon dialect, graceful dramaturgy, and—most telling of Wolf-Ferrari, half German but born and buried in Venice—revival of Venetian opera's duenna-sung-by-a-tenor (as in *Poppea's* Arnalta), here doubled into two characters. Wolf-Ferrari revived yet another ancient trope in *Il Segreto di Susanna* (Susanna's Secret), reminiscent of the short comic *intermedio* played on the bills with serious works. The secret is Susanna's cigarette habit; her husband thinks it's a lover. London (Chiara, Weikl; Gardelli) plays it all for charm, husband Weikl very sympathetic in his torment; we feel he would do anything to be reassured.

Columbia's digital disc (Scotto, Bruson; Pritchard) is more dramatic. Here the husband is not worried but furious; a close call for Scotto, at her best here, in rich sonics that send the overture swelling into one's living room.

Perhaps the essential verismo composer was Riccardo Zandonai. The great House of Ricordi, publisher of and agent for Verdi and most of his successors, handled Zandonai with great care, taking him for the next Puccini. This Zandonai was only more or less: more in his greater sophistication as a musician but less in his limited melodism. At least, if he is another "one-opera" man, it's a masterpiece: *Francesca da Rimini*, still popular in Italy. Here is a classic verismo prototype—a costume romance with *Tosca* principals taken from the theatre of Gabriele D'Annunzio. I could not recommend an opera more enthusiastically, for beauty of expression and integrity of form—but we lack a great recorded statement. Cetra's mono set, under the brilliant Antonio Guarnieri, offers Maria Caniglia in a part she was born to play, unfortunately some forty-five years before taping time, when she was beyond her prime, ravaged by overwork. As her brother-in-law and lover Paolo, Giacinto Prandelli is too light for a heavy role, but imaginative and resourceful, and Carlo Tagliabue, in the Scarpia part as the husband, supplies the needed danger. A very close near-miss. Only one other commercial entry touched *Francesca*, London's highlights with Olivero and del Monaco, made on time spared from their *Fedora*. They had sung the piece together at La Scala in 1959 under Gavazzeni, and MRF records the performance. This is *plenty* verismo, with rhythmic liberties, moments of *Sprechstimme*, and the odd scream: a sloppy but committed performance, albeit in such distant sound that the all-important viola solo in Act One that makes the first full statement of the love theme is almost obliterated. And the erratic Gavazzeni is at his least persuasive here.

Cetra's relay from Trieste in 1961 brings a more disciplined *Francesca* with one or two fewer cuts than heretofore and a forceful but unlovely cast: Leyla Gencer, Renato Cioni, and Anselmo Colzani under Franco Capuana. BJR counters with Eve Queler's New York concert with Raina Kabaivanska, Plácido Domingo, and Matteo Manuguerra, beyond question the prettiest reading: also the most heavily cut. No, slashed. No—*devastated*. Too bad, for despite the scrappy playing, Queler energizes a ready orchestra and has her singers coached and *pronti*.

MRF has apparently embarked on a Zandonai cycle, with *Conchita* (Zandonai's "Cav-Pag" verismo entry) and *I Cavalieri di Ekebù* already logged and *Giulietta e Romeo* promised. *Ekebù* gets its odd title from the Swedish location of Selma Lagerlöf's novel *The Story of Gösta Berling*, its source. Not astonishingly, the opera was a hit in Sweden, and the original Stockholm cast recorded a great deal of the piece for HMV and Odeon, in Swedish, including choral and orchestral segments. Swedish EMI collected fifty minutes of these 78s into a highlights disc in 1974, an odd excursion out of verismo in the inwardly lyrical approach of Einar Beyron, Kirsten Thorborg, and Brita Hertzberg under Nils Grevillius. MRF's Mirto Picchi, Fedora Barbieri, and Rina Malatrasi render verismo unto verismo again, in a heavily cut but superbly enacted performance under Alfredo Simonetto, Malatrasi very sensitive and Picchi and Barbieri two giants striding at their ease. Italians still speak of this performance when discussing Zandonai, so verismo students should take note, not least of MRF's fine notes and annotations.

The verismo era peaked in the 1920s, for Puccini's *Turandot* was the last world success that verismo produced. Even in Italy, verismo's practitioners were silent or in eclipse by 1930, and the two outstanding younger composers of opera, Gian Francesco Malipiero and Luigi Dallapiccola, adopted other approaches, the former favoring neo-Classicism and the latter a version of tone-row organization. (Shockingly, not one of Malipiero's many operas has been recorded, even on undergrounds. Dallapicolla's *Il Prigioniero* is discussed in chapter 22.)

A few Italian composers continued to treat *veristo* subjects—emphasizing, ironically enough, the lurid realism of verismo's very first days. Renzo Rossellini, for instance, set *Uno Sguardo dal Ponte* (A View from the Bridge), based very closely on Arthur Miller's play. As LR's recording reveals, the passionate bursts of melody that sparked Mascagni and Leoncavallo in their youth are snuffed out: here is verismo's form, not its spirit.

The most successful of these latter-day *veristi* is Gian Carlo Menotti, sometimes termed an American composer because he settled in the United States and for the most part set English texts. Like Leoncavallo, Menotti wrote his own librettos, reviving the slashing theatricality of *Cav* and *Pag*. But as with Leoncavallo (and most of his colleagues), Menotti's first flood of tunes soon gave way to a trickle, and only his earlier works are on disc. The earliest, *Amelia al Ballo* (Amelia Goes to the Ball), claims a competent, slightly cut mono LP in Angel's Scala series (Carosio, Prandelli, Panerai; Sanzogno), and Victor caught *The Saint of Bleecker Street* (in mono) and *Maria Golovin* (in stereo) in their premiere mountings on Broadway, underlining Menotti's close association, in the middle third of his career, with commercial stagecraft. This, at least—as we will see in Chapter 25—

is a very American notion. It happily provides us with a handsome reading of Menotti's best opera, *The Consul* (Decca mono), fresh from the Ethel Barrymore Theatre in 1950, with Patricia Neway, Marie Powers, and Cornell MacNeil under Lehman Engel. Oddly, Columbia's mono souvenir of *The Medium* (Odyssey) in its 1947 Broadway cast (with its comic curtain raiser, *The Telephone*) is vastly outmatched by Columbia's studio remake, and not simply because of the stereo advantage. Broadway's medium, Marie Powers, was an essential Menotti artist, and had more than a little of the pugnaciously eccentric Madame Flora in her. One might think that Menotti had based the character on Powers; in fact, he first met her at the eleventh hour of casting. Still, the later recording, conveniently stuffed onto one LP, boasts the fascinating Regina Resnik as Flora, sour above the staff but gripping and even touching as the fake spiritualist who ends up haunted by her own tricks. Judith Blegen employs a too-too diction totally wrong for the daughter of a nickle-and-dime seeress, but vocally Blegen improves on the mono's pallid Evelyn Keller. *The Consul* remains Menotti's most sustained melodrama, still timely in its look at Eastern Europeans trying legal channels to escape to Western liberty. But browsers in this odd corner of opera history, this one-man "verismo revival," may find the stereo *Medium* the choice Menotti performance.

One aspect of verismo we have yet to cover: its innovative emphasis on overtures and intermezzos. A long-forgotten Angel mono disc presented such excerpts of Zandonai, Mascagni, Wolf-Ferrari, and a few others under Alceo Galliera with the Philharmonia, a superb taste of verismo's expansive orchestration, far beyond what Verdi worked in. Think of the poignant colors in the *Manon Lescaut* intermezzo, the neo-Classical bustle of the overture to *Il Segreto di Susanna*. And, for an encore to all this, try Renata Scotto's *Serenata* (Columbia), an hour of songs by verismo composers. To John Atkins's splendid piano accompaniment, Scotto reveals an unexpected side of this art, one in which elegance and wit edge out fury and passion. After helpings of *Cav*, *Pag*, and *I Cavaleri di Ekebù*, it's a delightful way to clean the palate.

17

PUCCINI

☙❧

Of all so-called verismo composers, Puccini stands out for his very popularity: for retaining a broad hold on the international repertory long after his colleagues had dwindled into one-opera reputations everywhere but in Italy. Like them, Puccini was verismo purely by formality. He shares their vocal casting, delighting in the expressive artiste more than in the well-schooled singer. But a tour through his operas reminds us how many different genres verismo in fact contains.

Puccini's first two operas, *Le Villi* and *Edgar,* not only precede *Cav* and *Pag* chronologically; they look backward, to the *melodramma* of lyric voices and fantastic plotting. Columbia has both with Scotto, tactful in the brief *Le Villi* (The Witches) and untamed in the awkwardly Verdian *Edgar,* partnering Carlo Bergonzi. Neither work especially enchants the Puccinian, but Puccini's third opera, *Manon Lescaut,* gives us the composer's style in full flower—and what could be less like verismo, with a period setting, wigs and minuets, and a social outlook favoring glamour over realism? Nor is the singing truly of the emphatic style a Santuzza or Canio needs. Manon is essentially a lyric soprano, importunate in "In quelle trine morbide" and cunning in "L'ora, o Tirsi." Only in a few moments must she open up forcefully. Similarly, the tenor's "Ah, Manon" is disheartened, not desperate, and "Guardate! Pazzo son" is clarion, not lachrymose. Perhaps that's why Montserrat Caballé and Plácido Domingo (Angel) seem ideally cast, especially as conductor Bruno Bartoletti doesn't try to turn the show into *Andrea Chenier* but lets his singers *sing.* True, in mono years

Licia Albanese and Björling (Victor, Victrola) pointed up the characters more aptly, Albanese breathlessly apologetic in the second-act duet. But Albanese's mature timbre annoys some ears. At that, Callas (Angel, Seraphim) outdoes everyone in the sustaining of opulent tragedy in the final act. But elsewhere in the role she sounds out of sorts, wobbling direly on the high notes. Most recently, we have DG's digital set under Giuseppe Sinopoli, with the personable but hard-voiced Mirella Freni and, again, Domingo. Sinopoli is the most impassioned of *Manon* conductors, but this is virtually the Bayreuth version, *sehr romantisch*, the orchestra contending with the singers as much as supporting them. The CDs at least placate the noise, though the air of supervening verismo still jars.

Puccini is anything but noise, writing more parts for lyric voices than dramatic ones. Nor was he impressed by "realism." Consider *Gianni Schicchi*. The verismo approach would be entirely out of place in this precise little comedy. Hear how different Tito Gobbi sounds as Schicchi than as Tonio or Scarpia, on Angel in 1958, then Columbia in 1976, the two portrayals alike in every detail. Angel has Victoria de los Angeles's lovely "O mio babbino caro," but Columbia has Lorin Maazel's discerning baton and Plácido Domingo's Rinuccio—the sole time on disc that this abused role has been assigned to a world-class voice.

If Puccini is not strictly verismo, he is sometimes nothing else. This confuses some singers, who attack all Puccini in *verista* style, or avoid it entirely. Surely de los Angeles's shimmering heroine of *Suor Angelica* (Angel) is simply an expanded "O mio babbino caro," especially as compared with the intense Scotto (Columbia.) On the other hand, surely de los Angeles's partner, Fedora Barbieri, makes the Princess too fierce and chesty; one has the feeling that she coached the role with Mamma Lucia. Scotto's Marilyn Horne better observes the Princess's aggressive reserve, as does Christa Ludwig (London), unfortunately opposite Joan Sutherland, who somehow manages to do the right things in an unhelpful way. Angelica, along with Manon, Mimì, and Liù, is an essential Puccinian character, the sweet and helpless girl who dies because she loves. The pathetic beauty of her doom must carry in the very timbre of her voice, in the vulnerable arabesque of her high lines, the impetuous generosity of her parlando. We hear none of this in Sutherland. Even Tebaldi, on an earlier London disc, sounds hard, if in a portrayal of great appeal (and Giulietta Simionato's Princess is the best of all).

An amusingly instructive way to taste the *stile pucciniano* is to hear some outstanding all-Puccini aria recitals back-to-back. I sampled Callas (Angel mono), Virginia Zeani (London), and Mirella Freni (Angel): one lyric-dramatic, one lyric-verismo, and one plain lyric. As Callas only reluctantly identified herself with verismo on the way to reviving golden-age bel canto, as Zeani is a committed *verista* of little *réclame* outside Italy, and as Freni has the best-liked timbre of the three, it is interesting that all these discs prove stylistically valid. Callas most successfully presents a gallery of portraits, varying her palette from a pale Lauretta through a bright Butterfly, shyly rapt, on to a fiery Turandot. Zeani tends to the grand manner; where Callas is gravely poignant in Manon's "Sola, perduta, abbandonata," Zeani is desperate, wild. Freni, with the loveliest instrument, is less attentive to text but innately musical. Curiously, only she mars Liù's "Tu che di gel" with verismo excess, slipping a "Poor little me, I'm dying" noise into the final phrase. Puccini, then, is not one thing to all, rather a variety of possibilities.

When Puccini does adopt verismo, his verismo is pure—but he did it only once, in *Il Tabarro* (The Cloak). Here is the modern-dress urban realism, the laden atmosphere, and terse narration introduced in *Cav* and *Pag.* Here, also, are the abradantly overloaded voices that verismo called into existence; here, at any rate, we need them. An old Victor mono disc, now on Angel with the other two operas of *Il Trittico*—*Gianni Schicchi* and *Suor Angelica*—gave Tito Gobbi one of his best characterizations; in stereo, Columbia is choice for Scotto's testy Giorgetta, with Domingo and Ingvar Wixell under Maazel. The work is claustrophic, dense in its fog-lapping Seine and adulterous secrets, with little room for the languid soprano or swaggering tenor line that Puccini made his signature in larger works. However, a similar plot—but now in period costume—opened up into what for many is the height of Puccini and verismo both: *Tosca*.

Tosca has varied wildly on disc. Many of the great singers of the LP era have had their say, yet some are miscast (Freni as Tosca? too nice; Fischer-Dieskau as Scarpia? too small) and others uncommitted in three of opera's most passionate roles. A few *Toscas* stand among the worst recordings ever made, and one is, by common consent, one of the greatest. Why so many possibilities? *Tosca* hasn't the elusive richness of *Don Giovanni* or *Carmen,* infinitely renewable. There is only one way to do it well: as Callas, di Stefano, Gobbi, and conductor Victor de Sabata do it on Angel's classic Scala set of 1953, brighter and cleaner than ever in its digital remastering. It is not just that the singing is excellent, but that the storytelling is, especially in Callas's scenes with Gobbi and in the way de Sabata imbues the studio with a theatre atmosphere. De Sabata's precision in details of orchestration has such visual impact that we virtually hear the curtain rising and falling; and those who never experienced Callas onstage may fancy that they see her making her third-act entrance, so ecstatically does de Sabata play the music that describes it. HRE's 1952 Mexico City *Tosca* with Callas and Giuseppe di Stefano, in strained sound and with an intrusive prompter, fascinatingly prepares for the commercial reading. Here Callas is sweeter, less consistently determined, pleading in "Ma falle gli occhi neri" (But let her eyes be black), where on Angel she is more confident. She pours out her voice in Mexico in an almost spendthrift way, allowing us to appreciate all the more the subtleties of her Angel Tosca, the polished, sifted verismo of de Sabata's team.

Sets of the 78 years, on the other hand, recall to us a more pungent style. In 1929–30, Victor's Carmen Melis, Piero Pauli, and Apollo Granforte have the edge over Columbia's team featuring the gritty Bianca Scacciati. Nearly a decade later, Victor's Maria Caniglia and Beniamino Gigli (Seraphim) took the era's laurels, though they make an odd match, she better in the denunciations and outbursts than in the lyricism, he more comfortable singing than storming. Still, all these performers bring spontaneity to the microphone, and without it *Tosca* is a dud. Too many LP sets are well-intentioned but unsurprising—Herbert von Karajan's, for instance, a typical grand-slam international gathering in Leontyne Price, di Stefano again, and Giuseppe Taddei (Victor, London). Price sounds gorgeous but not remotely like Sardou's diva whose ferocious appetite for art and love inspired Puccini to create a second essential character, abrasive rather than sweet and anything but helpless—Tosca, Giorgetta, Minnie, Turandot. Nor does von Karajan's CinemaScope verismo keep the three principals in focus: his sound effects count more bells and cannon than the War of 1812 (and I don't mean the Overture; I mean the War).

Some sets aren't even well-intentioned—Victor's 1956 Met-flavored reading (Victrola) under Erich Leinsdorf, Jussi Björling's attractive Cavaradossi sandwiched between Zinka Milanov's matronly Tosca and Leonard Warren's graceless Scarpia. Georg Solti's digital set of 1986 (London) tries to make up in sonics for Kiri Te Kanawa's placid heroine. Then there are the flawed but interesting portrayals—Nilsson's Tosca for Maazel (London), her freedom on high and very spirited sense of character compromised by the lack of warmth in her timbre; or Galina Vishnevskaya, penetrating as the diva but in reproachable voice. Or the portrayals without flaw but trapped in flawed recordings—Régine Crespin's ravishing diva in an otherwise dumpy French highlights disc (EMI), or Ruggero Raimondi's Scarpia on von Karajan's remake (DG). On his entrance, unusually subdued where most

Scarpias bellow, Raimondi suggests the hypocrite imagining a blasphemy to be shocked at—the "bigoted satyr," as Cavaradossi describes him, who balances his comely prudery with a secret, plundering sensuality. But Raimondi's partners Katia Ricciarelli and José Carreras disappoint, she unimaginative and he in arduous voice.

Tosca, for all its solos, is the most collaborative theatre piece of a genre that plumed itself on its theatricality. It is less available than many operas to studio routine. It needs compulsion from its cast—more so even than Scotto, Domingo, and Bruson supply for James Levine (Angel digital). Soprano and conductor are refreshingly thespian, as witness her outrageously matter-of-fact "Questo è il bacio di Tosca." The others, too, are up to the mark. Here's *Tosca* crisp, tense, full. But where's the engagement, the motivation to love and sing, to free the world, and to debauch beauty that the principals, respectively, represent? At times, we get hints of all this in Tebaldi's old mono reading for London with Giuseppe Campora and Enzo Mascherini—not because any of the singers, or conductor Alberto Erede, is a dynamic interpreter, but because their unpretentiously traditional approach recalls a golden age of opulent Toscas, idealistic Cavaradossis, and saturnine Scarpias, an age when effective *Toscas* could be taken for granted.

Scarpia wants Tosca against her will, hating him; Jack Rance offers Minnie a thousand dollars for a kiss. Otherwise *La Fanciulla del West*, from David Belasco's *The Girl of the Golden West*, is *Tosca* in buckskin (though musically more advanced). Like *Tosca*, *Fanciulla* needs a powerful sense of involvement—for Belasco is Sardou in English. Angel's Scala set of 1959 (Seraphim) is an oddity: Birgit Nilsson flanked by the more naturally Puccinian João Gibin and Andrea Mongelli under Lovro von Matacic. It's fun to hear Nilsson riding the role's climaxes, but she's no cowgirl, and the all-important duet at the end of Act One lacks confessional intimacy. Two decades later, DG produced an even more international rendition with Carol Neblett, Domingo, and Sherrill Milnes under Zubin Mehta—not an Italian in the whole corral. The sound is superb, and the performance, drawn from a Covent Garden production, a great improvement on Angel's. Barring her woolly lower-middle register, Neblett makes an attractive Minnie, with some wonderfully ruthless top notes, and her partners are more engrossed than usual for them, the miners especially—another case of a studio set in effect sanctioning the live performance (albeit with starry Milnes in for the less glamorous Silvano Carroli, Rance at Covent Garden).

Still, the most impressive *Fanciulla* is Cetra's set, in clumsy mono and cast with singers who could be called, to be kind, uncelebrated:

Carla Gavazzi, Vasco Campagnano, and Ugo Savarese, under Arturo Basile. Don't listen for the sheen of Angel's or DG's teams—this is a provincial reading. But for "provincial" read "authentic," especially in Gavazzi's girlish, impetuous Minnie, eloquent at the end of Act One and a smash, to say the least, in the testy, pleading, hysterical Poker Scene, "due mani sopra tre" (two hands out of three). The sound, true, is poor mono. But London's big-name stereo extravaganza (Tebaldi, del Monaco, MacNeil, Tozzi; Capuana) could have used some of Cetra's small-town punch.

Puccini's verismo is the least pure of the era, counting heavily on the opposing quality of *morbidezza*—literally, "softness," denoting an almost sickly pathos. We think immediately of Angelica, Liù . . . but also of Magda, of *La Rondine* (The Swallow). A bittersweet comedy with but two important roles, *La Rondine* started out as a sort of Viennese operetta, and needs Vera Schwarz and Richard Tauber. In fact, Melodram gives us a relay from Vienna in 1955—in excellent sound—with Ljuba Welitsch and Anton Dermota, in German. It's nicely done, but, somewhat surprisingly, lacks *Schmalz*. Columbia's digital set with Kiri Te Kanawa and Domingo takes the palm.

La Bohème, another bittersweet comedy, is slathered with *morbidezza*, veritably revels in the sickly pathos of Mimì's wasting away. But there is much more here, in the propulsive energy of the bohemian life; *Bohèmes* need, above all, atmosphere. The 78 sets supply it. Victor's 1928 Scala album under Sabajno (now on LP on Bongiovanni) gives us not just a tenor and a baritone but a poet and a painter: they *sound* like artists. Indeed, the Marcello, Ernesto Badini, was virtually a character baritone, London's first Schicchi; and the Benoit/Alcindoro is the expert Salvatore Baccaloni. Columbia's 1929 Scala album ups the vocal stakes with the Mimì of Rosetta Pampanini, another of those verismo legends who don't match today's sopranos in voice but outdo them in expressive variety. Here, too, we believe in the bohemians, not least when, after Rodolfo's "Siamo in due" (There are two of us), the three hell-raisers downstairs let out delighted groans. Best of all was Victor's 1938 Scala box (Seraphim), laden with atmosphere and boasting Albanese and Gigli. As we cross over into the LP years, we lose the atmosphere, though we gain in voice, most typically in London's mono set with Tebaldi and Giacinto Prandelli under Erede. This is not unlike the reply to the more verismo-oriented 78 sets: this time out, everyone can sing. But the singing is somewhat monochromatic. The close of Act One has no insinuation, none of the interplay we get from Pampanini and Luigi Marini. But note the casting of Hilde Gueden, an acknowledged star, as Musetta. Heretofore, Italians

cast this part with minor contract players—Thea Vitulli, Luba Mirella, and Tatiana Menotti, for instance, on the 78 sets cited above.
Nowadays we expect a certified diva as Musetta—because phonograph
casting taught us to.

Five LP *Bohème* sets stand out. In mono, Toscanini's 1946 NBC
broadcast (Victor) is Most Historic, Votto's Scala set (Angel) Most
Traditional, Beecham's (Victor) Most Lush, especially in its stereo
rerelease (Seraphim). In stereo, von Karajan's (London) is Most Youthful
and Levine's (Angel) Most Modern. Comparing them through the
third-act quartet, virtually the heart of the opera, one finds surprising
differences. Toscanini is fast, his singers are sloppy, and the sound is
poor even for 1946. Votto, a former Toscanini protégé but famous for
his sympathy for singers' problems, is seductively expansive, with Callas, the young Anna Moffo, di Stefano, and Rolando Panerai at their
best in sonics that allow them to blend without overpowering each
other. Beecham beguiles with a subtle rhythmic pulse, but even de los
Angeles and Björling can't match Votto's lovers for giving warmth.
Von Karajan has Freni and Pavarotti in early stardom and the best of
comedians in Elizabeth Harwood and Panerai, nicely original in their
name-calling. Levine has a typical contemporary lineup in Scotto,
Neblett, Alfredo Kraus, and Milnes; Scotto is unsteady on the top B
flats, but note her fresh, catty reading of "Addio sospetti" (Goodbye,
jealousy). Von Karajan has the best voices, Votto the best singing.

For *Madama Butterfly* Puccini wrote his most central lead role, building
morbidezza into verismo by sheer force of drama. Characterologically,
the geisha should be a lyric soprano—she is only fifteen, remember,
when the opera begins. But lyrics may flounder in the role. Searching
for the perfect casting, the truest style, we can come as close as three
years after the first performances, to the Met production of 1907, with
Geraldine Farrar, Louise Homer, Enrico Caruso, and Antonio Scotti,
whose Victor 78s were collected on a Victrola LP. (Farrar's cuts alone,
in a better transfer, are on Rubini.) The Camden studio's acoustic and
cutdown orchestra do not make for conclusive deductions, but it is
notable that Farrar occasionally sings a line or two from the original
version of the opera, changed when Puccini shortened the wedding
scene, divided the second act into two parts, and performed other
surgical niceties after the disastrous Scala premiere. Also notable is
"Oh! quanti occhi fissi," the Love Duet, in which Farrar, miffed that
Caruso showed up for the session a touch moistened, supposedly replaces the line "Sì! per la vita!" with "He's had a highball!" It's *almost*
true; listen for yourself.

We get a better grasp of style in the 1924 HMV set sung in English, mainly because the style is so far off. No doubt it's a relief to hear a *Butterfly* without all the intrusive sobbing that was common among Italian singers at the time, but there is very little portamento, even on the famous sighing fall from high B flat to E flat in Butterfly's Entrance, and at the same phrase on its repetition in the Love Duet. Moreover, though Tudor Davies gives a spirited Pinkerton, Rosina Buckman's Butterfly lacks passion. She even seems sensible, which runs against not only the character but the neurotically sensual music. Eugene Goosens conducts well, getting a surprising amount of the score into the acoustic horn, but the voices lean into the ear, letting one catch most of the words—note that the decorous translator has upped Butterfly's age in the first act from fifteen to eighteen. It's a curiosity, and the curious may hear it today on a small British label, Claremont, a bargain on two discs.

The other 78 sets reassert the kind of Butterfly that Puccini might have heard, though one wonders how he took to Rosetta Pampanini's incessant little interjections, her "No!" and "Ah!" Still, her 1928 Columbia set preserves one of the most affecting Butterflys of the century; coevally, Victor's Margaret Sheridan (Club 99), an Italianized Irishwoman, is neater but dull. Victor tried again in 1939 with the most enduring of the 78 albums, featuring Beniamino Gigli's honeyed Pinkerton and, most notably, the unique Butterfly of Toti dal Monte (Angel, Seraphim). Like Pampanini, dal Monte scales her voice down and tricks up her phrasing to suggest a teenaged child, but where with Pampanini the effect comes and goes, dal Monte performs virtually the entire opera as a little girl. The result is heartrending. It was an influential portrayal: one hears Licia Albanese trying something comparable on Met audiences in various undergrounds, adding in the cries and flutters of the Pampanini School of Geisha Verismo. Like her colleagues, Albanese could work within a tradition yet create her own interpretation, another great one.

The LP years brought in some more sizable voices, such as Renata Tebaldi (London mono, Richmond; London stereo), lovely and resourceful but on the cool side after the avid 78 Cio-Cio-Sans. Callas, with Gedda, suavest of Pinkertons, under von Karajan (Angel mono), refers back to the childlike interpreters. As one expects, she adds many a special touch, as in her deadpan "Morto!" (Dead!) when the Consul asks about her disgraced father. Note too an early hint of later von Karajan in the slow tempos and overall delicacy of approach. We get none of this from the pedestrian Erich Leinsdorf on Victor's stereo entries with Anna Moffo and Leontyne Price. Moffo, partnered with Cesare Valletti, was to have reclaimed the piece for the light—the lyric—approach. Perhaps Price's all-out spinto reading is more persuasive, for she opens with the charm that captivated Pinkerton, then grows into the tragedy. Her "Morto!" is a whisper, her death scene a beautiful agony. An even bigger voice appeared on Angel's Sadler's Wells highlights disc (in the same translation that Buckman sang): Marie Collier. Her fluttery, tight tone annoys—but hear how vividly she narrates "One fine day."

The tenor gets short weight in *Madama Butterfly,* though the biggest stars routinely sing it—record it, anyway. De los Angeles has di Stefano on her mono set (Capitol, Seraphim) and Björling in stereo (Angel), but it may well be Richard Tucker who best brings the lieutenant to life. Tucker partnered Price, but he is in more ringing voice earlier in mono on Columbia with Eleanor Steber. Tucker's Pinkerton is less ardent than di Stefano's, less debonair than Björling's. But his naturalism is intriguing—the somewhat pensive tone of the opening, the genuine curiosity on "Quei pupazzi?" Columbia's set in general is creditable; what reads on paper as a routine night at the Met circa 1949 turns out to be a stylish and affecting performance, conducted with surprising verve by Max Rudolf.

Is *Butterfly* even remotely a conductor's opera? Herbert von Karajan seems to think so; his second try, on London (Freni, Ludwig, Pavarotti, Kerns) is *highly* conducted, with a wide dynamic range taking in a mesmerizing rustle in the Humming Chorus, a cathartic explosion at the sighting of Pinkerton's ship. But with such consistently slow tempos, a certain lassitude sets in. The singing, however, is excellent, Freni, lyric of lyrics, playing Butterfly's fragility right up to the death scene, and Pavarotti very engaging, genial and careless. Critics have generally hailed the set as the best ever, but I prefer the first of Scotto's two tries, under another conductor with stately ideas about tempo, John Barbirolli (Angel). Here the opera appears to be unfolding; under von Karajan it meanders. Then too, if Scotto lacks Freni's focused top, she is second to none, not even Callas, in interpretation of this role, possibly Scotto's greatest. Another strong point for Angel is Carlo Bergonzi's Pinkerton, delivered with that honeyed elegance that this underrated tenor uniquely possessed. Scotto's second Cio-Cio-San, another in Maazel's Puccini cycle for Columbia, may offer a few more telling points of character, but she was in better voice for Barbirolli.

In *Turandot* Puccini at last set his two basic heroines side by side: Liù for pathos and Turandot for flash. Sadly, flash is in short supply today, which gives us Turandots and Calafs who use the microphone to beef up insufficient instruments. Various pirate relays of excerpts from Covent Garden in 1937 with Eva Turner and Giovanni Martinelli under Barbirolli reveal *Turandot* in full true, with voices to fill a theatre. A year later, Parlophone's commercial set (Cetra) yields a less impressive but still correct performance under Franco Ghione, with the boisterous Gina Cigna, the surprisingly tentative Magda Olivero, and the unimaginative Francesco Merli, bettered, in early stereo years, by the genuinely heroic Mario del Monaco (London), the polished Jussi Björling (Victor), and the strenuous Franco Corelli (Angel). At that, Angel's mono Scala set under Tullio Serafin (Callas, Schwarzkopf, Fernandi) disappoints when it's stylish and has impact when it's incorrect. Callas should astound us in this of all roles, but she is, for her, mediocre; "In questa reggia" went better on her Puccini recital. Serafin, too, should show us how this bizarrely romantic, comically cynical piece should go, but he splits the difference between the enchantment and the alienation, trying to make the score sound like *Manon Lescaut*. Worse yet, the best performance comes from Schwarzkopf's Liù, heavenly of phrasing but more suggestive of a *Dynasty* schemer than a teenaged slave. On the other hand, the del Monaco set has Renata Tebaldi's wonderful Liù but the Brünnhildische Turandot of Inge Borkh.* This opera has always had casting problems. Even Liù, the role that ought to be easy, consists almost entirely of three piteous arias—a limited way of ingratiating oneself. Maria Zamboni, who created the part under Toscanini, rushed to the studio to preserve her "Tu che di gel sei cinta." It's nothing to write home about. Strangely, neither of her colleagues, Rosa Raisa and Miguel Fleta, left a note of their roles, though Cetra's Merli hails from the first Scala production, third to sing Calaf.

It's typical of the collapse of verismo singing that the best *Turandots* feature international teams; but then Turandot is the least *verista* of the era's operas. First-timers should try Angel's Nilsson-Corelli pairing (with Scotto's Liù) to taste what Met veterans recall. as a glory of the Rudolf Bing years. True, Victor's Nilsson–Björling partnership helped popularize this opera, and they have Tebaldi's second, more careful Liù. But Angel presents a more vivid theatre. London's second set, under Zubin Mehta, is less surely styled, bearing Sutherland's determined yet unconvincing Turandot and Pavarotti's resourceful but ultimately underpowered Calaf. Mehta's drive does lend excitement, though, all the more so on CD, and he has Caballé as Liù—a more apt portrayal than her Turandot (Angel).

* One advantage of London's Borkh album was the libretto booklet, apparently printed from some arcane source, bearing not what Puccini set but what his librettists Adami and Simoni wrote. This is a slightly longer text, containing lines we will never hear sung.

Thinking back to the intensity of Turner and Martinelli, we might venture into Columbia's digital performance, live from Vienna (in Hal Prince's staging), with Eva Marton, José Carreras, and Katia Ricciarelli under Maazel. Another very variable grouping: Ricciarelli pleasing as Liù, Marton solid but very dry, un-Italianate, as Turandot. Carreras is too lyric for Calaf, but he makes it work, letting his passion feed on his labor so that we really feel his obsession for the princess. Listen to his verve as he throws off the answers in the Riddle Scene—this is Calaf! Best of all is Maazel's barbaric conducting, taking us back to Gozzi's original—fierce, fearful, pestering.

But von Karajan's digital set (DG), also from Vienna, beats Maazel's, if not for authenticity, such as it is today, then for sheer sonic splendor. The CDs emphasize the unsteadiness of Ricciarelli's dullish Turandot, but they improve upon the already sumptuous LPs for detail of orchestration and shimmer of atmosphere (on three discs, albeit, to Mehta's two). Nor does von Karajan drag the score out, as he does *Butterfly*. This is a magical *Turandot*, really a fairytale for once—and note that Ricciarelli, whatever her failings, is only the second Italian to sing Turandot on records. Domingo's Calaf shares Carreras's vocal limitations but not his imaginative delivery, and Barbara Hendricks's Liù, though admirably youthful, sounds a bit out of sorts (again, more so on the CDs than the LPs). But the other roles have a sheen, a command, that we seldom hear in the theatre. Wagnerian heavyweight Siegmund Nimsgern sings the Mandarin, Ping, Pang, and Pong's trio scene in Act Two erases all competition, and Piero de Palma, familiar from three decades of comprimario work on Italian-made sets, takes the Emperor. (This has become a phonograph convention: Mehta has Peter Pears in the part, Maazel Waldemar Kmennt.) This is, then, a triumph of production more than of individual contributions. If we cannot have a pure verismo, or even a pure Puccini, we can at least have pure von Karajan.

18

MASSENET

꙳

In his day cursed by critics for his unstoppable success, Massenet has been cursed anew during his current revival—and lo, the man who, as Debussy pointed out, had the "pleasant form of glory" to be more popular than Johann Sebastian Bach, turned out to be stoppable after all. Now even the public doesn't like Massenet. Some find him thin, others soupy; and while Joan Sutherland can float a *Roi de Lahore,* an *Esclarmonde* through sheer force of (Richard Bonynge's) will, even Beverly Sills in her prime (though in a loudly condemned production) could not protect *Thaïs,* once a repertory staple.

Yet the phonograph has taken to the Massenet revival. As late as in 1960, only his three most popular works had been recorded complete. Now, including undergrounds, we have sixteen—seventeen if one counts the stageable oratorio *Marie-Magdaleine.* Listening to them all, one hears beyond the familiar legend of the vain *cuisinier* who designed feasts around personable sopranos. Instead, one comprehends Massenet as the last great composer of grand opera and *opéra comique*—great because he combined elements of the two into an elastic form of rich potential, and last because Massenet was the only one who worked in it: for during his career Debussy pointed French opera in a different direction, and soon after neo-Classicism and expressionism also vied for adherents. Massenet was closed out.

It is worth appreciating his hybrid genre, if only to learn another reason why grand opera, the outstanding form of the nineteenth century, was outmoded by the start of the twentieth. Like verismo's composers, Massenet was not attracted to grand opera's size, that sheer rhetoric of architecture. But where verismo is another form altogether, Massenet took grand opera out of the Opéra, retaining its musical sophistication and larger-than-life singers but mixing in the sentimentality and intimacy of *opéra comique*. The grotesque and the *gai primitif* Massenet largely banned (though *Grisélidis*, a modern miracle play complete with henpecked Devil, marks a return to the spirit of the old fairgrounds vaudeville). But Massenet did texture his recipe with pastiche. Scattered through his oeuvre are musical suggestions of India, Judeo-Roman Israel, Moorish, Cervantean, and late-Empire Spain, and medieval, eighteenth-century, and Revolutionary France. In particular, Massenet reinvented the recitative that so basically distinguished grand opera from *opéra comique*. (Massenet thought the traditional spoken dialogue between numbers in *opéra comique* harmful to the continuity of his narrative, though he would allow a few lines of dialogue here and there, always *over* the music.) A convention in Meyerbeer, recit in Massenet became as important as outright song, often the most incisive aspect of portrayal. Consider the evocative lines of Thaïs's first entrance, as sensual as we expect from Alexandria's most illustrious courtesan, yet as pensive as we need from the woman who will repent her fleshly past and die a Christian. So elastic is Massenet's use of singing speech that this little scene defies category, from recit to arioso—even to ensemble, for Massenet actually brings Thaïs's *protégeur* Nicias into the music, as if it were a duet.

After *Marie-Magdaleine*, caught in a New York concert with Régine Crespin (BJR), Massenet's earliest works on record, from 1877 to 1889, tend toward grand opera with exotic settings. *Le Roi de Lahore* and *Esclarmonde* claim Sutherland-Bonynge performances on London, the soprano monochromatic in character but in fine voice, Bonynge compellingly dramatic, and the casting more international than French. *Le Roi* came out when digital sound was new, and the sonics are ungimmicked, the strings warm but not too glossy, the woodwinds bright, and the big finales handsomely separated—note the theatrical "presence" of the offstage fanfares in the Act Two battle entr'acte. The singing is variable. Tenor Luis Lima is overparted, Sherrill Milnes, the villain of the piece, in splendid form, Nicolai Ghiaurov (as the god Indra—one act takes place in heaven) suffers one of his woolly seasons, and Huguette Tourangeau cannot make her lullaby the standout solo it should be. But this is surely the only *Roi de Lahore* we will ever have, and it repays curiosity, not least in Massenet's already secure gift for innocuously melodic pastiche, as in the ballet, wonderfully played by London's National Philharmonic, that includes an "Indian melody" for flute with five variations. *Esclarmonde,* Massenet's gently Wagnerian opus, written to exploit the freak high notes of Sibyl Sanderson (the score is dedicated to her, as was an interesting portion of Massenet's personal life), is similarly charming, and only somewhat well done on London. Giacomo Aragall's hero typifies the set: stylish singing but execrable French, Massenet's sound without his character. Still, it's fascinating to hear Massenet's version of Tristanesque ecstasy. Wagner set an entire night of love before us in *Tristan's* second act; Massenet discreetly draws his curtain at the climax for a passionate entr'acte.

Only the pirates give us a complete *Hérodiade.* MRF's set, also on Rodolphe, is rough and ready, but EJS preserves a performance from 1957 under Albert Wolff with Andrea Guiot, Mimi van Harden, Guy Fouché, Charles Cambon, and Germain Ghislain that reminds us how much energy a provincial repertory night (in Ghent, to judge by the cast) can deliver. Van Harden suggests a young Rita Gorr, and Guiot, as Salomé—not Strauss's egotistical minx but a nice kid with a conscience—turns the key into "Il est doux" with a confessional spontaneity. *Hérodiade* is rich in big-tune arias and duets, which kept it alive in the 78 years after *Le Roi de Lahore* and *Esclarmonde* had vanished, and Angel's highlights disc of 1963 became the Massenet buff's classic, especially for its top-line cast of Crespin, Gorr, Albert Lance, and Michel Dens. But only the women deliver.

Le Cid, the last of Massenet's out-and-out grand operas, claims Columbia's set drawn from Eve Queler's 1976 concert with Grace Bumbry, Plácido Domingo, and Paul Plishka, all at their best. But Massenet isn't. He's in form only in the romantic scenes and the big ballet (where Queler plays her ace), and *Le Cid,* from Corneille's tragedy, is about honor, not romance. Massenet's setting of "Ô rage, ô désespoir" (Oh rage, oh despair), Don Diègue's lamentation that age has impeded his heroism, rings as hollow as Thomas's setting of Hamlet's soliloquies. Then too, the premiere, at the Opéra in 1885, presented a historic cast: the two de Reszkes, Leon Melchissédec, Pol Plançon. Maybe this opera doesn't deserve such giants; but maybe it needs them to survive. Certainly, a Callas doesn't hurt, in her famous cut of "Pleurez, mes yeux." She makes the scene sound as if the opera were about honor *and* romance.

At this point Massenet moves into his own form, with *Werther.* After all that royalty, war, and sarong ballet, we come to a middle-class family disrupted by a self-indulgent poet. The 1933 set with Ninon Vallin and Georges Thill offers "timbre magic," the very sound of those characters for a generation. Angel's early stereo reading under

Georges Prêtre with Victoria de los Angeles and Nicolai Gedda is stylistically so solid that it should be a classic, but the sonics are shallow and the performance without atmosphere. This is a rare Massenet item without any scene-setting *divertissement:* no ballet, no picturesque solos, almost no chorus. Everything is left to Charlotte and Werther and, less so, to the rest of the family circle, especially husband Albert and sister Sophie. Angel's second try, with Tatiana Troyanos and Alfredo Kraus under Michel Plasson, does have atmosphere—but that of a tragedy, particularly in Troyanos's beautiful but grandiose Charlotte. "Souriant," Massenet directs in the Clair de Lune duet at the end of Act One: *smiling.* Troyanos is already in despair. Of all the characters, only Werther takes himself too seriously. Unfortunately, Plácido Domingo is not serious enough on DG with Elena Obraztsova under Riccardo Chailly. Domingo is musical, yes, but not the suicidal poet Goethe had in mind; and Obraztsova, like Troyanos, plays the whole opera as if it were the fourth-act death duet, missing the flighty shifts of mood in the Letter Scene.

Colin Davis's Covent Garden *Werther* (Philips) seems to me ideal in defining the bourgeois setting, proving that French opera doesn't necessarily need native performers. The character parts are rendered with great spirit, and Isobel Buchanan and Thomas Allen are the best Sophie and Albert on disc. In Frederica von Stade we have another Charlotte who tends toward the plangent, but von Stade is more sensitive than tragic; and José Carreras creates a persusive poet. His "Rêve! Extase!" in the Clair de Lune carries wonder to a rhapsodic epiphany, and the occasional sense of overparting in his lyric instrument is, for once, suitable: Werther *is* desperate. Moreover, Carreras attends to Massenet's markings better than anyone else since Thill. When, in the second-act duet, Davis carefully referees a kind of standoff between von Stade's reasonable pleading and Carreras's passion, the set beautifully brings Goethe and Massenet together.

What a change, then, to reencounter the more recognizably *massenétique* composer of *Thaïs,* another Sanderson vehicle, this one filled with colorful evocations: of the monastic life on the one hand and old Alexandrian decadence on the other. This is the opera in which Carol Neblett once dared a nude scene; imagine that in *Werther.* Sadly, no *Thaïs* set quite satisfies, though each has advantages. Urania's early mono album, reissued in a direly reverberant acoustic, is hurt by Geori-Boué's shrill heroine, though the soprano, a noted beauty, has the timbre to suggest a sumptuous courtesan. Vega's late mono set with Renée Doria and Robert Massard appeals to connoisseurs for its Gallic sureness of style; the American issue, on Westminster, cut some of the ballet and all of Act Three, scene two, needed to clarify Athanaël's change of heart from Thaïs's proselyte to her suitor.

The stereo years brought forth Anna Moffo (Victor) and Beverly Sills (Angel), troubled sets, though at least complete. Moffo is in terrible form, her upper register hard and her top notes disastrous; even the middle register crackles. Her Athanaël, Gabriel Bacquier, is very much the fanatic of the "barbe rude" (rough beard) and the "yeux pleins de feu" (fiery eyes) that the Alexandrian slave girls drolly admire in him, but the top lines are out of his reach. Too bad, for Julius Rudel conducts synoptically, to confront Massenet's two arenas of the chaste and the sensual, monk and harlot. Lorin Maazel, Sills's conductor, is less alert than Rudel, though he presents a vivid ballet scene and, for good or ill, plays the violin solo in the Méditation entr'acte himself. It's unfortunate that Moffo didn't have Sills's vocal trim to match Moffo's understanding of the part, or Sills Moffo's suave intensity. In any case, Sills is much better than the critical roasting of her Met Thaïs would suggest. Sherrill Milnes is no Athanaël, however good he sounds, but Nicolai Gedda's Nicias is first-rate, very much the big-city hedonist—Victor's mild Carreras is utterly out of his league here. However, this is virtually an opera for soprano and baritone (and violin), and if Rudel can't save Victor, Gedda can't redeem Angel.

Like most other prolific composers, Massenet tried verismo, most acutely in La Navarraise—brief, rural, and violent. Victor (Horne, Domingo, Milnes; Lewis) and Columbia (Popp, Vanzo, Souzay; de Almeida) waited some seventy-five years and then published discs almost neck and neck. Victor has the truer voices, Columbia the truer French and more guts. Sapho is Massenet's urban verismo, based on a play (from Daudet's novel) about an aging bohémienne and a young Provençal that was closed by the police on Broadway in 1900. It's like La Rondine, but with an edge; in revision, Massenet added a ferocious quarreling scene for the lovers. The hero's homesick reverie, "Qu'il est loin mon pays," inspired one of Thill's best 78s, but EMI's complete set under Roger Boutry, from 1978, reveals a piece rich in the strenuous saturnalia of the Paris salons: the better, of course, to set off the tenor's Provençal innocence. This is basic Massenet, then, the alliance of the innocent and the sensual. Lyric coloratura Renée Doria is a surprise in the part, written for the tempestuous Emma Calvé—a surprise because Doria is excellent, as is tenor Ginès Sirera, who sounds a bit like Alain Vanzo, especially in his high notes.

Now, in the late 1890s, Massenet concentrates on his unique developments in opéra comique. More than ever, we need not big international voices but singing personalities like Mary Garden, famous for the title roles in *Le Jongleur de Nôtre-Dame* and *Chérubin*, the further escapades of Beaumarchais's page from *Le Mariage de Figaro*. Garden's co-optation of the juggler as a trouser role mildly irritated Massenet, who set it for tenor. He would have been pleased by Angel's set, with Vanzo under Boutry, a fine reading of a modest work, built entirely on the juggler's modest drives: to perform, to eat and drink, and to wander. Liberty, he says, is his mistress. No wonder Garden liked the part; liberty and chastity were two of her favorite things, too. Her 1911 Columbia cut of the juggler's "Liberté!" rather spoils the legend that she had personality but no voice. She has both. Without Garden, *Le Jongleur* is a no-diva opera, but *Chérubin* counts three: the trouser lead, the winsome Nina, and Chérubin's more superb but temporary amour, La Ensolleiad. MRF offers a dull performance hectored by inexplicably niggling cuts, some as short as a bar or two. Voce preserves a marvelous Carnegie Hall concert with von Stade, Ashley Putnam, and Valerie Masterson under Henry Lewis. Only MRF includes a libretto, along with an undistinguished Italian radio performance of *Le Portrait de Manon*, Massenet's short sequel to his greatest success.

MRF has the only *Grisélidis* on disc, drawn from the 1982 Wexford Festival, but personality is in short supply—as are decent singing and acceptable French, except from heroine Rosemary Landry. As the sixth-side filler, MRF offers transcriptions of 78s from rare Massenet operas, and the singers, such as Léon Escalais and Vanni-Marcoux, have personality to spare. Wisely, MRF did not further embarrass its own singers by including the two most famous 78 sides from *Grisélidis*, Louis Cazette's honeyed "Je suis l'oiseau," an anthologist's favorite, and Aline Vallandri's "Il partit au printemps," one of the most Puccinian arias not by Puccini.

Cendrillon—Cinderella in the Perrault version—is delicately lovely, its magic gently coexisting with the comic stepmother and -sisters. Here is another three-diva opera, for soprano heroine, mezzo prince, and coloratura fairy. BJR's set, taken live at the Manhattan School of Music, suffers from a tenor prince and amateurish playing, but Martha Williford's Cinderella is superb and Marsha Bagwell's Stepmother a kind of Joanne Worley in French—one hears the audience greatly enjoying her capers. Columbia's stereo *Cendrillon* under Julius Rudel is a vast improvement for its French stylists. Jules Bastin is a surprisingly uninspired father, but Jane Berbié is another amusing stepmother and Ruth Welting quite on top of the Fairy's high line. As at Manhattan, we get a tenor prince. (Voce's *Chérubin* includes, as filler, an act of *Cendrillon* with Marilyn Horne as the Prince, for those who want to sample Massenet's original vocal color scheme.) At least Nicolai Gedda makes a real character of the Prince, at first disengaged, bored because loveless, then passionate, redeemed by devotion. Von Stade's Cinderella is ideal in timbre, technique, and coloration. Highly recommended.

Personality, if some lack of vocal glamour, justifies Bonynge's daring release of one of the few Massenet operas without a cult following, *Thérèse* (London). Period verismo, a love triangle set in the French Revolution, it is not memorable Massenet. London's handsome cover photo, of Huguette Tourangeau *en décolleté* trimmed with a rose, fairly sums up the work's content. But Tourangeau and Louis Quilico are really quite excellent; Ryland Davies, third point of the geometry, is overwhelmed but game. London also released a fine *Don Quichotte*, with Nicolai Ghiaurov in Shalyapin's shoes, supported by Crespin and Bacquier under Kazimierz Kord. One problem unique to disc: vocally, the two basses overcomplement each other, without the visual element of a theatre peformance to distinguish them. London might also have held the work to two instead of three discs; it's a short evening, less an adaptation of Cervantes than a kind of *Quixote* cabaret. Still, the set is theatrical and warmly conducted, though the death scene lacks the tactful sorrow of Vanni-Marcoux's famous 78 of 1934 (with Michel Cazette and Odette Ricquier).

I saved *Manon* for last because, while it dates back to Massenet's grand-opera period, it remains his most essential *opéra comique*, with its antique swank of minuet and gavotte; its distinctive use of recit and underscored dialogue; its *hommage* to Auber and his historically formative version, nodding fondly as it sweeps Auber aside; and especially in its voyage from innocence on to sensuality—note that, by the St. Sulpice scene, Manon is a harlot and Des Grieux a form of monk: *Thaïs* in wigs. Eminently excerptable, *Manon* threw off countless 78s, not least because the heroine is *opéra comique*'s Violetta— vivacious, sensitive, and tragic. Sopranos longed to display their faceted gifts in the numbers—sometimes a gift per selection, sometimes all gifts in one. Ninon Vallin's many cuts accord with the former approach, supremely playing a different mood on each side; Emma Luart spins the kaleidoscope with a more human figure. (Rubini collects seven of her *Manon* solos on LP; the flip side, also useful, finds Luart in aria and duet from the familiar—*Hoffmann*—to the piquant— Pierné's *Sophie Arnould*, on Gluck's fascinating prima donna—and yields further Massenet in Thaïs's Mirror Aria.) Fanny Heldy was another notable Manon of the day, but she presides over Pathé's undistinguished 1923 set (excellently transcribed onto LP in 1984 by Bourg)

with Jean Marny under Henri Busser. There are a few cuts, mostly in
the Transylvanie Scene, but ensembles are sloppy, and the music comes
alive only in the lovers' duets. The album's one point of interest is
the Lescaut, Léon Ponzio, who delivers the role as if a comic figure
out of Favart or Offenbach, thus relating Massenet to a century of
opéra comique traditions.

Columbia's 78 set, from 1932, under Elie Cohen, is, on the other
hand, a real theatre performance: Lescaut ad libs "en paradis?" during
"Je suis encore," the small parts have lots of life, the ballet sounds
dancey, and the standard cuts are observed. Germaine Feraldy's Manon,
however, pales somewhat next to Joseph Rogatchewsky's passionate
Des Grieux. A pirate from the next decade, with Bidú Sayão and
Charles Kullmann under Thomas Beecham at the Met (OPA), generally offers less voice but more character—Sayão's very free delivery
of and Beecham's conspiratorial accompaniment to "N'est-ce plus ma
main?" is the best on disc, a shocking magic.

The first years of LP brought London's heavily cut reading with
Janine Micheau, Libero de Luca, and Opéra-Comique forces. The set
is historic, for, given carte blanche by the front office, producer Max
de Rieux replaced the *massenétique* dialogues with spoken narration,
making a dullish performance downright perverse, and thus warning
the industry away from recorded opera as a thing-in-itself and recom-
mending theatre simulation as much as possible. Another curiosity:
London's Micheau is the only album Manon to omit the Gavotte in
favor of the Fabliau, "Oui, dans les bois et dans la plaine," written for
the original *Cendrillon* Fairy, Georgette Bréjean-Silver (who recorded
it, not well, in 1906).

If London's Opéra-Comique people are merely competent, Victor's
draft of the house forces but a few years later found them inspired, led
by Victoria de los Angeles, Henri Legay, Michel Dens, and Jean Borthayre under Pierre Monteux (Capitol, Seraphim). De los Angeles's
"On m'appelle Manon" typifies her portrayal, naïve, deft, lovely, and
in flawless French. As with all great Manons, hearing her is to redis-
cover the piece, from the artlessness of the first scene to the delicate
grasping in St. Sulpice, where her "Oui, c'est moi!" turns from terror
to ruthless determination in two repetitions. Legay is wonderful, a
more lyric Des Grieux than we hear nowadays, and Borthayre's senior
Des Grieux makes a great deal of a small part. In Monteux we have
the expert utterly at home. Too bad the original four discs (three on
Seraphim) couldn't have opened up the house cuts, or blended in the
dialogue more smoothly—it sounds like the singers' studio voice-overs.
Still, a noble performance.

Beverly Sills's set with Gedda under Rudel (ABC; Angel) is as French as Monteux's and more theatrical, with sonics that are almost too good. The timpani at Des Grieux's entrance come through so loudly that a moment of casual sentiment—the first meeting of young lovers—suggests a voodoo ceremony. (Angel's remastered rerelease, on three discs to ABC's four, soothes the problem somewhat.) Perhaps this is the industrial-strength Manon. When laughter is needed, we get hysterics; and Sills's "A Paris!" is so fervent she might be a hostile general mustering his troops. But this may have been Sills's very best role, and in sound and person she is Vallin and Luart's successor. How confidential Sills is in "Voyons, Manon," how scintillating in "Je marche sur tous les chemins." And at St. Sulpice, when Gedda is almost violent, Sills is sweetly rational, making the confrontation the very center of the performance. Only Sayão surpasses her.

Angel's digital set, with Ileana Cotrubas, Alfredo Kraus, Gino Quilico, and José van Dam, is most surpassing yet. Like others in Angel's series of French operas made under Plasson at Toulouse, it is stylish and theatrical, with imaginative stereo separation. The taping range is tight, but clear and warm; the voices are pleasantly forward in the snatches of dialogue. Cotrubas above all makes the set essential. Her naturally girlish timbre is perfect in Act One, and she prudently grows in the role as Manon collects experiences. We hear the breathless adolescent in "A Paris!," delicately ravished—but one act later we sense the woman, rueful in "Adieu, notre petite table." (There is a wonderful touch just after, when Cotrubas gives a hollow echo to Kraus's energetically unknowing "A table," underlining the imminent collapse of their idyll.) Cotrubas lacks some Manons's imposing radiance in "Je marche," and she avoids the high coloratura options. Still, she has a glittering high D—and, like Sills, is one of the very few Manons to bring off the awkward melisma on "voix" at the end of "N'est-ce plus ma main?" avec charme, as Massenet requests. Kraus, too, is estimable, if old-sounding and not as elegant in French diction as in French musical stylistics. His "Toi! Vous!" at his first glimpse of Manon in St. Sulpice typifies his performance, the entire set, and, to an extent, Angel's excellent Toulouse series in general. The deserted lover has of course taken priestly vows, and he thus corrects the involuntarily intimate "Toi!" with the formal "Vous!" Both words mean "you," but while "Toi!" attracts, "Vous!" distances. Most tenors hurl the words as an accusation, accurate enough. But Kraus changes tone at "Vous!"—going soft, sadly imploring even as he formalizes. A wonderful touch, blending Massenet's innocence and sensuality in a single note.

That Manon can produce so many worthwhile records is no surprise, for the work is singable and richly dramatic. But the LP years have proved that there is more to Massenet than a few early stabs at grand opera, followed by a series of show-shop vehicles for stars like Sanderson and Calvé. There is, above all, an alchemy of genre, a solution to opera's perennial problem of balancing music and text—in Massenet's case, balancing the "voice" parts and the "artistry" parts. When he left grand opera, he abandoned pure vocalism for acting vocalism, which is why all the great Massenet roles are *opéra comique* roles, and why the great Massenet stylists are great as Manon, Des Grieux, Werther, Charlotte, Cendrillon, Jean the Juggler, or Chérubin. *Avec charme*, Massenet directs: with personality.

19

STRAVINSKY, BARTÓK, AND WEILL

❧

Just as Massenet's operas serve as the culmination of nineteenth-century tradition, those of this Russian, Hungarian, and German who all ended up in the United States exemplify operatic trends of the twentieth century: Stravinsky in his neo-Classical antiquing and mixing of theatre genres into unique hybrids; Bartók in his emphasis on motivic transformation and the musical setting of the rhythms of language; and Weill in his blend of popular and classical forms and his attraction to vital stagecraft, whether with Bertolt Brecht or on Broadway.

The Stravinskyan experiments in form make it difficult for analysts to draw generic lines. Some of his ballets—*Les Noces, Perséphone,* and *Renard*—are almost operas; and *Oedipus Rex* almost isn't one. Oddly, Stravinsky's first opera, *Solovyey* (The Nightingale)—generally called *Le Rossignol* because it was translated into French for its premiere, in Paris—is almost conventional. In three acts but under an hour long, it is based on one of Hans Christian Andersen's tales, much as Tchaikofsky's comparably short *Iolanta* is. Typical Stravinsky, *The Nightingale* has its quirk: the second and third acts, composed five years after the first, sound stylistically more advanced.

Or so the scholars tell us. In performance, few unwarned ears detect the shift in style, perhaps because Stravinsky uses the unvarying Song of the Fisherman as a narrative frame in all three acts. There are two recordings, Angel's mono *Rossignol* with a French cast under André Cluytens and Columbia's early stereo *Solovyey* with an American cast under the composer. Stravinsky's singers are accomplished musicians—Reri Grist as the miraculously soothing bird, Elaine Bonazzi as Death, Loren Driscoll as the Fisherman, and Donald Gramm as the Emperor. But, except for Gramm, Cluytens's team has the edge, especially Jean Giraudeau's dreamy Fisherman and Janine Micheau's old-fashioned storybook nightingale. Vocal timbre is all-important in the title role, because, while it does lie rather high, it is not truly studded with high notes like Massenet's Esclarmonde (there is a single high F) or blessed with sensual tunes like Rimsky-Korsakof's Queen of Shemakha. In this miniature fairytale, each character must make an immediate impression with little more than the sound of his voice and a turn of phrase—which may be why veteran Christine Gayraud gives her tiny but crucial scene as Death a little more presence than does Bonazzi, then youthfully ahead of her days of greatness and in any case singing in an alien language.

Cluytens, too, has the advantage of a superior orchestra—note the expert oboe playing in the dance of the mechanical nightingale that replaces the living one in the Emperor's fashion-conscious court. Cluytens gives a better reading as well. Stravinsky's is hard-edged, stubbornly emphasizing the stylistic gap between the first two acts as if preparing a document for some critic's lecture. Cluytens irons it out. The Columbia disc is brittle metal, then, Angel's crystalline.

Mavra, Stravinsky's short four-character farce after Pushkin, also claims two performances in different languages. London's, in English under Ernest Ansermet, is sluggish, as if the conductor were counting out the intricate cross-rhythms with his fingers. Nor are the singers helpful; oddly, three of them sing Robert Craft's translation while Joan Carlyle delivers some other version, not clearly at that. Melodiya offers a vastly more vital performance under Gennady Rozhdestvensky in more spirited stereo. Listening to Ansermet, one sees why *Mavra* is neglected—but from Melodiya's first bars, Lyudmila Belobragina's maiden's lament followed by Nikolai Gutorovich's charismatic soldier's song, this delightful nonsense comes alive, and one shakes one's head at *Mavra*'s neglect.

With *Oedipus Rex* we come to an opera almost literally without action, sung in a language no one speaks. To the hieratic appearance of a Greek frieze is added a solemn touch of the *boulevardier:* a narrator in evening clothes outlining the plot in the language of the audience. Jean Cocteau, who wrote the text (a friendly Latin scholar made the translation), narrates on Stravinsky's mono recording (Columbia, Odyssey), giving it historical interest. But Peter Pears's Oedipus is vocally weak—though brilliant at "Ego senem kekidi," the four timpani-accompanied lines in which he first realizes what a snare of fate he was born into—and Martha Mödl's Jocasta is unsteady. Nor is London's mono disc under Ansermet any better, though Ernst Häfliger acts well and Hélène Bouvier fields a beautiful voice—as befits a former Dalila—if without the breath control for "Oracula, oracula."

In the stereo years, performances improved. Stravinsky's remake (Columbia) offers Shirley Verrett's superb Jocasta, very much the formidable and passionate woman this legend suggests. George Shirley is suprisingly human-scale, a good man who happens to be a king. The recording also offers English narration, from John Westbrook, as does London's under Solti, from Alec McCowen. But Solti has Pears again, still boxing above his weight and now unsteady as well, partnered by the woolly Kirsten Meyer.

To my mind, the two best performances are Leonard Bernstein's (Columbia) and Colin Davis's (Angel). Bernstein's Oedipus, René Kollo, is heard just entering upon the wobble that would dog his later career, but the performance as a whole is quite theatrical—something this piece always has trouble being. Tatiana Troyanos is the best Jocasta on disc, unfazed, as most of her colleagues are, by the 12/8 section of her duet with Oedipus, Tom Krause abets with a vigorous Creon, and Bernstein's narrator, the American Michael Wager, is very easy on the ear.

However, Davis's disc is drawn from a Sadler's Wells (now the English National Opera) production, giving the work theatricality in spite of itself. Here only do we hear a master thespian narrator (Ralph Richardson), and here, more than elsewhere, the orchestra seems not only structuring the action but urging it forward—as in the great aplomb that Davis gives to the famous accompaniment at the start of Jocasta's aria. Ronald Dowd's Oedipus is utterly on top of the role in singing and acting, Patricia Johnson a biting Jocasta, aware of the truth from the start, an interesting Freudian interpretation of a fascinatingly undiscovered character. Fans of the ENO Goodall *Ring* will be amused to encounter the young Alberto Remedios as the Shepherd, though he was at this point (1962) well ahead of his prime. The disc has one flaw, restricted sonics that, for instance, can't encompass the "Gloria" chorus at the end of Act One. Here, Columbia and Bernstein hold the palm. But Angel's remains the unique *Oedipus*, the theatre-defying score made theatrical.

The Rake's Progress, to W. H. Auden and Chester Kallman's libretto after Hogarth's picture series, is another of Stravinsky's *sui ge-*

neris entries, a somewhat Mozartean format using twentieth-century sounds. If Verdi, Massenet, and Berg are participants in their narratives, Stravinsky is a commentator on his, seating us at a remove, his welcoming fanfare and droll epilogue enclosing a sorrowful tale not precisely sorrowful in presentation. The piece is further distinguished by the text itself, unquestionably the wittiest and most poetic in opera, Kallman being the opera buff and craftsman and Auden the bard. Without Auden, *The Rake's Progress* might have been just another modern opera; but without Kallman it might not have been an opera at all.

And without Stravinsky it might not have been recorded for decades, for the composer leads the first three of a set of four. Cetra's relay of the 1951 premiere, staged by the Scala company in Venice before an audience of heavyweight Names, is distressing. The sound is barely listenable, the performance poor—shocking, considering the talent involved: Elisabeth Schwarzkopf, Jennie Tourel, Robert Rounseville, Otakar Kraus, with Hughes Cuénod supplying another of his many cameos as the auctioneer. One problem seems to have been a lack of rehearsal, for the ensemble is notably scrappy: in the last main entry in the Epilogue, *all* the principals fail to come in. (Schwarzkopf eventually rights things through force of musicianship.)

Another problem is the singers' polyglot background: only Rounseville is a native speaker of English (though Schwarzkopf has better diction), and the Scala chorus is risibly out of tongue. At least Schwarzkopf's Anne Trulove is superb, and it's interesting to hear the legendary Tourel in a rare live appearance. But Rounseville, just cresting the early fame of his Hoffmann in the celebrated film version, seems not to have learned his music. He is often off the mark by a considerable measure, and, floundering, his intonation suffers. By the end, he sounds as if he, not Tom Rakewell, is dying.

The Bing Met suffered one of its worst failures with the *Rake* in 1953, but Columbia recorded its competent team: Hilde Gueden, Blanche Thebom, Eugene Conley, and Mack Harrell. Gueden pales next to Schwarzkopf, and Thebom has none of Tourel's zest, but at least Stravinsky now has his forces in trim. His stereo remake, also on Columbia, offers his first set with a Hogarthian atmosphere, especially in Jean Manning's wonderfully cheesy Mother Goose. The four leads are youthful and generally pleasing: lovely Judith Raskin, Regina Sarfaty (wobbly and too placid), Alexander Young, and John Reardon.

London's digital *Rake* under Riccardo Chailly was the first *not* to sport a copy of Hogarth's "The Orgy" on its cover. Drawn from the John Cox-David Hockney Glyndebourne production, it offers Hockney's drop curtain—significantly, for this is the most stageworthy of the four sets, with a creative use of sound at, for example, Baba's intrusion into Tom and Anne's reunion in Act Two and at Nick's disappearance in Act Three. Musically, the reading is superior, clean and bright. Philip Langridge's Tom is more characterful than others'; significantly, he alone of the Glyndebourne principals joined Chailly when the production was staged at La Scala. Cathryn Pope's Anne is sensitive, but fields a wiry sound; and Astrid Varnay is ten years past her ability to do justice to Mother Goose. However, Samuel Ramey's Nick is excellent and Sarah Walker's Baba outstanding, bizarre and sensitive, the only portrayal in all *Rake* recordings that ranks with Schwarzkopf's Anne. Unlike other Babas, Walker has the high notes as well as the low; and a sense of humor to match Auden's. It is amazing to think that it was Walker who stole the show on the ENO's 1983 American tour as the humorless and insensitive Elizabeth in Britten's *Gloriana*.

Stravinsky wrote from four to eight operas, depending on how heavily one counts the vocal component in his polymeric stage works. But Bartók has only one, *A Kékszakállú Herceg Vára* (Duke Bluebeard's Castle). Like *Oedipus Rex*, it has little action, a language problem, and a speaking part (in a brief prologue, seldom recorded but usually printed in the album librettos), and sits nicely on one disc. In short, this is excellent home listening fare, especially as theatre performances are few. It is not a popular piece, but a renowned one, and Bartók's fascinating scoring procedures rendered it a stock hi-fi demonstration disc; records proliferated after stereo came in. There are discs in Russian, German, and English (Columbia's woefully dull effort with Rosalind Elias and Jerome Hines under Eugene Ormandy), but most singers tackle it in Béla Balázs's original Hungarian. Mercury's Olga Szönyi and Mihaly Szekely have a natural ethnic advantage, not least in their fellow Hungarian Antal Dorati's alert conducting, though the sound is dullish early stereo. Interestingly, the singers treat their roles quite differently from what is thought usual in the West, emphasizing lines that non-Hungarians glide through. Szönyi's gritty tone and Szekely's snarling black bass, too, make for an unusual experience. Not the best *Bluebeard*—but the most authentic?

Three more recent performances are recommendable. Connoisseurs prefer London's, with Christa Ludwig and Walter Berry under Istvan Kertesz. DG's Julia Varady and Dietrich Fischer-Dieskau under Wolfgang Sawallisch, however, offer competition in their subtle naturalization of the piece. This is, after all, a miniature myth, and most performers play it as an archetypal confrontation of questing woman and alienated man. Varady, instead, presents an importunate, domineering wife, Fischer-Dieskau almost a henpecked husband. A domestic drama. DG supports this with a tight, dry acoustic, the orchestra somewhat tamed. It's clear sound, but not the equipment-tester many want from this work. Possibly the best disc—certainly challenging London's seniority—is Columbia's, with Tatiana Troyanos and Siegmund Nimsgern under Pierre Boulez. The sound is spacious yet intimate and the singers are brilliant, Judith poignant, then desperate, then doomed; Bluebeard roaring and sad and beautifully intoned.

Kurt Weill's two careers, first as a German and then a naturalized American insisting on a patriotic reading of his last name as "while," might be viewed as mirror reflections, reversals each of each. After perfusing his German symphony and opera with popular sounds—Doktor Jazz—he came to Broadway, uplifting its vernacular sound with classical techniques—the Pop Maestro. Weill's work is still being reinvestigated, as witness the New York City Opera's revival (and revision) of Der Silbersee (Silverlake), recorded on Nonesuch in English with Joel Grey, William Neill, Elizabeth Hynes, and Elaine Bonazzi under Julius Rudel. Note the collaboration of opera and theatre people; and the librettist, Georg Kaiser, was a playwright rather than a librettist. But then, Stravinsky had his Cocteau and Auden; twentieth-century opera makes its own rules. Silverlake dates back to 1932, high Weimar, when symbolism and realism were trying to tolerate each other in the unique blend that might be called "Berlin expressionism": socially aware and theatrically adventurous. It's a heavy mix, and very dated, though Weill's music nicely exemplifies the grouchy sentimentality that marks his German years especially. The two discs include dialogue.

The rest of the German Weill discography emphasizes the Brecht collaborations; and here especially Weill's oeuvre stands apart from those of Stravinsky and Bartók. With the former, we think first of rhythm, of the dance; with the second, we think of folklore, of ethnic symphony. But with Weill we think of Brecht, the little tycoon of what the Nazis termed "cultural bolshevism." And with Weill-Brecht we think of Die Dreigroschenoper (The Threepenny Opera). Perhaps this work does not properly belong here, as a play with songs rather than an opera—a work strictly for actors. But it is central to Weill, and a useful complement to its source, The Beggar's Opera (see Chapter 2).

If Gay's satire is a "Newgate pastoral," The Threepenny Opera is

Weimar cabaret, savage where Gay is ironic and shifting the love plot to the side to concentrate on the social implications. Two hundred years after *The Beggar's Opera*, *The Threepenny Opera* opened in a small, out-of-the-way theatre after bellicose rehearsals. The smart money, to lend Broadway jargon to the Berlin of Pabst and Döblin, didn't give the show a week; the Mrs. Peachum, assuming a disaster, had accepted an engagement for the night after the premiere. The first minutes played to a cold house, but the public suddenly warmed to . . . no, not the Moritat ("The Ballad of Mack the Knife"), nor to "Pirate Jenny," but to the Kanonensong, and the rest is opera history: that of the ceaselessly stimulating appeal of a theatre piece unthinkable without song. Post-Wagnerian opera has more in it than revolts against *Leitmotive* and fantasy.

The basic *Threepenny* recording is Columbia's early stereo set (Odyssey) under Wilhelm Brückner-Rüggeberg with Lotte Lenya playing Jenny and, I have no doubt, watching over every detail down to the brand of reed employed by the clarinet. The use of a narrator, though out of text, is Brechtian, and the performance compelling. The elaborate booklet makes much of the inclusion of Mrs. Peachum's "Ballad of Sexual Slavery," dropped during rehearsals because of performer's outrage, though it was quickly reinstated and is on most recordings. However, Columbia does include Lucy Brown's aria, an opera spoof dropped because of performer's inadequacy and never reinstated. All told, this is Weill-Brecht at its truest, opera for actors, proud and correct.

A Telefunken LP gathers the fourteen 78 sides made in 1930, two years after the premiere, with whoever was playing the roles at the time—Lenya again (in three parts), along with Erika Helmke, Willy Trenk-Trebitsch (Macheath here; Mr. Peachum on the Columbia album), and Erich Ponto. American Weill buffs will be pleasantly startled by Lenya's sopranino, an indication of the high line Weill heard in his head while composing—for, he said, he always worked from her muse—as opposed to the bamboo bass she had become when his music later came into fashion here. Obviously, these are authoritative performances in a theatre atmosphere, even in antique sound. On the other hand, Heliodor's 1968 disc offers the corruptions of the studio— the second finale, for instance, accompanied solely on guitar. True, this suggests Brecht's own performances of his songs at parties, but it sounds decrepit. Too bad, for the program is unusually complete. Even less useful is a Vanguard mono entry combining opera veterans with *diseurs*, completely out of style.

Die Dreigroschenoper, more than most works, must be heard in one's own language. Luckily, both *Threepenny Opera* casts are drawn from the stage, MGM's mono disc from the famous 1954 Theatre de Lys production in the Marc Blitzstein "adaptation" and Columbia's, in stereo, from Richard Foreman's 1976 Lincoln Center staging, in Ralph Manheim and John Willett's more faithful rendering. Each disc offers a full text, and the choice between them will center on style of approach. MGM's off-Broadway troupe, including Jo Sullivan, Beatrice Arthur (later television's Maude), Charlotte Rae, Scott Merrill, and Martin Wolfson as well as Lenya's Jenny-as-antifascist-survivor, was struggling to institute a neglected work as a classic. Nineteen fifty-four can't have been a great time in which to argue the case for a strongly leftist polemic; Brecht himself had appeared before HUAC in 1947 and promptly left America. Blitzstein, then, had to be cautious. To pick one instance out of many: in the Moritat, Brecht cites as one of Macheath's victims one Schmul Meier, intending to shock with the blatantly Semitic ring of the name, to take anti-Semitism back from the anti-Semites. Unwilling to test sensitivities in a post-Holocaust age, Blitzstein renamed the victim Louie Miller. The whole disc suffers from this muzzling of the Brechtian bite, but it's a compelling performance—and one that duplicates the original's air of an uncelebrated company taking the town against the smart money's bets, for the tiny de Lys played host to the show into the 1960s.

The Foreman production competes with stereo sound, retranslated Brechtian truth, and Weill's original orchestration. MGM's Samuel Matlowsky had to rearrange the score for a kind of rinky-dink Palm Court orchestra. Foreman's conductor (and collaborator on a number of operas), Stanley Silverman, retrieved the sound of 1928, even unto constructing an acoustic Hawaiian guitar for the Tango Ballad. Some of his conductor's choices give the music a swing it doesn't have on any other disc. Purists may resent his speeding up of the trio of the overture, which gives it a slick oomph, a sort of classical rock—MGM's Matlowsky's even tempo retains the needed Bachian sarcasm. But surely everyone will appreciate the way Silverman builds the Moritat from a dirge into a raving fox trot.

What of the singers?—the actors, rather. In general, Silverman's cast is inferior to Matlowsky's in voice but superior in personal reverberation. I prefer Charlotte Rae's Mrs. Peachum and Beatrice Arthur's Lucy on MGM, but, on Columbia, Karoline Kava's Polly is more knowing, Raul Julia's Mac sleazier, and C. K. Alexander's Peachum more vicious than their predecessors; and, while Lenya's Jenny is indisputably the icon of the Weill revival in America, it is a relief to hear a fresh voice in the part for once, especially as Ellen Greene makes so much of it. Columbia includes a lyric sheet and detailed notes, and altogether has preserved one of New York's most memorable Weill productions.

In the days of Mozart and Beethoven, opera scores were commonly turned into woodwind divertimentos, and the neo-Classical rediscovery of the wind combinations—as well as a certain distaste for the Romantic *Schmalz* of the violin tone—led Weill to arrange a *Threepenny* suite, called *Kleine Dreigroschenmusik.* It's fascinating, the familiar tunes rescored and combined—essential listening for Weill buffs. Otto Klemperer introduced it and recorded it decades later, in stereo, on Angel; David Atherton has a competitive (and slightly more complete) reading on DG, as part of a three-disc box that also contains *Happy End,* something of a *Twopenny Opera,* set in Chicago. Columbia's *Happy End,* with Lenya and a chorus, is dynamic but really a studio rendering. Atherton's more theatrical presentation unfortunately reorders numbers and drops the show's hit, "The Bilbao Song."

With *Aufstieg und Fall der Stadt Mahagonny* (Rise and Fall of Mahagonny City) we come to an out-and-out Weill-Brecht opera, written for opera-house casts, productions, audiences. Atherton's album cues us in with the short early version of 1927, the *Mahagonny* Songspiel,* comprising six songs that turned up in the opera and three orchestral interludes that didn't. Atherton's chamber orchestra plays quite well, but an odd miking procedure renders some of the singers indistinct. It is nevertheless an atmospheric performance, though it surely goes against style to have the two songs in English rendered by English singers—without the natural German accents that enhance Brecht's sly suggestion that Pidgin Colonial, so to say, was the inevitable Esperanto of capitalism.

The full-length *Mahagonny* arrived in 1930, and vies with Křenek's *Jonny Spielt Auf,* Hindemith's *Mathis der Maler,* and Strauss's *Die Schweigsame Frau* as *Streitfragen,* "controversies," of late- and post-Weimar censorship troubles. Columbia's *Mahagonny,* in fine late mono, was another of Lenya's projects. It lacks the zing that makes Columbia's German *Dreigroschenoper* arresting, and Lenya herself cannot deliver the soprano Jenny that she sang in 1930, but it remains a great performance of a great—Weill's greatest?—work. With luck, some label may give us a stereo *Mahagonny,* this time in English so we can accept it as its authors intended us to, with the immediacy of line-by-line intelligibility.

*The *Mahagonny* Songspiel is not to be confused—it often is—with *Das Kleine Mahagonny* (The Little Mahagonny), an early capsule version of the later evening-length opera and as yet unrecorded.

The Weill-Brecht scores are as suited to LP recitals as Mozart or Puccini. The classic entry is another of Lenya's missionary exhortations on Columbia, *Berlin Theatre Songs,* choice Brecht cullings plus two numbers from *Silverlake,* a disc as famed for its cover painting of Lenya in her de Lys Jenny kit as for the authenticity of the performances. Lenya's energy, vulnerability, and tactless charm make this one of the most notable of all LPs, one in which art and artist are inseparable. Gisela May, hardier and in stereo, covers much the same material on Philips, and Laura Betti, on Orizzonte, offers unusual European material on one side (including a ten-minute cameo of *The Seven Deadly Sins,* in Italian) and Weill's American standards on the other—in, however, free arrangements from jitterbug to modern jazz. Lenya's American recital (Columbia) also—unforgivably—deals in ersatz arrangements. It refreshes to hear a rare, romantic Lenya, the Brechtian controversies put by for "Speak Low" and "September Song." Still, the outstanding cut is the wry "Sing Me Not a Ballad," with a deathless reading of a line about Lenya's ideal man, someone "strong and silent." He would be, Lenya adds, vehemently purring, "Inarticulate . . . but vi'lent." The texture of accent on the last word, from Vienna to Berlin for early triumphs, fleeing the Nazis to Paris, and off to America and transcultural reinvention, is a wonder of the phonograph.

This brings us to the American Weill. "An American opera," he wrote in 1947, "should be part of the living theatre." In short: Broadway. So Weill set out to reorient his sound along American lines, especially after the failure of his first American musical, the Weimarisch *Johnny Johnson.* This is a strange work, a surrealistic antiwar parable with a score now wistful, now louche, designed, like the *Threepenny* songs, to be performed by actors. Ironically enough, its sole recording (MGM, Heliodor), using New York actors, took in two people who abandoned Broadway for opera—Evelyn Lear and Thomas Stewart. Burgess Meredith plays Johnny, and of course Lenya is on hand for official Weill truth, in a single cut.

Weill's later works tend to the musical play rather than to opera. *Lady in the Dark,* however, is a play counting three little operas, each a Freudian dream-turning-nightmare. On LP, Victor's television cast with Ann Sothern is the better performance, Columbia's studio cast with Risë Stevens the more complete. Perhaps the only certain opera in Weill's American batch is *Street Scene,* beautifully caught by the original cast on a Columbia highlights album—one of the heftiest 78 sets of its day, crammed onto LP and kept in the catalogue virtually by *force majeure* (and the faith of Goddard Lieberson, Columbia's president and a friend of the Weills). *Street Scene* affirms the Weillisch mixture of opera and drama—the "living theatre"—in its gathering of the Met's Polyna Stoska and Brian Sullivan, operetta and Hollywood's Anne Jeffreys, and fancy dancers Danny Daniels and Sheila Bond, for the boogie-woogie *divertissement,* "Moon-Faced, Starry-Eyed"—unfortunately left off the record. Spoken cue lines allow the uninitiated to follow the plot, which, despite Weill's "living theatre" theory, is not a sturdy one: in fact a claptrap slice-of-life melodrama twenty years old even then. An odd comparison with the German Weill, whose every show was, whatever its source, contemporary in thrust; or with the ever self-renewing Stravinsky, the timeless Bluebeard of Bartók's opera. Yet Weill's supporters have been emphasizing *Street Scene* lately, banking, no doubt, on its television broadcast—the first such of a Weill piece in twenty years, from Ann Sothern to Catharine Malfitano.

In any case, the *Street Scene* disc is not a great one. Stoska is "operatic" and unsteady, Sullivan a nerd, the orchestra skimpy. But if the artistes are insecure, the thespians are game—and again we find Weill settling for actors, and getting the best of—out of—them. If Stravinsky mainly requires dancers and Bartók Hungarians, Weill needs twentieth-century performers: those to whom the living music theatre means the full art of transformation. And who—it must be asked—knows that better than Lenya? Newcomers should navigate around her discs, and, more currently, around Teresa Stratas's *The Unknown Kurt Weill* (Nonesuch), pulled from manuscripts Lenya passed on in a historical moment. Did Stratas shiver? I do. It's one of the great recitals on LP, not unlike Maria Malibran passing on her music to Maria Callas. For satiric relief, try a cut of *New Faces of 1968* (Warner), Madeline Kahn's "Das Chicago Song," a brilliant spoof of every "Surabaja Johnny" Brecht and Weill wrote.

20

MODERN FRENCH OPERA

※

The twentieth century saw the collapse of grand opera. Those who had briefly worked in the form, like Verdi or Wagner, had gone on to other things; those who had built their reputations on it, like Meyerbeer and Halévy, were about to fall into disrepute. The Opéra itself became a museum, incapable of presenting worthwhile new works—for, as Massenet had shown, the vitality of French music theatre lay in developing the verbal dexterity of *opéra comique*.

Thus, the popular sensation of the first days of the new era was Gustave Charpentier's *Louise*, the tale of a working-class girl who deserts her strict parents for the bohemian life of Montmartre. Charpentier, who wrote his own libretto, supplied so much character detail that he called his piece a "musical novel"—and note the jarring title. After exotic Lakmé, antique Manon, sensual Carmen: plain Louise. Sung throughout, the opera nevertheless observes *comique*'s confidentiality rather than grand opera's oratory; and the fiercely contemporary setting would have been unthinkable in grand opera. It was shocking enough in *opéra comique*, with its look at tenement housework and dinner and, by way of social defiance, its exhilarating view of the roofs of Paris as Louise sings "Depuis le jour" to her painter lover. It's the free artists against the intolerant householders, with Paris as a highly partial referee. Paris loves freedom, and Charpentier caught this mag-

241

nificently; and it was said that many a young woman of Louise's class frequented the Opéra-Comique as her counterpart today would read a romance novel.

Charpentier wanted too much money for the recording rights, so decades passed before he gave in in 1935, luckily to Columbia's classic cast—Ninon Vallin, Georges Thill, and André Pernet—but unfortunately in an abridgment (by the composer) that yields but half the work. Vallin is far more thespian than Thill, but it's a theatrical performance in general. Still, who can enjoy pages from a novel? In the 1976–77 season, Columbia and Angel issued nearly complete versions (both take the same whopping cut in the big Act Three duet), Columbia's Ileana Cotrubas winning the palm as the lovelier (and more youthful) heroine, Angel having in Nicolai Gedda and Julius Rudel the better Julien and conductor. Angel has other advantages: fine sound (Columbia displaces the orchestra and fumbles the crowd scenes) and the superb Father of José van Dam (Columbia's Gabriel Bacquier is in poor voice). Angel also has Beverly Sills's heroine, another in her gallery of utterly correct portrayals. Those who map their opera on sheer voice will want Cotrubas, but Sills's innocently passionate Louise pairs fascinatingly with Gedda's worldly artist.

However, a temporarily forgotten mono set made at the Opéra-Comique with Berthe Monmart, Solange Michel, André Laroze, and Louis Musy under Jean Fournet (Epic) captures the spirit of the piece better than any other. There are plenty of big cuts, but the entire cast, down to the many tiny roles Charpentier used to bring his city to life, play as if they held the author's patent. Monmart's very stimulated "Depuis le jour" lacks the vocal cream that Dorothy Maynor poured out in her classic 78 of 1940, conducted by Serge Koussevitsky; Laroze's painter has passion but lacks elegance; and Musy is past his prime (though he does sound like a work-weary father). Still, Epic gives us the libertarian elation of youth, the stingy disapproval of age, that energize Charpentier's tale. When the young Andrea Guiot launches Irma's shyly enthralled waltz in praise of Paris, we may well be listening in on what drew young women to the first performances: to hear what being young and free sounds like.

If Louise led the sociopolitical reaction to grand opera, Debussy's Pelléas et Mélisande led the artistic one: a few characters in conversation, without arias or act finales or processions or ballets—not even a chorus, save for a few bars, and offstage. Early recordings laid down the French style in this work: a lyric soprano Mélisande, very cleanly presented; a light baritone Pelléas, acting shy; a very musical Golaud; a conductor with the grace of a chanson accompanist. Columbia's 1928 highlights—a few scenes taken whole, not bits here and there—features Marthe Nespoulos, Alfred Maguenat, and Hector Dufranne under Georges Truc (Pearl) in a very free performance, the singers often a bit ahead of or behind the orchestra, unfortunately in sound that mutes the instruments. In 1942 came Victor's classic complete set under Roger Desormière (EMI), highly atmospheric (especially in the interludes), with Irène Joachim's marvelously indeterminate Mélisande—she seems to regard everyone in the opera equally as relative, friend, lover—Henri Etcheverry's surprisingly sensitive Golaud, and Jacques Jansen's demanding Pelléas, so willful that one blames him for the tragedy. Running into LP years, Angel issued a *Pelléas* in this French line under André Cluytens, with Victoria de los Angeles's almost knowledgable Mélisande, turning it into her, not Golaud's, tragedy. As Camille Maurane pleads and de los Angeles resists, we feel the air of adultery more keenly than elsewhere, though the two are technically innocent.

It is a strength of Debussy's vocal writing that different line readings result in different stories. *Pelléas* was Ernest Ansermet's favorite opera, one he conducted often and felt strongly about—yet his mono reading (London, Richmond) centers on Mélisande (the energetic Suzanne Danco), the stereo (London) on Golaud (the brutal George London). Ansermet's stereo Geneviève, Josephine Veasey, delivers the best reading of the letter on disc.

Conductors, too, shift the emphasis, as Pierre Boulez (Columbia) and Herbert von Karajan (Angel) do, in thunderous accompaniments and broad sonics. Boulez's derives from Covent Garden, with the elaborate Elisabeth Söderström and the sole recorded tenor Pelléas, George Shirley, his bright projection bringing a new color to the work after decades of barytons-martins. Von Karajan, like Boulez a passionate rather than tactful Debussyan, offers a mezzo Mélisande in Frederica von Stade—again, each set brings something new to the work. Received opinion prefers Desormière and von Karajan. Comparing the two, one finds equally authentic—but quite contradictory—readings, the older one a fairytale, the newer a love story.

Debussy wrote no other operas, though Angel issued the surviving fragments from his *Pelléas*-like Poe project, *La Chute de la Maison d'Usher,* digitally under Georges Prêtre. Paul Dukas write his one opera, *Ariane et Barbe-Bleue,* somewhat in the *Pelléas* style, at that using another Maeterlinck play—and one that includes Mélisande among its characters. (When she appears, Dukas pays *hommage* by quoting *Pelléas.*) *Ariane* is as positive a character as Mélisande is passive. Bluebeard's sixth wife, she finds the first five hidden in his castle and at-

tempts to liberate them. Like Debussy, Dukas chastely revels in music
as shape and color, catching the sounds, as it were, of great dark
spaces, of water, sunlight, even of cascading jewels. He is more generous, however, with song structures and use of chorus. MRF's relay
of a French radio broadcast offers Epic's Louise, Berthe Monmart, as
a very impetuous Ariane; Erato's digital set has the more sensitive
Katherine Ciesinski, feeling her way through the dire castle and life's
choices. This is an excellent performance, beautifully conducted by
Armin Jordan in atmospheric sound. The "Filles d'Orlamonde" chorus,
for instance—the first time we hear the imprisoned wives—builds to a
tremendous climax. As Ariane is another of those French falcon parts,
we have option of timbre, Monmart's bright soprano or Ciesinski's
slightly overparted but game mezzo.

Maurice Ravel is often linked with Debussy for a stylistic similarity
in some of their piano, chamber, and symphonic music. But Ravel's
operas are a different case, waggishly rhythmic where *Pelléas* tends to
flow dreamily. *L'Heure Espagnole* * does deal in the musical conversations
that many associate with *Pelléas*, but the tale is earthy and droll. Two
mono sets are the best: London's under Ansermet and Angel's under
Cluytens. Angel has the wittier delivery, but London wins the palm
for its clear, rangy sound and a more musical cast. In the Habañera
finale, at the moment wherein Don Inigo drops his voice so low that
the contrabassoon has to finish the phrase, Angel's Charles Clavensy
cuts off before the joke is in gear; London's André Vessières sinks
down so thoroughly that it's hard to tell where he ends and the bas-
soon begins. Then, too, Angel's narrow sound makes a hash of this
ensemble, while London spells it out cleanly. London's *L'Enfant et les
Sortilèges* (The Child and the Enchantments), also under Ansermet,
remains choice for similar reasons, but Angel's gives André Previn a
slightly livelier cast and digital sound, strategic in this uniquely scored
fantasy.

All these works premiered at the Opéra-Comique (*L'Enfant* at Monte
Carlo, a comparable house), underlining French composers' desertion
of the Opéra and its conventions. But note that all these titles as well
reinvented *opéra comique*. Nothing in the days of Gounod and Thomas
suggested that plays might be turned into opera virtually as they were
scripted, without adaptation (as Maeterlinck's were), or that an opera
might treat an hour of attempted, foiled, then successful adultery (as

---

* Literally reading as *The Spanish Hour*, the title puns on "heure" to mean something
like *How They Keep Time in Spain*.

L'Heure Espagnole does), or that the deviously sensual Colette might write a libretto whose protagonist is a child (as she did in *L'Enfant*).

What, then, of unreconstructed *opéra comique?* Henri Rabaud's *Mârouf, Savetier de Caire* is a facsimile, save that musical conversations outnumber arias and ensembles. An Arabian night, *Mârouf*—cobbler, the title goes on, of Cairo—enjoys the exotic setting that old *opéra comique* loved and the fanciful orchestration that new *comique* could not live without. Peters offers a decent if sparkless performance on three discs from Nantes with Michel Lecocq (in the tenor version of the title role; Rabaud left an alternate for barytons-martins) and Anne-Marie Blanzat under Jesus Etcheverry, a very close recording, with everyone tumbling out of the speakers. Little of the piquant, the alien, the grotesque—the sheer wonder of the fantasy—comes through. The first appearance of the sumptuous love theme in Mârouf's first duet with his Princess, *Très lent et très large*—slow and grand—is played as if it were Meyerbeer waiting music. MRF offers a smarter reading on two discs; and browsers may sample Mârouf's two arias in Georges Thill's evocative 78s.

Those in search of grand opera's descendants might enjoy Albert Roussel's *Padmâvatî,* an "opera-ballet," a form virtually as old as French opera. The Opéra hosted the premiere, but this is nonetheless a tight work, fleet, even impatient, three discs shorter than Meyerbeer. The setting is India, the time is war, and the question is, Will the unapproachable Padmâvatî give herself to the conqueror to save her people? MRF offers Rita Gorr, Albert Lance, and Gérard Souzay under Jean Martinon in acceptable sound; Angel has Marilyn Horne, Nicolai Gedda, and José van Dam under Michel Plasson in brilliant digital. Both performances are compelling, Horne emphasizing the heroine's sensuality, Gorr her strength.

Manuel de Falla often falls into chapters on French music, for his seven years' infatuated stay in Paris gave him access to Debussy, Dukas, and Ravel, and his music at times shows their influence. A Spaniard pledged to nationalistic art, however, de Falla chose subjects that set his two operas apart. Their length is also unusual: they sit better on one or three sides than on two or four, necessitating filler material, usually de Falla's ballet with song, *El Amor Brujo* (The Demon Lover). *La Vida Breve* (Life Is Short) finds de Falla conventional in approach with a story that might have served Giordano. The stereo competition pits Angel's Victoria de los Angeles, Ines Rivadeneyra, and Carlos Cossutta under Rafael Frühbeck de Burgos against DG's Teresa Berganza, Alicia Nafé, and José Carreras under Garcia Navarro. It's hard to choose. Angel has more passion and atmosphere, but Berganza is superb, earthily enchanting where de los Angeles is plangently sweet. Compare them on "Solo tengo dos cariños" (I love only two people), de los Angeles virginal, as befits a young woman addressing her grandmother, Berganza startlingly sensual, a young woman speaking of her lover.

De Falla intended *La Vida Breve* as an ethnic study, but its borrowed verismo compromises it somewhat. But then: setting a page of Cervantes as *El Retablo de Maese Pedro* (Master Peter's Puppet Show), de Falla provided one of opera's unique works, on the performance of a chivalric romance by Master Peter's puppet troupe, who so excite Don Quixote that he destroys the entire company. Yet Peter and Don Quixote, too, are puppets. With its piquant fanfares, pompously antique dance strains, and adolescent (actually a soprano) narrating in spare recit, *El Retablo* is the kind of opera that particularly appeals to people who don't usually like opera, and it goes well on disc despite the lack of the appealing visuals. Of the two mono recordings, Angel's Eduardo Toldra has a better Quixote than London's Ataulfo Argento (Richmond), and a more prominent harpsichord to bring out the score's haughty whimsey. For stereo sound and a more appropriate filler, de Falla's harpsichord concerto, try Argo's disc under Simon Rattle.

The reader may have noticed a minimum of the big "voice" stars in these post-*Pelléas* operas, those big names who show up in Meyerbeer, Gounod, Massenet, or, for that matter, Puccini, the bulk of whose career (from *Tosca* on) coincides with the years covered thus far in this chapter. True, we have Horne's Padmâvatî with Gedda and van Dam, a cast for *Le Prophète* or *Carmen*. Generally, however, *Louise* marks the end of French opera's great singing roles, for the pervasive influence of *Pelléas* calls in specialized talents as surely as does verismo or atonal expressionism. In these years, French singers must be, above all, reciters, declaimers, nearly *speakers* of song. It cannot be coincidental that, while German and Italian singers spent the 78 years recording excerpts from the newest operas, most of the famous French singers increasingly retrenched, concentrating on older and vocally more grateful composition. Granted, operas such as *Pelléas* and *L'Heure Espagnole* are not as readily excerptable as the "number" operas of the 1800s. Still, it is notable that the most prominent French voices of the twentieth century built their discographies mainly on the classics: Georges Thill, forthright and appealing, in the grand-opera heroes; Marcel Journet, suavely macabre, in the grand-opera villains; Germaine Lubin, effortlessly supreme, in Wagner. The three left samples of their work in Reyer's *Sigurd*, grand opera's version of *le Wagnerisme*.

By 1930, when all three were active (Journet after four deacades), *Sigurd* was dowdy next to *L'Enfant et les Sortilèges*. Yet Reyer had the chic, not Ravel. When we encounter contemporary French opera on 78 cuts, it most frequently belongs to the less-celebrated singers—Suzanne Balguérie, for instance, an Isolde and Donna Anna, exuberantly lovely in two solos from *Ariane et Barbe-Bleue*. Even Mary Garden, a relentless promoter of new work, somewhat avoided it on disc, though she did record a cut each of *Louise* ("Depuis le jour") and *Le Jongleur de Notre-Dame* ("Liberté!") when they were almost brand-new, and left a snippet of Mélisande with Debussy at the piano.

At least the century's first quarter is well covered in LP sets. Operas of the following generation, including those of such as Milhaud and Honegger, have been scarcely sketched in, and not till the pop-classical success of Francis Poulenc did an operatic oeuvre get full representation. Poulenc's, three settings of plays, claim the participation of his soprano of choice, Denise Duval: as a woman-turned-man in Guillaume Apollinaire's absurdist *Les Mamelles de Tirésias* (Angel mono, Seraphim), as a nun of questionable vocation in Georges Bernanos's very moving *Dialogues des Carmelites* (Angel mono), as the losing half of a spent affair in Cocteau's short monodrama *La Voix Humaine* (Victor stereo). Duval matches Poulenc in versatility, as facetious in Apollinaire as she is fearfully direct in Bernanos, and their colleagues, from the Opéra-Comique zanies of *Tirésias* to such Opéra stalwarts as Régine Crespin, Rita Gorr, and Denise Scharley in *Dialogues*, are exemplary. LR offers a somewhat shrill performance, in Italian, of *Dialogues'* 1957 Scala premiere with Virginia Zeani. But this album, like Seraphim's reissue of *Tirésias*, lacks a text booklet, a dire omission with the very theatrical Poulenc.

Comparably theatrical—and more deeply rooted in the pop world—is Gilbert Bécaud's *Opéra d'Aran* (Angel), which enjoyed a flash success in 1962 in an open run at a commercial theatre in Paris. A verismo tale of a shipwrecked Italian's disruption of a bleak Irish island, *Opéra d'Aran* is melodious and fierce, quite a respectable credit for a man who, albeit clasically trained, made his name as a cabaret troubador. The ruthlessly outré Poulenc set the moment of Thérèse-Tirésias's sex-change to a "Boston" (the European term for our "hesitation waltz"), recalling the days when Ravel and Milhaud flooded serious music with the sounds of the dance hall. But Bécaud speaks the common parlance of tuneful opera, a modern Puccini.

Opéra d'Aran is, above all, a vocalists' opera, needing the voices of the 1800s more than the textual clarifiers of the 1900s. Margherita Wallmann staged the premiere, and Angel wisely recorded her cast, all superb singing actors: Alvino Misciano as the Italian, a poet in a society of fisherman; Rosanna Carteri as the woman he dazzles; Agnès Disney as the mother of Carteri's betrothed, who left to make his fortune and never returned; and Frank Schooten as the betrothed, for he does return—just as Misciano and Carteri are about to board the steamer that will take them to a happier world. This moment, the close of Act One, typifies Bécaud's bold narration. As the villagers stand watching, the orchestra dies out, the steamer whistles its last call, the two thwarted lovers stare at Schooten. Silence. And the curtain falls.

21

STRAUSS

Richard Strauss's operas almost entirely coincide with the development of the phonograph. *Guntram,* his first opera, appeared in 1894, a bit after the first home machines and cylinders had been put on the market and a bit before Emile Berliner introduced the playing disc. *Intermezzo* enjoyed its first runs just as acoustic recording ceded to electric. And Strauss's fourteenth opera, *Die Liebe der Danae,* though composed in 1940, was first performed in 1952, just after Europe surrendered to the institution of the LP. Thus, we have a number of "creator" 78s (including some with the real creator conducting), tastes of what *Der Rosenkavalier, Ariadne auf Naxos,* and *Daphne* sounded like at their premieres.

This is no mean vanity, for a launching sensation was considered as crucial in Strauss's day as in Bellini's, and a Strauss premiere was virtually a Continental event. So it is instructive to hear his first casts, as well as other singers, such as Lotte Lehmann, who were closely associated with Strauss in his years of influence.

The first thing we learn is that the essential Strauss instrument—the vivacious, soaring soprano—seems not to have been born with these operas, but to have developed with time. Early recordings of *Salome*'s "Jochanaan, ich bin verliebt" from Emmy Destinn and Johanna Gadski reveal bright top ranges and bell-like, almost *pizzicato* effects on the high notes, but little vivacity, little soaring. The voices even lack body—this doubtless because of the primitive technology, because both were of Wagnerian weight. Still, we begin to see why

Strauss kept urging lyric sopranos like Geraldine Farrar and Elisabeth Schumann to try Salome: dramatic sopranos were not making the most of it.

Even the three original *Rosenkavalier* sopranos—Margarethe Siems, Eva von der Osten, and Minnie Nast—seem oriented more to the music than to the text. There is a feeling of "School of Lilli Lehmann" about them: a good soprano sings everything well and does not specialize. (Siems was not only the first Marschallin but the first Zerbinetta—two roles virtually no one of today could trade off.) There is, also, a reminder of the helter-skelter of the acoustic horn in these first *Rosenkavalier* 78s in that the celesta in the closing duet sounds like a dripping faucet—again, the primitive technology.

We sense a transition in the 1920s, as in Ariadne's "Es gibt ein Reich" by Maria Jeritza and Lotte Lehmann, two classic Strauss sopranos. Neither truly soars, but both locate the shocking low notes with which Strauss studded his soprano staves. Lehmann is more interpretive, Jeritza more radiant; both take an insulting breath right in the middle of Ariadne's most soaring line, "Du wirst mich befreien" (You will free me).

Rose Pauly's two solos from *Die Ägyptische Helena* point toward a more forward, even impetuous vocal placement. Perhaps Marjorie Lawrence's four Victor sides of *Salome*'s final scene—in French, because recorded in Paris—at last give us the true Straussian soprano, gorgeous of voice, decanting the text, dominating the orchestra. (Preiser has an ideal LP transcription.) From Lawrence it is a small step to Elisabeth Schwarzkopf, Leonie Rysanek, Marianne Schech, Lisa della Casa, Eleanor Steber, Christa Ludwig, Gwyneth Jones, and Hildegard Behrens. Perhaps Leontyne Price, in Helena's "Zweite Brautnacht!" (Second honeymoon!), marks the completion of the instrument, the winged brilliance matched by a dark, telling weight in the lower register.

Other voice types are less relevant to Strauss, though the bassbaritone, in such roles as Jochanaan, Orest, and Mandryka, can be crucial. Early recordings of Strauss baritones tend toward the lyrical, with little of the verbal dynamics we expect today. Theodor Scheidl emphasizes this in two excerpts of Jochanaan, calmly sung, barely inflected. At least Strauss wrote well for baritones; tenors he set as wooden figures, and wooden tenors, accordingly, have gravitated to Strauss. *Guntram,* nicely served on Columbia digital, sports a mockup of the Wagnerian hero, and *Feuersnot,* similarly well served on Acanta, doesn't even have a tenor lead.

At that, *Salome*'s tenor, Herod, is not always a "tenor" as opera understands the voice, but a performer—as opposed to a singer. Solti's Gerhard Stolze (London) epitomizes that Schoenbergian Herod, fetid and clammy, marring an otherwise superb set, the sound so good even the mono glows and Birgit Nilsson's Salome a wonderfully spendthrift thunder. A purer *Salome* may be heard on MRF's 1949 Met broadcast with Ljuba Welitsch under Fritz Reiner, for Welitsch's voice carried the girlish quality the role needs. (Still, her notorious 1944 broadcast of the final scene under Lovro von Matacic, on Seraphim, provides a last word in poised decadence; one wants to bathe after hearing it. Remember, Salome not only was scandalous art: it *is* scandalous art.) Certainly Gwyneth Jones, also caught live, at Hamburg in 1970 (DG), gives us few clues to Salome's amoral sensuality; and Dietrich Fischer-Dieskau, her Jochanaan, has to work against his hundred Schubert discs, putting something of a bow tie on his portrayal. *

This Hamburg *Salome* is conducted by Karl Böhm, Strauss's artistic confederate on the personal level. Yet von Karajan wins the palm, for a most beautiful yet authentic *Salome* (Angel: Behrens, Karl-Walter Böhm, van Dam). Victor's Caballé suggests Strauss's dream come true, a "pretty" voice withstanding the orchestra's roar, but Victor's set never comes together, and this is where von Karajan triumphs. Sifting the querulous expressionism for its poetry, he idealizes cast and work. His Salome, Behrens, is lovely, thoughtless, dangerous—listen to her "Ah!" when, failing to get the guards to drag Jochanaan before her, she spots the smitten Narraboth. This is Salome.

Strauss retained the expressionistic commentary in *Elektra,* vocally unique in Strauss for its revisionist use of Wagnerian types in its ultra-Brünnhilde (Elektra), lurid Fricka (Klytemnestra), frantic Wotan (Orest), and cheesy comprimario Siegfried (Aegisth). Only Chrysothemis holds the main line in Straussian vocal writing, as the expected soaring soprano, the Leonie Rysanek part, so to speak. Rysanek herself was to have sung the role for Solti (London), but she had to cancel. Marie Collier took over, disputing what is otherwise one of the phonograph's great stereo documents, spectacular in sound and monumental in performance. Regina Resnik preserves her Klytemnestra, an important portrayal for two decades; Tom Krause corrects Scheidl's lyric baritone with a darker, more dramatic approach to Orest; and, for that matter, Collier's supporters note how valiantly this Kunstdiva filled in what is basically a Stimmdiva part. Nilsson and Solti, mainly, are what make the set go. They have no rivals, even if Nilsson lacks that

---

* All credit, though, to DG, whose booklet presents Wilde's original French text along with German and English translations, showing where Strauss cut to turn a play into an opera libretto.

measure of tragic majesty to pour into "Ja, ich diene hier im Haus" (Yes, I'm a servant here) when her returning brother takes her for a supernumerary.

Of other *Elektras*, there is Thomas Beecham's famous 1947 broadcast (Erna Schlüter, Welitsch, Schoeffler), its final scene released commercially (Victor) and the whole pirated on many a label—a wonderful reading. There is Decca's mono highlights disc under Ferdinand Leitner—Elektra's monologue, her scene with Klytemnestra, and the Recognition—with Christel Goltz, Elisabeth Höngen, and Ferdinand Frantz, important as a souvenir of a different grade of Strauss soprano, voice-poor, who gets by on expertise. Inge Borkh, who sings Elektra for Böhm (DG mono), is another such. They can't touch Nilsson; still, Goltz's interview with her mother is startlingly good, and Frantz, Furtwängler's choice Wotan, is admirably rugged.

Just as Strauss had found his *Salome* libretto by cutting down a play, so did he take his *Elektra* text. It was the work of Hugo von Hofmannsthal, and the famous collaboration continued with *Der Rosenkavalier*, recorded in 1933 with a classic cast: Lotte Lehmann, Maria Olszewska, Elisabeth Schumann, and Richard Mayr (HMV, Angel, Seraphim). It might have been even more classic, as HMV had invited Strauss to conduct. His fee was too high, so Robert Heger stepped in. Only half the opera is here, but this is the closest any of the four principals came to recording any role complete, and Heger, in the event, leads the Vienna Philharmonic with verve. In fact, the performance is fresher than some recent versions, the big moments and celebrated lines often indelibly delivered—Mayr's oddly matter-of-fact reading of his exit line, "Leopold, mir gengan" (Let's go), for instance, as if Ochs has given up all fight and just wants to get home. Lehmann, of course, was the era's Marschallin, and her authority sweeps one away. It must have swept her away, too, for she left the studio without delivering *her* exit line, one of the most famous in opera: the heartbreakingly renunciatory "Ja, ja." Schumann filled in for Lehmann, apparently in flawless imitation.

The complete *Rosenkavaliers* of the LP years revealed the piece as a prime phonograph study, for at home we can follow every line of the libretto, one of opera's richest. Von Hofmannsthal is one of the few librettists whose psychology has not only insight but wit. With such beautifully drawn characters and so many comprehensive portrayals, we become impatient with albums that aren't entirely excellent— Kempe's (Urania mono) and Bernstein's (Columbia), with Marschallins in questionable voice, or deWaart's (Philips), generally decent but enchanted only by Frederica von Stade's gorgeous Octavian, or even

Angel's highlights LP, with della Casa and Anneliese Rothenberger switching off roles in the duets, reminding us how often sopranos are graduated from Sophie to Octavian or Octavian to the Marschallin (some have sung all three over the course of a career). It's nice to be reminded; but the disc is uninflected when della Casa (a famous Octavian) tries the Marschallin, a bit light when Rothenberger (a great Sophie) tries Octavian.

Böhm's *Rosenkavalier* (DG) is as delightful as his *Salome* is disappointing. This is an energetic reading, persuasive in the rhapsody of the prelude, in complementing Irmgard Seefried's impulsive Octavian, in the bracing preparations for the Presentation of the Rose, in the blatant mockery of Ochs in the Tavern. Marianne Schech, so often unworthy on disc, is here at her best, playing beautifully with Seefried in the last third of Act One, Octavian bewildered and the Marschallin briefly giving way to her fears at "Heut oder morgen," then quickly retrieving diplomatic cover. As Ochs, Kurt Böhme is so vital and spontaneous that, at the filthy giggle he drops into his speech to the Marschallin about seducing women, one is disgusted at the character before one remembers to admire the singer. With Rita Streich as Sophie, a young Fischer-Dieskau as her father, and Dresden forces, this is the first fine complete set, not as beautiful as Erich Kleiber's Vienna entry (London mono: Reining, Jurinac, Gueden, Weber) but more delightful. However, London struck back in stereo in the marvelous Solti reading (Crespin, Yvonne Minton, Helen Donath, Manfred Jungwirth), sometimes too forceful but nonetheless graceful in Crespin's Marschallin, so *boulevardière* that she makes even Maria Reining *hausfrauisch* by comparison.

Angel's quartet of Schwarzkopf, Ludwig, Teresa Stitch-Randall, and Otto Edelmann under von Karajan remains the modern classic, despite a few idiotically tiny cuts and mere mono, reproachable in 1956, when London and Columbia were hedging the risk with emergency stereo masters and EMI was dragging its feet on stereo as it had done on LP. All the more shocking, then, that producer Walter Legge went to great lengths to make this the world's permanent *Rosenkavalier*, casting for strength and novelty even in the small roles. (Ljuba Welitsch is the duenna; Nicolai Gedda sings "Di rigori armato" in the levée; Kirsten Meyer tackles Annina with gusto and a wink; and Schwarzkopf, Ludwig, and Meyer double as the three orphans.) Legge himself ran up the booklet's English translation, to make sure the Hofmannsthalian flavor came through. It is notable that von Karajan, nearly thirty years later, and this time complete to the note, could not outdo his mono reading. He clearly meant to, for the almost arrogantly slow and detailed prelude to Act One implies a "this time for sure." But the new cast (Tomowa-Sintov, Baltsa, Janet Perry, Moll), however impressive as sheer sound, is lovely, not wise (DG digital).

Legge's multistar approach to *Der Rosenkavalier* held up over the years. Many Vienna stalwarts enrich Solti's album, and Pavarotti, Domingo, and Carreras have sung "Di rigori" on various sets. But no crew matches Legge's for the perfection of *Schmalz*. Note, too, how fastidiously Legge cast Sophie, bringing in an American with a somewhat cold, vibratoless tone. Next to the almost psychopathically stylish Germans, Stitch-Randall sounds culturally virginal—exactly as her character should. The producer as genius.

Legge did it again with Angel's *Ariadne auf Naxos*, still with Schwarzkopf and von Karajan in mono. Leinsdorf's (Victor, London) is heavy-handed, though Sena Jurinac is a treasurable Composer and Roberta Peters a superb Zerbinetta, elated and confidential as she explores the shifting moods of her aria. Kempe's (Angel) suffers stiff *seria* characters, even if Gundula Janowitz is the loveliest of Ariadnes (no intrusive breath mars *her* "Du wirst mich befreien"). Solti's (London) is beautifully balanced, with Leontyne Price's luminous heroine, Tatiana Troyanos's direly fretful Composer, René Kollo's poised Bacchus, and Erich Kunz's grand Major-Domo, a study in facetious tact. Aficionados revel in Böhm's 1944 Vienna performance honoring Strauss's eightieth birthday (DG mono), with the youthful Seefried's exuberant Composer and Maria Reining's handsome heroine (but Alda Noni's Zerbinetta is too chirpy and Max Lorenz's Bacchus unimaginative). Yet, of all *Ariadnes*, von Karajan's offers the most sophisticated presentation of this most sophisticated of operas, *seria* framed by *buffa*, the daring oxymoron prepared by a prologue carefully integrating satire, despair, and wonder.

Here, on Angel, we find the truest heroine (Schwarzkopf), fascinatingly distraught in "Ein schönes war" and purely soaring in "Es gibt ein Reich." Here, also, the most musical comedians, the haughtiest Major-Domo. Seefried improves greatly on her work with Böhm; Rita Streich delivers a zesty Zerbinetta; in such company even Rudolf Schock (Bacchus) behaves himself. In short, von Karajan and company best understand the lavish humanism of Strauss–von Hofmannsthal, the sorrow sensed in sweetness, the inner torments of the heroic, the complexity of self-image in apparently simple personalities.

Oddly, the authors put much of this aside in *Die Frau Ohne Schatten* (The Woman Without a Shadow). Suddenly, we are dealing with the archetypal figures of the storybook: immortal princess and mortal prince, shrewish wife and patient husband, the two couples set into interaction by the princess's viciously scheming nurse. So hieratic is the piece that most of its characters have no names: the Spirit Messenger, the Voice of the Falcon, even just Empress, Emperor, Nurse. (The most interesting character, the Empress's father Keikobad, never appears.) *Die Frau*, furthermore, is a long opera, nearly four hours of music. Strauss had long been accused of sycophantic Wagnerism, especially for the general tone of *Guntram*'s story and the volume of *Elektra*'s orchestra. But *Die Frau* is his only really Wagnerian work, the one made entirely of permutations of *Leitmotive* and employing voices that also sing Isolde, Ortrud, Tristan, Sachs. An extremely Straussian cast introduced it, in Vienna in 1919: Jeritza, Lehmann, Mayr—and Karl Oestvig, not Straussian, but then neither is the Emperor. The staging was inadequate, and this colossal fairytale needs visual magic; also, its length daunted; and the music was not heard enough to become familiar. (Not a single 78 side was cut.) The usual know-nothing critics enforced its neglect, but revivals in the post–World War II years have revealed it as a masterpiece, though one that is improved by cutting.

In fact, none of the complete sets is complete. London took the cast of the 1955 Vienna staging into the studio, wisely making a stereo tape just in case. It came in handy when the new Met had a smash with *Die Frau* in the 1960s and Richmond rereleased the decade-old performance with a Met stage design on the cover, unfortunately without the original's table of *Leitmotive*, keyed into the text booklet so one could get a grip on this complex, restless score. London's major advantage is its near-completeness. Böhm conducts Rysanek, Goltz, Elisabeth Höngen, Hans Hopf, and Schoeffler, only the last at his best, though Goltz's unlikable timbre at least suits the shrew, and Höngen is the least unsteady of the recorded Nurses, a lucky strike in that London offers by far the fullest reading of her part.

DG's first of two *Fraus* comes live from Munich in 1963, with Ingrid Bjoner, Inge Borkh, Martha Mödl, Jess Thomas, and Fischer-Dieskau under Josef Keilberth. It's heavily (sometimes absurdly) cut, but the stereo sound is clear and the performance better than it looks on paper. Keilberth's lyricism misses Böhm's intensity, but Borkh delivers a telling shrew, one of the opera's few characters—her husband Barak is the other—who truly come alive psychologically. Mödl is a fascinating Nurse, if vocally painful, and Fischer-Dieskau makes an ideal Barak, the character's wistful patience built into the very sound of his voice. Hear how Schubertian he makes the downward melisma on "Damit ich sie stille" (So I could soothe them) when begging his wife to give him children.

DG brought *Die Frau* back to Vienna in 1977, taping—live in the

Staatsoper—a celebrated grouping of the day: Rysanek, Nilsson, James King, and Walter Berry. As with the *Puritani* Quartet of Grisi, Rubini, Tamburini, and Lablache, with Mario later in for Rubini, this *Frau* quartet bore an alternate: Christa Ludwig had sung Barak's wife earlier in this company, an amazing stunt for a mezzo, as the role runs from a low F to high C sharp. Böhm again conducts, far more vitally than before, though he was by now taking slashing cuts, even during the Emperor's "Falcon" monologue in Act Two. Still, this is the greatest *Frau* of all, a performance that quickly became legendary in Vienna, though DG waited till 1986 to release the discs.

The singing is not flawless: Rysanek takes most of the evening to warm up (she skips the difficult top D in her entrance scene), King was always a stolid Emperor, and Ruth Hesse's Nurse is, like the other Nurses, overblown. Still, everything fits together decisively, and the great moments are truly great, as when Nilsson gives a taste of Schoenbergian *Sprechstimme* to "Dritthalb Jahr," underlining Strauss's on-and-off flirtation with expressionism. Böhm matches her note for note. Their collaboration, for a page or two, is hair-raisingly brilliant, creating one of those rare readings in which a key scene is enlightened for you forever.

If all the *Fraus* suffer erratic vocalism, all its LP excerpts are notable for sure singing (and King, on Angel, gets a shot at the complete "Falcon" scene). For a taste of the original Met *Frau* quartet, try Ludwig and Berry's Act Three duet (Seraphim), then sample, for a change, two American Empresses, Eleanor Steber (ST/and mono) in the opening scene and Leontyne Price (Victor) in the second-act nightmare. Steber's cut, caught live at a Carnegie Hall recital, suggests the improvisational make-do of the early 78 years, with a piano accompaniment and no theatre fidelity. (Steber takes the Falcon's lines herself.) Price's scene exemplifies contemporary recording style, which gives us not only a full orchestra but all secondary singers as needed (including a Falcon, Patricia Clark). If one were to tape these selections in story order, appending Leinsdorf's *Frau* suite (Seraphim)—Leinsdorf's own arrangement, a harmless potpourri—one would have the equivalent of the highlights albums that opera buffs assembled on a freelance basis in the early 78 years: the most popular bits rendered in a variety of styles (not to mention languages) by different singers over a period of twenty-five years, plus the odd "gems" medley thrown together by a small band.

For instance, an admirer of *Arabella*, having no complete set to purchase, would put together his own album, comprising, say, "Aber der Richtige" by Viorica Ursuleac and Margit Bokor of the original cast, Lehmann's overaged but vital "Mein Elemer!," the second-act duet of Marta Fuchs and Paul Schoeffler, and the final duet of Tiana Lemnitz and Gerhard Hüsch, beautifully rendered. Not till the stereo age were we to hear what goes on between these excerpts in the last Strauss–von Hofmannsthal collaboration, often compared to *Der Rosenkavalier* because the setting is again Vienna and the same cast could sing both operas (though here the von Faninal takes a lead and the Sophie is merely a bit.) London's Solti (della Casa, Gueden, London) is stylish, Angel's Sawallisch (Varady, Donath, Fischer-Dieskau) perfunctory, however digital, completely missing the swing of the waltz that irrupts into the end of "Mein Elemer!" Angel's mono highlights gives the most telling performance, very lyrical. The orchestra, for once, never overpowers, and Anny Felbermayer (Zdenka), Nicolai Gedda (Matteo), and Josef Metternich (Mandryka) wield smaller voices than one is used to. Schwarzkopf's Arabella is perfection, the singer's opulent deliberation mirroring the character's pensive approach to life. But this brings us back to excerpts. For a whole *Arabella*, Straussians swear by a 1947 Salzburg cast on recent undergrounds: Reining, della Casa, and Hotter under Böhm, in brittle but listenable sound. Reining is, as always, marvelous but disappointing, lovely in "Mein Elemer!", then embarrassing in the last measures of the Act Two duet. Georg Hann is a strong Waldner (the Ochs role), Julius Patzak Elemer; and Böhm uses the two-act revision, telescoping Acts Two and Three into an entity.

After von Hofmannsthal, Strauss comes into question: did he run out of melody, as some think? *Die Schweigsame Frau* (The Silent Woman) counts a Böhm underground (Gueden, Wunderlich, Hotter; Salzburg, 1959) and Angel's studio reading, less starry but without Böhm's cuts. It's not a great piece. *Daphne* has its admirers: of Victor's two 78s of the original production (Teschemacher, Ralf; Böhm), of Böhm's lush stereo set (Gueden, King, Wunderlich), and of Angel's more intimate digital reading (Popp, Reiner Goldberg, Schreier). Strauss's most successful post–von Hofmannsthal piece is *Capriccio*, the opera about opera. Böhm (DG) has stereo and a wonderful cast, but Angel's Sawallisch counts the incomparably *soignés* Schwarzkopf, Ludwig, Gedda, and Fischer-Dieskau, with Hotter as La Roche, the theatre impresario, and Anna Moffo as the Italian Soprano, an amazingly elitist recording for 1959.

Strauss was almost as well known for conducting as for composing, Hear his stick technique on two 78s of orchestral extracts from *Intermezzo*, Strauss's autobiographical comedy about a woman who nearly destroys her marriage because of a supposed infidelity. The work—

extremely light in texture, almost a play in recit—dates from Strauss's von Hofmannsthal years, but the composer wrote his own libretto, for the poet would have nothing to do with such inflamed naturalism. (Strauss twitted his partner in a private joke, when the wife, Christine, excoriates her husband's "schamlosen Dichter, die alle ihre Erlebnisse auf die Strasse tragen": shameless librettists, who put all their adventures right on the stage.) Far more to von Hofmannsthal's taste was *Die Ägyptische Helena*, on the reconciliation of Helen and Menelaus, filled with magical passes and totemic imagery—and as vigorously lush as *Intermezzo* is sparing. Compare the two, which fall directly between the loaded *Frau* and the intimate *Arabella* in Strauss's canon. London's *Helena* finds Gwyneth Jones now soaring and now just getting by, and Antal Dorati working hard to convince us that the music is worth hearing. It isn't, though Barbara Hendricks pulls off a nice turn as the seeress Aithra. EMI's *Intermezzo*, under Sawallisch, enjoys the aid of the expertly verbal Lucia Popp and Fischer-Dieskau, so comfortable as, virtually, Herr und Frau Kapellmeister Richard Strauss that we become as embarrassed as von Hofmannsthal was . . . pleasantly so.

It may seem an odd note on which to leave the notoriously Wagnerian Strauss. However, it reminds us how often, after von Hofmannsthal died, Strauss brought his texts forward and his orchestra back, how carefully he worked up to the most textual of operas, *Capriccio*. This typifies the twentieth century, the age of the post-Romantic, of the passing of Wagner and the coming of Debussy. The words begin to matter more, even to composers.

22

TWELVE-TONE OPERA

※

"There has been a total rupture between artist and public," Jean Cocteau observed, "since about 1914." Cocteau was speaking essentially
of the Parisian theatregoing public. But his statement aptly sums up
the history of twelve-tone composition, Arnold Schoenberg's technique that is for some the most significant development, and for others the bane, of twentieth-century music.

The technique itself—by which a set arrangement of the twelve
available notes of the chromatic scale is infinitely varied and recom-
bined to furnish the entire content of a given piece—might be regarded as the logical extension of expressionism, the artistic movement that uses distortion, fragmentation, and collage to disclose man's
inner torment. It might also be regarded as expressionism's contain-
ment, expressionism as a rigorous discipline rather than the babble of
private jokes it was threatening to become. But expressionism in Strauss's
Salome and *Elektra* does not overwhelm the melodic material. In
Schoenberg, expressionism is the melodic material itself.

Thus, Schoenberg's short monodrama *Erwartung* (Waiting) presents
a woman wandering through a forest, eventually encountering the corpse
of her lover. It is axiomatically expressionistic that we never learn
whether this is actually happening or a nightmare; Columbia's performance under Robert Craft (in the eight-volume series of two-LP sets
collectively called *The Music of Arnold Schoenberg*) conveys this ambiguity in Helga Pilarczyk's exact rendering of the Schoenbergian
Sprechstimme and in vivid stereo separation. We hear the piece theat-

rically, as a representation caught between imagination and reality, something like a musical version of Edvard Munch's *The Scream*. London's Vienna *Erwartung*, under Christoph von Dohnányi, fails to exploit its digital sonics, and Anja Silja, as always in this repertory, keeps trying to soothe Schoenberg's vocal line, to *sing Sprechstimme's* pitched declamation. In fact, her pitching is very approximate and her top wobbles unsongfully. This is an almost apologetic performance, as if the album bore the warning "Avant-garde material herein." Craft and Pilarczyk, more in command, fold themselves into the art: the music rather than the performance.

The same Columbia box includes Craft's reading of *Die Glückliche Hand* (The Lucky Hand), awkward on disc because the staging turns on a symbolistic use of colored lighting flashing on vicious pantomine. (Columbia's libretto, however, gives a detailed impression of the action.) More amenable to home study in Schoenberg's comedy of manners, *Von Heute auf Morgen* (From Today to Tomorrow), a kind of drawing-room expressionism, suavely satiric rather than lurid, and based, apparently, on an incident in the life of Herr und Frau Franz Schreker (himself a master of expressionist opera: see Chapter 23). Craft's cast, in another of Columbia's Schoenberg boxes, is excellent: Erika Schmidt, Heather Harper, Herbert Schachtschneider (a bit too much the "tenor" here, but then he's supposed to be), and Derrik Olsen.

None of these three works is much appreciated even now, three generations after they were written. However, Schoenberg's one evening-length opera, *Moses und Aron*, has enjoyed considerable popularity, partly for the sensationalist aspect of the Orgy of the Golden Calf, but also because the score is more involving than the other three, keenly characterized in almost pictorial music—the Burning Bush, for instance, chillingly launches the piece in four-part chorale. *Moses* is very difficult to prepare, so stagings are few; once again the phonograph, in default of the theatres, keeps a classic accessible. Barring Columbia's competent mono reading under Hans Rosbaud, there are three fine sets, under Pierre Boulez (Columbia), Michael Gielen (Philips), and Georg Solti (London digital), each with its difference of emphasis.

Boulez leads the BBC Symphony in a highly romantic performance; Gielen's Austrian Radio forces suffer pallid sonics and the conductor's somewhat academic approach, as if he were "demonstrating" twelve-tone procedures. One wouldn't demonstrate *Tosca*, and *Moses und Aron* is as fiercely delineated, its patriarchal protagonist as tormented by his faith as stimulated by it, his eloquent brother Aron as much rival as deputy, and, for background, there are the restive people who need a God they can feel more than One they must imagine. It's tempting to think of Moses as Schoenberg, his people as Cocteau's alienated public, and Aron as . . . well, Tosca. Certainly Boulez' Günter Reich (Moses) and Richard Cassilly (Aron) project well the duel of the pure artist and the artist-magician, Cassilly lyrically forthcoming and Reich intently measuring out the Schoenbergian *Sprechstimme* that expresses but cannot sing. Reich repeats his Moses for Gielen, but here he seems to be merely indicating Moses' tragedy, rhetorical rather than involved. Consider the famous last page, the close of the middle act, but the last page that Schoenberg actually set to music. (The third act stands as unscored text.) Having shattered the Tablets of the Law, Moses cries out, "O Wort, du Wort, das mir fehlt!" (O Word, you Word that I lack!). For Gielen, Reich delivers it as a proclamation, ending in irate despair. But for Boulez Reich laments, ending in wonder at the catch-22 of a God who demands understanding but cannot be understood.

Solti has the advantage of both Boulez and Gielen, in opulent sonics, for one thing, and the Chicago Symphony, for another. He also has the most captivating Aron in Philip Langridge, hauntingly beautiful in the falsetto close to the second scene of Act One. Franz Mazura's Moses is not as impressive, interesting here and there but uninflected at the most telling moments. The last page seems to trickle away, emphasizing the opera's unresolved state but cheating the performance of its finale. Still, in all, Solti's is the most successful *Moses*, an absorbing reading and quite the exhibition piece for the CD player.

Alban Berg, Schoenberg's pupil, found somewhat more traditional forms for expressionism: common-man tragedy in *Wozzeck* and femme-fatale guignol in *Lulu*. *Wozzeck* is not even a twelve-tone work, binding some post-Wagnerian *Leitmotive* in an extremely liberal harmonic background. Often, several strands of melody seems to be competing as they collaborate, as if two or three operas about one set of characters were going off at once, a conflicted expansion typical of expressionism. This makes *Wozzeck*, like *Moses und Aron*, prime equipment testing, and Columbia's early mono set with the New York Philharmonic under Dimitri Mitropoulos is obviously handicapped, even if the sound is very clear. Then, too, Eileen Farrell, at the time more experienced as a radio pop singer than as an opera soprano, is uncomfortable in *Sprechstimme*. She can sing her lines, or declaim them, but expressionism's "half-and-half" defeats her: she simply speaks her pitched dialogue. She is, at least, the prettiest of Maries, and Mack Harrell the most severely expressionistic of Wozzecks, very precise in *Sprechstimme* and more concerned with nightmarish suggestion than with naturalistic portrayal.

The three more modern *Wozzecks* claim opera-house origins. DG's from Berlin's Deutsche Oper, has three most notable exponents of the score in Dietrich Fischer-Dieskau, Evelyn Lear, and Karl Böhm, who conducts dramatically, romantically, as if he had never heard a note of Schoenberg. Lear's Marie is so musical she finds rhapsody even in *Sprechstimme;* but is not Fischer-Dieskau's Wozzeck *too* musical? Wozzeck is a demented oaf. Fischer-Dieskau's very timbre is laden with the sensitivity of the *Liederabend,* and, resourceful as he is, we never quite forget the singer and hear the song.

Walter Berry (Columbia), on the other hand, makes Wozzeck naturally crass as well as sympathetic, though he hits the note of hallucinating madness a little too heavily too early on. His Marie, Isabel Strauss, is much too approximate in the *Sprechstimme* pitches. But Columbia rivals DG, for the Captain (Albert Weikenmeier) and Doctor (Carl Doench) are the best on disc, balancing realistic theatre with their commentative roles as symbols of the exploitative system. Moreover, Pierre Boulez, leading Paris Opéra forces, has not only the measure of the score but very personable sonics, vivid and intimate.

London's digital *Wozzeck,* from Vienna under Christoph von Dohnányi, is even better, with a deep, full bass and a vibrant treble, smashingly separated in the beery waltz in Act Two, scene four. (At places, however, where the melodic architecture is most dense; the sound muddies—the ensemble that closes Act Three, scene three, for instance, is no clearer here than for Böhm or Boulez.) The performance is imposing, Eberhard Wächter an excellent Wozzeck and Silja, though still wayward vocally, a touching Marie. The Captain (Heinz Zednik) and Doctor (Alexander Malta) seem too villainous, almost savage; are they not more the tools of system than its auteurs? The best *Wozzeck* would have been Berry, Lear, and Mitropoulos in London's sound on CDs. That failing, try DG for an old-fashioned Middle European melodrama and London for the cold-school modern approach.

With *Lulu* we have, again, four sets (discounting Columbia's justly forgotten mono entry). These vary in quality more than the *Wozzecks.* In the late 1960s, Angel and DG released live performances from, respectively, Hamburg and Berlin. Bergians recoiled at the sloppy executions and a few blundering portrayals, but the spirit is there, less in Angel's Leopold Ludwig, more in DG's Böhm. Each has a notable Lulu of the day, Anneliese Rothenberger and Evelyn Lear, so connoisseurs should investigate. London's studio set of 1976, again with

Silja under von Dohnányi in Vienna, is much better, precise and forceful, Berry the most fully drawn of Dr. Schöns—note his comically exasperated "Postscription?" during Lulu's dictation of the letter at the end of Act One. Indeed, the cast is quite accomplished—Brigitte Fassbaender sings Countess Gerschwitz, Hans Hotter Schigolch—and Silja does some of her best singing ever here, right up to high D.

Even as critics praised London's set, however, they lamented that it used the same incomplete text as older albums: for *Lulu*'s third and final act, long sequestered by Berg's widow, had been secretly developed from short score to a full performing edition by Friedrich Cerha. Helene Berg's death in 1976 made complete performances possible, and DG wisely recorded Patrice Chéreau's excellent Opéra production under Pierre Boulez, with Yvonne Minton's Geschwitz, Franz Mazura's Dr. Schön, Kenneth Riegel's Alwa, Toni Blankenheim's Schigolch (demoted from, but better played than, his Schön for Angel), and, mainly, Teresa Stratas, *the* notable Lulu of the day. More sensual than Lear and Rothenberger and more beautiful in sound than Silja, Stratas gives us something comparable to Louise Brooks's Lulu in G. W. Pabst's film *Die Büchse der Pandora*, drawn, like Berg's opera, from Frank Wedekind's plays. Stratas is less the femme fatale than a reckless elf. Her "Er schlagt mich tot!" (He'll beat me to death!) suggests the wail of a baby. She is as well the most fastidious Lulu in following Berg's notes and observing his markings. But most crucial here is the institution of the third act. Any work deserves a complete reading, but *Lulu* in particular demands it, to play out the intricately symmetrical arch-form of its structure, a kind of incantation mirrored in recantation, Lulu on the rise for the first half, Lulu in decline in the second. Remember, Schoenberg's school was devoted, above all, to form.

The generation that inherited Schoenberg's technique freely adapted it, developing styles that suggest *Wozzeck*'s liberal atonalism, with a limited use of tone-row constructions at key points, Luigi Dallapiccola's *Il Prigioniero* (The Prisoner) is perhaps the best-known work in this line of "compromise serialism," so cleanly articulated that one can hear Dallapiccola's rowlike patterns, as in the orchestra's statements of the notes corresponding to the line "Fratello" (My brother). The last hour in the life of victim of the Spanish Inquisition, *Il Prigioniero* is an ideal phonograph opera, too short to command an evening but perfect timing on a single LP. However, contemporary opera is no longer the draw that it was in 78 years, when companies would leap to excerpt the latest premiere. First performed in 1950 (at the Florence May Festival), *Il Prigioniero* was not commercially recorded till 1975. Earlier, FWR had released a New York concert reading, in English, under Leopold Stokowski, with Norman Treigle as the Prisoner, Richard Cassilly in the dual role of the Jailer (who purports to be a fellow liberal) and the Grand Inquisitor (who leads the hero to his doom), and Anne McKnight as the prisoner's mother. Here are familiar names (McKnight was Toscanini's broadcast Musetta), a rarity in this repertory, for while no worthy star turns down Wozzeck or Marie, other advanced compositions seldom field the lavish star voices that the phonograph emphasizes in Mozart, Verdi, or Massenet. Why is there no *Prigioniero* under Riccardo Muti with, say, José van Dam, Plácido Domingo, and Montserrat Caballé? They would justify Dallapiccola's masterpiece better than FWR's reading, for while Harold Heiberg's translation comes through cleanly, the orchestra and especially the chorus fade under the solo voices, so much so that the extraordinary *fortissimo* explosion of the chorus's "Fiat misericordia tua" as the lights black out on the prologue is almost unheard. London's disc offers good sound and a gripping performance under Antal Dorati, with Maurizio Mazzieri, Romano Emile, and Giulia Barrera.

If Dallapiccola is very free serialism at most, some contemporary expressionist operas are even more free, rather a discordant impressionism than a use of tone rows. Alberto Ginastera, prominent in this arena, actually enjoyed some popularity, in North America rather than in his repressive homeland, Argentina. Ginastera's *Don Rodrigo,* which launched Plácido Domingo's stardom at the New York City Opera, is unrecorded. But Columbia caught the difficult *Bomarzo,* luckily with the superb cast of its world premiere by the Opera Society of Washington: Salvador Novoa as the hunchbacked duke of late Renaissance Florence, Claramae Turner as his sage grandmother, Joanna Simon as the courtesan Pantasilea, Richard Torigi as his astrologer, under Julius Rudel. Turner and Simon are especially impressive in their ability to generate sympathy for threatening characters, most difficult in expressionism's nightmarish aesthetic. "The shocking new opera," Columbia's *Bomarzo* album cover exults, "of 'sex, violence, hallucination,' " the blurb courtesy of the *New York Times.* (Something new in hype: prestige sensationalism.) Actually, sex, violence, and hallucination are essential elements in expressionist art, even in works based on plays of considerable vintage. Two such classics as *King Lear* and Lenz's *Die Soldaten* provided contemporary expressionist masterpieces, in settings by Aribert Reimann and Bernd Alois Zimmermann.

Reimann's *Lear* was recorded live (DG) in its premiere production in Munich in 1978. For once, we note mainstream singers as well as "modernist" specialists—von Karajan's Brünnhilde, Helga Dernesch, sings Goneril, Julia Varady Cordelia, and Dietrich Fischer-Dieskau is

Lear. They join Hans Günter Nöcker (Gloucester), David Knutson (Edgar), Werner Götz (Edmund), and Colette Lorand (Regan), under Gerd Albrecht, in a truly brilliant reading. It is all the more admirable given the extremes of vocal writing that Reimann resorts to, with a historical compendium of character voices—Goneril a Wagnerian soprano, Edgar a Baroque counter-tenor, the Fool, commentatively alienated from music, a speaker. The source material is timeless, of course, but virtually unthinkable except as a post-Schoenbergian opera of, yes, sex, violence, hallucination. Did not Verdi, one of the ablest masters of opera's preceding century, pursue *King Lear* all his life without success? In fact, opera has seen a number of *King Lear* adaptations, but perhaps the century of Auschwitz and the gulag is the one to comprehend it.

Zimmermann's *Die Soldaten* is both smaller and larger than *Lear*, centering on a young woman's seduction by a Prussian officer but expanding at its edges to swing through history, through the social paradigms of Western civilization. *Die Soldaten* is also opera's most complex score, designed to be mounted complexly, on a series of stages, each event crowding out another in what Zimmermann called the "Kugelgestalt der Zeit," the "ball-shape of time." Vastly simplified, *Die Soldaten* was given at Cologne in 1965, and Wergo took the brilliant first cast into the studio: Edith Gabry, Liane Synek, Anton de Ridder, Claudio Nicolai, and Zoltan Kélémen under Michael Gielen. If *Lear* is the heir to *Moses und Aron*, *Wozzeck*, and *Lulu*, *Die Soldaten* strikes off on its own, though Zimmermann uses the *Grundreihe* (the all-basic tone row on which the entire composition is built) essential to Schoenberg's conception.

If ever a work needed the familiarizing indoctrination of phonograph study, it is *Die Soldaten*. Unfortunately, Wergo includes no texts— only detailed notes in German only. *Lear* fails here, too; DG furnishes Munich's lavish program book with the German text, but no English translation. Too bad: for a day spent listening to the tonal *Salome*, the atonal *Wozzeck*, then the experimentally twelve-tone *Die Soldaten* would encapsulate the history of expressionism in opera.

23

MODERN GERMAN
OPERA

※

Twentieth-century German opera is the saga of styles at war: the neo-Classicists challenging the Romantics, the contemporaries of jazz wandering into ageless myth, *Der Rosenkavalier* on the one hand and *Wozzeck* on the other. By the late 1920s, there was a distinctly political side to all this, as some composers took to regarding themselves as positive, nationalistically traditional, even ethnically correct—while calling other composers decadent and corruptive.

Wagner's shadow hung over nearly everything—but not over Eugen D'Albert's *Tiefland* (Lowlands), a Germanic verismo. This is rather like Catalani's *La Wally* cast for Mascagni's singers. It would be interesting to hear a *veristo* gathering try it—Olivero, Scotto, Picchi, and Guelfi, say. Victor's fine digital set under Marek Janowski has a more appropriate team led by Eva Marton and a slightly wobbly René Kollo.

Consider that *Tiefland* hit theatres then celebrating the tenth anniversary of *Hänsel und Gretel*, Engelbert Humperdinck's Wagnerian miniature; consider that *Märchenoper* ("fairytale opera") was as much in fashion as verismo. Von Karajan's mono set with Elisabeths Schwarzkopf and Grümmer has not been out of the catalogue since its appearance in Angel's inaugural release in 1953, for good reason. No, four good reasons: von Karajan's magical conducting, the two kids (Schwarzkopf carefully beating all the Marschallin *Schlag* out of her

266

delivery), and Josef Metternich's vivacious Father. Else Schürhoff's flavorless Witch dulls the set's fourth side, but Angel was an immense improvement on Columbia's 1947 set, sung in English by Risë Stevens, Nadine Conner, and a typical Met cast under Max Rudolf, and about as magical as a Boy Scout Jamboree. Moving into stereo, we find, once again, a fine Angel set (Rothenberger, Seefried; Cluytens) spoiled on side four, here by Elisabeth Höngen's blowsy Witch. Solti (London) is ordinary, Pritchard (Columbia) lacking in storybook atmosphere, though he has faultless singers—Ileana Cotrubas and Frederica von Stade up front, Christa Ludwig and Siegmund Nimsgern as their parents, and Elisabeth Söderström as the Witch, with forest cameos by Kiri Te Kanawa and Ruth Welting. The choice is Victor's set under Kurt Eichhorn (Donath, Moffo), as well sung as any and more atmospheric. For once, side four actually improves on the rest, with Ludwig's superlative Witch, one of the phonograph's great portrayals. German theatres regularly cast the role with aging stars; here's a rare chance to hear a star Witch in her prime.

Humperdinck's *Königskinder* (Royal Children) may look like a second *Hänsel*, with another witch, another children's chorus, and yet more folklike ditties. But this is a more expansively Wagnerian piece, most beautifully performed by Helen Donath, Hanna Schwarz, Adolf Dallapozza, Hermann Prey, and Karl Ridderbusch under Heinz Wallberg. EMI's original box bore only the German text. Arabesque's American release has the English as well. Strongly recommended— but more to Wagnerians than to *Hänsel* fans.

A more basic artistic conflict of the age was the battle between the diehard practitioners of Romanticism and the innovators of neo-Classicism. *Spätromantik* ("late Romantic") opera was showing signs of exhaustion, falling into burlesques of itself, while the spare, clean techniques of the Classical style seemed purgative as well as evolutionary. Erich Wolfgang Korngold's *Die Tote Stadt* (The Dead City), admirably served on Victor (Neblett, Kollo, Prey, Luxon; Leinsdorf) in full, warm sound, evokes the gushy heart of *Spätromantik*, in a tuneful but often shapeless score obsessed with typical images of death and rebirth. More extreme, and somewhat influential, was Franz Schreker, who specialized in sickly-sweet stories of human dissolution in complexly perfused orchestrations, a sort of expressionistic Puccini. Schreker's *Der Ferne Klang* (The Distant Sound), in a superlative radio broadcast under Ernst Märzendorfer (MRF), makes an ideal audition piece in its picaresque look at a young composer in search of a mystical ideal embodied in a musical theme. MRF's airwave stereo cannot encompass Schreker's rich noises, melody fondling melody; and there is some cutting (irritating especially in the dismembering of the heroine's big solo, "Im Walde entschlief ich"). But the performance itself is riveting, not least in Maria de Francesca's *Ewig-Weibliche* heroine icon, who loses the composer to his quest, meets him long after in a bordello in the Venetian lagoon, and comforts him at his death.

Schreker's *Die Gezeichneten* (The Doomed)—available in two performances, on Voce (without a libretto) and MRF—looks beyond *Der Ferne Klang*'s art nouveau languor into outright depravity, putting the neat, even austere world of neo-Classicism into perspective. Ferruccio Busoni's double bill of *Arlecchino* and *Turandot* recalls *commedia dell'arte*'s lively arena of love chastely pledged and pomposity outwitted. *Turandot* is particularly interesting for its close adherence to Gozzi's play; Puccini's version Romanticizes. Then, too, where Puccini goes in for spectacle and an almost Stravinskyan *colorito*, Busoni holds to eighteenth-century proportions, everything trim, firm, fair. Victor's mono *Arlecchino*, from Glyndebourne in 1956, is disappointing. The lovers don't glisten; the comics need more snap. Various undergrounds of *Turandot* present a more successful performance, from Bern in 1979 with Melitta Muszely and Fritz Uhl under Otto Ackermann. The singing is only serviceable, but the projection generally spirited. DG's *Doktor Faust* under Ferdinand Leitner is best of all Busoni on disc, an excellent performance of a darkly brooding masterpiece. Dietrich Fischer-Dieskau turns in one of his absolutely correct and beautifully designed characters as the questing magician-philosopher. Of the rest, only Hildegard Hillebrecht fails, in a role that would have loved Elisabeth Söderström. Fischer-Dieskau similarly takes major hold of the lead in Paul Hindemith's *Cardillac*, under Josef Keilberth (DG). Later, Hindemith Romanticized somewhat in the affecting *Mathis der Maler*, another of Fischer-Dieskau's notable parts (Angel). But *Cardillac*'s overt "techniqueism," discrete structuring, and shockingly poised delineation of a murder scene to the accompaniment of a flute duet all mark a resistance of *Spätromantik* excess. This time DG gives us Söderström.

For an extreme but telling comparison, we might set Hans Pfitzner's *Palestrina* next to Ernst Křenek's *Jonny Spielt Auf* (Jonny Strikes Up the Band). Pfitzner, so reactionary that he was avant-garde, wrote almost pre-Wagnerian music for a story about a sixteenth-century composer. Křenek's hero is a black American musician who steals a violin to conquer the world with jazz, and Křenek's form, *Zeitoper*, was, literally, "opera of the day." *Jonny Spielt Auf* is opera of the minute, with its Kurt Weillisch saxophone and Paul Whiteman cymbal stingers, the sort of opera the Nazis loved to hate. As with *Shvanda the Bagpiper*, their ban killed the piece not only for its day but for ours as well. Thus, we have DG's fine *Palestrina* (Gedda, Weikl, Fischer-Dieskau; Kubelik), a committed performance of a frankly rather subdued opera, not for every taste. And, for the aficionado, undergrounds bear the *Palestrina*s of Fritz Wunderlich (EJS) and, most celebrated of all, Julius Patzak (Melodram). But there has never been a complete *Jonny*, even on the pirates. There are some 78s—Ludwig Hoffmann, Berlin's first Jonny, recorded two sides, and Bela Dajos's orchestra put down a double-sided medley (a very popular form at in 78 years, when complete sets were bulky, expensive, and sometimes hard to find). But all we have on LP of this once sensational hit is Mace's highlights disc under Heinrich Hollreiser, a kind of running summation of the narrative, the whole opera cut down rather than a selection of a few big numbers. Evelyn Lear is appropriately dotty as an opera singer; the young Lucia Popp is vivacious as Jonny's girlfriend; and Thomas Stewart sings a superbly menacing Jonny, relishing the elated solipsism that Křenek hears in the sound of American pop music, sees in American movies, fears in American war power. It would be fascinating to hear what Simon Estes might do with the part in a complete version.

German opera's major conflict was not that of composers disputing aesthetics, but that between the Nazi regime and progressive creators. After the war, Carl Orff's stark, shrill, percussive settings of Greek tragedy seemed to exult in experimentalism for its own sake, to exploit the fresh air. DG recorded both *Antigone* (Borkh, Uhl, Häfliger; Leitner) and *Oedipus der Tyran* (Varnay, Stolze; Kubelik), the former the superior performance, but both very hard to take. Strange to say, his Nazi-era *Märchenopern*, *Der Mond* (The Moon) and *Die Kluge* (The Wise Woman), are square-cut and tuneful, perfectly realized on Angel's famous albums, made in London with Wolfgang Sawallisch conducting under the composer's supervision. *Die Kluge*, in mono only, counts Gottlob Frick and Elisabeth Schwarzkopf as the peasant and his almost fatally wise daughter. *Der Mond*, taped in stereo, has Hans Hotter's Petrus. Still, these performances are triumphs of spirit rather than of individual portrayals, exercises in folk feeling and timeless storytelling, as in the ribald character of the big choral scene in which *Der Mond*'s four townsmen present the stolen moon to their uproarious fellow citizens; or in *Die Kluge*'s clashing of fairytale and morality play in the brutal comedy of the three vagabonds—Gozzi rewritten by Schikaneder. Oddly, the vagabonds' lurid ditty, "Als die Treue ward geborn" (When horror was born), seems to have sailed right over the censors' heads despite its savage commentary on the quality of life in Germany in 1943. Angel's two sets point up another of the phonograph's virtues: its preservation of performances made under the stylistic guidance of the author himself. Just as well, that, for few of the operas of this time get a second chance in the studio. *Die Tote Stadt, Cardillac, Doktor Faust,* and *Palestrina* simply don't have the market appeal for an alternate reading. By hap, *Der Mond* did get a second recording, in 1974 in Leipzig under Herbert Kegel (Philips)—an excellent performance, if not up to the gala vulgarity of Angel's.

Kegel and his Leipzigers, however, hold the monopoly on Paul Dessau's setting of Bertolt Brecht's *Der Verurteilung des Lukullus* (The Condemnation of Lucullus), on Telefunken. In the world of Brecht adaptations, there are two kinds of composer: the ones who sound like Kurt Weill and the ones who don't. Dessau is both kinds. Some scenes recall *Die Dreigroschenoper,* as if touching base with a political-artistic ontology. Other scenes confidently strike out on their own, as is to suggest that, if Weill were still setting Brecht today, he would sound like Dessau. The Telefunken *Lukullus* is first-rate, though the text booklet is in German only.

Postwar German opera has been dominated by Hans Werner Henze, a one-man conflict, glorifying leftist totalism in a nation still recovering from the totalism of the right, and doing so in the complex compositional forms that police states loathe. Outside the fatherland, Henze has had spotty success, and his home company, DG, has recorded only two of his dozen operas, much more of his symphonic work. At that, *Elegy for Young Lovers* counts only highlights (in the German translation of the W. H. Auden and Chester Kallman text), conducted by Henze and vividly enacted by Caterina Gayer, Martha Mödl, and especially Fischer-Dieskau, who seems to have recorded just about everything in modern German opera except "The Ballad of Mack the Knife."

Der Junge Lord, at least, was recorded complete. This is Henze's most ingratiating piece, a black comedy about a Biedermeier town's enthusiastic aping of the dress and manners of the title's visiting young lord, unmasked at the end as an ape. Berlin's Deutsche Oper hosted the world premiere in 1965, and this cast, under Christoph von Dohnányi, gives the score a delicious reading filled with character portraits. There is no protagonist (which explains why Fischer-Dieskau, for once, does not appear), but rather a town's worth of types; Sir Edgar's retinue (including American mezzo Vera Little, who delivers a few lines in Caribbean English), the circus troupe that provides the ape, and a pair of young lovers (Edith Mathis and Donald Grobe) who serve somewhat as our agents in the action. DG's album, released in 1966 as the opera was making its rounds from house to house, emphasized how the phonograph can amplify the premiere of an important new opera to international proportions, moving beyond the theatres into the homes of "witnesses" thousands of miles away. Angel's Orff operas, albeit excellent, were studio constructions, platonic essences. DG's *Der Junge Lord* is a piece of opera history, with the crackle of the stage in it. Some buffs no doubt would rather have had discs of the first *Norma* with Pasta and Grisi, or of Nourrit's Masaniello, Arnold, Raoul, Eléazar. Alas, the phonograph came late, and even then was slow to find its mission in the experiential chronicling of opera history. But with such albums as DG's *Der Junge Lord,* we leave a taste of what we knew for the future to learn.

And who knows? What if *Der Junge Lord* turns out to be the *Norma* of the twenty-first century?

24

MODERN ENGLISH
OPERA

༺༻

This chapter oversees a phenomenal success story. Around 1900, the English opera scene was anything but English, its repertory, stars, and traditions Continental rather than native. In such a world, Nellie Mitchell, despite a spectacular voice, would bill herself as Melba, and Mary Wilson would sensibly become Florence Austral, the foreign tang of the last names (from Melbourne and Australia) mitigating the useless plainness of the first names. English opera was Royal Opera, gala opera, grand. *Foreign.*

It seemed reasonable that Frederick Delius would set *Koanga* on an American plantation, *A Village Romeo and Juliet* in an archetypal German village, *Fennimore and Gerda* in Scandinavia. Angel recorded them all in stylish stereo performances, and Arabesque released the BBC broadcast that unveiled, eighty-two years late, *The Magic Fountain—* this set in old Florida. (Katherine Pring plays an Indian.) Most listeners find Delius's impressionistic, elegiacal approach to opera underwhelming; his symphonic and choral pieces have more bite. Angel's *Fennimore* is representative, not only a fine performance (Söderström, Tear; Davies) but, as if emphasizing Delius's cosmopolitan muse, a Danish production. However, a tour through Delius's discography should start with Thomas Beecham's 78 set of *A Village Romeo and Juliet*, reissued on World. The cast—Lorely Dyer, Margaret Ritchie, René

Soames, and Gordon Clinton—is variable, but Beecham, for decades Delius's most decisive advocate, gives a masterly reading.

Gustav Holst both embraced native style and rejected it, as a kind of unintelligible stopgap. His Indian chamber opera *Savitri* (Argo) enjoys Janet Baker's unflappable legato. *The Wandering Scholar* (Angel) opens up into Chaucerian farce (though set in France). Sample the Celtic revival in Ronald Boughton's *The Immortal Hour* (Hyperion digital), a fairytale beautifully set to a great deal of strophic ballads, *a cappella* ditties, and Romantic magic. The performance, dramatically a bit sluggish under Alan G. Melville, lacks the charisma of Angel's Delius crew, which includes Wendy Eathorne, John Shirley-Quirk, Benjamin Luxon, Robert Tear, and conductors Charles Groves and Meredith Davies.

These and many other of the present generation of British singing actors provide the key advantage of Angel's series of operas by Ralph Vaughan Williams—and here, at length, we reach a genuinely English music theatre: "an opera," in the composer's own recipe, "written to *real* English words, with a certain amount of *real* English music and also a *real* English subject." The opera Vaughan Williams was cooking up at the time, his first, was *Hugh the Drover*. If its librettist, Harold Child, didn't take his composer's advice—the text speaks quaint English, not real—still Vaughan Williams went ahead and set it to real English music. He termed it a "romantic ballad opera." Unlike the classic ballad operas, *Hugh* has no dialogue; but like them it constantly halts the action to parry a tune.

Hugh's tunes are exemplary, almost contentiously folkish, with a swagger for the men and "sympathy" for the women. HMV found it irresistible, and put out an album with much of the original cast under Malcolm Sargent in 1924, the last year of acoustic recording. Pearl's fine LP stuffs it all onto one disc, not so much a highlights album as the whole opera with much connecting material slashed to emphasize the songs. Often, British singers of this era brought the genteel air of the Victorian parlor ballad into the opera house, but Tudor Davies and Mary Lewis head a lusty crew. In fact, it is Angel's modern cast under Charles Groves (two discs, complete but in absurdly wide-ranging stereo) who lack energy, Robert Tear and Sheila Armstrong too polite for the bluff drover and his impulsive sweetheart.

As with Delius, Angel made a project of Vaughan Williams. Meredith Davies leads *Riders to the Sea*, from Synge's one-act tragedy, somewhat Debussyan and, interestingly, often sliding into unaccompanied recit. Adrian Boult directs *The Pilgrim's Progress*, as sprawling and episodic as *Riders* is concentrated. It's good Bunyan, if not good opera. (Many find it . . . well, slow.) Angel has an ace, however, in Dennis Noble's Pilgrim, ecstatic and terrified. By far the best performance, and probably the best opera, is *Sir John in Love*, from *The Merry Wives of Windsor* but more Shakespearean than Verdi's version, with a greater share of the original's lines and characters and a kind of subterranean concerto of English folk tunes running through the score. After Gobbi's Sir John or Giulietta Simionato's Quickly, it is fetching to audition Raimund Herincx and Helen Watts in the roles, along with Elizabeth Bainbridge's Mrs. Ford, Felicity Palmer's Mrs. Page, and Tear's Fenton, under Davies. This *is* real English music.

All the foregoing makes a kind of apprenticeship to the modern, decades of sifting. By the postwar years, English opera was on a roll, with Benjamin Britten turning out an *oeuvre* that in some ways compares to those of Puccini and Strauss. Alongside Britten, William Walton's *Troilus and Cressida* seems fatuous, certainly old-fashioned. Angel wisely held to a highlights disc, in mono, with Elisabeth Schwarzkopf and Richard Lewis under the composer. Later, EMI caught Walton's revision of the score for Janet Baker, with high notes and even keys lowered. We lose the anguished brightness of the soprano setting, but the new registration takes on a brooding glamour perfect for Baker. Hear also, on London's Covent Garden anniversary album, Marie Collier and Peter Pears (the original Pandarus) in "At the haunted end of the day" and pages before and after, a treasurable souvenir of Collier, like Olive Fremstad and Mary Garden a great performer but not a phonographic singer. Her Minnie and Elina Makropulos are legendary—but opera history is "written" in recordings now, not in legend.

Michael Tippett may be viewed as Walton's opposite, seeking unorthodox subjects, melodies, orchestration. Philips recorded excellent Covent Garden productions of *The Midsummer Marriage* and *The Knot Garden*, both under Colin Davis. But *King Priam* (London digital) is Tippett's masterpiece, avoiding the mythic pretentiousness of the earlier work and the self-dramatizing *Angst* chic of the later. *Midsummer* is largely for youngsters—Joan Carlyle, Elizabeth Harwood, Alberto Remedios, Stuart Burrows: something of an *opéra comique* cast. *King Priam* is the grand opera for the senior contingent, boldly matching up with Homeric archetypes: Norman Bailey (Priam), Heather Harper (Hecuba), Thomas Allen (Hector), Felicity Palmer (Andromache), Yvonne Minton (Helen), Robert Tear (Achilles), under David Atherton. A great cast. Perhaps the work's unique element is its scoring, as when Allen berates Philip Langridge (Paris) for his hedonism to irate timpani, nattering piano, and wry woodblock. ("I wish," Paris replies, "you were not so like a living hammer.") Or when Palmer attacks Minton for bringing war to Troy, to ripples of plucked strings; or when Tear laments his homesickness, in "O rich-soiled land," to solo guitar. Tear sings it well—as does Richard Lewis, the original Achilles, in the Covent Garden anniversary album, to John Williams's vividly struck guitar. However, it is Achilles whom Tippett fails as creator, for the scene in which Priam begs for the body of his slain son Hector goes for nothing in this opera. It is an epic moment, for Hector has killed Achilles's lover Patroclus and Achilles, in turn, by the savage logic of war, has killed Hector. Priam finds Achilles brooding over the corpse, the victor's honorable spoils, and persuades him to honor instead a father's grief. Achilles does: barbaric man, the warrior, ceding to democratic man, the citizen. In Homer, the scene is devastating. In Tippett, it is a paragraph (though the composer understood Homer's relevance well enough to present the premiere at Coventry Cathedral, a site of World War II's calamitous logic). This one failing allowed, *King Priam* is a noble work, nobly recorded.

Benjamin Britten is the name with which the era reckons, from *Peter Grimes,* the vital revelation of a new voice, to *Death in Venice,* so evident as will and testament that it was staged virtually posthumously, though Britten was to survive the premiere by three years. He enjoys a unique relationship with the phonograph, as the only major composer who saw most of his oeuvre to disc with *his* singers under *his* direction, all on London. Britten's casting invariably centers on tenor Peter Pears, Britten's lifelong lover and artistic collaborator; Pears's eccentric timbre, which suggested an old man even in his earliest records, irritates some ears. However, there is no denying Pears's artistry. If he is unsuitably mature for the shy young hero of *Albert Herring* or the ardent suitor Lysander in *A Midsummer Night's Dream* (at the premiere, more aptly, Pears played Flute), he is excellent as *Billy Budd's* Captain Vere, as General Wingrave, and as *Death in Venice's* Aschenbach, deftly sifting Vere's sorrowful gentility, the General's self-righteous fire, and Aschenbach's poetic amazement. As with Puccini and Gilda dalla Rizza, or Kurt Weill and Lotte Lenya, the composer's first choice may depend more on expression or "atmosphere" than on sheer beauty of tone.

This does not, however, apply to the rest of Britten's London casts. His regulars, many of them longtime participants at Britten's Aldeburgh Festival and in his English Opera Group, form a virtual company, devoted to emphasizing the theatre in music while keeping theatre musical. It is a pleasure to follow such stalwarts as Jennifer Vyvyan, Janet Baker, Benjamin Luxon, and John Shirley-Quirk as they proceed from role to role: as Baker passes from saint (in the title role of *The Rape of Lucretia*) to fury (in *Owen Wingrave*), as Shirley-Quirk rises to the challenge of one of the most heterogeneous roles in opera, the seven tempter figures who lead Aschenbach to doom. Throughout Britten's London sets one senses logic as well as loyalty in the casting, so that if, say, Sylvia Fisher's Lady Billows in *Albert Herring* is gusty and wobbly, surely this only helps her capture the grumpy majesty of the rustic Dame. In the style of Restoration satire, the lady really does billow.

It helps, too, that Britten himself is an able conductor. He not only knows how his music best sounds, he shows us. Perhaps his most resonant issue is *Owen Wingrave*, with a kind of "festival of Britten" ensemble: Benjamin Luxon as the scion of a military family who turns pacifist, Pears and Fisher as his outraged family, Shirley-Quirk as his teacher, Nigel Douglas (Pears's alternate in the first *Death in Venice* performances) as his schoolmate, Heather Harper as a sympathetic confidante, Baker as the pacifist's fiancée, who locks him up for a night with the family ghost, and Vyvyan as Baker's mother. To wrap it up, Pears also sings the opera's theme song, "There was a boy, a Wingrave born." And of course Britten conducts. London's album affords a unique opportunity to hear the Britten style up close, word by word, for this is the most chamber-sized of chamber operas, expressly written for the intimacy of television (and lost, as subsequent Covent Garden performances proved, in a big house). On disc, we are not lacking an essential component of the experience, as with *Death in Venice*'s dance sequences, or the mystic rituals of the three No-flavored Church Parables, *Curlew River*, *The Burning Fiery Furnace*, and *The Prodigal Son*. We have, in fact, something of a conclusion to the question posed by Richard Strauss's *Capriccio:* words and music indivisibly dramatized.

Even more successful as phonograph theatre is *A Midsummer Night's Dream*, with a libretto by Britten and Pears drawn from the original text. What other Shakespearean work needs music more?—as in the deep groans of the strings as the forest stirs alive, shimmering with harps; the facetious trombone glide when Bottom auditions his lion's roar; the muted trumpet fanfares chasing a gurgling celesta and eluding impetuous drumming as Puck speeds in and out of sight; the recorder, cymbals, and woodblocks played (onstage) by the four elfs attending the "translated" Bottom. The vocal casting is unique in opera, almost a congeries of genre: a counter-tenor Oberon and coloratura Titania as if out of Baroque romance, an almost Brahmsian quartet for the lovers, an all-male *opera buffa* for the thespian workmen—and Puck is an acrobat! True, the three discs offer none of the play's extraordinary visuals. But Britten is more imaginative than many a director. He even makes the farcical play-within-the-play phonographic by setting it as a spoof of mid-nineteenth-century *melodramma*, opera-within-the-opera—and London's sound effects dazzle. Elizabeth Harwood's ravishing Titania and Owen Brannigan's absurd Bottom stand out, but here again is a generally fine cast and an ideal experiment for the newcomer ready to taste modern opera.

Britten has actually become almost popular, to the point where some of his titles count competing versions. Challenging London's *Peter Grimes* is Philips's newer set under Colin Davis, neither box clearly preferable. London is more theatrical in sonics, with Pears's rather deranged hero. Philips is drier in sound, with Jon Vickers's more inward Grimes—though, paradoxically, he outdoes Pears for passion in the "Great Bear" outburst in the tavern scene. Both sets use Covent Garden forces, as do HMV's seven 78 sides made in 1947 with the original leads under Reginald Goodall: the opening of Act Two, Ellen's Embroidery Aria, and the scene in Grimes's hut. Here is the most perfect casting of all, with Pears in budding energy and Joan Cross the absolute spinster in sound and approach. London's Claire Watson is lovelier, Philips's Heather Harper more expressive. But Cross, on these discs at least, *is* Ellen Orford. The highlights, unreleased when new, came out on LP in EMI's *Stars of the Old Vic and Sadler's Wells* album.

HMV also caught *The Rape of Lucretia*'s original cast, again under Goodall, on sixteen 78 sides. These *were* released, to disappointment that Kathleen Ferrier's alternate, Nancy Evans, took the title role. EMA has Ferrier in scenes from a Holland Festival performance, a disappointing reading in terrible sound. In any case, HMV's highlights preserve an exciting ensemble, more worthy even than London's complete set in stereo. However, given the English Opera Group's stated intention of bringing poets into the librettist game, it is rewarding to hear Ronald Duncan's text uncut, for his cynically idealistic world view goes beautifully with Britten's often abrasively sweet melodies: "The Romans being wanton worship chastity," for instance, or "That rude politeness at which a servant can excell."

Philips and Davis challenged London again with *The Turn of the Screw*, and where it does not equal the older set, it betters it. Gorgeous though Jennifer Vyvyan is, she plays the Governess as pure victim, while Davis and Helen Donath reach back to Henry James's ambiguously disturbed heroine, as involved in the horror of Bly as her two charges. The children, too, are better on Philips, as is Ava June better than London's unsteady Joan Cross. Too, it's a relief, after the inevitable Pears, to hear Philip Langridge's more pleasing instrument in the Prologue. Lastly, the London set was made in mono, giving Philips the sonic advantage, especially when ghost Robert Tear "materializes" from afar.

Two of Britten's major operas have yet to be recorded: *Gloriana* and his version of *The Beggar's Opera*, so thoroughly recomposed that it is nearly a resetting of Gay's text. Some company lost a priceless chance to catch it at the Edinburgh Festival with Baker, Harper, and Pears, a juicy performance known only to the tape underground. *Gloriana*, thus far counting only an orchestral suite of the dances and big scenes (Angel), may never reclaim its premiere Covent Garden cast of Cross, Vyvyan, Pears, and Geraint Evans under John Pritchard, unless a tape is released. But the superior English National Opera staging led by Sarah Walker's astonishing Elizabeth I—the sensation of the ENO's American tour—should be preserved.

Britten's standing discography of house experts is one phenomenon of postwar British music theatre. Rock opera is another. This genre was born on LP, on two-disc song cycles. Within a mere fifteen years, the form underwent evolution from an audio to a theatre experience, to be *recaptured* on discs. Yet, despite a highly commercial market, it remained an elusive form, and strictly British: for American attempts to co-opt it repeatedly collapsed. *Tommy*, as written and performed by The Who (Pete Townshend, Roger Daltrey, John Entwhistle, and Keith Moon), was the instigating work, MCA's superb stereo frankly putting forth the rough-and-ready vocals, uncharacterized except by the cues we read in the text sheets. "See me, touch me, feel me, heal me"— immortal catchwords of the 1970s—are the signature of a psychosomatically deaf and blind boy who has the healer's gift. The work, sung or played throughout, was stageable. Finally, Ken Russell filmed it. Polydor's sound track (also with text sheets) retained The Who, but now the figures in Tommy's life are portrayed: Ann-Margret as his mother, Elton John as the Pinball Wizard, Tina Turner as the Acid Queen. The Who wrote some new material, and the new cast more carefully delivers lines that were chanted or wailed on MCA. *Tommy* had become art.

Andrew Lloyd Webber, in collaboration with librettist Tim Rice, pursued the process: two-disc song cycle, then cast recordings of stagings. *Evita* best displays rock opera's strengths (versatility of musical style, showy ingenuity of production) and weaknesses (monotonous recit, insistent plugging of big tune—*Evita*'s audiences leave the theatre with "Don't Cry for Me, Argentina" engraved on their eardrums), most impressively in MCA's West End highlights, MCA's more complete New York cast, and Jupiter's Vienna cast, entered into scandal when the Evita's understudy was convicted of hiring bravos to throw acid in the star's face.

Webber's *Cats*, to T. S. Eliot's whimsical poems, duplicated *Evita's* international success, throwing off countless albums—West End, Broadway (with new music), Australian (most complete), Viennese (one disc of highlights only, in the at times poor German of the many American dancers slotted into the Theater an der Wien company), Japanese (caught live), even a Hungarian cast, and all with the trademark "cat's eyes" cover art.

Such is the British charisma in rock opera that a French entry based on Victor Hugo's *Les Misérables* has come to prominence, in translation, as a *British* work, rescored (by the original orchestrator, John Cameron) and restaged (by the *Cats* crew—Trevor Nunn, John Caird, and John Napier). First Night has the usual two discs, this time not the bulk of the show but merely selections. First Night also reissued the original French cast on a single disc, almost demoralizing in how much must be left out of this extraordinary score. The French Fantine bears a bemusing resemblence to Polly Bergen that the West End's Patty LuPone rises above—literally, as her settings range more operatically.

Unlike *Tommy* and the Weber shows, *Les Misérables* doesn't center on a protagonist. Here, Jean Valjean is but one of several principal "outcasts"—the *misérables* of Hugo's valiantly political document. But then, rock opera is still in its early development. One hard fact; it has lost its rock. *Les Misérables* observes the characteristic eclecticism, but the echoes are those of Weill, Janáček, Puccini, Trenet, Monnot—the tunesmiths of the century. There is a vestige of blue wail in the delivery of the West End Jean Valjean, Colm Wilkinson. Still, rock as *rock*—rock as The Who would hear it—has been expunged. Rock opera has become . . . opera.

25

AMERICAN OPERA

❧

No nation has had as much trouble establishing a popular and artistic base for opera as the United States. What *sounds* should composers emulate? Wagner? Verdi? Gounod? Or some eclectic projection?

This was the trouble: American opera was so busy borrowing from other cultures that there was no American opera. Or yes, there was one, but almost no one heard it till sixty years after it was published: Scott Joplin's *Treemonisha.* Printed in 1911, privately performed in concert style in 1915, and at last reclaimed for the public in the 1970s (in a new orchestration by Gunther Schuller), *Treemonisha* is folk opera. The scene is local, the folk are American, the sound is idiomatic and the theme topical: blacks must become educated to become good citizens.

DG's album of the Houston Grand Opera production offers the excellent Carmen Balthrop, Curtis Rayam, Ben Harney (later the ruthless manager in *Dreamgirls*), and Willard White, with only Betty Allen disappointing, her voice spreading and her diction poor. The Frank Corsaro–Franco Colavecchia staging emphasized childlike naïveté, suiting the simplistically rhyming libretto, the tuneful parlor ballads and ragtime dances—not to mention Joplin's primitive sense of narrative. He was not comfortable with recitative (a foreign element, after all, in American art, European and ancient), so he built his piece almost entirely of songs. The result is unique, comparable to *Der Freischütz* or *The Bartered Bride* but for *Treemonisha*'s tragic lack of exposure in Joplin's lifetime. Note how the folkish derivation of

Joplin's style is made manifest in the irresistible finale, "A Real Slow Drag," in that its arching first phrases seem to reach from spiritual into ragtime; and the last cadence pulls in "operatic" coloratura, to complete the détente of pop and art.

None of *Treemonisha*'s contemporaries has been committed to disc, save on 78 excerpts. New World's *Toward an American Opera* LP collects some of the more distinguished of these: Alma Gluck and John McCormack (excellent!) in arias from Victor Herbert's *Natoma;* Lawrence Tibbett in three operas he helped squire into brief fashion at the Met—Deems Taylor's *The King's Henchman,* Louis Gruenberg's *The Emperor Jones,* and Howard Hanson's *Merry Mount.* Now, this much *is* toward an American opera: in Herbert's use of native history (three races at odds in mission California), in Gruenberg's use of jazz and a Eugene O'Neill text, in Hanson's startling penetration of puritan chorale with a clanging xylophone. Too, the period covered here, roughly the first two generations of the century, was one of earnest attempts to conceptualize American opera. But side two of the disc runs into the postwar era in LP excerpts of Aaron Copland and Gian Carlo Menotti, somewhat after the "toward' had been surpassed by George Gershwin and Virgil Thomson among others. And how does Menotti contribute to an *American* opera? Perhaps the disc should have concentrated on 78 material from the genuinely "toward" years, say in something from Herbert's *Madeleine,* a score in the arioso, parlando manner of Debussy. Those interested in a solid sample of one opera rather than in tastes of many might investigate Mercury's *Merry Mount* highlights, an Eastman School of Music performance conducted by Dean Hanson himself. The orchestra plays well, but the students are uneasy; the Wrestling Bradford is especially overparted. Worse yet, Mercury gives only thirty-four minutes of the work, with two fillers, only one of which—the prelude to Horatio Parker's *Mona*—is relevant.

Sometime between New World's side one and side two, the more imaginative composers began to break away from derivative exercises and, like Joplin, invent their forms. Virgil Thomson is especially instructive here in his collaborations with Gertrude Stein, *Four Saints in Three Acts* and *The Mother of Us All. Four Saints,* says Thomson, was designed to dodge both symbolism and realism to portray "the childlike gaiety and mystical strength of lives devoted in common to a nonmaterialistic end." Well, no doubt saints are an airy gang. But such lines as "Saint Ignatius with it Tuesday" or "To be interested in Saint Teresa fortunately" (leaving alone the celebrated "Pigeons on the grass alas") do not make for cogent narrative, and the event becomes two hours of Mother Goose dada. Still, like Joplin, Thomson found his unique form, basic in the use of all-American tunes and chording. Thomson himself chose the excerpts for and conducted Victor's 1947 abridgment, a much more spirited performance than Nonesuch's complete digital set, undermined by Joel Thome's stodgy conducting. It is part of *Four Saints'* charm that the cast, for no good reason (except that Thomson admired their diction), is all black. Both sets use prominent black singers of their respective eras—Inez Matthews, Ruby Greene, Charles Holland, and Edward Matthews on Victor; Clamma Dale, Florence Quivar, Betty Allen, and Benjamin Matthews on Nonesuch.

A similar air of the absurd informs *The Mother of Us All*, but this look at the life of feminist pioneer Susan B. Anthony is merrier and more focused than *Four Saints*. New World's recording of the 1976 Santa Fe production under Raymond Leppard has a vitality that makes up for the erratic vocalism of the many young Americans, though their senior, Mignon Dunn, could do with a little of Anthony's legendary formidability. Thomsonites should also sample the composer's four-movement *The Mother of Us All* Suite (Columbia mono) under Werner Jansson, a neat summation of the work's elated marches and oompah waltzes and, in the extract from the prelude to Act One, scene four, an arresting chromatic vista of ice crinkling on leaves.

Few European composers have neglected opera; in America, many avoid or simply fail in it. Aaron Copland's long association with Columbia yielded discs of *The Second Hurricane* and *The Tender Land* that few opera buffs possess. The earlier work, "a play-opera for high school performance," reflects the condescending *faux naïf* of the leftist Popular Front of the 1930s in its tale of teenagers flying aid to flood victims. Two choruses—kids and parents—and as little solo work as possible (plus a load of dialogue) were to have facilitated amateur production, but even New York's High School of Music and Art under Leonard Bernstein (also narrating) is no more than competent. Columbia's stereo separation of the choruses is amusing, but this is a witless work. *The Tender Land*, which reclaims the folk rhapsody Copland made special in *Appalachian Spring*, claims a highlights disc, happily with grownups—Joy Clements, Claramae Turner, Richard Cassilly, and Norman Treigle, under the composer.

Samuel Barber's two brushes with opera are better known and more successful than Copland's, if only because both received their premieres at the Met. Neither added much to a repertory that could be called American; this is not toward a native art but away from it. RCA preserved the original *Vanessa:* old-fashioned, tuneful, plotted not unlike a Gothic romance, and without Maria Callas, who refused the title role when she realized that Vanessa's "niece" and rival, Erika, has all the great moments. Eleanor Steber excellently assumed the lead—luckily, as she had few chances to document her important Met career on disc. Regina Resnik as her mother and Giorgio Tozzi as the family doctor are fine, and Rosalind Elias is a touching Erika, albeit lacking a notable instrument—the role wants Frederica von Stade or Delia Wallis. Nicolai Gedda, however, is all too excellent as the aphrodisiac Anatol—as suave, worldly, and *continentale* as the part demands (and in superb English). But what is this smoothy doing in an "American" opera? In revision, Barber reset Menotti's libretto from "a northern country" to upper New York State, not unlike resetting *The Lord of the Rings* in Bridgeport.

Launching the new Met with *Antony and Cleopatra*, Barber took his text from Shakespeare through Franco Zeffirelli. The elaborate production overwhelmed the music, the poetry, and the crew (all Americans in the leads and on the podium: Leontyne Price, Jess Thomas, Justino Díaz, Thomas Schippers). All anyone could hear was scenery. Barber later trimmed the piece, deleting subsidiary characters and episodes—a scene here, a line or two there—and it is this slimmer, unspectacular *Antony* that we hear on New World, live from the 1983 Spoleto Festival, with Esther Hinds and Jeffrey Wells under Christian Badea. It's a good performance, though the orchestra is too forward. But in rescuing Shakespeare's intimacy from Zeffirelli's pagent, Barber also stripped away much of the work's color. The important element of grotesquerie, -as in the eunuch's falsetto solo, "Now the master's gone away," is gone—not because it has no place in Shakespeare (on the contrary) but because such scenes failed originally: because the Met didn't have able comprimarios to tackle them. Similarly, Cleopatra originally died on the line "What should I stay . . ."—leaving her heartbroken confidante Charmian to conclude with ". . . in this vile world?" A marvelous moment, also gone.* Barber now treats only the love plot and Roman politics. But if Shakespeare's sensuality comes through in the music, the political scenes are loud and dull.

We are left, then, with half an opera, little more than a diva vehicle. Just as well, for if Wells is stolid, Hinds is in glory: a great portrayal and great singing. Oddly, she sounds a bit like Price, who left her memento with Schippers on Victor. There are two scenes,

---

*Other deletions include the Stick Dance and the unnotated, choose-your-pitch recitative that runs over it (one of Barber's few original touches), Antony's earlier, longer armor scene, and Charmian's eulogy of Cleopatra. There is one addition, a love duet, "Take, o take those lips away," drawn from *Measure for Measure*.

one LP side—but the selection is suitelike, giving a flavorful taste of the score, and Price, in gala voice, obeys all the markings, as befits the original Cleopatra singing during the composer's lifetime.

The group most identified with movement toward an American music theatre is the New York City Opera, and records of City Opera productions document the company's struggles to attract an audience to compelling native art; or, that wanting, to American operas. All too typical is CRI's two-disc set of Robert Ward's *The Crucible*, to Bernard Stambler's reduction of Arthur Miller's play. Here is a classic indictment of township politics co-opting due process to overwhelm justice, as the antics of a few girls send innocent people to the gallows. Mixed into this is the triangle of a good but adulterous man, his frigid wife, and a whore intent on killing the wife as a witch and—when the husband intercedes—turning against the husband. Imagine what Berg could have done with it, or Britten—the wails of the "afflicted" girls, the ruminations of the townspeople, the attack, defense, counterattack. All Ward gives is sound-track burble under Miller's lines—accompaniment, not dramatization. The cast, under Emerson Buckley, recalls the great old days of the underdog City Opera in the old City Center: Patricia Brooks as the whore Abigail, Frances Bible as the wife, Chester Ludgin as the husband. Ludgin's bass, at least, contrasts dramatically with the shrill tenor judges, and Brooks has plenty of high notes, apparently indicative of destructive tendencies. But giving Miller's play an orchestra pit doesn't make it into an opera.

Carlisle Floyd's *Susannah* is preferably representative, as a work conceived for music. Private labels have released two favorite casts; one has Maralin Niska, the Lincoln Center Susannah, but history is better served by HRF's City Center cast of Phyllis Curtin, Richard Cassilly, and Norman Treigle under Knud Anderson, caught in 1962. The mono sound is decent, though diction is erratic and no libretto is included—and Floyd's libretto leans to Tennessee mountain dialect. Curtin's touchingly vulnerable heroine will spark many a memory, and the set usefully recalls the days when City Opera complemented the international Met with singing actors at ease in the odd speaking line, as here. Imagine Nicolae Herlea or Zinka Milanov trying to pull that off. Niska, on BJR, sings with Harry Theyard and, again, Treigle.

Yet another case entirely in this search for an American style in opera is that of Douglas Moore. Desto has his *Carry Nation*, to William North Jayme's family melodrama on how the saloon-wrecker became, in her youth, a fanatic. Beverly Wolff (Carry), Ellen Faull, Julian Patrick, and Arnold Voketaitis fill in more of City Opera's vocal profile under Samuel Krachmalnick—but only the opening scene, Carry and her sorority in action, has vitality.

How, then, to explain the marvelous theatricality of Moore's *The Ballad of Baby Doe* (MGM, Heliodor, DG), one of City Opera's most enduring productions? Perhaps John Latouche's expert libretto made the difference. *Baby Doe* is an American epic: the romance of a miner-turned-plutocrat and a fortune hunter seen against the rise and fall of the silver economy. Conservative opera buffs who shy away from "modern" rep flock to *Baby Doe* for its glimpse of Beverly Sills before her days of stardom, for she has one of her best roles here. The voice burns and glows. Walter Cassel as Horace Tabor and Frances Bible as his cast-off wife help Sills lead a cast of grand vivacity under Emerson Buckley; the three discs have the fervor of a Broadway cast album. One warning: the first issues suffer garish reverberation and a distant, tinny orchestra. The DG remastering is much suaver.

Perhaps the best in this City Opera series is Marc Blitzstein's *Regina* (Columbia), for the solid stereo, committed performance, and Blitzstein's ability to re-create faithfully: to transform Lillian Hellman's *The Little Foxes* into an opera. Generally, the blend of aria, arioso, rhythmic speech, and dialogue is apt. More specifically, a few lines about music in Hellman yield, in Blitzstein, an aria outlining Birdie's fluttery pathos. A dinner party is punctuated, *andante,* by the harmonized commentary of the guests. Hectic preparations for a dressy soirée force upon Regina breathless lines on a single note. And an astonishing second-act finale reinvents Regina's vicious baiting of her ailing husband by setting its climax on high C, then dropping the curtain in silence, as if the orchestra were too shocked to reply. Krachmalnick again conducts, leading Brenda Lewis, Elizabeth Carron, Carol Brice, George S. Irving, and Joshua Hecht. Lewis sang the lyric Birdie in the Broadway premiere, but sounds perfect as the ruthless Regina, Carron's Birdie sorrowfully representing the doomed beauty of southern gentility that Regina's capitalist cohort will overrun. Helen Strine's unsteady Alexandra is a drawback, but she has the right spirit for Regina's rebellious daughter, reminding us that the best performers of American opera are strong in what Broadway is strong in: thespian smarts.

Thus far we have dealt with relatively conservative forms. A more recent group provides new wave—all the better, as American operas are most impressive when least traditional. We have no Puccini. Center Opera of Minnesota, in CRI's *Postcard From Morocco,* illustrates a typical condition of contemporary opera: committed performers delivering a now-inventive, now-tired composition of recycled dada as a group of strangers bouncing stream-of-consciousness off each other in a public place. It is a pleasure to have one of Dominick Argento's stage works on disc, as he is the most prolific of living American theatre composers. But John Donahue's libretto is weak when the dada is most active, and only competent elsewhere; and the cast of unrenowned young Americans offers a few of the voices that are supposed to be more forgivable in, say, Argento than in . . . well, Puccini.

A newer wave flows through Philip Glass's *Einstein on the Beach* (Tomato), a very typical sample of minimalism, the troupe handpicked by the two most typical minimalists, as this is one of Glass's collaborations with thespian Robert Wilson. As the term suggests, the art is reduced to utter simplicity, with a great deal of repetition. In this context, the occasional syncopation is almost wrenching. An unusual orchestration, spoken lines of no narrative intent, and nonsense chorales add a certain savor, as when an adult and then child utter "This court of common pleas is now in session" over and over while women drone "mi-mi-mi" in the background. Tomato's recording is expert, with illustrative stereo effects, but four records may be more of minimalism than most people want to hear.

Of twelve-tone scores, or other offshoots of atonal expressionism, America knows little. There is no public for it, and America's hack music journalists of course flatter the public. We have none of the climate in which a *Lear* or *Die Soldaten* may become at once a scandal, a status symbol, and a major provider in the cultural food chain. Andrew Porter, one of our few distinguished critics, put his weight behind John Eaton's *Danton and Robespierre,* and CRI recorded the premiere, by the Indiana University Opera Theatre. It is an impressive performance of an intriguing work. Eaton is no ersatz modernist, miscellaneously purveying the expressionist's clichés—the anemically screechy solo violin, the scornfully repetitive timpani whacks, the tactless tone clusters. They are there—but not miscellaneously; Eaton composes narratively, with verismo's incisive sense of tempo, drive. The three discs zip by. Porter hailed Eaton's "mastery of vocal gesture which is the mark of the born opera composer," and many of the big scenes strike tellingly, such as the opening of Act Two, Robespierre's address of the starving Parisian women punctuated by their insistent cries of "Bread!," followed by St. Just's bloodthirsty rallying call. (Eaton makes him sound like a vampire.) The cast, though students, is excellent.

Stanley Silverman and Richard Foreman's *Elephant Steps* is in some ways the all-basic avant-garde American opera, for Foreman's stren-

uously opaque libretto and Silverman's pastiche gallimaufry, from vo-
de-o-do to quarter-tones. Columbia's album dubs itself "a multi-media
pop-opera extravanganza" promising "pop singers, opera singers, orchestra, rock band, electronic tape, raga group, tape recorder, gypsy
ensemble, and elephants." And *"All,"* the album insists, "under the
direction of Michael Tilson Thomas." This is not hype: *Elephant Steps*
is everything at once; or, rather, everything one after another. Despite
Foreman's Steinesque puzzles, the work is enjoyable as much for its
narrative as for Silverman's winsome parodies. The performance is first-
rate.

One reason why American opera is such a jumble—lifeless re-creations
of Americana and adaptations from the stage side by side with one-of-
a-kind works—is that many composers followed Kurt Weill's lead to
the "living theatre" of Broadway, to raise up an American opera of a
communicative immediacy beyond anything that opera companies can
readily supply. The New York City Opera was exceptional, of course,
and it is notable that City Opera singers regularly worked on Broadway, not to mention the appearances of Ezio Pinza, Helen Traubel,
and Cesare Siepi. But then, many a piece first heard on Broadway
might easily have been written for an opera company, and some—
Regina and *Sweeney Todd*, for instance—have been taken up by the
music world after the thespians were through.

Much of American opera has thus splintered off into a neither-here-
nor-there sector, for the use of vernacular melody as opposed to something roughly identifiable as a "European" style distracts the hack journalists and academicians. If it's popular, they reason, surely it can't be
respectable. Those interested in tasting of this unique method of fash-
ioning singing theatre out of the common tongue, should investigate
the original cast recordings of Jerome Moross's updating of Homer,
The Golden Apple (RCA, Elektra—highlights only), Frank Loesser's *The
Most Happy Fella* (Columbia—complete on three discs), and Henry
Krieger's *Dreamgirls* (Geffen—highlights only, unfortunately emphasizing the "arias" rather than the recitative and ensembles). Here we
find a vitality and originality that many Europeans—theirs and ours—
lack, as well as librettos far wittier than those of Piave or Scribe (except for that of *Dreamgirls*; Piave is Auden compared with Krieger's
collaborator, Tom Eyen). The singing, too, may have great commitment, no less from *Dreamgirls'* blues diva Jenifer Holliday than from
The Most Happy Fella's Met baritone Robert Weede. In fact, this ea-
gerness to throw off received generic inhibitions—to put opera into
the musical, the musical into opera—is what sets American music
theatre apart, and why its discography counts so many titles that jus-

tified themselves in the commercial milieu, from *Treemonisha* through *Porgy and Bess* on to *Sweeney Todd*.

Sample *The Golden Apple*'s clean-cut Americana in its brassy, dancing overture, then go on to its ticker-tape march, main-street speechifying, and procession to the church supper that welcomes the local boys back from the Spanish-American War. Do you truly hear a more secure panorama in Thomson's pastiches? I don't. Nor is Gertrude Stein the equal of Moross's poet, John Latouche. Consider the aria of Penelope awaiting Ulysses, "Wind Flowers." Has Puccini more propelling melody, more poignant harmony? Hear the *Odyssey* transformed into a vaudeville of antique struts and turns as Ulysses' men are overwhelmed by the ruthless processes of the post-Newtonian technocracy. "The city itself," sings Troy's Jimmy Walkeresque mayor, "will be our stratagem," and he gives us civilization as destroyer in instant fame ("Calypso"), market speculation ("Scylla and Charybdis"), space travel "(Doomed, Doomed, Doomed")," libertarian sex ("Goona-Goona"), and power ("Circe"). "Watch me take the city!" Ulysses gloats—but the city has taken his comrades, and the country boy, affirming country hearth and wife, returns alone. Where in the "European" school can one find such ingenuity? In *The Crucible*? In *Carry Nation*? And note that it was in collaboration with Latouche that Moore rose to greatness in *The Ballad of Baby Doe*. As Weill noted when he reached America—rather, Broadway—almost exactly between *Show Boat* and *Oklahoma!*, *this* is where opera lives.

Marc Blitzstein offers a case in point here, for just as *Regina* has bounced back and forth between Broadway and the opera house, Blitzstein himself was a fully trained musician who made Broadway his atelier. Some opera composers are natural melodists: Mozart, Verdi, Britten. Some are not: Gluck, Meyerbeer, Hindemith. Blitzstein was of the latter class, and this, combined with a hectoring leftist dogmatism, makes much of his output sound as if Lenin had composed it on a whoopie cushion. Still, *The Cradle Will Rock* is renowned. Bertolt Brecht urged Blitzstein to write it, after hearing its key song, "Nickel Under the Foot," and the result is not unlike an American *Threepenny Opera* in its cross-section of types in Steeltown, U.S.A., from the bosses and their stooges down to working people and a prostitute—the first of all to suffer in hard times. ("I'd like to give you a hundred bucks," a prospective client sings, "but I only got thirty cents.") Originally written for the Federal Theatre, one of Franklin Roosevelt's relief programs, *The Cradle Will Rock* was only rehearsed under government auspices—not performed. Blitzstein's class-conscious honesty unnerved heavyweights in D.C., and on opening night the theatre was padlocked. But Blitzstein's troupe went freelance on the spot and gave their own concert version in an abandoned theatre to one spotlight and piano accompaniment (by Blitzstein)—against, by the way, the strict veto of Actors Equity, defied on the technicality that the performers delivered their parts from the auditorium and did not grace the stage. This boldly shabby demonstration not only promoted the show into legend, but supplied an unofficial mandate for bare-stage performance and neglect of the orchestrations. (A City Opera staging in 1960 was famous for its revision of this pretentiously unpretentious aesthetic: sets, costumes, and players in the pit.)

All three *Cradle* recordings serve the piano-only plan. Musicraft's hefty 1938 album is, by hap, Broadway's first original-cast recording, in crackly sound but historically enticing, with Blitzstein narrating at the keyboard. There are some worthy performances, especially Olive Stanton's vulnerable prostitute, an Americanized Jenny. The private label American Legacy crammed the 78s onto a single LP, and MGM caught, on two discs, the 1964 off-Broadway revival, with Gershon Kingsley following Blitzstein's style but playing a surer piano. This set, however, breaks with Blitzstein's Brechtian approach of an opera for actors, as some of the cast field decent pop voices. No doubt Lauri Peters brings more tone to "Nickel under the Foot." But Stanton's plainer sound better suits the piece. Another cast of actors appears on That's Entertainment's disc of the Acting Company's production, the best yet, though even Patti LuPone can't rival Stanton.

Blitzstein's most impressive work—as theatrical as *Regina* but, for once, endearingly melodic—is *Juno* (Columbia), from Sean O'Casey's *Juno and the Paycock*. Who but Blitzstein would have written an opera around Shirley Booth and Melvyn Douglas? But opera it is; those who know O'Casey's "tragi-comedy of Dublin" will be fascinated by Blitzstein's scrupulous rendering yet development of the original, more advanced than his adaptation of Hellman. *Juno*'s opening, "We're Alive," Irish defiance of the British that starts as a capering anthem and—on the same tune—becomes a requiem for a slain rebel, remains one of the most stirring invocations in theatre.

Leonard Bernstein, a close colleague of Blitzstein, separates the "classical" from the "popular" somewhat more carefully, though Bernstein's one-act opera, *Trouble in Tahiti*, was heard on Broadway. Another gloating dissection of America's second-favorite subject, marital instability, *Trouble in Tahiti* takes its title from a sarong-and-volcano movie that the wife has seen; her report on it, hard-driving camp, is the only time the work comes alive. The mono disc (MGM, Heliodor), with Beverly Wolff and David Atkinson under Arthur Winograd, is preferable to the stereo (Columbia), with Nancy Williams and Julian Patrick under the composer. True, stereo allows for a brighter sound and an amusingly ersatz sound-track effect in the main statement of the movie's theme song, "Island Magic." Also true, Patrick puts more menace than Atkinson did into the husband's solo in the gym. ("There are men who can make it," he crows, "and men who cannot.") But Winograd's less emphatic and very musical performance sits better on the ear. Bernstein is a bit overblown. It's not *that* big a piece.

Stephen Sondheim, a colleague of Bernstein, places easily: the original cast albums preserve the significant performances, coached by the author, save that Victor's digital *Follies* is more complete than Capitol's Broadway reading, in vastly better sound; the CDs glitter. Sondheim meets Bernstein on *Candide*, as Sondheim provided some new lyrics for the 1973 revision. Many writers have put in time on this score. A Broadway joke told of two savants meeting. One says, "You and I belong to an exclusive club."

"Oh?"

"We're among the few *not* to have written lyrics to *Candide*." (Richard Wilbur, John Latouche, Dorothy Parker, Lillian Hellman—"Eldorado," surprisingly—and Bernstein himself preceded Sondheim.)

New World bills its 1986 digital *Candide* as "the opera house version." What do they think the 1956 original (Columbia) was, honkytonk? Here we are torn between the great performance and the copious one. Columbia's disc, with Robert Rounseville, Barbara Cook, Irra Petina, and Max Adrian under Krachmalnick, is a perfect *Candide*, most musicianly and most theatrical, albeit bearing witness to the fatal flaw in the adaptation: there is as much romance as satire. Oddly, Bernstein and Hellman began composition out of a wish to use Voltaire's Lisbon auto-da-fé as a comment on McCarthyism, sheer satire. After a revision in London also failed, Hellman bowed out of the case, and Hugh Wheeler wrote a new book for a shortened version of the score. Harold Prince staged it, Columbia recorded it, and this— the 1973 version—is honky-tonk, puerile and, except for June Gable's condignly husky Old Lady, poorly rendered.

A third version expands the Prince-Wheeler edition, and it is this *Candide* that we hear on New World with David Eisler, Erie Mills, Joyce Castle, and John Lankston under John Mauceri leading City Opera forces. This is an expert performance in crisp, full sound; and the two discs naturally audition music that couldn't fit onto the 1956 LP: the Wedding Chorus and ensuing battle, the auto-da-fé, "Dear Boy" (deleted from the show in Boston), the Pilgrims' Chorus, the music denoting Candide's return from Eldorado, with its unmistakable quotation of "Tonight" (Bernstein worked on *Candide* and *West Side Story* simultaneously), the Money Chorus, even the *Poco meno mosso* section of the Paris Waltz, while we're listing, with its two *soli* violins. However, except for Eisler's Candide and Mauceri's conducting, New World does not rival the original. Students would do well to buy both, for the vitality of 1956 and the completeness of 1986. Every note in this score counts, for it is one of American opera's most distinguished stylistic experiments: a European form built on a European subject yielding a pure American sound—synthesized, in the main, on major sevenths and ninths. In the hollow harmony of the pilgrims' "Alleluia," the disturbingly soothing effect of the 5/8 beat of "Eldorado," the spoofs of twelve-tone rows in "Quiet," the hurdy-gurdy ritornello of "What's the Use," and, perhaps most basically, the fanfares of the overture, *Candide* invents an indigenous sound. And, once again, the venue is the "opera-house version" of Broadway.

Note again the ministrations of City Opera, which has yet to get to *West Side Story*, the other Bernstein-Sondheim collaboration. The composer conducted DG's digital album, musically complete (except for the dull overture, not Bernstein's work) and cast—note again the insistent American stylistic crossover—with opera people such as Kiri Te Kanawa, Tatiana Troyanos, Marilyn Horne, and José Carreras. Excellent—though Carreras, for all his Bellini and Verdi, seems befuddled by the tricky changes in meter in "Something's Coming."

Colleague to all these, and the man who negotiated the first settlement in the suit to establish a living theatre of American opera, was George Gershwin. He arrived on the scene in a time comparable to that of Gluck: their predecessors in music theatre had been relying too much on song forms that impeded narration and too little on musical storytelling. In Gluck's day, of course, the "song" was the *da capo* aria, occasionally varied by full-scale ensembles at the ends of acts. In Gershwin's day the song was not invariably a solo and of course hardly the vehicle for singer dandies that the *da capo* aria was. Still, there was a leaden feeling to the American musical when Gershwin set out, in 1919. Like Gluck, Gershwin did not launch his career with reform. But by the time of the three political satires *Strike Up the Band, Of Thee I Sing,* and *Let 'Em Eat Cake*—in 1927, 1931, and 1933 respectively—Gershwin was helping break ground for the kind of show Bernstein and Sondheim would write.

Gluck did not take to the ensemble finale. His reform operas are essentially soloistic, with choral commentary spliced in here and there. But Gershwin loved ensembles. *Of Thee I Sing* is really an operetta, as Capitol's recording of the 1952 Broadway revival make clear in the full-scale ensembles depicting a beauty pageant, the Presidential Inauguration, and an impeachment trial. Two years later, Gershwin redoubled the sport by setting almost all of the score to the sequel, *Let 'Em Eat Cake*, contrapuntally. Little of *Strike Up the Band* has made it onto records, but Turnabout caught a very representative slice of *Let 'Em Eat Cake* on a disc also incorporating Gershwin's first stab at opera, *Blue Monday Blues*.

This one-act opera, also called *135th Street*, started as a section of the *Scandals* revues Gershwin was composing for showman George White—another unique aspect of American opera: commission by producer rather than impresario. *Blue Monday Blues* was savaged in the first-night reviews and dropped. It's a humdrum black version of the Frankie and Johnny story, and gives not the slightest taste of what, ten years later in 1935, was to prove Gershwin's salient lesson in how to write an American opera, *Porgy and Bess*.

Porgy and Bess's record history reflects the general confusion in perceiving what is American in opera: the howls of the cheap critics, the Broadway flotation followed by opera-house reconstitution, the popularity of aria excerpts preceding popularity of the entire score, and the sometimes unquestionable nonoperatic vocalism of certain performers. Was *Porgy* opera or entertainment? The first album tended to opera: Victor's four twelve-inch 78s borrowing the Met's Lawrence Tibbett and Helen Jepson with the original chorus and conductor, Alexander Smallens, and Gershwin "supervising." These are essential discs, not least for the stupendous Tibbett, amazingly in style whether as Porgy, Jake, or Sporting Life. Jepson, too, sings solos from more than one part, as do Todd Duncan and Anne Brown at the time of the 1942 revival, again under Smallens (Decca). Because Decca went through the decade pioneering the "original cast album" in such long-lived albums as *Oklahoma!*, *Carousel*, *Song of Norway*, and *Annie Get Your Gun*, and because Duncan and Brown created the title parts in 1935, Decca's two 78 albums, transcribed complete onto one LP, became a sort of honorary "original cast." But the sporadic use of supporting principals and the cut-down orchestra rule this set out except as nostalgia. Even less appropriate, though typical of *Porgy*'s catholic appeal, is Decca's other 1942 set, a cycle of dance-band cuts by the Leo Reisman group with vocals by Helen Dowdy and Avon Long, both of the revival.

It is worth remarking that few of these voices truly engage their characters. Tibbett presses forth simply by force of virility, but Brown and Jepson suggest Sunday-school teachers correcting minor villainies in the cloakroom, not a whore torn between a decent and a heavy man. Yet in a strange way Brown and Jepson are not miscast, for innocence has long been the institutional sound of American opera, innocence against the system. In *Treemonisha, Johnny Johnson, The Mother of Us All, The Golden Apple, Candide, The Ballad of Baby Doe, Susannah, Sweeney Todd,* even *The Crucible,* and certainly in *Porgy and Bess,* American opera deals with people of peaceful mentality and the most basic drives forced into conflict with sweeping social or historical forces. If Schwarzkopf is the sound of "European" art, what is American? Marian Anderson, perhaps. No doubt she, too, would have lacked the temperament for Bess; but at least her participation in a *Porgy* recording would have made it easier to hear its opera.

Studio versions of the LP era continued to temporize as to genre, *Porgy* as "greatest hits." However, casting was vital, drawn from revivals; surely *Porgy and Bess* is the essential phonograph opera in that it built its popularity as much on these highlights albums as on theatre performances. Music for Pleasure's disc is typical, its erratic vocalism enlivened by theatre expertise, including a healthy selection of the traditional ad libs, contributed over the years by performers who virtually built their careers around *Porgy* tours and revivals. (Smallens was perhaps the most notable of these, running the pit from the 1935 premiere into the 1950s; but Georgette Harvey was the most versatile, playing Maria in the 1927 straight play as well as in the opera, right through the 1940s.)

MFP's is not a virtuous *Porgy.* Sporting Life takes a solo in "Oh, I Can't Sit Down," "It Ain't Necessarily So" becomes a chorusless duet with vaudeville patter, and "I Got Plenty O' Nuttin' " is accompanied on piano and drums. (The record does preserve a taste of Irving Barnes and Martha Flowers, a favorite lead team of the 1950s, though Flowers gets only "Summertime" and the Strawberry Woman's Call.) Still, MFP has an authentic savor that we miss in the abominable sound track of the 1959 Goldwyn film (Columbia). Most of the leads were dubbed by others, yet the Sporting Life, Sammy Davis, Jr., sings on the sound track but—for contractual reasons—*not* on the record! Singers who don't appear, actors who don't sing: this is canned opera, not to mention the fake potpourri overture, revised orchestrations, "My Man's Gone Now" lowered to d minor, and lurid sonics.

The most intently narrative *Porgy* highlights, Philips's digital LP with Roberta Alexander and Simon Estes under Leonard Slatkin, stands out also for unhackneyed choices. "A Woman Is a Sometime Thing," "What You Want Wid Bess?," an "There's a Boat That's Leavin' " are missing, but Jazzbo Brown's blues precede "Summertime," "I Can't

Sit Down" leads into the recit in which Maria drags Bess off to the picnic (the act that precipitates the tragedy), and a few numbers are given as whole scenes, not just in the hit-tune approach favored on most albums.

Still, the choice single LP is RCA's from 1963 with Leontyne Price, William Warfield, and the original Sporting Life, John Bubbles, delightfully game if dry of tone. The choice of Skitch Henderson to conduct implies a pop approach, *Porgy* as jazz musical, but no: the full orchestration is used, and of course the cast is authentic, Price taking liberties with "Summertime" that only the most entitled soprano might dare. As on earlier discs, the two stars dip freely into the stock, sharing the numbers between themselves. But who would want a Price *Porgy* without a Price "Summertime" and "My Man's Gone Now"? (Purists resent the fondness of various Besses for "Summertime," which belongs to Clara, the third of the soprano leads. But Bess does in fact take one verse of the song in a reprise in Act Three, scene one.)

Black pop singers, too, made soloistic albums, *Porgy* as cabaret— Ella Fitzgerald with Louis Armstrong (a broad program on two discs), Sammy Davis, Jr., and, in duo, Lena Horne and Harry Belafonte. The best is that by Diahann Carroll with the André Previn Trio (United Artists). Carroll's modern-jazz "Summertime" will shock traditionalists, and, if Previn accompanies "My Man's Gone Now" right off the piano-vocal score, Carroll sings it an octave below pitch with a lazy, after-hours feeling that offends the aria's context. But her "I Got Plenty o' Nuttin'," to Previn's tinny Dixieland piano, is irresistible, and it is arresting to hear the jazz world stake its claim to a work that numbers jazz among its informing influences.

That is the problem with American opera, some may say: this insincere *canto,* to be shared by Leontyne Price and Diahann Carroll, by the Singer and the singer. In the European school, would a Carroll dare Aida? Would a Price attempt Brel or Weill? But American music theatre comprehends a broader range of voice than European, and can do more with "less." In fact, the *canto* is more sincere precisely because theatre—expression of character, intensity of presentation—became American opera's first imperative, the *canto* of Carroll as well as Price, who, for that matter, may be heard in theatre music on *Right as the Rain* (Victor), accompanied, not unlike Carroll, by André Previn. A sub-Dietrich "Falling in Love Again" fails badly, but otherwise, in Kern, Rodgers, Arlen, and Previn—a Rodgers-Hart *hommage* called "It's Good to Have You Near Again"—Price is utterly accomplished. If American musicality teaches anything, it is that the study of genre is useless. American opera is practical, impulsive; is it possible that

Kurt Weill would have had to come to America even without Hitler as an incentive, to institute his living theatre?

Surely Gershwin, had he been German, would have done so. Try by try, experimenting, testing, he rose to *Porgy and Bess,* and, at length, so did the nation. *Porgy* demands a complete set, if only because the "hits" work best in their dramatic setting. How else, for instance, to understand why Porgy tells Bess she "must laugh and sing and dance for two instead of one" unless one knows he is talking her into attending the picnic that he alone of Catfish Row will not attend— thereby sealing their letter of tragedy, as it is at the picnic that Bess comes again under Crown's power, leading Crown to seek her out in Catfish Row and Porgy to strangle him, and Porgy to be arrested, and Bess, assuming he is lost to her, to let Sporting Life spirit her off to the north?

The first complete *Porgy* was Columbia's 1951 set under Lehman Engel (Odyssey)—ironically, not hailing from Columbia's opera wing but part of Goddard Lieberson's project to record classic American *musicals.* With Camilla Williams, Inez Matthews, Helen Dowdy, Lawrence Winters, Warren Coleman, and Avon Long's Sporting Life, it's a persuasive performance despite early mono sound and an astonishing number of frittering little cuts. The ad libs are observed, Engel (an underrated conductor who hurt his reputation by concentrating on Broadway) is dynamic and sensitive, and Williams offers a great Bess— again, a City Opera alumna reminds us of that great company's sturdy sense of song-as-character. Williams's colleagues, generally veterans of *Porgy* revivals, uphold a style that some of them may have learned from Gershwin himself.

Not till the American Bicentennial was Columbia challenged, and lo, both London and Victor opted for complete readings, *Porgy* as opera. London's Lorin Maazel presents the conservatory version, *Porgy* as sacred text, precise but uninvolving, though the singers themselves—Leona Mitchell, Florence Quivar, Barbara Hendricks, Barbara Conrad, Willard White, McHenry Boatwright, and François Clemmons—stand among the top of the class. Victor's Houston Opera cast, under John DeMain, has a theatre bite, and thus Clamma Dale, Wilma Shakesnider, Betty Lane, the stupendous Carol Brice, Donnie Ray Albert, Andrew Smith, and Larry Marshall offer more than Maazel's cohort can. *Porgy* as opera! The détente of pop and art! As Robin Williams says, What a concept! But *Porgy* is an opera, always was. True, the new generation cannot face up to Harlem flash as John Bubbles, Avon Long, and Cab Calloway could, and the ad libs are dying out in this age of Do As Written. Yet the musical program holds true: truer as we go on. *Four Saints in Three Acts* made the short-lived Mini-Met and *Porgy* made the Met. What's next? *Street Scene? The Golden Apple? Susannah?* Or does American opera need established companies at all? As Gershwin, Weill, Bernstein, and Sondheim tell us, America has an alternate arena: that's the Broadway melody.

INDEX

❧❧

*Numbers in boldface type denote a composer's
or work's significant discographic entry.*